A Note About the Author

J. Douglas Smith is the author of *Managing White Supremacy: Race, Politics, and Citizenship in Jim Crow Virginia*, which received the 2003 Library of Virginia Literary Award in Non-fiction. He is the executive director of the Los Angeles Service Academy, a program that teaches high school students how the political, social, and environmental infrastructure of metropolitan Los Angeles works. He lives in Los Angeles with his wife and two children.

ALSO BY J. DOUGLAS SMITH

*Managing White Supremacy: Race, Politics, and Citizenship
in Jim Crow Virginia*

ON
DEMOCRACY'S
DOORSTEP

ON DEMOCRACY'S DOORSTEP

|||||||

THE INSIDE STORY OF
HOW THE SUPREME COURT
BROUGHT
"ONE PERSON, ONE VOTE"
TO THE UNITED STATES

J. DOUGLAS SMITH

HILL AND WANG

A DIVISION OF FARRAR, STRAUS AND GIROUX | NEW YORK

Hill and Wang
A division of Farrar, Straus and Giroux
18 West 18th Street, New York 10011

Library of Congress Cataloging-in-Publication Data
Smith, J. Douglas, 1965– author.
    On democracy's doorstep : the inside story of how the Supreme Court
brought "one person, one vote" to the United States / J. Douglas Smith. —
First edition.
        pages   cm
    Includes index.
    ISBN 978-0-8090-7423-5 (hardback) — ISBN 978-0-374-71208-2 (e-book)
    1. Apportionment (Election law)—United States—Cases.
    2. United States. Supreme Court.   I. Title.

KF4905 .S65 2014
342.73'072—dc23

                                                            2013040784

Designed by Abby Kagan

Hill and Wang books may be purchased for educational, business, or promotional use.
For information on bulk purchases, please contact the Macmillan Corporate
and Premium Sales Department at 1-800-221-7945, extension 5442, or write to
specialmarkets@macmillan.com.

www.fsgbooks.com
www.twitter.com/fsgbooks • www.facebook.com/fsgbooks

1   3   5   7   9   10   8   6   4   2

FOR JULIE

I maintain that the moment a majority in a republic assumes to draw a distinction with the intent that certain men shall be enabled to enjoy twice or thrice the amount of political power which an equal number of other men are to possess, that is the hour when tyranny begins.

—CHARLES FRANCIS ADAMS, 1853

On a shoestring, we changed the world.

—CLARKE STALLWORTH, newspaperman,
Birmingham, Alabama, 2005

CONTENTS

ON
DEMOCRACY'S
DOORSTEP

PROLOGUE

On Friday, July 5, 1968, Chief Justice Earl Warren greeted close to one hundred journalists who had gathered in the elegant oak-paneled East Conference Room of the Supreme Court of the United States. The chief justice rarely met with the press, but since his recent resignation, effective upon the qualification of his successor, reporters had been clamoring to speak with him. Described by one newspaper as "more relaxed, carefree and far more communicative than he had been in a long time," the seventy-seven-year-old Warren fielded questions on many of the momentous and deeply divisive opinions rendered by the Court during his fifteen years on the bench. When asked which of these was the most important, Warren did not hesitate. He identified *Baker* v. *Carr*, *Reynolds* v. *Sims*, and a series of companion cases that, taken together, established the principle of "one person, one vote" in all state legislative and congressional apportionments.[1]

When asked the same question in later years—and he was asked frequently—Earl Warren acknowledged that his choice came as a surprise to most people. The vast majority of Americans familiar with the work of the Supreme Court might have expected the chief justice to pick one of the many other landmark decisions handed down during his controversial tenure: perhaps *Brown* v. *Board of Education*, the 1954 decision that ruled racial segregation in schools unconstitutional, or *Gideon* v. *Wainwright*, the 1963 ruling that granted all criminal defendants a right to legal representation, or maybe *Miranda* v. *Arizona*, the 1965 decision that required police to inform all suspects, prior to interrogation, of their right to remain silent and, therefore, avoid self-incrimination, and their right to have counsel present before answering any questions. But Warren never wavered in his conviction. From his last day as chief justice in June 1969—a Senate filibuster and a presidential election postponed the confirmation of a successor—until his death five years later, Warren time and again insisted that the reapportionment decisions trumped all others. To him, they were the most important to the realization of a truly democratic nation.[2]

Prior to the *Baker* and *Reynolds* rulings, American democracy was a deliberately misshapen enterprise. Because most states based representation in at least one chamber of the legislature on factors other than population, district boundaries could readily be drawn to give some citizens a far greater voice than others. A lawmaker from one area of a state, for example, might have represented ten thousand voters, while a colleague from another region might have had two, or five, or even ten times as many constituents. Like Jim Crow, this practice seemed to defy the most elementary notions of democracy as a system of popular self-rule—and yet it had many defenders. From the Pacific to the Atlantic, from the Gulf Coast to the Great Lakes, from the Hawaiian Islands to the Alaskan peninsula, residents of small towns and rural areas enjoyed disproportionate political power, while their metropolitan counterparts struggled for an effective voice in state government. Malapportionment allowed rural lawmakers free rein to appropriate state funds, drawn largely from urban and suburban taxpayers, to pay for roads, bridges, and schools in their home districts. And since state lawmakers typically control districting for the U.S. House of Representatives, it guaranteed that residents of more populous regions lacked adequate representation at the federal level as well.

Numerous individuals and interest groups with ties to the nation's metropolitan regions also benefited from this entrenched system of minority rule. Urban-based corporations and capitalists have always vied for power in the halls of state capitols and in Congress. In the late nineteenth and early twentieth centuries, the railroads, among other corporations, simply bought state legislators and members of Congress. Beginning in the 1930s, the business lobby fought tenaciously to limit the effects of the New Deal. In the mid-twentieth century, the leaders of many business and trade groups, who believed representatives of remote and lightly populated districts to be more reliable allies than their urban counterparts, actively defended malapportionment in order to promote a probusiness, antilabor agenda of low taxes, limited government spending, and minimal regulation.[3]

Throughout the United States, malapportionment was entangled with fundamental struggles for civil and voting rights, as well as related contests between labor and business. In the industrial Northeast and Midwest, and especially in populous states such as Illinois, Michigan, Pennsylvania, and New York, whose vast cities teemed with blue-collar workers and ethnic minorities, malapportionment circumscribed the political power of labor and civil rights advocates. In the American South, by contrast, where labor unions were weak, malapportionment served as a cornerstone of white supremacy, ensuring the overrepresentation of the most ardent segregationists and thus further delaying the realization of civil and voting rights for African Americans. And as the twentieth century proceeded, minority rule only intensified in all regions of the country as urban and suburban populations swelled dramatically while legislative districts remained roughly the same.

After World War II, individual citizens, municipal officials, and civic organizations such as the League of Women Voters began to seek relief, but they repeatedly failed, thwarted by a conspiracy of inaction. Not eager to apportion themselves out of their jobs, lawmakers ignored state constitutional mandates, fearing no legal or political recourse. State courts frequently granted that malapportionment violated state constitutional requirements, but then ruled that apportionment was the province of the legislature and refused to intervene. In 1946, Justice Felix Frankfurter temporarily foreclosed the possibility of federal judicial relief with his majority opinion in *Colegrove* v. *Green*, in which he wrote that the federal courts must not enter the "political thicket." Though he saw that extreme disparities existed in the Illinois congressional districts under review in *Colegrove*, Frankfurter nevertheless argued that state legislatures and state courts alone had the power to resolve apportionment disputes. For the next fifteen years, federal courts cited Frankfurter's opinion in *Colegrove* as they declined to accept jurisdiction in state legislative and congressional reapportionment cases.[4]

In 1959, representatives of Tennessee's largest cities filed what became known as *Baker* v. *Carr* after the state legislature again dismissed the idea of reapportioning, just as it had done every year since 1901. Three years later, a divided Supreme Court deferred ruling on the specific merits of the Tennessee case but still handed proponents of reapportionment a major victory. Though Frankfurter made a vigorous and impassioned dissent, the Court decided that federal courts had jurisdiction to consider whether or not legislative malapportionment violated the Equal Protection Clause of the Fourteenth Amendment. Deliberations in the Tennessee case took an unusual toll on the justices and contributed to the resignation of two of the Court's nine members.[5]

Baker v. *Carr* did not, as is often erroneously claimed, establish a standard for states to follow in drawing legislative districts, but the decision did open the doors of the federal courts to litigants to challenge the overrepresentation of rural and small-town communities. And challenge they did. A movement soon came together, as attorneys and plaintiffs in more than three dozen states brought suits alleging legislative and congressional malapportionment.

During a tumultuous term that began in October 1963 and was tragically interrupted by the assassination of President John F. Kennedy, the Supreme Court heard oral arguments and issued full opinions in seven of these cases, each of which asked the justices to answer the fundamental question they had avoided in *Baker* v. *Carr*: What standard of apportionment did the Equal Protection Clause require? In February 1964, the Court announced in *Wesberry* v. *Sanders*, a case from Georgia, that each state's districts for the U.S. House of Representatives must contain, as nearly as possible, the same number of people. The Court had taken a crucial first step in addressing the malapportionment of congressional districts, but what came next proved far more consequential and controversial. On June 15, 1964, the Court stunned many observers, including many advocates of reapportionment, when it declared that the Equal Protection Clause required that both chambers in a bicameral legislature be apportioned according to the principle of "one person, one vote." Selecting *Reynolds* v. *Sims*, a case that originated in Alabama, as the vehicle through which to announce its decision, the Court ruled that the "federal model"—with one chamber apportioned primarily by population and the second chamber on the basis of other factors, as with the U.S. Congress—would no longer be permitted on the state level. Although less well known than *Reynolds*, a companion case from Colorado, *Lucas* v. *Forty-Fourth General Assembly of Colorado*, turned out to be the most important decision handed down that day. In it, the Court made clear that its ruling in *Reynolds* left no room for states to deviate from straight population equality in either branch of a bicameral legislature, even if a majority voted for a less rigorous standard. By the end of the decade, the Supreme Court had determined that apportionments for all elective municipal and county offices—including city councils, boards of supervisors, and school boards, among others—must adhere to the same standard.[6]

The Supreme Court's reapportionment decisions had profound and far-reaching consequences, forcing almost every state in the nation to reconsider its scheme of apportionment. The *Washington Post* referred to the rulings as "magnificently liberating," a step "toward establishing democracy in the United States." But for every editorial or column that supported the Court's action, another saw the rulings as evidence that the Warren Court had yet again exceeded its authority. Conservative columnist David Lawrence, for instance, claimed that the reapportionment decisions constituted the most significant "usurpation of power by the judicial branch" in American history, while William S. White alleged that the Court's mission was to "make the urban parts and interests of this nation the unchallenged and total masters of our affairs."[7]

Such objections came as no surprise and fit within a broader critique of the Supreme Court that animated conservatives throughout Warren's tenure. Expanding the reach of the Constitution, and the Fourteenth Amendment in particular, to carve out and defend a series of previously unrecognized rights for individuals, the Warren Court condemned racial segregation, abolished state-sponsored prayer in the schools, affirmed the rights of couples to decide for themselves whether or not to use birth control, and ordered that criminal defendants, no matter how destitute, be provided access to legal counsel. With every one of these decisions, conservatives and right-wing extremists criticized the Court, directing their most withering rhetoric at Warren. In 1961, soon after the justices ruled that courts could not consider evidence found in unlawful searches, the fiercely anticommunist John Birch Society launched an "Impeach Earl Warren" campaign. So far to the right that its members considered Dwight Eisenhower a communist and a traitor, the Birchers published pamphlets and newsletters and posted their message on billboards along highways across the nation. Although their campaign never gained traction in Congress, it lasted until Warren's retirement and helped legitimize more mainstream critiques of the chief justice and his conception of American democracy.[8]

The conservative response to the Warren Court's reapportionment decisions was swift. In Congress, southern Democrats, joined by a bipartisan collection of representatives from rural districts, proposed drastic measures to strip the Court of certain powers. Soon, the anti-reapportionment push coalesced around Senator Everett Dirksen of Illinois, the Republican minority leader who enjoyed close ties with national business organizations such as the U.S. Chamber of Commerce and the National Association of Manufacturers. Dirksen championed a constitutional amendment that would have allowed state legislatures to apportion one branch of a bicameral legislature on factors other than population, but when this failed to draw enough support in the Senate, he and others began encouraging state legislatures to petition for what would have been the first constitutional convention since the founding convention of 1787. Dirksen hired Whitaker & Baxter, a California firm that had pioneered modern political campaign management, to carry out a massive lobbying effort, which the firm did relatively quietly, even as it raised large sums from many of the nation's richest corporations. Over the course of five years, from 1964 to 1969, Whitaker & Baxter made remarkable and, to many observers, frightening progress.

No one person stands at the center of the story of reapportionment. Rather, a vast number of individuals and organizations figure in the dramatic narrative that follows. Members of the League of Women

Voters and other civic groups educated one another and the public on the costs of malapportionment. Reporters, opinion writers, and editors devoted thousands of column inches to the subject. Litigants and plaintiffs' attorneys across the country filed suit after suit in federal court, typically without compensation. Attorney General Robert Kennedy and Solicitor General Archibald Cox, along with other officials in the Department of Justice and the White House, debated sharply, at times contentiously, what position the federal government should take. Earl Warren faced vociferous opposition, most especially from Felix Frankfurter (even after the latter's retirement), as he attempted to engineer consensus support for a position considered radical by some. Indeed, Warren likely did not realize at the outset just how far he, and the Court, would go in transforming the political structure of almost every state in the nation.

The Supreme Court's reapportionment decisions unified various political opponents—in Washington and at the state level—on both sides of the issue. Elected officials who faced the threat of losing their seats as a result of the decisions, no matter what party they represented, fought against them with tremendous resolve. Liberal senators in favor of the Court's rulings launched a filibuster—a tactic usually employed at the time by opponents of civil rights—to block attempts to weaken the Court's actions. Big-city mayors and labor leaders perceived the importance of reapportionment to their agendas, while business and trade associations committed significant resources to overturning the Court's decisions. President Lyndon Johnson, eager to maintain a broad coalition behind his Great Society legislation, did his best to stay out of the fight. Meanwhile, most Americans, when polled, expressed support for the Court's decisions but observed from the sidelines as both sides claimed to represent their interests: supporters of the Court's decisions spoke of "one person, one vote," while Dirksen and the business lobby claimed, less convincingly, that they wanted to "Let the People Decide."

However they participated—working behind the scenes or in public, writing letters to editors and lawmakers, filing lawsuits, raising money from corporations, lobbying lawmakers, setting national policy, or interpreting the Constitution—the people involved in the question of reapportionment in the 1950s and 1960s demonstrated at once the great potential to remake American democracy and the eventual limits of serious attempts to do so. What follows is a story of democracy in action, even as it is a story about the very meaning of that word in this country.

1 ||| ROTTEN BOROUGHS

The problem of apportionment, like many episodes in the contested history of democracy in the United States, reflects one of the deepest and most long-standing political and cultural divides in American society—the divide between city and countryside, between coast and heartland. Addressing delegates to the 1894 New York Constitutional Convention, Henry J. Cookingham, a lawyer and former state representative from Oneida County, disparaged residents of the state's rapidly growing cities, and especially their corrupt political leaders, as he argued passionately in favor of an "honest, fair and just apportionment" that would ensure continued rural control of the state. "I say without fear of contradiction," he said, "that the average citizen in the rural district is superior in intelligence, superior in morality, superior in self-government, to the average citizen in the great cities."[1]

More than three decades later, Baltimore journalist and satirist H. L. Mencken reached a decidedly different conclusion. Looking ahead to the 1928 presidential election, Mencken noted that "the essential struggle in America, during the next fifty years, will be between city men and yokels. The yokels have ruled the Republic since its first days—often, it must be added, very wisely. But now they decay and are challenged, and in the long run they are bound to be overcome." He added, with his typically unsparing disdain, that "the yokels hang on because old apportionments give them unfair advantages. The vote of a malarious peasant on the lower Eastern Shore counts as much as the votes of twelve Baltimoreans. But that can't last. It is not only unjust and undemocratic;

it is absurd. For the lowest city proletarian, even though he may be farm-bred, is at least superior to the yokel . . . In the long run he is bound to revolt against being governed from the dung-hill."[2]

While guilty of employing the crudest stereotypes in their rhetoric, Cookingham and Mencken were right that apportionment was one of the fundamental political issues of their time. Mencken's city dwellers did indeed revolt, although it would take another thirty-five years and the further erosion of their political voice before they succeeded. In the interim, the rural and small-town citizens so admired by Cookingham saw their numbers thin and demographic forces turn against them. From his vantage point in the 1890s, Cookingham looked back to an earlier day, prior to the waves of immigration and urbanization that so profoundly shaped and changed the United States, and imagined a Jeffersonian golden era in which a few learned men governed wisely on behalf of the entire populace. Even as he noted the contributions that such men made in the early years of the American experiment, Mencken mocked those who struggled to cope with the changes occurring around them and who clung to power in a manner at odds with the basic principles of representative democracy. In assuming that the advance of civilization moved in one direction, from farm to city, Mencken set aside his predilection for slandering the intelligence of most people, no matter where they resided, and offered an alternative vision to Cookingham's, one based on the conviction that the voice of every individual should carry the same weight in the political process.

Disputes over the proper basis of representation in the United States have their origins in the British method for determining parliamentary representation, from which colonial practices derived. In the British model, towns, or "boroughs," were assigned representation in the House of Commons. As British citizens moved around and once flourishing population centers declined, representation remained fixed and ultimately produced what was called a "rotten borough" parliament in which sparsely inhabited regions, typically controlled by an absentee landlord, enjoyed considerable political clout. When Lord John Russell rose before the House of Commons in March 1831 to introduce a Reform Bill aimed at eliminating more than fifty rotten boroughs and reducing the representation of thirty other sparsely populated constituencies by half, he cited as evidence one village, Old Sarum in Wiltshire, that contained three houses and fifteen persons yet sent two members to the House of Commons. Fourteen houses in the village of Newtown and twenty-three houses in Gatton also sent representatives. By contrast, tens of thousands of inhabitants of rapidly growing cities, such as the rising industrial centers Manchester, Birmingham, and Leeds, had no representation at all. Imagining the reaction of a visitor to Britain, Russell asked his colleagues, "Would not such a foreigner be much astonished if he were taken to a green mound, and informed that it sent two members to the British Parliament?—if he were shewn a stone wall, and told that it also sent two members to the British Parliament; or, if he walked into a park, without the vestige of a dwelling, and was told that it, too, sent two members to the British parliament?" Finally passed more than a year later, the Reform Act of 1832 eliminated the rotten boroughs and expanded the franchise in Great Britain. While it did not produce the same kind of extremes as the English model, representation in the early American colonies also emphasized place over population. Virginia allotted two seats in the House of Burgesses to each county, regardless of the number of people living in each, while most towns in New England sent a representative to their legislature.[3]

In the mid-eighteenth century, mounting revolutionary fervor in the colonies, and in particular the notion of no taxation without representation, contributed to demands for greater political equality. In his *Notes on the State of Virginia*, Thomas Jefferson took issue with the malapportionment of his state's governing body and proposed instead a model constitution in which each county sent delegates to the legislature "in proportion to the number of its qualified electors." As he argued elsewhere, "For let it be agreed that a government is republican in proportion as every member composing it has his equal voice in the direction of his concerns . . . by representatives chosen by himself." Responding to the threat of violence from frontiersmen who felt politically powerless, Pennsylvania adopted a new constitution in 1776 based on the idea that "representation in proportion to the number of taxable inhabitants is the only principle which can at all times secure liberty, and make the voice of a majority of the people the law of the land." In Massachusetts a year later, citizens from Essex County denounced the manner in which the commonwealth granted a delegate to every township and demanded that "representatives be apportioned among the respective counties, in proportion to their number of freemen."[4]

Such pronouncements did not, of course, lead to political equality for all citizens in the new nation. Women, most African Americans, and many whites were denied the right to vote from the outset. But even among those who had access to the ballot, one person's vote could prove substantially more or less consequential than another's. At the state level, a general fear among the propertied classes that the laboring masses and frontier settlers lacked the necessary qualities for self-government led to the imposition of various suffrage restrictions and ensured that residents of certain locales continued to exercise greater power than their numbers would have otherwise indicated. Even as states abolished suffrage restrictions for all white males, a process largely completed by the 1830s, malapportionment limited the political power of the newly enfranchised and ensured that a well-to-do minority in most states maintained control of at least one legislative chamber, and thus a veto power over the entire legislative process. At the federal level, of course, the architects of the U.S. Constitution had reached a compromise by allowing small states the same number of representatives in the Senate as their much more populous neighbors. The Founders did apportion seats in the House of Representatives according to population, but they guaranteed at least one representative to every state, no matter its population, a significant caveat that would figure prominently in the reapportionment debates of the 1960s.[5]

The formation of new states in the late eighteenth and early nineteenth centuries pushed the nation toward a greater embrace of political equality for all white men. Aided by the Northwest Ordinance of 1787, which set forth a method for the establishment of future states beyond the Appalachian Mountains and guaranteed "a proportionate representation of the people in the legislature," a number of new western states adopted apportionments based on population. With the admission of California in 1850, the citizens of the new state, the Union's thirty-first, wrote into their constitution an explicit population-based apportionment for both branches of their legislature. Meanwhile, some older states, such as Massachusetts, abandoned systems of representation that had allowed distinct minorities to control the state's legislative

chambers. Addressing the residents of Quincy at the 1853 state constitutional convention, Charles Francis Adams had helped the cause by
denouncing the tyrannical power accumulated by residents of small
towns. Within a few years, Massachusetts adopted a new system of
apportionment that tied representation more closely to population. A century later, Massachusetts remained one of the most equitably apportioned
states in the nation.[6]

In most states, however, the trend toward fairer representation lost
momentum in the late nineteenth and early twentieth centuries as massive waves of immigration swelled the populations of the nation's cities.
Millions of Catholics and Jews, primarily from eastern and southern
Europe, began to flock to the factories and mills of the industrializing
nation. These laborers not only joined a growing urban-based working
class but also provided the votes municipal political machines, such
as New York's Tammany Hall, used to assume control over local governments. Meanwhile, significant internal migrations were in motion, as
hundreds of thousands of rural Americans, white and black, left their
farms in search of industrial jobs. The political implications of such
demographic transformations—and in particular the empowerment of
urban, working-class, Catholic, Jewish, and African American voters—
terrified Henry Cookingham and like-minded men and women throughout the United States.[7]

Residents of small towns and rural areas, often still in control of their
states despite what was happening in the cities, introduced numerous
measures to maintain political control. In state after state, they forced the
adoption of constitutional and statutory provisions that protected rural
and small-town minorities. Delaware and Mississippi based representation in both branches of the legislature on area and gave no consideration whatsoever to population. A dozen states did apportion both
legislative chambers without regard to area and instead counted people,
qualified voters, or, in the case of Indiana, male inhabitants over the age
of twenty-one. But the remaining states relied on some combination of
population and area, and more often than not added qualifiers that diminished the effectiveness of individual voters. States as geographically
and demographically distinct as New Jersey and New Mexico, for example, apportioned one state senator to each county and ostensibly based
representation in the second chamber on population, but only after

guaranteeing each county at least one legislator in *this* chamber as well. New York and Pennsylvania set limits on the maximum number of senators from a given county, while Florida, Georgia, and Maine did the same in the apportionment of their lower chambers. Vermont and Connecticut ignored the example of Massachusetts and continued to allow each township, no matter how minuscule, its own representative.[8]

Legislative inaction was just as effective a tool as constitutional and statutory provisions. Most states had long mandated the reapportionment of at least one branch of the legislature at regular intervals, typically after each decennial census, and more than half of the states required the regular reapportionment of both branches. Lawmakers, however, frequently chose self-interest over the law. Opting for what became known as the "silent gerrymander," they allowed district boundaries to remain fixed for decades. Only eighteen of forty-eight states redrew boundaries in the wake of the 1940 census. Legislators in Oregon ignored their obligations for a half century after 1907. Illinois established districts in 1910 that remained in place until 1955, while Pennsylvania and Indiana reapportioned in the early 1920s but not again for thirty and forty years, respectively. Despite constitutional requirements to reapportion every ten years, Alabama and Tennessee set districts in 1901 that did not change for more than sixty years.[9]

With each passing decade, the political influence of urban residents shrank even more in relation to their proportion of the population. Whether the result of legislative initiative or intentional neglect, by 1960 malapportionment had produced staggering inequality in virtually every state in the union. A town of 38 residents in Vermont constituted the smallest legislative district in the United States and elected the same number of representatives—one—as the state capital, Burlington, population 33,000. In New Jersey, the state's twenty-one senators represented as few as 48,555 people or as many as 923,545. In Georgia, house districts contained between 1,876 and 185,422 constituents. Senate districts in Georgia ranged from 13,050 to 556,326, in Idaho from 915 to 93,460, and in Arizona from 3,868 to 331,755. In California, more than 6 million residents of Los Angeles County, nearly 40 percent of the state's total population, elected just one state senator, as did the 14,294 inhabitants of three sparsely populated counties. California's thirty-eighth senatorial district (Los Angeles County) was not only the most populous legislative district in the United States, but had five times more residents than the second largest, a senate district in Texas.[10] (See appendix.)

In addition to comparing the populations of the largest and smallest districts in a given legislative chamber, political scientists measured malapportionment by looking at the percentage of the population living in districts represented by a majority of a legislative body. In January 1962, only five states—Massachusetts, New Hampshire, Oregon, West Virginia, and Wisconsin—apportioned districts so that majorities in both chambers of the legislature represented at least 40 percent of the population. In twenty-three states, by contrast, the theoretical minimum in the state senate was less than 30 percent, and in ten of those, the figure did not reach 20 percent. Lower legislative chambers tended to be slightly more representative. In fifteen states, theoretical minimums of less than 30 percent controlled a majority in the lower chamber, and in five of those states, 20 percent or less proved sufficient. Florida held the distinction as the only state in which legislative majorities in both branches of the legislature represented less than 20 percent of the residents. In California, a majority of the forty-member senate represented as few as 10.7 percent of the state's nearly sixteen million residents, making the California senate the second most malapportioned legislative body in the United States. Only the Nevada senate, in which a majority represented 8 percent of the state's 285,278 residents, was less representative of the population as a whole.[11]

In most states, state legislators drew, and still draw, boundaries for the U.S. House of Representatives. Consequently, congressional districts within individual states had also become severely malapportioned by the mid-twentieth century. Although not generally as excessive as legislative malapportionment, congressional disparities prompted one observer in 1954 to refer to the lower chamber of Congress as the "House of Un-Representatives." James Madison, the lead architect of the Constitution, had foreseen such a possibility and warned that "the inequality of the representation in the legislatures of particular states would produce a like inequality in their representation in the national legislature." To restrain the potential for this kind of abuse, the Founding

Fathers empowered Congress to regulate the time and manner of congressional elections. Between 1842 and 1872, Congress passed a series of laws requiring that its members be elected from single-member districts with "as nearly as practicable an equal number of inhabitants." Subsequent legislation mandated compact and contiguous districts, a clear attempt to minimize gerrymandering.[12]

The 1920 census revealed that, for the first time, a majority of Americans lived in urban areas. Not coincidentally, Congress that year failed to reapportion the House of Representatives for the first—and, as it has turned out, only—time in American history. The farm bloc and prohibitionists, in particular, feared the consequences of congressional reapportionment. Members of Congress from states set to lose representation opposed reapportionment, as did shortsighted congressmen from states set to gain representation, more concerned, as they were, that members of the opposing political party controlled the state legislature and thus the redistricting process. The national press lambasted Congress for its failure to act, while several commentators emphasized the coincidence between the discrimination suffered by people in states underrepresented in Congress and the plight of urban residents who lacked adequate representation in state legislatures. After nearly a decade of gridlock, Congress finally passed the Reapportionment Act of 1929, but only after gutting key provisions put in place over the previous eighty years.[13]

The act freed states to draw congressional districts that were neither compact nor contiguous, and that made no pretense of containing equal numbers of inhabitants. Even by the relatively forgiving standards suggested at the time by the American Political Science Association, more than 35 percent of the congressional districts in the United States were malapportioned by 1960. In nineteen states, the largest district had more than twice the number of residents as the smallest. In six of those states, disparities were simply staggering. Districts in Arizona, Colorado, Georgia, and Maryland exceeded a three-to-one ratio, while the largest district in Texas contained more than four times the number of residents as the smallest district. No state, however, approached Michigan, home to a large nonwhite population and a bastion of unionized labor, in its embrace of congressional malapportionment. The state's Republican-controlled legislature created districts that ranged from

117,431 to 802,994 residents, a ratio of nearly seven to one. Into the 1960s, Detroit constituted one of the thirteen largest congressional districts in the United States; the others comprised all or parts of Houston, Dallas, San Antonio, Atlanta, Indianapolis, Birmingham, Seattle, Miami, Columbus and Dayton in Ohio, and Bridgeport and Hartford in Connecticut.[14] (See appendix.)

Those who most clearly benefited from the drawing of America's rotten boroughs included a disproportionate number of congressional leaders. House Speaker Sam Rayburn, a Democrat from Texas, represented the fifteenth least populous district in the United States. His district was so small, and his hold on the district so complete, that Rayburn received fewer than sixteen thousand votes when he was reelected in 1958. At least eight of twenty committee chairs in the House of Representatives came from overrepresented districts, including Wayne Aspinall of Colorado, who hailed from the fourth-smallest district in the nation, and Wilbur Mills of Arkansas, who represented the eleventh-smallest district. On the other side of the aisle, at least two members of the Republican leadership represented small districts in Michigan.[15]

Malapportionment proved consequential in Washington, D.C., and in every region of the United States. Across most of the nation, but especially in states with large metropolitan centers, malapportionment limited the ability of working-class Catholics, Jews, African Americans, and progressive reformers of all races and creeds to improve working conditions, increase funding for education and health and welfare programs, and advance civil rights protections. In the South, malapportionment solidified the power of a small percentage of rural white voters who dominated state and regional politics and allowed them to stifle substantive racial reform for decades. To cite one example, when the Virginia legislature voted in 1956 to close public schools rather than integrate, the twenty-one state senators who voted in favor of the action represented fewer Virginians than did the seventeen senators who opposed it.[16]

Malapportionment was certainly about race and ethnicity, about nativism and distrust, about fear of the other. But malapportionment served, above all, as a practical and eminently useful tool for maintaining power. This was its allure, but also its weakness. By ensuring minority control of government in a purportedly democratic nation, it stood on a shaky foundation. The plaintiffs and lawyers responsible for the reapportionment revolution of the 1960s, including those from southern states, chose not to dwell on race in their legal briefs and oral arguments. Rather, they emphasized the broader denial of the rights of individual citizens, abridged not on account of race but on the mundane realities of residence.

Both major political parties relied on malapportionment to further their own, often minority, interests. In the South, Democrats benefited most clearly from malapportionment. In the rest of the country, Democrats tended to enjoy more support in urban areas and thus the Republicans in these states gained more from malapportionment. As one journalist noted in the late 1950s with reference to New York, Illinois, and Michigan, the upper chamber "has been given, virtually in perpetuity, to the Republicans. It has become a rural conservative fortress, a kind of petty House of Lords almost above the swings of majority rule." He added, "This follows the political rule that Republicans where possible shortchange Democrats, and Democrats where possible shortchange Republicans, and both shortchange city-dwellers."[17]

Where existing malapportionment did not suffice, legislators turned to the old and familiar tactic of gerrymandering, of crafting political boundaries for distinctly partisan advantage. Gerrymandering took its name from Elbridge Gerry, who, even though he did not invent the practice, employed it so flagrantly that his name defines the practice two centuries later. Gerry was the governor of Massachusetts in 1812, when he sanctioned his party's creation of a district so twisted and contorted that critics likened it to a salamander.[18] A century and a half later, operatives in the employ of both major political parties proved as adept at picking their constituents as had Gerry's lieutenants. Writing in the *Christian Science Monitor* on the eve of the reapportionment revolution, George Merry remarked, "If a preschool child was turned loose with a pencil and a map of the United States, he couldn't possibly scribble more irregular, jagged-shaped patterns for congressional districts than have been contrived already by some state legislatures."[19] As Gus Tyler, the political director of the International Ladies' Garment Workers' Union and a leading voice in reapportionment debates in the

1950s and 1960s, put it, gerrymandering "viciously multiplied" the inequities created by malapportionment.[20]

By the middle of the twentieth century, England, the original home of the rotten borough, had passed a series of reform laws that had led to parliamentary districts that were, in the words of New York Times reporter Anthony Lewis, "carved out with sterile precision" and that tolerated "no population inequalities of any significance." In the United States, by contrast, the situation was becoming worse. One report concluded that three-fourths of state legislatures were less representative in 1955 than they had been twenty years before. In this regard, Michigan was certainly typical.[21]

In the wake of the 1954 elections, a pair of memoranda labeled "confidential" and addressed to Republican Party employees in Michigan laid out in detail the degree to which their power was based in malapportionment. Credited to a fictitious Republican state senator ("Mossback McKinley") from a nonexistent district, the memos were almost certainly the creation of Democratic Party operatives, but they nevertheless reveal the absurdity of Michigan politics. In that year's elections, the memos emphasized, more than 55 percent of voters in Michigan reelected the Democratic incumbent governor G. Mennen "Soapy" Williams, who romped to a fourth two-year term by more than 250,000 votes. But just as in each of the six terms that he eventually served, Williams found himself facing a legislature controlled by the opposing party. In balloting for the state house, Republicans received 47.6 percent of the vote but held on to 53.6 percent, or 59, of the 110 seats. In the state senate, GOP candidates tallied 48.7 percent of the ballots but claimed an amazing 67.6 percent of the seats. Twenty-three Republican senators in Michigan represented an average of 142,579 people, while eleven Democratic each voted on behalf of 281,131 constituents. Malapportionment in the Michigan senate was so extreme and so entrenched that Democrats would have needed to win 70 percent of the votes to take control of the chamber.[22]

Republicans in Michigan in the 1950s, like Democrats and Republicans elsewhere, continued to exert minority control as long as they were able to beat back reform efforts led by municipal officials, civic organizations such as the League of Women Voters, and labor unions. As Mossback McKinley warned, "We must be ever vigilant against the Democrats and other elements of our society who are sure to propose another scheme of equal legislative representation which would result in nothing short of putting control of our Government in the hands of the majority of the people." It is perhaps telling that the Democrats in Michigan attempted to find some sort of political and psychic refuge in parody. They and their opponents were confident that the state's artfully rigged electoral system would continue indefinitely. Little did they or other politically engaged Americans appreciate how quickly their world was about to change.[23]

2 ||| CALIFORNIA, 1948

The consequences of malapportionment became more pronounced during and immediately after World War II, as the rapidly expanding population of the United States moved in unprecedented numbers. No state was affected by this demographic change as much as California. Not coincidentally, therefore, the first significant midcentury effort to reapportion a state legislative chamber took place in California, where the state Federation of Labor spearheaded a highly contentious initiative that appeared on the November 1948 ballot. Shaped by the dramatic growth of California's highly urbanized population and the state's distinctive history of reapportionment, the 1948 initiative introduced many of the issues that would define reapportionment debates in the 1950s and 1960s. Most important, the 1948 campaign to reapportion the California senate laid bare the stakes involved for both sides as corporations and business groups, in particular, went to great lengths to maintain malapportionment as a means of keeping taxes low, regulations to a minimum, and labor unions politically weak. Furthermore, the 1948 campaign marked the first substantive foray into reapportionment politics for two of the prime adversaries in the reapportionment revolution of the 1960s: Earl Warren, the Republican governor of California, and the campaign management firm of Whitaker & Baxter. In 1948, Warren stood with Whitaker & Baxter on the same side of the reapportionment debate; that would not be the case in the 1960s.

In California, a unique coalition of rural and regional interests coalesced in the 1920s and succeeded in entrenching minority political rule as effectively as in any other state. From statehood in 1850 until the 1920s, the California senate and assembly were both apportioned on a population basis. The 1920 census, however, revealed that two-thirds of the state's residents resided in urban areas. Although substantially more urban than the nation as a whole, California was still home to influential rural residents. Like their counterparts throughout the nation, these people were not the rubes and hillbillies imagined by H. L. Mencken, but rather farmers, lawyers, bankers, doctors, teachers, and small-business owners who saw in the census numbers a clear threat to their control over the legislature.[1]

Rural Californians were not alone in worrying about the political implications of the latest census figures. The decennial count also confirmed trends that had been evident for some time: Southern California was growing at a much faster rate than the rest of the state, and Los Angeles had surpassed San Francisco in total population. In 1880, Los Angeles County was home to a mere 4 percent of the state's population; by 1920 that figure had exploded to 27 percent. By 1940, four out of every ten Californians lived in Los Angeles County. The percentage of the population living in San Francisco fell almost as quickly as that of Los Angeles grew. Twenty-seven percent of the state's population resided in San Francisco in 1880, but by 1920 that figure had fallen to 15 percent. Twenty years later, only 9 percent of the state's residents lived in San Francisco. This great demographic shift meant that reapportionment battles in California were not delineated in terms of crude urban-rural divisions. Instead, a much more complicated and intricate web of regional rivalries between urbanites in Northern and Southern California formed the foundation of the state's system of reapportionment. As a 1965 legislative report explained, "By 1920 rural groups were determined to control at least one house of the Legislature while the continual decline of San Francisco encouraged an alliance with the other northern groups to prevent Los Angeles and southern California from gaining additional seats in relationship to population gains."[2]

The California constitution called for reapportionment after each federal decennial census. Yet in the wake of the 1920 count, a deadlocked legislature, much like the Congress of the same year, failed repeatedly to pass a reapportionment measure. In 1926, the issue came before the state's electorate. The bipartisan All-Parties Reapportionment Commission sponsored Proposition 20, an initiative that would have maintained a population basis in both houses and empowered a Reapportionment Commission to draw new legislative boundaries if the legislature refused. In response, a coalition led by the California Farm Bureau Federation and the San Francisco Chamber of Commerce supported Proposition 28, a measure that proponents dubbed the "Federal Plan" because it created a legislature with an assembly based on population and a senate based on geography.[3]

California was by no means the first state to model its legislature on Congress. But no state's plan created disparities as large as California's. Opponents of Proposition 28 objected above all to the provision mandating that no county could have more than one senator, and that no senator could represent more than three counties. In practical terms, this would mean that Los Angeles, Alameda, and San Francisco Counties—with a combined population of more than 50 percent of the state's total—would elect only three of the forty total senators. In November 1926, the state's voters overwhelmingly supported the plan, despite the opposition of most Los Angeles County voters. It would remain in place until 1965.[4]

Spurred by the climate and the promise of federally funded, defense-related jobs during World War II and the cold war, California's population rose from 6.9 to 10.6 million between 1940 and 1950, the equivalent of more than one thousand new residents every day. Such growth resulted, of course, in more clout in Washington; California was apportioned twenty-three members in the House of Representatives after the 1940 census, and its congressional delegation numbered thirty a decade later. Virtually all of this growth occurred in the state's already populous metropolitan areas. In 1940, 71 percent of Californians lived in areas categorized by the census as urban. By 1950, that number had risen to just over 80 percent, as California trailed only New York, New Jersey, Rhode Island, Massachusetts, and Washington, D.C.[5]

And yet, given the system of apportionment adopted in the 1920s, control of the state senate remained in the hands of a shrinking rural and small-town minority that jealously guarded its ability to veto any legislative action. Unlike voters in many other malapportioned states, though, residents of California had at their disposal the initiative and referendum. In the fall of 1947, the California Federation of Labor began collecting signatures for a revised apportionment plan, and qualified Proposition 13 for the 1948 ballot (this Proposition 13 should not be confused with the famous tax-cutting initiative of 1978).

Emphasizing California's spectacular urban growth, backers of Proposition 13 derided the state's federal plan as "outmoded" and presented their alternative as an attempt to "restore more representative government" to the state. They acknowledged the widespread anxiety about the size and potential political muscle of Los Angeles County, which stood to elect as many as sixteen of forty senators given a strict population-based apportionment, by making the tactical decision to limit an individual county to a maximum of ten senators. Consequently, Proposition 13 proposed to apportion nineteen, rather than twenty-five, senators to the four most populous counties—Los Angeles, San Francisco, Alameda, and San Diego. In an attempt to broaden support, backers of Proposition 13 pointed out that residents of the ten most populous counties paid 81 percent of state sales taxes and 94 percent of income taxes but elected only ten of forty senators. They added that three-quarters of the state's veterans lived in these same ten counties. Surely, they argued, these citizens and taxpayers deserved more equitable representation.[6]

Opponents of Proposition 13, by contrast, defended California's "balanced system of representation," an effective rhetorical slogan that would soon appear in reapportionment debates throughout the nation. Warning against the virtual disfranchisement of fifty-four of the state's fifty-eight counties, opponents claimed that the state's federal plan was the only reliable obstacle preventing the trampling of minority rights by unscrupulous majorities. Noting that the "great cities" already controlled the election of the governor, lieutenant governor, both U.S. senators, and a majority in the state assembly, the official statement in opposition to Proposition 13 concluded that "rural California . . . has only one forum where it can demand adequate consideration of its problems—the State Senate. If Proposition 13 is adopted, that forum would be lost." Opponents attempted to assuage fears that a "balanced legislature" would ignore the needs and interests of more populous regions of the state by denying that the rural-controlled senate had conspired to block legislation supported by municipal officials and residents.

They cited the state's "splendid educational system" and a host of social welfare programs, including workmen's compensation, minimum wage, and assistance for the elderly and unemployed, all of which had passed with the support of the existing senate, and trumpeted California's record as "one of the most progressive States in liberal legislation."[7]

Both advocates and critics of Proposition 13 saw value in presenting the debate rhetorically as a dispute between a frustrated urban majority and a frightened rural minority. But, in fact, an intense tug-of-war between the state's business interests and labor unions lay at the heart of the campaign. Proposition 13 was not primarily a referendum on the appropriate balance between urban and rural representation but rather a proxy for looming legislative battles over a range of contentious issues dear to the state's dominant economic interests. In this regard, too, the threat of reapportionment in California in 1948 foreshadowed debates elsewhere in the United States.

No organization took a stronger position in opposition to Proposition 13 than the California State Chamber of Commerce. In February 1948, the chamber reaffirmed its support, first articulated in the 1920s, for a "balanced legislature" and warned that the passage of Proposition 13 would lead to the "complete domination" of the legislature by metropolitan groups indebted to, and therefore controlled by, the state's major labor unions. Over the next nine months, the chamber joined with its affiliates to secure the endorsements of local government officials and dozens of probusiness lobbying groups, including those of crop farming, citrus, cattle, petroleum, real estate, retail, and manufacturing interests. Operating primarily through a San Francisco–based front called the Northern California Committee Against Reapportionment and its Southern California satellite, the Committee Against Senate Reapportionment, the Chamber of Commerce and its allies issued grim warnings about the takeover of state government by radical, left-wing labor unions and big-city political bosses. In the final run-up to the November 1948 election, the Northern California Committee warned of "a political conspiracy of radical labor bosses to grab legislative control." In its October newsletter, the state Chamber of Commerce declared that "this proposal is backed by Organized Labor, whose purpose is to gain control of our State Legislature. Don't let THEM get away with it. Keep the American form of government." (Apparently the chamber felt no need, at the start of the cold war, to explain who constituted "THEM," and what danger "they" posed.)[8]

Underlying the rhetoric, opponents of Proposition 13 did, in fact, have a concrete agenda: to maintain control of the state senate in order to forestall an aggressive urban and liberal agenda that included increased workmen's compensation; higher unemployment, sickness, and disability insurance; public ownership of water and power utilities; passage of a Fair Employment Practices Act, similar to a measure defeated at the polls in 1946; and the creation and funding of a state public housing agency, which appeared alongside Proposition 13 on the 1948 ballot and which the Chamber of Commerce denounced as "socialistic." No single issue raised the ire of business groups more than the threat of compulsory health insurance. Beginning in 1945, the California Medical Association (CMA), a staunch ally of the chamber, waged an intense and acrimonious battle with Governor Earl Warren over a proposal that he championed as a pragmatic solution to the problem of insuring California's rapidly expanding middle class, but that the CMA and the Chamber of Commerce lambasted as "socialized medicine." Warren's widespread popularity—the state's Democrats did not bother running a candidate against him when he won reelection in 1946 to the second of three terms—was not sufficient to overcome the massive lobbying effort of the CMA against the health care bill. The experience, according to one biographer, deepened Warren's "conviction, which he never abandoned, that lobbying was a pernicious business that served to undermine democracy."[9]

Local affiliates of the Chamber of Commerce joined the state leadership in opposing Proposition 13, including even the Los Angeles Chamber of Commerce. In 1926, after a great deal of debate, its Board of Directors formally endorsed Proposition 20, which provided for a population-based apportionment of both branches of the legislature, and refused to support Proposition 28, the federal plan. By 1948, however, members of the Los Angeles chamber had come to believe that rural control of the state senate more effectively protected their interests than did an increase in representation from their own county. Voting unanimously to take a position of active opposition to Proposition 13, the board extolled the virtues of the state's balanced legislature and warned of the dangers of domination by labor unions and urban political machines.[10]

The position of the Los Angeles Chamber of Commerce provides an early example of the extent to which urban business interests across the United States supported malapportionment and rural political control. Indeed, opposition to Proposition 13 was funded almost entirely by urban business groups. Of the $294,772 the opposition raised, just under half came from Southern California and the rest from the San Francisco Bay Area. The agricultural valleys and rural regions of the state, the areas supposedly most vulnerable to a population-based reapportionment, contributed a negligible amount. In a study of the California legislature conducted in the mid-1940s, Dean McHenry, a political scientist at the University of California at Los Angeles, explained this apparent paradox: "Certain business interests in the state have found it easier to make their influence felt in the legislature through senators from rural areas. Privately owned utilities, banks, insurance companies and other concerns with crucial legislative programs have discovered some 'cow county' legislators more responsive to their demands and less committed to contrary points of view on key social and economic questions than are urban representatives." Bill Boyarsky, a journalist and astute observer of California politics, noted at the start of his distinguished career in the 1960s that the businessmen and farmers were not just friends, but "often the same person."[11]

Just days before the election in November, opponents of Proposition 13 turned for help to Earl Warren. Even though the moderate governor advocated compulsory health insurance and other issues that the Chamber of Commerce and its allies found abhorrent, he did support California's existing system of apportionment. The 1948 Republican nominee for vice president of the United States, Warren had spent the fall campaigning across the country on behalf of Thomas Dewey and had not spoken out in support of or in opposition to Proposition 13 or any of the other state ballot initiatives. During the final week of the campaign, however, Warren found himself back home, traveling the state. In response to a request from Joseph Beek, the secretary of the state senate and an ardent opponent of Proposition 13, the governor publicly affirmed his belief in the status quo. "Our state has made almost unbelievable progress under our present system," he explained at one campaign stop. "I believe we should keep it." Warren then essentially reiterated the comments he had made the previous November, when

Proposition 13 first qualified for the ballot. On that occasion, the governor remarked, "I have always believed the rural counties are of much more significance in the life of our state than the population of those counties would represent. And I also believe the principle of balanced representation in the two houses of the legislature is in keeping with the federal system of representation." Precisely what effect Warren had on the final tally is impossible to know, but despite the overwhelming urban orientation of California's citizenry, more than two-thirds of the state's electorate agreed with their governor. Proposition 13 suffered a staggering rebuke, losing in every county, including Los Angeles, with only 1,069,899 votes in support and 2,250,937 in opposition.[12]

The lopsided margin of defeat did not surprise Carey McWilliams, a social critic and author, most notably of *Factories in the Field*, a deeply sympathetic look at migrant farmworkers in California and a searing indictment of those who employed them. (The book was published in 1939, the same year as John Steinbeck's *The Grapes of Wrath*.) "This amazing spectacle of a people approving their own disfranchisement," concluded McWilliams, "can only be explained by the control which the present system of representation gives to the dominant economic interests." Writing in the immediate aftermath of the defeat of Proposition 13, McWilliams, who served as the head of California's Division of Immigration and Housing under Culbert Olson, Warren's liberal predecessor, added that the unwillingness of the electorate to abandon the federal plan ensured that "Sacramento has become, not so much the capital of a great state, but the headquarters of the lobbyists," a place where "interests, not people, are represented."[13]

While sharing Earl Warren's abiding distrust of lobbyists, McWilliams and the governor rarely saw eye to eye in the 1940s. Derided as a "left winger" by the politically conservative *Los Angeles Times* and regularly attacked by the moderate Warren, McWilliams publicly criticized Warren's record as attorney general and governor, especially with regard to civil liberties issues and most intensely over the internment of Japanese Americans during World War II. Only after both men left California—Warren to Washington in 1953 to become chief justice, McWilliams to New York in 1955 to begin a twenty-year tenure as editor of the *Nation*—did McWilliams find reason to admire his onetime antagonist. Toward the end of his life, McWilliams accepted with pleasure, and a touch of irony, the Earl Warren Civil Liberties Award from the ACLU Foundation of Northern California.[14]

The campaigns for and against Proposition 13 prefigured the national reapportionment debate in the 1960s, in which Californians would play seminal roles on both sides. As chief justice, Earl Warren would come to understand reapportionment in starkly different terms than he had as California's governor. In contrast, Whitaker & Baxter, the San Francisco political consulting and campaign management firm that had been hired by the California State Chamber of Commerce to defeat Proposition 13, would spearhead state and national efforts against reapportionment well into the 1960s.

In 1933, thirty-four-year-old Clem Whitaker, a former political journalist who had moved into public relations work, and twenty-six-year-old Leone Baxter, the manager of the Redding, California, Chamber of Commerce, made their first mark on California politics when they partnered to run a referendum campaign on behalf of the Central Valley Water Project, an irrigation and flood-control initiative opposed by the corporate behemoth Pacific Gas & Electric. Operating on a shoestring budget, the political neophytes scored a narrow and unexpected victory against their deep-pocketed opponent. It proved to be the last time in their long and successful partnership that Clem Whitaker and Leone Baxter took up the cause of an obvious underdog. PG&E soon put the pair on retainer, as did a slew of other corporations and business associations.[15]

It was not until the following year, however, that Whitaker and Baxter emerged as a powerful force in state politics. Just two months prior to the November 1934 election, alarmed conservatives hired them to defeat gubernatorial candidate Upton Sinclair, whose End Poverty in California (EPIC) program appeared to be gaining traction with voters. Despite the late start, Whitaker and Baxter changed the trajectory of the campaign by developing and employing tactics that soon became their trademarks: a vigorous, sustained attack that made effective use of innuendo to impugn the character of the opposition; a commitment to what Baxter referred to as "fighting prose" and the coining of brief but dramatic slogans that instilled doubt and fear in voters and prompted them to take action; a belief in tailoring the message for different seg-ments of the electorate; overwhelming voters with a barrage of pam-phlets and flyers; and launching an all-out assault in the final days of a campaign. Sequestering themselves for three days, the pair pored over Sinclair's voluminous writings from his three decades as a muckraking journalist and novelist, and identified quotations that could be used to paint him as a socialist or communist. Whitaker and Baxter then hired an artist who produced a series of alarming images, which they paired with Sinclair's most disturbing and seemingly dangerous utterances. Thousands of these images ended up in newspapers and on billboards throughout the state. Sinclair lost by a wide margin.[16]

If Whitaker and Baxter's methods and tactics seem mundane, that is only because they helped create the kind of political campaign manage-ment we know so well today. Prior to them, party functionaries ran cam-paigns with little thought to planning or budgeting, and only occasionally hired specialists to write speeches and generate positive publicity. By contrast, as journalist Irwin Ross explained in a 1959 profile in *Harper's*, Whitaker and Baxter "provided the entire management of a campaign—overall strategy, organization, financial supervision as well as publicity and advertising." *Time* magazine identified the two as "the acknowledged originals in the field of political public relations" and, as late as 1955, "still the world's only permanent specialists." At both the start and end of their careers, Whitaker and Baxter perceived the importance of new forms of mass communication—first radio and then television—and understood the implications for campaigns. In his profile, Ross predicted that "no future Presidential campaign will be able to dispense with the five-minute TV speech, the thirty-second spot, the canned interview, and the carefully scripted political rally." He concluded that "Whitaker and Baxter can reasonably boast that they have led the way."[17]

Clem Whitaker and Leone Baxter emerged onto the scene at an es-pecially propitious moment. The California public's embrace of direct legislation, in the form of the ballot initiative, referendum, and recall, guaranteed that an ever-increasing number of issues would be con-tested at the polls rather than debated in the legislature. Facing virtu-ally no competition, Whitaker and Baxter found a steady supply of clients willing to pay handsomely for their expertise. In 1935, Whita-ker, the father of three children, separated from his wife; three years later he married the widowed Baxter. By all accounts, they managed their campaigns as true partners, sharing oversight of every aspect of their work. Operating through their firm and a subsidiary, Campaigns, Inc., they dominated California electoral politics for a quarter century, managing eighty campaigns and ballot initiatives from the early 1930s to the late 1950s, losing on just six occasions. Both claimed to work only for clients and on behalf of causes in which they genuinely believed, typically Republicans who favored small government and low taxes. Throughout their career, they took on only a single Democrat, a candidate for mayor of San Francisco who eventually lost. Leone Baxter once remarked that they could have won most of their campaigns if they had taken the other side, but "it wouldn't have been worth it."[18]

Among the many suitors who recognized the value of having Whitaker & Baxter in their corner was the incumbent attorney general and former district attorney of Alameda County, Earl Warren, who hired the firm to run his first gubernatorial campaign in 1942. From the outset, Whitaker and Baxter saw that most Californians knew Warren only as a stern law-enforcement official, and thus they set out to create a more approachable and appealing image. According to *Time*, Whitaker and Baxter "taught Warren how to smile in public, and were the first to recognize the publicity value . . . of his handsome family." In this regard, they succeeded magnificently. Throughout the campaign, however, Warren's political views evolved as he embraced moderate positions that strained relations with some of his supporters and led him to rely less on the advice of his campaign managers. Ten days prior to the election, Warren had a falling-out with Whitaker. Whatever the actual spark that precipitated the split, Warren effectively dismissed the pair, coasted to an easy victory, and refused even to return a congratulatory phone call from Whitaker.[19]

Whitaker and Baxter did not forget the slight, and before long they would exact their revenge. When Governor Warren introduced his plan for compulsory health insurance in 1945, the California Medical Association immediately paid the consultants a retainer of $25,000 a year for three years, placed substantial resources at their disposal, and charged them with torpedoing the initiative. It was Whitaker and Baxter who succeeded in labeling Warren's bill "socialized medicine" and ensured its defeat.[20]

Their fight against compulsory health insurance in California turned out to be a tune-up for their debut on the national stage. In Chicago, the leaders of the American Medical Association took notice of their success and hired them to kill the Truman administration's proposal for national health insurance. Now commanding a fee of $100,000 per year, Clem Whitaker and Leone Baxter moved full-time to Chicago in January 1949. Warning that the "virus of socialized medicine had spread from decadent Europe and taken root here," they orchestrated a nationwide campaign that eventually cost the AMA $4.7 million but that achieved the desired result.[21]

Given their track record and in particular their success in turning back initiatives opposed by business groups, it should have surprised no one when the California State Chamber of Commerce engaged the firm to lead the campaign against Proposition 13. It was Whitaker and Baxter who established the Northern California Committee Against Reapportionment, secured endorsements from leading political figures and business and trade associations, churned out regular press releases, wrote speeches and advertising copy, designed brochures and pamphlets, and disseminated tens of thousands of pieces of campaign literature on behalf of their client. And it was they who were responsible for the rumors of plots and conspiracies by radical labor bosses. In fact, they had been making these types of claims for years. Proposition 13 marked but one more victory on a very impressive record.[22]

In the late 1950s, Clem Whitaker and Leone Baxter turned over their firm to Whitaker's son, Clem Jr., who had joined the family business in 1946 and had become a partner in 1950. Borrowing heavily from the playbook created in 1948 by his father (who died in 1961) and his stepmother, Clem Jr. and his staff at Whitaker & Baxter successfully defeated statewide reapportionment initiatives in 1960 and again in 1962. As a result of the firm's work in those campaigns, Whitaker & Baxter caught the attention of Everett Dirksen. In due time, the firm would lead the campaign to overturn the Supreme Court's reapportionment decisions, though in this endeavor it would encounter more formidable opposition.[23]

3 ||| THE SHAME OF THE STATES

O f the organizations on the losing side of the Proposition 13 vote, the League of Women Voters (LWV) had been, at best, a minor player in the debates leading up to it. But outside California, members of local and state chapters of the LWV led the way in making the public aware of the problem of malapportionment. Joining forces with civic activists, municipal officials, labor union leaders, and proponents of good government, members of the LWV set out to educate the public, lobby elected officials, and make reapportionment a legislative and constitutional priority. Although not immediately successful in most instances, statewide campaigns led by the league in the 1950s did more than the efforts of other organizations to lay the groundwork for the constitutional revolution of the 1960s.[1]

Founded in 1920 just prior to final ratification of the Nineteenth Amendment giving women the right to vote, the League of Women Voters endeavored from its inception to promote good government and the rights of citizens, with a special emphasis on "the well-being of the least-protected members of society." By the 1950s, these priorities spurred the LWV into the arena of civil rights, voting rights, and reapportionment. Avowedly nonpartisan in its affiliations, the LWV appealed to women of a certain social and economic stratum who were deeply engaged in politics. Members of the LWV tended to be in their thirties, forties, and fifties. Two-thirds had attended college, a substantial number had done some graduate work, and one in four held a full-time job. Eighty-five percent of members were married, more than likely to a professional. Very much a grassroots organization, the LWV empowered members at the local level to decide on an agenda, carry out research, and develop a plan of action. After concerted study, local affiliates made recommendations to the state branch for further action. Thus the LWV's engagement with reapportionment began at the local level, and only later, when enough local branches had expressed an interest, did state branches become involved.[2]

Though it became especially active in reapportionment battles in the Pacific Northwest and Midwest, the LWV helped make the issue visible in every region of the country, with the exception of the Deep South, where advocacy on behalf of reapportionment remained minimal prior to the late 1950s. In a number of grossly malapportioned states, including Connecticut and Pennsylvania, the league made absolutely no headway despite years of active lobbying. In other states, however, chapters of the league achieved some measure of success. Given the wide range of statutory and constitutional standards in place at the time, each state chapter faced starkly different challenges and thus supported a distinctive range of solutions. But every state chapter that studied the issue in the late 1940s and 1950s recognized an urgent need for drastic reform and agreed in substance with the Minnesota LWV, which summed up its study with a clear and direct title, "Reapportionment in Minnesota: Democracy Denied."[3]

Still, the positions taken by various chapters of the League of Women Voters in the late 1940s and 1950s reveal that a commitment to more equitable reapportionment did not necessarily entail a push for population equality in both branches of a bicameral legislature. Indeed, a close look at the LWV shows that the standard of "one person, one vote" that the Supreme Court ultimately made the law of the land was not inevitable and, in fact, was unimaginable to most proponents of reapportionment in the 1950s. Some did press for population equality in both chambers as early as 1951 or 1952, but a far greater number of concerned citizens throughout the United States accepted the premise that "balanced legislatures" and "federal plans," because they were consistent with the structure of Congress, should be the ideal model for the states. Many political scientists and law professors criticized the federal analogy as "fallacious" on the grounds that counties lacked autonomy and represented mere administrative creations of the states, whereas the federal-state rela-

tionship depended upon a compact among recognized sovereign entities. In the 1960s, the Supreme Court embraced this line of argument,
but in the 1950s most voters did not. Theodore Sachs, a young labor
lawyer in Detroit who supported population equality in both houses
when he argued Michigan's reapportionment case, remarked quite aptly
toward the end of his life that the very concept of a "balanced legislature" appealed to many in the 1950s as a "beguilingly" attractive and
logical option.[4]

Members of the LWV in several states, most notably in Wisconsin,
Oregon, and Washington, did push for straight population equality in
both branches of the legislature. They succeeded in Wisconsin and Oregon in 1951 and 1952, respectively, and both states subsequently ranked
among the most equitably apportioned legislatures. In Washington, the
LWV spent years studying the issue, weighing the merits and nuances
of federal plans and straight population reapportionments, and looking at practices in other states. Emphasizing the extreme variations in
the populations of senate districts—they ranged from 18,830 to 140,000
people—the Washington LWV garnered more than eighty thousand
signatures to place an initiative on the ballot in 1956 that would have
required majorities in both houses to represent at least 47 percent of the
state's voters. The measure passed at the polls, a tribute to the educational campaign led by the LWV, but the rural-dominated legislature
managed to gut the substance of the measure at its next session.
The state's highest court deferred to the legislature, leaving the LWV no
choice but to continue its advocacy into the next decade.[5]

In most states, the LWV, which operates based on consensus decisions of its members, supported instead some variation of the federal
plan. League members in Colorado recognized the preeminence of
population equality among districts but acknowledged the importance
of area considerations and expressed a preference for "a different basis
for the two houses." In Iowa, the league called for a lower chamber
based solely on population and a senate based on a combination of area
and population. In Indiana, a majority of members expressed a preference for a straight population-based reapportionment of both houses
but could not reach a consensus and settled for a federal plan as a compromise. Members of the Indiana league faced an additional hurdle:
Indiana was the only state in the nation that based reapportionment

solely on the number of male inhabitants (and, more specifically, only those over the age of twenty-one). Women literally did not count for the purpose of reapportionment. Any substantive reform in Indiana, therefore, first required the passage of a constitutional amendment, a cumbersome and lengthy process.[6]

The activities of the LWV in three midwestern states—Michigan, Illinois, and Minnesota—underscore the organization's commitment to reapportionment in the 1950s, but also the political obstacles that imposed real limits on the possibility of reform. Beginning with its origins as a territory carved out of the Northwest Ordinance of 1787, Michigan adopted a series of constitutions that based reapportionment primarily, albeit not exclusively, on population. But the Michigan constitution lacked an adequate enforcement mechanism to ensure that later reapportionments reflected demographic change. The state courts repeatedly found that excessive population imbalances in the size of districts violated the state constitution, but they declined to order the legislature to remedy the situation. By the mid-twentieth century, less than one-third of the state's residents lived in districts represented by a majority of state senators.[7]

The increasingly disproportionate power of a rural minority proved especially troublesome for Michigan's urban-based labor movement, whose ranks swelled in the 1940s as hundreds of thousands of migrants arrived to work in the relatively well-paying war-related industries that made Detroit the "arsenal of democracy." By the early 1950s, legislative inaction, especially in the senate, whose district boundaries had not been redrawn since 1925, prompted August Scholle, the president of the Michigan Federation of Labor (after 1958, Scholle was president of the combined Michigan AFL-CIO), to identify malapportionment as the chief obstacle to the union's legislative agenda. Scholle and the state Federation of Labor soon after sponsored an initiative campaign with the goal to reapportion both branches of the legislature on a "strict population" basis, and to establish a workable enforcement mechanism in the event that the legislature refused to reapportion. The initiative qualified for the November 1952 ballot.[8]

As in California four years earlier, a coalition of business interests

came together to defeat the labor-backed measure and to protect minority rule in Michigan. Led by the State Chamber of Commerce, the
Farm Bureau Federation, and the Michigan Manufacturers Association,
opponents of the Scholle initiative demonized the measure as a big-city
power grab hatched by venal labor leaders. In an effort to legitimize
existing disparities, they sponsored a competing measure, Proposition 3,
which they claimed would establish a "balanced legislature" but which in
fact would perpetuate significant disparities in both chambers of the legislature. Pitched to voters as a safe, logical, and appealing alternative to
the Scholle initiative, Proposition 3 easily carried the day.[9]

The LWV, though among the most ardent proponents of meaningful reapportionment in Michigan, interestingly chose not to endorse
either ballot measure. Like chapters of the league in other states, the Michigan LWV had begun to study reapportionment in the late 1940s, and
several years later reached consensus on a plan that apportioned one
branch of the legislature on a "straight population basis" and the second
branch on a combination of area and population, subject to certain
limits. Because neither the Scholle initiative nor Proposition 3 satisfied
the LWV, the league sat out the 1952 campaign altogether.[10]

Across Lake Michigan, the Illinois chapter of the League of Women
Voters initiated its own in-depth study of reapportionment in the late
1940s, its ultimate goal to combat the state's notorious corruption, in
addition to many of the same glaring inequities in state funding and
resource allocation found in other malapportioned states. To a greater
extent than in Michigan, voters in Illinois had committed themselves in
the nineteenth century to the population-based apportionment of both
branches of the legislature; between 1818 and 1901, the state reapportioned both houses fourteen times to reflect population changes. But
once the population of Chicago and Cook County reached a certain
point, lawmakers in Illinois refused to reapportion. Home to 14 percent
of the state's population in 1870, Cook County had grown to 38 percent
by 1900. Not coincidentally, the reapportionment after the 1900 census
proved to be the last for more than a half century. By 1950, the 4.5 million residents of Chicago and Cook County elected nineteen senators
(plus fifty-seven representatives to the lower chamber), while the 4.2
million residents of the remaining 101 counties sent thirty-two senators
(and ninety-six representatives) to the state capitol. The most populous

legislative district in the state had more than seven hundred thousand residents, while the least populous had fewer than forty thousand.[11]

After four years of inquiry, members of the Illinois LWV chose to abandon the existing constitutional mandate to reapportion every ten years on a straight population basis. Reaching the consensus that residents of Chicago and Cook County should not elect a majority to both chambers of the legislature, the nonpartisan league instead favored a legislature with one chamber based on a "strict population basis" and a second chamber on an "area-plus-population basis."[12]

The Illinois LWV concluded its study in time to take a leading role in support of the Blue Ballot Reapportionment Amendment, a constitutional amendment presented to the state's voters in 1954. The initiative, named for the actual color of the physical ballot, proposed to establish a lower chamber based on population that would be reapportioned after each decennial census. The Blue Ballot, therefore, initially apportioned Chicago and Cook County a slim majority of representatives in the lower chamber but ensured that Downstate voters (all of Illinois outside Cook County) maintained a substantial majority in the senate. The most potentially influential part of the Blue Ballot was that it proposed to make the current senate seats permanent.[13]

A remarkable and most unusual coalition, unlike anything even contemplated in Michigan or California, supported the Blue Ballot Amendment. In addition to the support of the LWV, the Blue Ballot garnered the unwavering support of the Illinois State Chamber of Commerce, the Illinois Agricultural Association, the Illinois State Federation of Labor, both political parties, and scores of civic groups in Chicago. Working together under the auspices of the Illinois Committee for Constitutional Revision (ICCR), these usually antagonistic groups all found in the amendment something that appealed to their own self-interest. Members of the Citizens of Greater Chicago and other leading urban-based organizations had lacked clout for so long in either chamber of the legislature that substantial representation in one branch seemed like an important step forward, even if it meant forgoing already existing, but unenforced, constitutional rights in the second chamber. The Illinois Agricultural Association and the Chamber of Commerce, on the other hand, understood that majority rule in the lower chamber posed no threat to their agendas as long as sympathetic officials controlled the senate in perpetuity. The ICCR sold the Blue Ballot as "a fair compromise restoring true representative government to Illinois" by simultaneously appealing to urban voters to "Eliminate the Rotten Borough" and to Downstate residents to "Protect Fair Rural Representation."[14]

Opposition to the Blue Ballot proved tepid, at best. A handful of Downstate legislators from both parties, seeing that reapportionment of the lower chamber would mean the end of their seats, attempted to fight the initiative, but they were ultimately stifled by the official position of both parties. Among liberal and progressive groups, only the Illinois Council of Industrial Organizations (CIO) withheld its support. Joseph Germano, the president of the Illinois CIO, explained that the national office supported only "true representation" and thus his organization could not sanction an initiative that permanently left one branch of the legislature in the hands of a rural minority. The Blue Ballot passed easily.[15]

Like its counterparts in Michigan and Illinois, the Minnesota LWV devoted years to a thorough study of reapportionment. Representing 5,500 members from fifty-four local affiliates spread across the state—including urban, suburban, and rural districts that were either adequately represented, underrepresented, or overrepresented—the Minnesota LWV reached an "overwhelming consensus" in the mid-1950s that the legislature, which had not been reapportioned since 1913 despite a constitutional mandate to do so "in proportion to the population," was in "serious, even dire need, of immediate reapportionment."[16]

During the 1957 session of the state legislature, Mrs. Stanley Kane, the league's reapportionment lobbying chair, appeared before a house committee and explained her organization's position. "Our form of government demands equitable representation of all citizens in all legislative bodies," she declared in words that appear at first glance to prefigure a call for strict population-based reapportionment. But in a clear recognition of the political realities faced by the LWV as well as lingering concerns that urban residents should not be trusted with too much power, Kane asked residents of the state's most populous urban center, where she herself resided, to be "content with some measure of underrepresentation." To that end, Kane announced the league's support for a pending bill that would have increased the legislative strength of greater Minneapolis and St. Paul from 22 to 29 percent, but not as much as the 34.5 percent required by a strict population plan.[17]

Despite the concessions favored by the LWV, the Minnesota legislature refused yet again to reapportion. In response to a growing sense among certain politicians and political groups that the situation had become intolerable, Governor Orville L. Freeman appointed a joint committee of legislators and citizens, including two members of the LWV, to examine the issue and make recommendations. But before the legislature had a chance to consider the committee's final report, residents of Minnesota's four most populous counties filed suit in federal court, claiming that chronic underrepresentation violated their Fourteenth Amendment rights to Equal Protection.[18]

Faced with the threat of federal judicial intervention, the legislature met in special session in 1959 and adopted a reapportionment act that generally followed the proposal supported by the LWV in 1957. Significant population disparities still existed in the wake of Minnesota's 1959 reapportionment; nevertheless, the plaintiffs in the lawsuit felt sufficiently satisfied with the outcome of the special session that they moved to dismiss the suit. Taking their cue from the LWV, these plaintiffs were apparently "content with some measure of under-representation."[19]

The activities of the LWV indicate significant interest in reapportionment at the level of state politics, but in the mid-1950s the reapportionment of state legislatures and of Congress began to emerge as a national political issue as well. In 1953, newly elected president Dwight Eisenhower appointed a twenty-five-member commission to inspect the relationship among federal, state, and local governments, and to recommend changes to the structure and practice of American governance. Chaired by Chicago industrialist Meyer Kestnbaum, the Commission on Intergovernmental Relations was composed of five U.S. senators, five members of the House of Representatives, and fifteen prominent citizens.[20]

In its final report, submitted to the president in 1955, the Kestnbaum Commission identified malapportionment as a leading cause in the erosion of the "power and influence" of state governments. Addressing critics of expansive federal government, the commission noted that residents and officials of urban areas had turned to Washington for help precisely because of the neglect of state authorities, who had refused for decades to provide adequate funds for public housing, slum clearance, urban renewal, metropolitan transportation and infrastructure projects, and other legitimate needs resulting from massive population shifts and industrial development. The necessity of meaningful reapportionment, concluded the commission, was obvious and paramount. "Reapportionment should not be thought of solely in terms of a conflict of interests between urban and rural areas," the report added. "In the long run, the interests of all in an equitable system of representation that will strengthen State government is [sic] far more important than any temporary advantage to an area enjoying over-representation."[21]

John F. Kennedy, the junior senator from Massachusetts, embraced the logic and conclusions of the Kestnbaum report as he began to prepare his bid for the nation's highest office. Fully aware that urban voters would make up a large portion of the electorate in 1960, Kennedy (or, more likely, one of his staffers) wrote an article for the *New York Times Magazine* in which he condemned urban blight and decay as a clear consequence of rural overrepresentation in state governments. Citing Lincoln Steffens and other turn-of-the-century muckrakers who exposed endemic municipal political corruption as the cause of staggering poverty and other social ills deemed the "shame of the cities," Kennedy argued that substantial progress had been made in the intervening half century and that urban political machines, many of them still scapegoated by opponents of reapportionment, had, for the most part, "given way to honest, efficient, democratic" municipal governance. Now, he claimed, cities suffered from the "shame of the states" in the form of malapportionment, which made it exceedingly difficult for municipal officials to address the most pressing problems, such as overcrowded schools, hospitals, and jails, dilapidated housing, and congested roads and freeways. At the federal level, Kennedy explained, the malapportionment of the House of Representatives was responsible for the recent failure of Congress to pass important housing, education, and labor legislation.

Kennedy's article was meant to appeal to Americans who lived in metropolitan areas, made up the majority of the nation's voters, and paid the preponderance of the nation's taxes. "The apportionment of representation in our Legislatures and (to a lesser extent) in Congress," he wrote, "has been either deliberately rigged or shamefully ignored so as to deny the cities and their voters that full and proportionate voice in government to which they are entitled." Pointing out the fallacy in federal plans that assigned representation in one chamber to every county or town, Kennedy concluded that "what sounds like equality is in reality rank discrimination."

In his commentary, Kennedy specifically cited the Kestnbaum Commission, and added his assent to that group's conclusion that Congress and the federal government must act "as long as our state legislatures are not fully responsive to the urban areas and their needs." He wrote that "our politics should not become a battle for power between town and country, between city-dweller and farmer. . . . For whenever a large part of the population is denied its full and fair voice in government, the only result can be frustration of progress, bitterness, and a diminution of the democratic ideal. Country and city are interdependent."

Kennedy recognized that equitable apportionment provided no "panacea for the city's ills" and that identifying the problem was far easier than finding a solution. The presidential aspirant had no faith that state legislators—"the perpetrators and beneficiaries of the present malapportionment"—would put aside their own self-interest, a conclusion for which there was already abundant evidence. Similarly, Kennedy expected little from the judiciary as state courts deferred to the legislatures and the federal courts declined to provide relief. In view of such grim prospects for institutional change, Kennedy called on "an aroused public, a vigorous press, and the force of the democratic tradition" to bring about equitable relief. Certainly, he concluded, "one hundred million citizens—constituting a majority of the nation—will not forever accept this modern day 'taxation without representation.' "[22]

As John F. Kennedy prepared his piece, Anthony Lewis, a young reporter in the Washington bureau of the *New York Times*, wrote an article in the *Harvard Law Review* that established him as one of the nation's foremost experts on reapportionment and soon attracted the attention of litigants and lawyers frustrated by the continued recalcitrance of lawmakers. In contrast with Kennedy, Lewis, who had delved into the intricacies of reapportionment jurisprudence while a Nieman Fellow at Harvard Law School in 1956 and 1957, not only embraced the possibility of federal court intervention but also identified it as offering the only meaningful avenue for change. By the time the Supreme Court handed down its reapportionment decisions in the early 1960s, Lewis was the *Times*'s Supreme Court correspondent and, in that capacity, played an important behind-the-scenes role in the unfolding drama.[23]

Like all students of reapportionment at the time, Lewis understood the obstacle posed by the 1946 Supreme Court decision in *Colegrove* v. *Green*. At the turn of the twentieth century, Illinois's congressional districts adhered closely to constitutional guidelines: each district had between 160,000 and 184,000 residents. But by 1928, after the population upheavals of World War I and the initial Great Migration, and after three decades without reapportionment, the population of congressional districts in Illinois ranged from 158,000 (the Fifth) to 560,000 (the Seventh). After World War II and the Second Great Migration, Illinois's Seventh Congressional District grew to 914,000 people, the most of any congressional district in the United States, while the Fifth District had shrunk to 112,000 residents, the least populous in the nation. Frustrated by the unwillingness of the legislature to alleviate such massive disparities within their state, residents of the most underrepresented districts turned for relief to the federal courts.[24]

The Supreme Court nevertheless turned aside the resulting suit, with Justice Felix Frankfurter authoring the decision's most famous line: "Courts ought not to enter this political thicket." No matter how firm the grip of minority rule or how remote the possibility of reform through the electoral process, Frankfurter insisted that "the remedy for unfairness in districting is to secure State legislatures that will apportion properly, or to invoke the ample powers of Congress." For more than a decade, the decision had been interpreted to mean that federal courts could not assert jurisdiction in reapportionment disputes. But where most others saw an insurmountable barrier, Anthony Lewis imagined possibilities. He was quick to point out that only three members of the Supreme Court, led by Frankfurter, actually took the position most associated with *Colegrove*. Three other justices, most notably Hugo Black and William O. Douglas, who remained on the Court through the 1960s and would play a central role in overturning the case, rejected Frankfurter's admonition and argued that the federal courts should intervene to address an obvious constitutional infraction. The spring of 1946 marked a rare moment when two members of the Supreme Court were absent—Chief Justice Harlan Fisk Stone had died in April and Associate Justice Robert Jackson was in Germany, where he was serving as the chief prosecutor of the Nuremberg war crimes tribunal. Consequently Associate Justice Wiley Rutledge cast the seventh and determinative vote in *Colegrove* v. *Green*. Rutledge sided with Frankfurter on the particular merits of the case, but on the larger point, he agreed with Black, Douglas, and Frank Murphy that the federal courts did, in fact, have the power to adjudicate reapportionment disputes. The apparent contradiction at the heart of Rutledge's decision masked the work of a savvy jurist whose tactical acumen would become apparent more than fifteen years later, after *Baker* v. *Carr*.[25]

Satisfied that *Colegrove* v. *Green* had not foreclosed federal court intervention in reapportionment disputes, Lewis urged the courts to correct what he referred to as an "evil" or a "disease incurable by legislative physic." Lewis knew that "the federal courts cannot remake politics," and so instead of calling on the courts to redraw legislative and congressional boundaries, he encouraged the judiciary to order at-large elections that would force lawmakers to undertake meaningful reapportionment.[26]

Lewis perceived that at some point in the future the courts would have to resolve the difficult question of what does or does not constitute "equality of representation." Malapportionment in most states, he argued, lacked a rational basis and therefore violated the Fourteenth Amendment's guarantee of equal protection and due process. But he made no attempt to put forth a particular mathematical standard that had to be met to satisfy the Fourteenth Amendment. "How is a court," he asked, "to determine when the disparity passes the allowable limit?" Neither the federal government nor any of the states provided such specific guidance at the time, although Representative Emanuel Celler of New York, the Democratic chairman of the House Judiciary Committee, had introduced legislation to require congressional districts to vary by no more than 20 percent from the average or ideal. Lewis also acknowledged with regard to state legislative apportionments that "there is no constitutional assumption that representation should be based on units of equal population." States, he admitted, were free to base apportionments on population, area, or other factors, but only so long as the schemes were reasonable and rational. Therefore, as late as 1958, one of the nation's leading proponents of legislative and congressional reapportionment, an individual who repeatedly referred to malapportionment as evil, did not push for strict population apportionments in both chambers of a bicameral legislature. Within a few years, however, this very question of standards would dominate reapportionment litigation.[27]

Although Lewis targeted a rather narrow, albeit influential, legal audience, the publication of his article coincided with the appearance of a burgeoning literature that reflected growing national concern with malapportionment. Aside from Lewis, no journalist did more to educate the general public about the politics of malapportionment than George B. Merry, a staff writer for the *Christian Science Monitor*. In late 1958, Merry wrote a five-part series on state legislative malapportionment, the first part of which covered an entire page of newsprint; the following year the *Christian Science Monitor* ran an equally informative four-part series by Merry on congressional malapportionment.[28] At the same time, *Harper's Magazine* ran its own piece on the subject with the title "The Next Election Is Already Rigged." Toward the end of the piece, its author, Richard Lee Strout, wondered if "the urban voter needs a psychiatrist." Even *Redbook: The Magazine for Young Adults* took notice. Not typically known for political reporting, it asked its subscribers, "How Much Does Your Vote Count?"[29]

As the 1960 presidential election approached, a contentious reapportionment measure once again appeared on the ballot in California. This time, however, the initiative, known as Proposition 15, was championed not by the California Federation of Labor but by increasingly frustrated metropolitan officials in Los Angeles County. The stupendous growth of California in the 1940s actually accelerated over the next decade: the state added 5.1 million residents, nearly 1,400 per day, between 1950 and 1960, enough for an additional eight members of Congress after the 1960 census. Once again, the increase was almost entirely in metropolitan areas, with the urbanites in the state rising from 80 percent to more than 86 percent. The population of Los Angeles County alone jumped from 4,151,687 to 6,038,771, but its residents continued to elect just one state senator—as did the 14,294 inhabitants of Inyo, Alpine, and Mono Counties on the eastern side of the Sierra. Not surprising, citizens and officials of the most underrepresented regions chafed at the absurdity of their predicament.[30]

Proponents of California's so-called balanced legislature maintained that the rural-controlled senate had consistently supported legislation favored by urbanites, but by 1960 officials in Los Angeles County were vociferously challenging this notion. Arguing that "the Legislature should represent people and not trees"—language that would appear almost word for word in Earl Warren's 1964 majority opinion in *Reynolds* v. *Sims*—Frank Bonelli, a member of the Los Angeles County Board of Supervisors and the chief sponsor of Proposition 15, attacked the legislature for its failure, during its 1959 session, to allocate gas tax revenue for highway and road construction in an equitable manner, as well as for defeating a much-needed air pollution control measure and a tax on factory inventory, land, buildings, and machinery that would have netted Los Angeles County $7 million to $8 million per year. Perhaps more than anything else, Southern Californians continued to worry about their access to an adequate supply of water from Northern California's rivers and reservoirs.[31]

The Bonelli initiative enjoyed critical support from an unexpected ally: the Los Angeles Chamber of Commerce. Unlike the California Chamber of Commerce, which continued to oppose reapportionment with every fiber of its institutional being, the Los Angeles branch changed tack once again. After supporting reapportionment in both chambers on a population basis in 1926 and actively opposing Proposition 13 in 1948, by 1960 members of the Los Angeles Chamber had come to question whether rural legislators, many of them Democrats, would continue to protect their interests in the senate. Led by James L. Beebe, the chair of the organization's State and Local Government Committee, the Los Angeles Chamber turned on these rural senators. As Beebe derided California's system as a "cow county plan" rather than a federal plan, his committee concluded in a private memorandum that rural legislators, "once considered a conservative influence in matters of legislation . . . have become exceedingly liberal with other people's money, piling the State tax load heavily on the populous industrial centers" while handing out subventions to the smaller counties. Furthermore, Beebe added, the state's major labor unions endorsed most rural senators in 1958 and 1960. He and others concluded that increased representation for Los Angeles County, especially in the region's burgeoning suburban neighborhoods, would mean more Republican state senators and congressional representatives. Noting that forty-three of fifty states had fewer

residents than did Los Angeles County, the Los Angeles Chamber demanded additional representation.[32]

Having assumed the reins of Whitaker & Baxter from his father and
stepmother, Clem Whitaker Jr. was hired to coordinate the attack on
the Bonelli initiative. No longer able to treat labor as the bogeyman
behind reapportionment, Whitaker & Baxter attempted to unify the
fifty-seven counties outside Los Angeles by defining Proposition 15 as a
blatant power grab by the state's most populous county. Working with a
budget of more than $250,000, double the amount raised by proponents
of the initiative, Whitaker & Baxter saturated the state's newspapers and
airwaves with language such as "You Are in Danger: California Must
Defeat State Senate Reapportionment" and "Don't Be Squeezed Off the
Map! Vote No on Proposition No. 15, The Senate Packing Reapportionment Scheme." The campaign succeeded spectacularly; Proposition 15
won barely one-third of the state's support and only one county, Los
Angeles. Two years later, Bonelli tried again, but for the third time since
World War II, Whitaker & Baxter turned back an effort to reapportion
the California senate. Outspending the opposition nearly three to one
in 1962, the firm ensured that its clients would remain in control of the
legislature a bit longer.[33]

As Whitaker & Baxter fended off another assault on minority rule on the
West Coast, residents of suburban Long Island threw a mock Tea Party—
complete with a ship and colonial and Native American costumes—to
protest their underrepresentation in the New York legislature and in
Congress. Staged by Nassau County Democrats just weeks before the 1960
election, the spectacle featured participants who declared that "taxation
without representation is tyranny," held up signs decrying the underrepresentation of Nassau and neighboring Suffolk County, and dumped
casks of fake tea into the harbor. As an exercise in political theater, the
Long Island Tea Party proved a bit silly, but in fact it focused attention
on a development that so far had eluded most critics of malapportionment: by 1960, residents of the nation's suburbs—whether Republicans
in Los Angeles or Democrats on Long Island—had as much to gain from
meaningful reapportionment as did urban dwellers.[34]

In the 1940s and 1950s, supporters of reapportionment framed the issue as a debate between rural overrepresentation and urban underrepresentation. Most observers, including Anthony Lewis and the authors of the Kestnbaum Report, said next to nothing about the suburbs, while John F. Kennedy referred to suburbanites only in passing. Not until late 1959, when the most prescient analysts began to predict the findings of the 1960 census, did the suburbs, and suburbanites, begin to merit serious attention in discussions of malapportionment.[35]

If the beginning of the twentieth century in America was defined demographically by the rapid influx of immigrants and the growth of the nation's cities, the period starting around 1950 witnessed another mass movement of Americans, this time from the cities to the suburbs. Between that year and 1960, the number of residents in almost all the central cities of the nation's largest metropolitan regions declined while the corresponding suburban populations increased dramatically. New York City experienced a small decline in its population, while the outlying suburbs of Nassau and Suffolk grew by more than 75 percent. Chicago, whose size had long been seen as a threat by opponents of reapportionment in Illinois, shrunk by nearly 2 percent, while its suburbs grew by more than 70 percent. In Minneapolis and St. Paul, where the League of Women Voters aggressively pursued reapportionment but not on a straight population basis, the central-city population declined by more than 4 percent, while the suburban populations of Hennepin and Ramsey Counties more than doubled. Similar demographic shifts took place in Detroit, Philadelphia, San Francisco–Oakland, Boston, Pittsburgh, Cleveland, Baltimore, Newark, St. Louis, and Buffalo; the central-city populations of these metropolitan regions declined between 1 and 12 percent as growth in the corresponding suburbs ranged from 17 to 79 percent. Among the fourteen largest metropolitan regions, only Los Angeles and Long Beach, California, witnessed an increase in their core populations. But even there, the suburbs exploded by more than 82 percent; these were the neighborhoods that the Los Angeles County Chamber of Commerce identified as full of potential conservative, and Republican, voters.[36]

J. Anthony Lukas, who later earned two Pulitzer Prizes, most notably for *Common Ground*, a stunning portrait of the busing crisis in Boston and its effect on three families, was among the first journalists to fully grasp the importance of the link between suburbanization and malapportionment. Looking at the 1960 census figures in Maryland, where the underrepresented suburbs around Baltimore had grown more than 72 percent in the previous decade, Lukas quipped that "Maryland suburbanites have purchased split-level splendor at the price of gradual political disfranchisement."[37]

On January 5, 1961, just two weeks before the inauguration of John F. Kennedy as president, Edward R. Murrow hosted an hour-long special on CBS, the first half of which he devoted to malapportionment. Murrow highlighted the extraordinary political power exercised by inhabitants of small towns from Vermont to California, as well as the effect of minority rule on residents of Los Angeles and Long Island, among other underrepresented regions. He included a bit of footage from the Long Island Tea Party, which might, in fact, have been staged as a prop for the broadcast. Among Murrow's viewers, few were more interested than Mrs. Edward Reisman Jr., a resident of Nashville and the president of the Tennessee League of Women Voters. The day before the broadcast, Reisman telegrammed members of the Tennessee legislature and encouraged them to tune in. For years, the Tennessee LWV had tried without success to spur the legislature to reapportion itself and finally had joined a lawsuit filed in 1959 that challenged the state's apportionment. As a new administration prepared to assume control of the nation's executive branch, that case, *Baker* v. *Carr*, awaited oral argument before the Supreme Court of the United States.[38]

4 ||| IT HAS LOTS TO DO WITH THE PRICE OF EGGS: THE MAKING OF *BAKER* V. *CARR*

Prior to the opening session of the Tennessee General Assembly in January 1959, three members of the League of Women Voters— Joan Harap, the state legislative chair; Sebby Billig, the president of the Nashville chapter; and Molly Todd, a former president of the Nashville chapter and a prominent member of the state committee— placed red signs on the desk of every lawmaker. The signs, bearing the signature of the LWV of Tennessee, read STOP, BEFORE you take your oath of office as a member of the General Assembly of Tennessee, and SWEAR TO UPHOLD our State Constitution, read Article II, Sections 4, 5, and 6 of the Constitution of the State of Tennessee. These parts of the state constitution required the Tennessee legislature to reapportion both its chambers on a population basis, and to do so every ten years.[1]

The Tennessee LWV, which had made reapportionment its top legislative priority in 1957, was led primarily by well-educated urban residents. Harap was a native of New York City, a 1923 Wellesley graduate with a master's degree in English, and a mother of four, who moved to Nashville in 1937 when her husband took up a professorship at Nashville's Peabody College for Teachers, now part of Vanderbilt University. Billig, who served as president of the Nashville LWV for four years, was also married to a professor. She and her husband, Otto, an Austrian Jew educated at the University of Vienna who fled his homeland after Hitler's rise, arrived in Nashville in 1948 when he was appointed to a position in clinical psychiatry at Vanderbilt's medical school. Molly Todd, a

Brooklyn native and 1925 graduate of Vassar, was the driving force behind the LWV's effort to reapportion the Tennessee legislature. Prior to moving to the state capital in 1939 with her second husband, she was a social worker focusing on birth control. In 1948, she rejuvenated the dormant Nashville chapter of the LWV, served as its first president, and spearheaded the organization's efforts to increase government support for schools, libraries, and child welfare services. "An activist to her fingertips," according to Harap's daughter, Todd helped bring Planned Parenthood to Nashville and served as a founding member of the city's chapter of the American Civil Liberties Union and the Tennessee Council on Human Relations. Like its counterparts in other southern states, the Tennessee council was established by the Southern Regional Council after the Supreme Court's *Brown* decision and tried to address the worst inequities caused by segregation and to prepare the state's citizens for the actual end of Jim Crow. When John Lewis, Diane Nash, and other local college students launched the Nashville sit-in movement in February 1960, the fifty-five-year-old Todd took a seat at the lunch counters, supported covertly by her husband, an executive at one of the department stores targeted by the protesters.[2]

From the moment the Tennessee LWV identified reapportionment as a top priority, the organization worked to educate the general public about the costs, both financial and otherwise, of inaction. Mrs. Murray Rosenthal, a mother of two and a member of the local LWV in Oak Ridge, explained to a reporter from her local paper precisely how malapportionment directly affected her. A three-cent tax on every dollar spent at the grocery store, she pointed out, funded most of the state's contribution for education, while the improvement and maintenance of the roads and streets in her neighborhood depended upon the allocation of the gasoline tax. Rural control of the legislature, however, ensured that residents of cities such as Oak Ridge did not receive back a fair share of such revenues. "Housewife Agrees," Rosenthal's hometown newspaper proclaimed in one of the more unlikely headlines focusing on malapportionment, "It Has Lots to Do With the Price of Eggs."[3]

As members of the LWV looked toward the 1959 session of the General Assembly, they agreed to support only legislation that adhered to the existing state constitutional formula, and not, as their midwestern colleagues had done, to accept any measure that deviated from a population-based apportionment of both chambers. The Tennessee LWV designed, printed, and distributed 7,000 copies of a flyer that high-lighted the legislature's failure to protect existing state constitutional guarantees, and pointed out that individual legislators represented as few as 3,800 people and as many as 70,000. A clear and concise sum-mary of the position of the Tennessee LWV, the flyers declared WE HAVE TAXATION WITHOUT FAIR REPRESENTATION! WE HAVE MINOR-ITY RULE IN TENNESSEE![4]

Todd, Harap, Billig, and the other members of the LWV knew that the likelihood of shaming lawmakers into passing a meaningful reap-portionment bill was slim at best. After all, the legislature had ignored its constitutional obligation since 1901, as the state's population continued to move from small towns and rural hinterlands to cities such as Mem-phis, Nashville, Clarksville, Knoxville, Chattanooga, and Johnson City. Despite these massive demographic upheavals, the Volunteer State re-mained in the firm control of a coterie of rural and small-town Demo-crats, led by "the unholy trinity" of James H. Cummings, I. D. Beasley, and Walter N. "Pete" Haynes. For more than a quarter century, accord-ing to a Nashville journalist, "these three were the men to see at the state legislature . . . the cloak-and-dagger men of the cloakroom." Unafraid of urban political bosses or governors, but terrified of majority rule, the tri-umvirate (and, after Beasley's death in 1955, the duo of Cummings and Haynes) consistently turned aside reapportionment bills, ensuring that two-thirds of the state's lawmakers continued to represent only one-third of the state's residents. Their goal was not merely legislative dominion—it was control of the state's financial resources. As Cum-mings acknowledged to one reporter, "I believe in collecting the taxes where the money is—in the cities—and spending it where it's needed—in the country."[5]

In 1955, a collection of mostly young lawyers in Johnson City, Knox-ville, and Nashville banded together to take on Tennessee's rural inter-ests, signing up a baker's dozen of civic activists as plaintiffs, and filing *Kidd* v. *McCanless* in state court. Arguing that minority rule stood "con-trary to the philosophy of government in the United States and all Anglo-Saxon jurisprudence," the lawsuit asked the judiciary to declare the existing apportionment in violation of the state constitution. In his brief, Nashville attorney Tom Osborn included a section that he labeled "pure argument." Imagining what the current demographic trends would leave the state looking like in the year 2000, Osborn predicted that the population of rural Cannon County, the home and political base of Jim Cummings, would shrink to only two residents—with both individuals sitting in the legislature, one in the house and one in the senate. Meanwhile, hundreds of thousands of residents of the state's most populous regions would be even more grossly underrepresented than they were in 1955.[6]

Tennessee's highest court rebuked Osborn for this speculation—he himself freely characterized his predictions as a fable—and threw out the case, leaning entirely on *Colegrove* v. *Green* to justify its refusal to intervene. In response, Osborn publicly questioned the integrity of the justices and was nearly disbarred as a result. In a one-line, unsigned opinion, the Supreme Court of the United States also cited *Colegrove* when it refused to hear an appeal.[7]

Osborn and his cocounsel launched this initial attack on the malapportionment of the Tennessee legislature without any support, financial or otherwise, from municipal officials in Nashville or Memphis. Authorities in Memphis avoided involving themselves in *Kidd* v. *McCanless* because Edward Hull Crump, better known as "Boss" to admirers and detractors alike, and who had ruled his Memphis political machine for nearly fifty years, had entered into a bargain with Jim Cummings and his cronies. The legislature directed more funds to Memphis than to other urban centers, and the Crump machine, in turn, supported the legislature's rural leadership. In Nashville, by contrast, Mayor Ben West feared antagonizing the legislature and losing the little state support his city did receive. The lack of assistance from the two largest and most important metropolitan regions meant that Osborn and the other attorneys in *Kidd* v. *McCanless* personally bore the cost of litigation. In fact, when Osborn agreed to join a second lawsuit against the Tennessee legislature in 1959, he confided to his cocounsel that he had only just recovered from the "monetary injury" he suffered as a result of his involvement in *Kidd* v. *McCanless*. "I bled awhile," he added, "but learned not enough from the experience to be permanently discouraged."[8]

By the end of the decade, however, officials in Memphis and surrounding Shelby County faced a new, and more daunting, reality. Crump had died in October 1954, just months before *Kidd* v. *McCanless* was first filed, and no one emerged to replace the Boss. Within a few years, the remains of his machine had crumbled and the city and county were struggling financially. Desperate for a greater share of state revenue, David Newby Harsh, the chair of the county governing board, saw a potential opportunity when he learned about the recent ruling of a federal court in Minnesota.[9]

In July 1958, a three-judge panel of the U.S. district court ruled in *Magraw* v. *Donovan* that the Minnesota legislature had an "unmistakable duty . . . to reapportion itself periodically in accordance with recent population changes." Not yet ready, however, to enter the "political thicket" enunciated by Felix Frankfurter in *Colegrove* v. *Green*, the district court elected to "defer a decision on all the issues presented (including that of the power of this Court to grant relief)." The district court, therefore, did not order the legislature to carry out a reapportionment but instead allowed lawmakers a final opportunity to act on their own initiative.[10]

In granting the Minnesota legislature a final chance to reapportion itself, the three-judge panel uttered a single, but critical, sentence that caught David Harsh's attention. "The Court has jurisdiction of this action because of the federal constitutional issue asserted," claimed the district court, hinting that it remained open to the possibility of tossing aside *Colegrove* v. *Green* if the legislature did not reapportion. The final outcome of *Magraw* v. *Donovan* not yet decided, David Harsh perceived in the Minnesota case a blueprint for a successful challenge in Tennessee, as both state constitutions required regular reapportionments on a population basis, with the single difference that Tennessee counted qualified voters while Minnesota included all residents. Furthermore, Harsh interpreted the federal court's apparent embrace of the Equal Protection Clause in the Minnesota case as evidence that the U.S. Supreme Court's landmark decision in *Brown* v. *Board of Education* had opened the door to an expanded definition of federally recognized individual rights. If federal judges did not sanction discrimination based on race, Harsh reasoned, they should not allow it on grounds of residence either.[11]

During the first week of January 1959, as Molly Todd and her friends in the Tennessee LWV prepared to lobby the legislature for a meaningful reapportionment bill, Harsh asked Memphis attorney Walter Chandler to look into the feasibility of filing a lawsuit along the lines of the Minnesota case. A former member of the state legislature and the U.S. House of Representatives, and president pro tem of the 1953 Tennessee Constitutional Convention, Chandler was one of the most respected and politically connected individuals in the state. He had served the Crump machine as the mayor of Memphis in the 1940s and yet simultaneously maintained his independence and reputation for competence and fairness, resigning the city's highest office with a year left on his term after a dispute with the Boss. Known to many of his friends and admirers as "Captain" for his exemplary service as an infantry officer in France during World War I, Chandler returned to the mayor's office for a short spell in 1955, completing the term of an incumbent who had died in office. In this second stint as mayor, Chandler chose not to lend support to Tennessee's first reapportionment lawsuit.[12]

By January 1959, however, Chandler had come to understand the implacable hostility of the legislature to even minimal reapportionment and the mounting costs to urban infrastructure and education. Now seventy-one, his most vigorous years behind him, Chandler nevertheless accepted Harsh's proposed case and immediately set out to learn everything he could about *Kidd* v. *McCanless* and *Magraw* v. *Donovan*. Chandler began an extensive correspondence with the attorneys in both cases and assembled a team of his own.[13]

No doubt intent on a second chance at the verdict that had eluded them several years earlier, Tom Osborn and Hobart Atkins, both veterans of *Kidd* v. *McCanless*, quickly agreed to join Chandler. Osborn was more than thirty years Chandler's junior. He had grown up poor, the son of a circuit-riding Presbyterian minister, and moved to Nashville after dropping out of college. There he took night classes in law at the local YMCA and passed the bar at age twenty-one. Lacking family connections, he relied instead on his sharp mind and determination in order to earn a position at a prestigious Nashville firm, and soon after moved to the city attorney's office, where he became acquainted with the stifling effects of malapportionment. By the time of his involvement in *Kidd*, he had returned to private practice. Hobart Atkins, for his part, had tried in vain for years to reform the Tennessee legislature from within. He represented heavily Republican Knoxville in the state senate for four terms and also served as general counsel for the state Republican Party. He devoted most of his practice not to corporations and the well-heeled but to the defense of the unlettered and the unsophisticated who swelled the population of Knoxville in the mid-twentieth century.[14]

In 1959, with the Tennessee legislature in session, Chandler, Osborn, and Atkins plotted strategy and began to draft their complaint. Chandler and Atkins warned every member of the General Assembly that they had one final chance to pass a meaningful reapportionment plan, or else risk a lawsuit. Simultaneously, Chandler arranged for the introduction of a population-based reapportionment bill, which he knew had no chance of passing. Predictably, the legislature killed Chandler's bill before adjourning in late March.[15]

Chandler, Osborn, and Atkins were pleased that the legislature had stepped right into their trap by adjourning without even a pretense of satisfying its constitutional obligations. They began carefully recruiting plaintiffs from across the state, all qualified voters entitled to cast ballots in state legislative elections. This bipartisan group, most of whom had long exhibited a commitment to reapportionment, included Guy Smith, a Knoxville newspaper publisher and the chairman of the state Republican Party; John R. McGauley, the president of a citizens' committee in Chattanooga; and Molly Todd, who was a neighbor of Tom Osborn's and whose inclusion represented a modest recognition of the role that the LWV had played in bringing attention to the issue. Charles W. Baker, the chairman of the Shelby County Quarterly Court, which functioned less as a traditional court and more as a tax-levying body, also joined the suit. Even though he figured only tangentially in the events that followed, he earned a lasting place in the annals of constitutional jurisprudence because the attorneys chose to list some, but not all, of the plaintiffs in alphabetical order. Chandler and his team sued Joe C. Carr, the secretary of state, whose duties included overseeing the commonwealth's election machinery, and five other state officials. Like Baker, Carr owes his place in history to the first letter of his last name as much as his actions (or lack thereof).[16]

Osborn, Chandler, and Atkins filed their lawsuit on May 18, 1959, with the clerk of the federal district court in Nashville. At the time, the Minnesota legislature was meeting in special session to resolve its reapportionment dilemma, and Chandler and his team had crafted their strategy with the expectation that they would be able to cite a final judicial order in *Magraw* v. *Donovan* as precedent for their motion. But as their date with the district court drew near, Chandler learned from Daniel Magraw that he and the other Minnesota plaintiffs were leaning against going back to the federal court. The Minnesota legislature had passed a bill that maintained unsatisfactory discrepancies in both chambers but that nevertheless represented a massive improvement from the preexisting arrangement. In a letter to an official with the National Municipal League, Magraw explained, "We feel that to jeopardize the progress we have made in the case so far by going back into court and risking an unfavorable opinion would be a serious error." In August, the lead attorney for the Minnesota plaintiffs drafted a motion asking the federal district court to dismiss all proceedings in *Magraw* v. *Donovan*. In October, the federal panel complied.[17]

Though a federal court order in Minnesota would have lent considerable weight to their cause, Chandler and his team remained cautiously optimistic when they appeared before Judge William Miller in early July to ask that he convene a three-judge panel. The United States Code mandates that such panels, made up of two district court judges and one appellate jurist, hear certain constitutional challenges, including all congressional and state legislative apportionment claims; if appealed, decisions rendered by these panels go directly to the Supreme Court. The first ruling in *Baker* v. *Carr* was welcome news to the plaintiffs: Miller determined that the issues raised in the complaint did, indeed, merit consideration by a three-judge court.[18]

Within days of Miller's order, Chandler and Osborn decided on the two central components of their strategy, both of which ultimately proved crucial when *Baker* v. *Carr* reached the Supreme Court. First, they set out to establish the total unwillingness of the Tennessee legislature to meet its constitutional duty and the corresponding inability of the people of the state to obtain relief through any alternative means, such as the initiative or referendum. To this end, they relied on Dr. Robert H. White, the state historian, who dug into old editions of the legislative journal, dating back to the 1870s, and methodically documented the recalcitrance of the legislature since the turn of the century. Chandler was pleased with White's final report, telling Osborn, "I do not think that it is necessary to show that war broke out every ten years, but it is worthwhile to show that the question of reapportionment came up frequently and nothing was done."[19]

Chandler and Osborn had determined early on that their entire case hinged on their ability to prove that the failure of the legislature to reapportion did, in fact, constitute a violation of the Equal Protection and Due Process Clauses of the Fourteenth Amendment. The second component of their strategy was based on this notion and came from Chandler. He suggested that they focus on not only the maldistribution of state revenues but also the passage of various acts of the legislature which, taken together, could be seen to demonstrate a pattern of discrimination against citizens of urban areas.[20]

In mid-September, as Chandler, Osborn, and Atkins prepared for their appearance before the three-judge court in late November, they received word that they would not, at least to begin with, have an opportunity to present their entire case. Instead, they would be limited to the issue of jurisdiction. They were deeply disappointed by this, but their spirits were soon lifted by the long-awaited news that Nashville mayor Ben West had finally taken an interest in the case.[21]

Ben West had been slow to commit himself to the reapportionment fight, but he became a dedicated and invaluable ally once he entered the fray. First elected mayor in 1951, West had remained a neutral observer during *Kidd* v. *McCanless*, fearful of antagonizing the legislature and convinced that the courts should not get involved. During his second term, he shed his fears as he acquired a national reputation. In 1957, as he completed a year as president of the American Municipal Association (later renamed the National League of Cities), West spoke all across the United States, and in a few foreign countries as well. In speech after speech, he highlighted the plight of city dwellers by facetiously telling his audiences that the cows, pigs, and people in rural Moore County had three times more representation per capita than residents of Nashville and Davidson County. Not surprising, members of the legislature failed to see the humor in West's statements, especially as the mayor sharpened his critique while cruising to a third term in the spring of 1959. By late summer, West knew that his relationship with legislative leaders could not be mended, yet he was still reluctant to join the reapportionment lawsuit. It took the urging of Atlanta mayor William Hartsfield, a prominent supporter of reapportionment, to convince West to lend his, and the city's, support to Chandler and Osborn.[22]

One of West's most important contributions was to place the staff of the Advance Planning Division of Nashville's City Planning Commission at the disposal of Chandler and his team. From his residence in Nashville, Osborn supervised the Advanced Planning Division as it went to work preparing, in Osborn's words, "the necessary proof supporting our due process violation allegations." Analyzing mountains of financial and demographic data, city planners meticulously detailed the discriminatory effects of malapportionment, especially as it affected state aid for education and the disbursement of gasoline and motor fuel tax revenues that paid for roads, bridges, and other infrastructure. The Planning Division, which had only three weeks to prepare for the first hearing, revised and refined its reporting throughout the two-year course of litigation. By the time *Baker* v. *Carr* was argued before the U.S. Supreme Court for a second time in October 1961, the final product, an eighty-page document, reflected the results of the 1960 census and made a significant impression on the Court.[23]

In early November, West and the City of Nashville formalized their entry into *Baker* v. *Carr* and instantly provided the plaintiffs with badly needed financial support. Responding to a request from West, the city council passed a resolution authorizing him to "intervene and participate" in the lawsuit and "to take any and all necessary steps in proving the long continued mistreatment of the people of the City of Nashville at the hands of the unlawfully apportioned General Assemblies of Tennessee." As one journalist pointed out, the resolution "amounted to a blank check." The commitment nominally cost the taxpayers of Nashville at least $35,900 between November 1959 and May 1961, and, in reality, probably a good deal more. Memphis and Shelby County, by contrast, had contributed $6,000 to get the plaintiffs through the initial stages of the lawsuit. In mid-November, less than a week before the three-judge panel met, West officially petitioned the district court to allow him to intervene as a plaintiff on behalf of the citizens of Nashville.[24]

Despite grim weather, a sense of anticipation coursed throughout the U.S. district court in Nashville on the day of the hearing. Among interested parties, the LWV, whose members had spent weeks poring over the briefs of both the plaintiffs and defense, was especially well represented. But as the hearing got under way, the LWV members in attendance confronted a disappointing reality. Questions and comments from the bench signaled that the judges did not appear inclined to side with the plaintiffs.[25]

Attorneys for the state of Tennessee stipulated that the legislature had failed to meet its constitutional obligations and that extreme malapportionment did discriminate against urban residents, but they predictably fell back on *Colegrove* v. *Green*, arguing that the case foreclosed any possibility of judicial intervention. Three weeks later, the three-judge panel unanimously granted the state of Tennessee's motion to dismiss the complaint. In their opinion, the judges not only determined that the state legislature was "guilty of a clear violation of the state constitution" but added in the strongest language possible that "the evil is a serious one which should be corrected without delay." Nevertheless, the panel concluded that the remedy "does not lie with the courts." The decision, of course, came as a blow to the plaintiffs, but Chandler vowed to press on. "We are appealing the case," he told one correspondent, "and have no intention of relaxing our efforts until we win."[26]

Although they had ostensibly been defeated, Chandler and his team simultaneously scored what would eventually be a more important victory when the judges allowed West to remain a party to the lawsuit and to amend and supplement his petition. Whether or not defense attorneys fully appreciated the importance of this ruling—it is more than likely they did not, convinced as they were that no federal court would overrule *Colegrove* v. *Green*—West's amended petition, and its twelve exhibits, became the vehicle through which the plaintiffs, on appeal, introduced into evidence the report of state historian Robert White and the financial analysis of the Advance Planning Division. West's continued involvement also ensured the funds necessary to make the appeal, funds that only Nashville was in a position to provide.[27]

Once the taxpayers of Nashville assumed financial responsibility for *Baker* v. *Carr*, Ben West nudged aside Walter Chandler, Tom Osborn, and Hobart Atkins, and asserted himself as the key decision maker among the Tennessee plaintiffs. As soon as the three-judge court formally dismissed the complaint in February 1960, West flew to Washington with the aim of hiring an expert in Supreme Court litigation to shepherd the appeal to the nation's highest court. After consulting with his contacts in the American Municipal Association, West settled on Charles Rhyne, a former president of the American Bar Association with deep ties to the Washington establishment, who was also a friend of then vice president Richard Nixon. (During the Watergate scandal, Rhyne and his son represented Nixon's secretary, Rose Mary Woods, who famously erased eighteen and a half minutes of crucial tape detailing the president's role in the cover-up.) By the early 1960s, Rhyne had built a lucrative private practice, its success a result in part of nearly a quarter century of continuous service as the general counsel of the National Institute of Municipal Law Officers, plus additional stints as general counsel of the American Municipal Association and the United States Conference of Mayors. In these positions, Rhyne became a highly specialized expert in constitutional law as it pertains to municipal issues, guiding more than one hundred cases to the Supreme Court. When approached by West, Rhyne demanded absolute control of *Baker* v. *Carr* in return for his involvement. West agreed and paid him an initial retainer of $5,000 in mid-February 1960. Chandler, Osborn, and Atkins each called Rhyne to assure him that they welcomed his participation in their lawsuit (though Osborn, in actuality, chafed at the intrusion throughout the course of the litigation).[28]

In an interview in the late 1960s, Rhyne claimed credit for convincing the federal government to enter *Baker* v. *Carr* as amicus curiae, or friend of the court, a process by which a brief is filed by a person or persons not directly involved in the complaint but who have an interest in the legal questions before the court. The decision of the federal government to enter the Tennessee case as amicus curiae turned out to be a crucial development that immeasurably strengthened the case of the plaintiffs, now officially recognized as the appellants. Rhyne did count Solicitor General J. Lee Rankin and Attorney General William Rogers among his friends, and West did select Rhyne in part for his connections within the Eisenhower administration. But the solicitor general needed no prodding from Rhyne to take notice of *Baker* v. *Carr*; Rankin had been searching for several years for the right case with which to launch a direct attack on *Colegrove* v. *Green*. In fact, he had contacted

Walter Chandler several days before West hired Rhyne and asked Chandler for a copy of the case file.[29]

The solicitor general occupies a unique position in the American system of government. A high-ranking official in the Department of Justice who reports to the attorney general, the solicitor general in theory represents the executive branch before the nation's highest court. In practice, however, the solicitor general serves an additional function and carries extra weight with members of the Supreme Court. Whether appearing on behalf of the United States as a direct party in a complaint or as amicus curiae, the solicitor general is expected by the justices, in the words of one observer, "to look beyond the government's narrow interests" and "to help guide them" to the proper decision. As a result of what former associate justice Lewis Powell referred to as the solicitor general's "dual responsibility" to the executive and judicial branches, the solicitor general has been referred to as the "tenth justice." Consequently, the office of the solicitor general has served as a stepping-stone for individuals aspiring to the nation's appellate courts, including the Supreme Court.[30]

Lee Rankin was appointed solicitor general in August 1956, at the tail end of the first Eisenhower administration. He initially tried to maneuver the Department of Justice into challenging *Colegrove* v. *Green* in 1958, when he favored filing a short amicus curiae brief in *Hartsfield* v. *Sloan*, a case that attempted to overturn Georgia's county-unit system (which is discussed in chapter 6). The Supreme Court had ruled in favor of the state of Georgia twice in recent years in factually similar cases and, in doing so, had reaffirmed *Colegrove*, but Rankin interpreted the recently passed Civil Rights Act of 1957 as providing authority for a reversal. Yet Assistant Attorney General Wilson White, the first head of the newly created Civil Rights Division, argued that *Hartsfield* v. *Sloan* did not, in fact, "constitute a good vehicle" to test *Colegrove*. White shared Rankin's desire to overturn *Colegrove* but saw no chance of success and worried that a failed challenge in *Hartsfield* would have the unintended consequence of strengthening *Colegrove*. Attorney General William Rogers sided with White, the Department of Justice chose not to file an amicus brief, and the Supreme Court declined to overturn the lower court in *Hartsfield* v. *Sloan*.[31]

As Rankin pored over the case files in *Baker* v. *Carr*, Rhyne formally notified the Supreme Court of the plaintiff's intention to appeal the lower-court decision. Throughout March, April, and May, Rhyne and his staff devoted a collective thirteen hundred hours to preparing a jurisdictional statement. Chandler, Osborn, and Harris Gilbert, a young Nashville attorney hired by West to represent the city's interests, flew to Washington on several occasions to consult with Rhyne and his assistants, but Rhyne remained very much in charge. On May 26, 1960, he formally filed the jurisdictional statement with the clerk of the Supreme Court. With the Court heading into its summer recess, a decision would not be forthcoming until the fall.[32]

Neither side knew it at the time, but the Supreme Court decided that same day—May 26—to postpone any further discussion about *Baker* v. *Carr* until it reached a resolution in *Gomillion* v. *Lightfoot*, a racial gerrymandering case from Tuskegee, Alabama, scheduled for oral argument that October. "Held for *Gomillion* v. *Lightfoot*," noted Associate Justice Tom Clark on his docket sheet, a record kept by each justice of the votes in each case. The terseness of Clark's remark gave no hint of the importance of the connection between the two cases.[33]

Robert Carter, the general counsel of the NAACP, considered *Gomillion* the most consequential case handled by his organization since *Brown* v. *Board of Education*. But *Gomillion*—which concerned the subdivision of black voters, who made up the majority of voters in Tuskegee, by a white minority intent on retaining political control of the city—placed the plaintiffs, and the justices, in a bind. Whites in Tuskegee had not prevented black voters from casting ballots; they had instead nullified the effectiveness of the black vote through gerrymandering. The question at the heart of the case asked whether racial gerrymandering constituted a violation of individual Fourteenth Amendment rights to due process and equal protection, or a Fifteenth Amendment requirement that the right to vote not be infringed on account of race. And if it was the former, did this in turn imply that malapportionment—a form of residential gerrymandering—also violated individual rights to due process and equal protection?[34]

In other words, Carter was concerned that arguing the case on Fourteenth Amendment grounds would be risky in light of *Colegrove* v. *Green*. He sounded out Thurgood Marshall and other leading black attorneys, as well as Theodore Sachs, the young labor lawyer in Detroit who had filed Michigan's reapportionment suit in late 1959. Sachs was among those who favored a more direct attack on *Colegrove*, but Carter settled on a less confrontational approach and attempted to skirt the issue. Yet during oral argument, Justice Hugo Black, who, along with William O. Douglas, had dissented vigorously from *Colegrove*, asked Carter point-blank if the Court needed to overturn *Colegrove* in order to rule for the black voters in Tuskegee. Carter demurred and responded that he did not think the Court needed to declare all forms of gerrymandering and, by implication, malapportionment, unconstitutional, since his case concerned only racial discrimination; nevertheless, he added that the Court should overturn *Colegrove* if the justices saw that as the only path to condemning racial gerrymandering.[35]

At that point in the proceedings, Felix Frankfurter began to nimbly lead Carter through a series of questions and answers designed to build an argument for deciding *Gomillion* on Fifteenth Amendment grounds. The journalist Bernard Taper, who was present in the courtroom, wrote that "one had the sense that complicated strategies were involved—for the justices as well as the attorneys." Frankfurter, a staunch critic of racial discrimination and himself a former lawyer for the NAACP, wanted to condemn the racial gerrymandering in Tuskegee, but not at the expense of challenging the core conviction he had enunciated in *Colegrove*. Black and Douglas, by contrast, appeared eager to use *Gomillion*, according to Taper, "as a wedge for breaching the entire judicial blockade against discussions of gerrymanders."[36]

On November 14, 1960, the Court delivered a stinging rebuke to whites in Tuskegee when it ruled 9–0 on behalf of the city's black voters. But by accepting Frankfurter's rationale and deciding the case on Fifteenth Amendment grounds, the Court sidestepped for the moment any judgment on *Colegrove* v. *Green*. At conference, Frankfurter had argued that "*Colegrove* is not even remotely relevant here." Black and Douglas disagreed sharply and left no doubt that they were prepared to overturn *Colegrove*, but in the end they signed Frankfurter's unanimous opinion after Frankfurter agreed to cut most of the portion in which he distinguished *Gomillion* from *Colegrove*. Charles Whittaker filed a concurrence, in which he expressed his belief that the facts of the Tuskegee case required a decision on Fourteenth Amendment grounds but not in such a manner that required reconsideration of *Colegrove*.

Whittaker and his line of reasoning immediately caught the attention of the plaintiffs in *Baker*.[37]

On November 21, 1960, a mere seven days after the decision in *Gomillion* v. *Lightfoot*, the Supreme Court announced that it had accepted probable jurisdiction in *Baker* v. *Carr*. The Court does not make public how individual justices vote when considering what cases to hear, but the rules of the Court require at least four votes to grant such petitions. Court watchers at the time assumed—correctly, as it turned out—that Black, Douglas, Warren, and William Brennan had provided the necessary votes to hear arguments in *Baker* v. *Carr*. "They want to overrule *Colegrove*," Richard S. Arnold, a law clerk for Brennan, wrote in his diary. "The boss doubts they will have the votes. So do I." Given a chance to present their case to the Supreme Court, the petitioners from Tennessee would need to find one additional vote in order to prevail.[38]

Just weeks before the Supreme Court agreed to hear *Baker* v. *Carr*, John F. Kennedy narrowly defeated Richard Nixon in the 1960 presidential contest. Kennedy's election meant not only that a committed proponent of reapportionment would occupy the White House when the Court sat for oral arguments, which were scheduled for April 1961, but also that Kennedy's appointees in the Department of Justice would determine the government's official position.

Though the end of the Eisenhower administration and his own term as solicitor general were imminent, Rankin's interest in the Tennessee case did not abate. He formally requested the views of others within the Department of Justice as to whether or not the government should file an amicus brief. On November 30, Harold R. Tyler Jr., the head of the Civil Rights Division since January 1960, responded in the affirmative, noting that "there is apparently general agreement within the Department that everything reasonable should be done to secure a reversal or modification of the *Colegrove* decision, since judicial action appears to be the only practical method of realizing Fourteenth Amendment objectives in this area." Tyler did not elaborate on those objectives, but the Eisenhower administration had in recent months committed itself to an expansion of Fourteenth and Fifteenth Amendment protections, especially where voting was concerned, and had fought for the passage of the 1960 Civil Rights Act against stiff opposition from southern Democrats.[39]

Tyler believed that the possibility of obtaining a desirable ruling had improved since the Department of Justice had elected not to get involved in *Hartsfield* v. *Sloan* three years earlier. He noted that the eight justices who took part in *Hartsfield*, and who remained on the bench, had split four to four in a procedural vote (the Court never heard arguments in *Hartsfield*). And he thought that Charles Whittaker's concurring opinion in *Gomillion*, and, in particular, Whittaker's belief that the case should have been decided on Fourteenth Amendment grounds, offered "some hope that he might be willing to switch his vote on the reapportionment issue." Furthermore, the views of the most recently appointed justice, Potter Stewart, remained unknown. At the very least, Tyler concluded, dismissing Felix Frankfurter's claims to the contrary, the *Gomillion* decision demonstrated "that there are exceptions to *Colegrove*."[40]

Bruce Terris, a twenty-seven-year-old in his fourth year as an assistant to the solicitor general, took a more circumspect view than Tyler. A nonpolitical appointee who accepted the position after graduating from Harvard Law School, Terris would serve in the solicitor general's office into the Johnson administration. He would figure centrally in shaping the federal government's argument, and in drafting amicus curiae briefs in each of the seminal reapportionment cases decided by the Supreme Court in the early 1960s. That was all to come. In the lead-up to the *Baker* oral arguments, Terris identified clear weaknesses in the arguments of the Tennessee appellants and was the first person within the Department of Justice to suggest an alternative strategy for overturning *Colegrove* v. *Green*.[41]

Terris wrote in a memorandum to Rankin that a strong legal argument could be made either in support of or in opposition to *Colegrove* v. *Green*. "No matter how convinced one may be of the serious evil resulting from failure of the states to apportion properly in congressional and state elections," Terris explained, "it does not necessarily follow that judicial action should be used to remedy the situation." Justice Frankfurter, he concluded, had made a "strong case for judicial abstention." On the other hand, Terris pointed out that the Court itself had not yet reached consensus on Frankfurter's political question doctrine.[42]

Terris hesitated to recommend an alternative course of action. "Frankly," he admitted to Rankin, "I am not sure what I would do if the decision were mine." But if the federal government did eventually intervene, Terris wanted to make sure that the DOJ argued the most credible case possible, which in his view would mean taking a distinctly different line from that of Rhyne and the Tennessee appellants. Terris objected to the complaint's "lack of substance" and, more specifically, to what he saw as the semantic nonsense of the appellants, who were arguing that a deprivation of Fourteenth Amendment rights had occurred because the state had violated its own constitutional mandate for equality of representation. To Terris, this was a "completely frivolous" and "obvious attempt to convert a state ground into a federal constitutional ground," and as such unlikely to win over the Supreme Court and lower federal courts.[43]

Terris submitted that the case be made on a fairly simple proposition: "the Fourteenth Amendment forbids inequality of representation where this inequality becomes extreme." In his most revelatory (and ironic, given Terris's own evolution on the issue in subsequent years) paragraph, he conceded that history imposed certain limitations on Fourteenth Amendment claims; as he wrote, "it has been a standard feature of American government" since the eighteenth century to allow some apportionment on factors other than population. But, Terris went on, "there is no doubt a line beyond which the inequality would doubtlessly be considered so extreme as to raise a serious Fourteenth Amendment question."[44]

Terris urged his superiors to separate "the threshold political question issue completely from the issue whether malapportionment violates the Fourteenth Amendment." As he put it, "I would argue the political question issue fully and then give the Fourteenth Amendment issue rather summary treatment, merely indicating that there is a line where discrimination is extreme enough to violate the Fourteenth Amendment." Terris recommended asking the Supreme Court to send the case back to the three-judge panel for consideration of the merits, thus freeing the Court, at least for the time being, from being forced to decide whether or not the alleged discrimination in the Tennessee case constituted sufficiently extreme inequality to violate the Fourteenth Amendment. "By so separating these two issues," Terris predicted, "we would be making it easier for the uncommitted Justices to decide one difficult issue at a time. In this way, I think our chances of winning on either or both issues would be increased considerably." The assistant to the solicitor general could not have imagined how accurate his initial instincts would turn out to be.[45]

5 ||| INTO THE POLITICAL THICKET

ee Rankin's designation of the United States as amicus curiae in *Baker* v. *Carr* was one of his final acts as solicitor general. His decision, however, was not binding on his successor, Archibald Cox, who was confirmed after a ten-minute Senate hearing in mid-January 1961 and sworn in on January 23. A specialist in labor law at Harvard Law School who had served as an adviser to the Kennedy campaign, Cox had not been the new president's first choice. Kennedy preferred Paul Freund, the preeminent constitutional law expert in the nation and, like Cox, a professor on the Harvard Law faculty. But much to Kennedy's surprise, Freund declined the offer and recommended Cox in his place.[1]

By his own admission, Archie, as he was known to his friends, had given little thought to reapportionment prior to becoming solicitor general, in part because he lived in Massachusetts, a predominantly urban commonwealth that consistently ranked among the most equitably apportioned states in the nation. Nevertheless, by all accounts, Cox had no doubts about following Rankin's lead on *Baker* v. *Carr*. On Friday, February 3, just ten days after being sworn in and not yet settled in his stately office, which offered sweeping views of the Capitol, Supreme Court, and National Archives, Cox received a visit from Tom Osborn, Harris Gilbert, and John Jay Hooker, a young Nashville attorney who was a friend of Attorney General Robert Kennedy's and an acquaintance of Cox's from the campaign. The solicitor general met with the trio for twenty minutes. Bruce Terris, who had briefed his new boss and onetime teacher—he had studied labor law under Cox at Harvard—on the case prior to the meeting, also attended. The Tennesseans tried to convince Cox to enter *Baker* v. *Carr* as amicus curiae. At the time, the federal government rarely participated in cases in which it was not directly involved, but Cox was persuaded to file a brief. When Robert Kennedy asked Cox several days later if he thought he would win, he replied, "No, I don't think so, but it will be a lot of fun." Recounting that exchange years later, Cox explained his belief, as a law professor, that the Court was unlikely to find in favor of the plaintiffs. A former student of Felix Frankfurter's at Harvard, Cox took seriously the justice's concerns. On the other hand, he believed that the "cancer of malapportionment" would continue to metastasize if the Court did not intervene.[2]

Cox and his staff had only five weeks until the mid-March deadline to file the government's brief. Drawing on the assistance of attorneys in the Civil Rights Division and in his office, Terris most of all, Cox crafted an argument and submitted an amicus brief that embraced many of the suggestions put forward by Terris in his December memorandum to Rankin.[3]

After a nerve-induced sleepless night, Archie Cox spent the morning of Wednesday, April 19, 1961, polishing his oral argument and then made his way, just after lunch, to the elegant sanctuary of the Supreme Court of the United States, where he greeted Charles Rhyne and the attorneys from Tennessee. At approximately two thirty, Chief Justice Earl Warren gaveled the Court to attention and invited Rhyne to begin. In his opening remarks, Rhyne defined *Baker* v. *Carr* as an individual voting rights case and alleged that the voting rights of the appellants had been "diluted and debased to the point of nullification" by the actions of the state of Tennessee. When Rhyne took a shot at *Colegrove*, Justice William O. Douglas interrupted with a query intended to distinguish *Baker* from *Gomillion* and, more specifically, to make the point that the Court could not find for the appellants in *Baker* by hiding behind the Fifteenth Amendment as it had done in *Gomillion*. Douglas, who did not ask another question during the entirety of the nearly three-and-a-half-hour argument, undoubtedly raised the issue primarily to annoy Frankfurter. The two, who had served together for more than twenty years, disagreed sharply about the role of the judiciary in the American system of government, a divide that widened after *Colegrove*. By the time of the *Baker* argument, their relationship bordered on contemptuous.[4]

Frankfurter did not respond to Douglas's barb, but he did shift the discussion onto less certain ground for Rhyne. Challenging the attorney on the point that Terris and Cox had identified as the weakness in the appellants' case, Frankfurter asked why a violation of the state constitution necessarily offended the federal Constitution. After several uncomfortable moments, Rhyne found his way back to more defensible terrain, turning to a discussion of the facts of the case. He reminded the justices that district court judge William Miller, despite refusing to accept jurisdiction in *Baker*, had concluded that federal judicial assistance offered the only possibility of relief. "I think it is a fair summary of the facts," Rhyne said, that "there is no way you can get out of this illegal straightjacket without some Federal assistance."[5]

Cox followed Rhyne to the lectern. In a calm and steady voice, he cut straight to the heart of the government's argument. Emphasizing that the "complaint alleges a deprivation of rights under the Fourteenth Amendment," he insisted that the federal courts did have jurisdiction to hear the complaint.[6]

Before Cox could move past his opening remarks, Potter Stewart interrupted and remarked that Cox's argument failed to address "the basic substance of this case": the question of whether or not an actual violation of the Fourteenth Amendment had occurred. "It does not seem necessary, nor indeed even appropriate," Cox replied, following a line of reasoning that Terris had suggested to Rankin four months earlier, "for the Court to rule now whether there has or has not been a violation of the Fourteenth Amendment." Instead, he explained, if the Court recognizes a reasonable claim on the part of the petitioners, it must accept jurisdiction and send the case back to the lower court to determine whether Tennessee's system of apportionment actually violated the Fourteenth Amendment. At this point, Justice Charles Whittaker jumped into the fray. If the Court accepted the government's position, he asked, "need we do more than hold that the complaint states a cause of action and that the district court must exercise it?" Cox assured the justice that the Court did not need to go any further.[7]

Previous challenges to malapportionment had stumbled in the face of *Colegrove* v. *Green* and its perceived ban on federal jurisdiction in such disputes. But rather than arguing the most contentious issue before the Court, Cox "took for granted," in the words of one courtroom observer, that only three of the seven justices who participated in *Colegrove* had assented to Felix Frankfurter's political question doctrine. "The Court," he confidently asserted, "has never held that it lacks power to deal with controversies over apportionment."[8]

Cox, challenging the Court's reluctance to accept jurisdiction, asserted that "the right to be free from hostile or capricious discrimination by a state in defining the class of people to vote, or in the exercise of the franchise, is a Federal right protected by the Fourteenth Amendment. It's also a right enforceable by the courts." Referring to a string of Supreme Court decisions handed down over the previous quarter century, he recognized that "the closest precedents do involve racial discrimination" but insisted that "the Fourteenth Amendment proscribes other arbitrary and capricious distinctions affecting the right to vote." To illustrate his point, Cox suggested a pair of obviously absurd restrictions, saying that no court would sanction a law denying the franchise to redheaded women or to any individual who had visited the British Commonwealth. Shifting closer to the facts of the Tennessee case, he claimed that Justice Black was correct when he wrote in an earlier dissenting opinion that the Fourteenth Amendment would ban a statute that assigned twenty-five votes to residents of the western half of a state but only a single vote to those who resided in the eastern half of the state. Therefore, Cox concluded, "where the apportionment statute has the same effect as allowing voters in the sparsely settled west half to elect five representatives for every one that the populous counties in the east half can elect . . . there must equally be a violation of the Fourteenth Amendment."[9]

Cox's line of reasoning prompted Potter Stewart to ask how far a state must go to avoid offending the Fourteenth Amendment. "I am not suggesting," Cox responded without hesitation, "that the Fourteenth Amendment requires the apportionment of representatives in both houses of the legislature in the ratio to the population. It's quite plain to me that that is not a Fourteenth Amendment requirement. Our history makes it plain that other considerations—geographic distribution, historic association, political subdivision, and things of that kind—may be taken into consideration, certainly in one house, and I would assume, for present purposes, may be taken into account in both houses." He added, "What I do insist on is that the state must have some rational basis for its apportionment." In a brief rebuttal the following day, Rhyne echoed Cox's position, assuring Justice John Marshall Harlan that the appellants did not seek mathematical equality but would accept "any reasonable classification."[10]

Assistant Attorneys General James Glasgow and Jack Wilson, representing the state of Tennessee, spoke after Cox. They argued that the federal courts had no jurisdiction. Glasgow conceded that the state was not in compliance with its own constitution, but he repeatedly referred to *Kidd* v. *McCanless* and *Colegrove* v. *Green*. Wilson denied that any private, individual rights were at stake in the case and insisted that Fourteenth Amendment claims were therefore not germane. Among the justices, Whittaker appeared especially troubled by the implications of Glasgow's and Wilson's arguments and had trouble understanding how a state could knowingly ignore a constitutional provision and then claim that no authority had the power to correct the abuse. Whittaker asked about this provision in a tone of disbelief: "Well, as long as it's there, is it to be ignored? . . . I don't follow that. It's there now. It means something."[11]

Brief rebuttals from Osborn and Rhyne brought the oral argument to an end. It had spanned two days, and by the end of the second, attorneys for the appellants allowed themselves a measure of optimism. Stewart, the most junior justice, had not tipped his hand, but in his active participation he had revealed no obvious hostility to the arguments of the appellants. Even more encouraging, the questions posed by Whittaker indicated at least some sympathy for the appellants. The Tennessee petitioners began to hope that one of the two—Stewart or Whittaker—might be willing to provide the critical fifth vote.[12]

On Friday, April 21, the justices gathered for their regular conference to consider recent motions and discuss cases argued that week. But this would not be an ordinary meeting. Supreme Court conferences, in general, are shrouded in mystery; they are one of the most opaque aspects of the practice of American democracy. Major decisions of constitutional importance are literally made behind closed doors. No one other than the justices is allowed to enter the room during conference. If law clerks or secretaries need to reach members of the Court, they must knock on the door and relay messages or pass information through the most junior justice. No official records or minutes are kept. Individual justices may choose to take notes of the otherwise private exchanges that take place, and these notes provide the only direct record of conference proceedings. Like others before him and since, Hugo Black considered these meetings to be so confidential that he ordered thirty-four years' worth of his conference notes burned when he retired in 1971.[13]

When the April 21 conference turned to discuss *Baker* v. *Carr*, Earl Warren led off and voted to reverse the lower court for the reasons proposed by Cox. But according to notes kept by Justices Brennan and Douglas, Warren thought that Cox had been "too cautious" in urging the Court to assert jurisdiction only. Black, the senior associate justice, who had been appointed in 1937 by Franklin Roosevelt, went next. A former U.S. senator from Alabama and a member of the Ku Klux Klan in the 1920s, Black had become persona non grata in his native state by the 1960s, as a result of his support for a string of Supreme Court decisions that eroded the legal underpinnings of white supremacy and racial segregation. Citing his dissents in *Colegrove* v. *Green* and *South* v. *Peters*, a 1950 per curiam opinion in which seven members of the Court leaned on *Colegrove* as they dismissed a challenge to Georgia's county-unit system, Black also voted to reverse the lower court.[14]

Then Felix Frankfurter took his turn. Born into a Jewish family in Austria, Frankfurter immigrated to America in the 1890s. He grew up on New York's Lower East Side, graduated from City College, and then distinguished himself at Harvard Law School. Prior to taking his seat on the Supreme Court in January 1939, Frankfurter had been associated with a number of progressive, even radical, causes. As both government appointee and Harvard Law School faculty member—he moved between the two worlds numerous times—Frankfurter lent his legal expertise to the American Civil Liberties Union and the NAACP, among other organizations, and championed the rights of workers, racial minorities, and even the anarchists Nicola Sacco and Bartolomeo Vanzetti. Throughout, Frankfurter maintained a staunch belief in judicial restraint, a position he articulated most clearly in his opinion in *Colegrove*. At the conference on April 21, 1961, he warned his colleagues that "unless we affirm we will get into great difficulty and this Court will rue the results." Lambasting his former student Cox as "irresponsible" for "stating that there is a permissible remedy," he insisted that "the subject matter is not proper for judicial inquiry."[15]

Appointed to the Court just months after Frankfurter, William O. Douglas grew up poor in eastern Washington State, attended Whitman College on a scholarship, and then traveled east to attend Columbia Law School. After graduation, he joined the faculty of Yale Law School, gravitating toward colleagues who focused on the sociological effects of the law rather than the more traditional view of the law as a series of rules and procedures meant to be memorized and applied rigidly (in his autobiography, Douglas described Frankfurter as a "brilliant traditionalist"). In 1934, Douglas was appointed to the Securities and Exchange Commission and moved to Washington, D.C., where he joined the legions of New Deal reformers. Three years later he became the chair of the SEC, and in 1939, Roosevelt appointed him to the Supreme Court. When Douglas took his oath as an associate justice in April 1939, he had not yet turned forty. When he retired from the Court in 1975, he had served longer than any other justice in the institution's history—36 years and 209 days, a mark that remains unsurpassed. Douglas time and again drew the wrath not only of Frankfurter but also of political conservatives, who at various times called for his impeachment in response to his opinions, and pointed to his four marriages to successively younger women as a sign of immorality. Like Black, Douglas had staked out clear positions in *Colegrove* v. *Green* and in *South* v. *Peters*. Without further comment, he voted to reverse.[16]

Tom Clark spoke after Douglas. A native of Dallas, Clark moved to Washington in 1937 when he joined the Department of Justice. In 1945, Harry Truman named him attorney general, a position he held until his elevation to the Supreme Court in 1949. Clark would step down in 1967 when Lyndon Johnson appointed his son, Ramsey, to his father's old job as attorney general. Confirming the assumptions of lawyers on both sides of *Baker* v. *Carr*, Clark voted to affirm, although not with the conviction of Frankfurter. "The precedents are against us," he stated. "Equality is not a basic principle in American political voting."[17]

After Clark, the Court's four most junior associate justices, all Eisenhower appointees, took their turns. John Marshall Harlan, a Princeton undergraduate and Rhodes Scholar at Oxford, had built a prosperous corporate legal career in New York (his clients included the Du Ponts), interrupted only by his service as a military intelligence officer in the Army Air Force during World War II. In 1954, Harlan took a seat on the United States Court of Appeals for the Second Circuit but remained there only a year prior to his confirmation to the Supreme Court in 1955. The grandson and namesake of the lone dissenter in *Plessy* v. *Ferguson*, the 1896 Supreme Court decision that sanctioned "separate but equal" and gave constitutional imprimatur to racial segregation, the younger Harlan was Frankfurter's most reliable ally. "I agree wholly with Felix's views," he stated with reference to *Baker* v. *Carr*. "I think that the Solicitor General was reckless in his desire to inject the judiciary into this field. There is no federally protected right in an individual based on equality of voting. . . . This Court is not competent to solve this type of problem. I affirm."[18]

William Brennan, a graduate of the University of Pennsylvania and Harvard Law School, and, like Harlan, an army officer in World War II, sided with Warren, Black, and Douglas. A former judge on the New Jersey supreme court, Brennan, who was a Roman Catholic and a Democrat, was appointed to the U.S. Supreme Court in 1956, with Eisenhower hoping to improve his bipartisan credentials heading into his reelection campaign. "Our decisions have not yet held that this is not a federally protected right," Brennan said, rejecting *Colegrove* as a precedent for staying any action. "The purpose of the Fourteenth Amendment was to give equality. Much of its history pertained to voting rights. I would rely on the equal protection clause. I do not believe that the remedies are insoluble."[19]

Thus far the initial round of voting had produced no surprises. The tally stood at four to three in favor of reversing when Charles Evans Whittaker ventured forth with his views. A native of Kansas City, Missouri, Whittaker had enjoyed a meteoric and unlikely rise to the nation's highest court. A well-regarded corporate attorney in his hometown, Whittaker lacked the pedigree of his colleagues. In 1954, Eisenhower appointed Whittaker to the district court, and two years later elevated him to the Eighth Circuit Court of Appeals. Whittaker was on the Eighth Circuit for less than a year before he took his seat on the Supreme Court. During his brief five-year tenure on the nation's highest court, Whittaker struggled, according to his biographer, with feelings of "inferiority and self-doubt" that were compounded by crippling anxiety and depression. *Baker* v. *Carr* alone did not force Whittaker off the bench, but the deeply held convictions of his colleagues, and his own ambivalence about the case, did contribute to a psychological breakdown that forced him to resign just three days after the Court announced its decision.[20]

At conference, Whittaker expressed substantive sympathy for the plight of the appellants but felt constrained by Frankfurter's opinion in *Colegrove.* "If we wrote on a clean slate, I would say that the petitioners have standing to sue and that they are being denied equal protection of the laws," Douglas recorded Whittaker as stating. "Precedents, however, say that this is a 'political' issue. I am reluctant to overrule those cases. So I affirm." Each term, Justice Brennan asked his clerks to prepare detailed histories of the most important cases. In their account of *Baker* v. *Carr,* Brennan's clerks reported that "Justice Whittaker disagreed with Justice Frankfurter on the law (as newspapers had inferred from his questioning at argument), but felt that *Colegrove* should not be abandoned by a majority of five, or, at the very least, that he would not join a majority as slim as five." Black relayed a similar version of Whittaker's position to his clerks and reported that Whittaker had told the other justices, "I'll be the sixth vote for jurisdiction, but not the fifth."[21]

Whittaker's ambivalence infuriated Frankfurter. According to Brennan's clerks, Frankfurter lit into Whittaker for ninety minutes as he "unleashed a brilliant tour de force, speaking at considerable length, pulling down *Reports* and reading from them, and powerfully arguing the correctness of *Colegrove.*" Black told his clerks that Frankfurter's tirade lasted four and a half hours, a seemingly impossible length of time. Whatever the duration, Frankfurter fixed a withering gaze at Whittaker and "really berated him," according to Black.[22]

As the junior associate justice, Potter Stewart was the last to weigh in. Born into a prominent Republican family in Cincinnati, Stewart exuded controlled self-confidence. He had gone to Hotchkiss, earned his undergraduate degree from Yale, where he was a member of Skull and Bones, and finished first in his class at Yale Law School while serving as editor of the law review. After graduation, Stewart suffered a rare setback when J. Edgar Hoover refused to hire him at the FBI because a field report indicated that Stewart's mother was a member of the League of Women Voters and supported a peace group considered suspect by the bureau. Stewart joined the Naval Reserves just before Pearl Harbor and ended up serving three years on active duty. In 1949, he launched his political career and was elected to Cincinnati's city council. In 1954, Eisenhower appointed Stewart, not yet forty, to the Sixth Circuit Court of Appeals, making him the youngest federal judge in the country at the time. Four years later, Stewart took his seat on the Supreme Court.[23]

At conference on April 21, Stewart professed uncertainty about the Tennessee case. "I am not at rest on the issue," he said. He was not convinced that *Colegrove* prevented judicial intervention, but neither did he believe that the petitioners would succeed on the merits. "I have trouble seeing that disproportionate voting is a violation of equal protection. A state can divide up its jurisdiction into unequal political units," he suggested, as he had in his exchange with Cox. On the other hand, Stewart believed that "Tennessee is different, because it has a law that requires equality, and the state's failure to apply it may raise an equal protection point." Years later, a Stewart clerk observed that the justice's discomfort had stemmed from the fact that "he was looking down the road to One Man, One Vote, and he didn't like it." Not yet ready to commit himself, the junior justice declined to cast a vote, leaving the Court deadlocked at 4–4. A week later, Stewart was no closer to a decision. Telling his colleagues that he considered *Baker* v. *Carr* "as important a case as our school desegregation cases," he asked the Court to take the rare step of assigning the case for reargument in October. His colleagues agreed and, on May 1, the Court announced that *Baker* v. *Carr* would be reargued at the start of the new term.[24]

Between April and October, Frankfurter and Harlan waged a campaign to bring Whittaker and Stewart around to their position. As early as April 24, Frankfurter wrote to Stewart and offered to "serve as a punch-bag on whom to try out the problems with which you are wrestling." Frankfurter reiterated his own belief that "egalitarianism, however determined, in the electoral distribution of legislative representation is not a constitutionally protected right." Such an idea, warned Frankfurter, threatened to "bring the Court in conflict with political forces and exacerbate political feelings widely throughout the Nation, on a larger scale, though not so pathologically, as the Segregation cases have stirred." These had enjoyed support everywhere except the South, whereas federal intervention in apportionment, Frankfurter predicted, would be felt, and opposed, across the United States.[25]

Frankfurter continued to press his most junior colleagues, keeping Harlan informed of his efforts by sending him blind copies of this correspondence. Frankfurter simultaneously flattered and cautioned Stewart when he expressed agreement with the latter's observation that "a decision has a momentum of its own and we must take account of the direction that is opened up by a decision." Several weeks later, Frankfurter gently went after the fragile Whittaker. "One of these days," he began, "I would like to have a talk with you regarding your general philosophy on the overruling of cases in which new members of the Court had not participated." Taking a swipe at Douglas and his casual disdain for precedent, the author of *Colegrove* warned against any action that might encourage a "lack of respect for that desirable continuity which is of the essence of law." By early October, as the justices prepared for the second oral argument, Frankfurter had begun to lose patience with Whittaker. Responding to his junior colleague's remark that Tennessee could have devised a different reapportionment system that did not guarantee population equality but that it was "stuck" with the one it had, Frankfurter belittled Whittaker's reasoning. The Tennessee supreme court, he argued, not the Supreme Court of the United States, was the appropriate arbiter of the state's constitution. "Please tell me," he wrote, his words dripping with sarcasm, "what provision of the United States Constitution disallows the Tennessee Supreme Court from construing the Tennessee Constitution."[26]

The fact that *Baker v. Carr* would be reargued was by itself a sign of its significance; that round two began on Monday morning, October 9, 1961, at ten o'clock, the first time in history that the Supreme Court heard arguments before noon, added to the excitement leading up to that day and to the tension in the courtroom. As the justices emerged from their cloakroom and took their seats on the bench, one glance at Frankfurter confirmed Rhyne and Cox's worst fears. During the first argument, the author of *Colegrove* had remained uncharacteristically subdued, but now he appeared primed for a fight. He would take on Rhyne first, Cox second. The solicitor general, who had spent the previous four days refining his argument, later suggested, perhaps only half joking, that Felix Frankfurter had devoted the entire summer preparing to embarrass him.[27]

For the most part, the arguments in October reprised those made in April. The Tennessee petitioners did provide one new substantive contribution, however—updated statistical evidence derived from just-released 1960 census data that had not been available in time for the April argument. Prepared by the Advanced Planning Division of the Nashville Planning Commission, the new figures further confirmed the arbitrary and capricious nature of Tennessee's system of reapportionment, prompting Justice Brennan to say that "at the very least, the data show a picture which Tennessee should be required to justify if it is to avoid the conclusion that the 1901 Act applied to today's facts, is simply caprice."[28]

The updated census figures buttressed the federal government's central contention that Tennessee's system of reapportionment was unconstitutional because it lacked any rational basis. In the government's redrafted amicus brief, the Kennedy administration insisted even more forcefully than it had in April "that the legislative apportionment in Tennessee is so grossly discriminatory as to violate the Fourteenth Amendment and that judicial relief is available against this violation." As the revised brief put it, "This Court has repeatedly invalidated discriminations against a class of voters based on race. The prohibitions of the Fourteenth Amendment are not confined to discriminations based on race, but extend to arbitrary and capricious action against other groups." But in contrast with its more general condemnation of other forms of discrimination in the spring, the government more pointedly insisted now that "a geographical classification may be so irrational as to violate the Fourteenth Amendment." Its brief again addressed the issue of standards by stipulating that the guarantees of the Fourteenth Amendment "do not lend themselves to mathematical formulas" but asserted with greater conviction than before that "the starting point must be *per capita* equality of representation, a fundamental American ideal." Any deviation from per capita equality, Cox told the Court during reargument, must be based on a "rational justification . . . other than sheer caprice, indifference, or the perpetuation of unjustified political power." The state of Tennessee, according to the solicitor general, provided no such justification, nor had it made any attempt to do so.[29]

With similar confidence, Cox argued that the federal courts could, in fact, provide relief, and he offered a few possible solutions. These sparked an animated Felix Frankfurter to warn that judicial intervention in the segregation cases, which had met stiff resistance, would prove far "simpler" than what lay ahead if the Court got involved in reapportionment. "You think the prejudices on this business of urban versus rural, which is just as strong in New York as it is in Tennessee, isn't even more deep-seated and more pervasively deep-seated?" Frankfurter asked. "Well," replied Cox, holding firm, "I would myself have doubted that. I may be wrong. But I would doubt whether it was as deep-seated."[30]

In the final few minutes left to him, Cox attempted to turn the logic of *Colegrove* on its head and to render irrelevant the distinction between *Colegrove* and *Gomillion* that Frankfurter had so carefully constructed. Cox claimed that the Court's failure to intervene in *Colegrove* stemmed not from a lack of jurisdiction but because it lacked enough time "to frame fair and effective judicial relief" in the face of an impending congressional election. In *Gomillion*, by contrast, "the remedy was plain" and the Court accepted jurisdiction. "I do not see why a case should be more justiciable because it arose under the Fifteenth Amendment rather than the Fourteenth," Cox said, "and it does not seem to me that the principle should be limited to racial discrimination. There are other forms of discrimination that may be equally invidious." Sitting in the courtroom, one of the attorneys who argued for the plaintiffs in *Colegrove* fifteen years earlier turned to Nashville attorney Harris Gilbert and remarked, "*Colegrove* is in serious trouble." Gene Graham, a Nashville journalist who followed the case closely, provided a wittier, if exaggerated, evaluation of the solicitor general's performance. "The pupil," he wrote, "had speared the master with his own weapon."[31]

Cox took no personal pleasure from challenging his former professor, or from asking the Court to reject Frankfurter's most deeply held and consequential judicial belief. Just before his time expired, Cox acknowledged that the Court faced an exceedingly difficult decision and attempted to ameliorate any concerns among the wavering justices about the consequences of a decision to intervene. "This is obviously a very important case," he said, "one which will affect our representative institutions for a long time, so far as anyone can judge. The issue is not confined to Tennessee. It affects a number of states all over the country."

He urged the Court not to shy away from accepting jurisdiction in this potentially momentous case. "I suggest to you," he passionately concluded, "that judicial inaction through excessive caution or through a fancied impotence, in the face of crying necessity and very serious wrongs, may also do damage to our constitutional system, may also do it, indeed, greater damage."[32]

In addition to seven hours of oral argument, spread over three days in April and October, and the multiple briefs submitted by both Tennessee parties and the federal government, the justices heard from a half dozen parties who filed hundreds of pages of amicus briefs, all in support of the petitioners. The National Institute of Municipal Law Officers filed two briefs signed by the city attorneys of Los Angeles, New York, Dallas, Richmond, Portland (Maine and Oregon), Cleveland, Minneapolis, and Detroit, while taxpayers on Long Island, New York, and in the Louisville suburb of St. Matthews, Kentucky, reminded the Court that they were grossly underrepresented as well.[33]

Urban residents of Mississippi, who had already filed a suit against officials in their state, characterized malapportionment as a "moral and political malignancy." Howard Edmondson, the governor of Oklahoma who had won election in 1958 on a platform calling for reapportionment, warned that, at a time when the United States and other Western democracies were engaged in a worldwide struggle against communism, malapportionment circumscribed the democratic aspirations of more American citizens than did segregation. In Kansas, echoing the Tennessee petitioners, the leadership of the *Hutchinson News*, which won a Pulitzer Prize several years later for its coverage of the effects of malapportionment, filed a brief that focused on the "practical effects of inequality," citing political domination by one party and a long litany of abuses associated with the distribution of state sales, liquor, and gasoline revenues. Although the Supreme Court denied the petition of the Kansas group to file its amicus brief, perhaps because it did not raise substantially different questions from those already posed in *Baker*, the Kansans aptly summarized the bipartisan nature of malapportionment when they noted in their brief that the situation in their state mirrored that in Tennessee, except for "the accident of history having made the

Democrats the offender in Tennessee and the Republicans guilty in Kansas."[34]

Having been briefed and argued and rebriefed and reargued on every conceivable point of law, *Baker* v. *Carr* went back to the justices. On October 10, just one day after the second argument, Frankfurter circulated a sixty-page memorandum outlining his well-known views on the case. He may not, as Cox suspected, have spent the summer recess purposefully devising ways to embarrass the solicitor general, but he had devoted much of it to the preparation of this document, which, with the exception of a few minor edits and four introductory pages that he added later, would become his dissenting opinion. On October 11, Harlan made his most forceful attempt at influencing Stewart and Whittaker, writing to the pair, "Unless I am mistaken, past events in this case plainly indicate that your votes will be determinative of its outcome." Sending a blind copy of his letter to Frankfurter, Harlan described *Baker* as among the most important cases to come before the Court in its history and heavily criticized the lack of "statesmanship" shown by the Department of Justice in urging the Court to accept jurisdiction. Expressing his belief that the federal government should have "stayed out of the case altogether," he appealed to his junior colleagues to recognize that a great responsibility now rested "entirely in our laps." Later that day, Frankfurter sent Harlan a handwritten note, in which he noted the "soul searching" that must have preceded so obvious an attempt to lobby fellow members of the Court. "I restrict myself to saying," Frankfurter wrote, "that you have rendered an important service to the Court, whatever the outcome."[35]

Familiar with the views of most of their colleagues, the justices spent less time discussing *Baker* at conference in October than they had in April. Attempting to secure a fifth vote, Earl Warren took a more limited position than he had six months before. He recommended that the Court "reverse solely on jurisdiction" and decided to withhold any judgment as to whether or not "the state must give precise equality." Invoking Cox's argument, the chief justice added, "All we need to do here is to say that this shows an arbitrary and capricious practice." When his turn came, William Brennan seconded the chief's position. Hugo Black and William O. Douglas preferred to go beyond the issue of jurisdiction. Describing Frankfurter's lengthy memorandum as "a good brief for a weak cause," Black told his colleagues that he adhered to his dissent in *Colegrove*, in which he and Douglas not only argued for jurisdiction but also expressed their view that while the Constitution did not necessarily require precise equality, "the constitutionally guaranteed right to vote and the right to have one's vote counted clearly imply the policy that state election systems, no matter what their form, should be designed to give approximately equal weight to each vote cast." For his part, Douglas added only that he considered the decision in *Gomillion* determinative as well. "The Equal Protection Clause is not designed just for Negroes," he explained, "even he has [sic] to show an arbitrary discrimination."[36]

Frankfurter, who had already laid out his views so fully in writing, said little at conference. Tom Clark embraced his core position and then added, according to Brennan's account, "that what really was at stake here was, at least in the South, the whites' control of the power structure" and that "it was impossible . . . for the Court to get into that." It was left to Harlan to fully elucidate the argument against accepting jurisdiction. He did so with "intense emotion," Brennan recorded. "I would plead, for the protection of this Court, against getting into these political contests," he begged as he recited a list of problems likely to result from intervention. When he added that "the protection of this Court has been in refraining from getting involved in these problems," Douglas wrote in his conference notes, "My God—what does he think the *Segregation Cases* were—or the *Tuskegee* case?"[37]

The passage of six months had done nothing to lessen Charles Whittaker's uncertainty about the case. When his turn came to speak, he told his colleagues that he had "written two memos diametrically opposed to each other—one for asserting jurisdiction and one for affirmance." This exercise, however, had apparently not helped much. He launched into a tortured explanation as to why the federal courts did have jurisdiction but could not exercise it in this case. He announced that he had decided to affirm the lower court's decision.[38]

By contrast, reargument did offer Potter Stewart some clarity and prompted him to cast the vote that he had withheld in April. Informing his colleagues that "I more or less agree with Bill Brennan," he concluded that the district court did, in fact, have jurisdiction. But he made it very clear that in his view states enjoyed wide latitude in designing systems of apportionment that were not based on population and that the plaintiffs, therefore, would have a difficult time prevailing on the merits. "I do not know whether there has been a deprivation of equal protection," he explained. "I would give the state *wide* leeway and impose a great burden on petitioners. I completely disagree that equal protection requires representation mathematically proportionate to the number of voters. Our whole history and tradition teach the contrary."[39]

Stewart seemed to provide the crucial fifth vote, without which the appeal from Tennessee would have foundered, and without which re-apportionment would have been dealt a major setback. But the junior justice still had to formally join a majority opinion. After the October conference, the task of assigning that opinion fell to Warren, as the senior justice in the majority. A consummate politician, he considered the assignment from every conceivable angle. He consulted extensively with Black and Douglas, both of whom had been on record since *Colegrove* as favoring a more sweeping ruling than Stewart was prepared to join. Consequently, Warren, Black, and Douglas agreed that either Brennan or Stewart would have to write it. Black worried that Stewart's vote was tenuous enough that the other four might lose him if Stewart did not write the opinion, but Douglas told Warren that he might not be willing to join an opinion by Stewart given the wide latitude that the junior justice would give to the states to design systems of apportion-ment. After ten days pondering the matter, the chief justice selected Brennan to write the opinion.[40]

Brennan set out to craft an opinion that would hold Stewart and si-multaneously satisfy Douglas. He chose not to address the question of what standard was required by the Equal Protection Clause. Instead, he focused on three specific issues: the jurisdiction of the federal district court; the standing of the petitioners to seek relief in federal court; and justiciability, a somewhat arcane concept—related to, but legally dis-tinct from, the question of jurisdiction—that ruled certain subjects be-yond the reach of the courts. Frankfurter had based his claims in *Colegrove* on his belief that all apportionment disputes inherently in-volved nonjusticiable political questions. In his *Baker* opinion, Bren-nan meticulously traced the history of the Court's decisions regarding the justiciability of political questions and then leaned on Wiley Rut-ledge's decisive opinion in *Colegrove* to conclude that apportionment disputes did, in fact, fall within the purview of the federal courts. As he explained in a memorandum to Warren, Black, and Douglas, he felt that such an approach was necessary "if we are effectively and finally to dispel the fog of another day produced by Felix's opinion in *Colegrove* v. *Green*."[41]

In late January, Brennan circulated a first draft only to Stewart, who responded that he had no substantive objections but was unwilling to consider the issue of standards. Brennan sent a subsequent draft to Warren, Black, and Douglas, and informed them of Stewart's position. On January 31, Brennan circulated his majority opinion to the entire Court. The following day, Frankfurter responded with his dissent, which Harlan and Clark joined immediately, the latter telling Frankfurter, "Your dissent is unanswerable." When Stewart formally joined Brennan's opinion, also on February 1, the majority appeared solid. A day later, however, Clark informed Brennan that he planned to write a concurring dissent—justices write concurring opinions, both in support of the majority or in dissent, when they agree with the conclusion of the main opinion but not necessarily the logic or reasoning, or when they wish to address a point not discussed in the main opinion—but would not be able to do so until he, Brennan, and Warren returned from a ten-day judicial conference in Puerto Rico. The delay almost proved the undoing of Brennan's majority.[42]

Warren and Black, with Stewart's vote still not assured, had agreed to Brennan's narrow opinion, but Douglas became increasingly impatient as the Court delayed handing down its decision. Brennan returned from the conference to discover that Douglas had drafted a separate concurrence in which he reiterated his view, stated originally in *Colegrove*, that the Equal Protection Clause required that legislative districts must be based on population. This assertion, of course, irritated Stewart, who felt compelled to draft his own concurrence in which he stated forcefully that the opinion of the Court extended only to the issues of jurisdiction, standing, and justiciability. Nervy days and nights followed in late February as Brennan attempted to hold together the majority. Eventually he prevailed upon Douglas to tone down the language that most troubled Stewart. The majority remained intact.[43]

Meanwhile, Frankfurter encouraged both Harlan and Clark to write separate dissents, and asked Clark to focus on the availability of other remedies not yet explored by the Tennessee petitioners. Clark agreed to do so after he returned from Puerto Rico. In drafting his dissent, Harlan took one last stab at changing Stewart's mind and asked the Court's junior justice to wait for his final draft "before casting what will be the decisive, and if I may say so, fateful vote in this case." Stewart promised to keep an open mind, but he did not switch his vote despite his irritation with Douglas. On February 14, Whittaker informed both Frankfurter and Harlan that, despite significant trouble in making up his mind, he had decided to join their opinions. The vote still stood at 5–4. But not for long.[44]

Upon his return from Puerto Rico, Clark sat down to write the concurring dissent Frankfurter had asked of him. But as he informed Frankfurter on March 7, he had scrutinized the record and reached the conclusion that no avenue other than the federal courts remained open to the Tennessee petitioners. This realization led Clark, rather remarkably, to reexamine all of his assumptions about *Baker* v. *Carr* and to conclude that he could not logically sustain his dissent. "Tennessee's apportionment," he wrote in a concurring opinion that turned out to support the majority, "is a crazy quilt without rational basis." In switching his vote, Clark expressed a willingness to consider not only the question of jurisdiction but also the actual merits of the Equal Protection Clause claim. In other words, Brennan, Warren, Black, and Douglas no longer needed Stewart's vote to write an opinion that reached beyond the narrow issue of jurisdiction. After a brief discussion, however, Brennan and the chief justice decided not to redraft the majority opinion at so late an hour. The vote now stood at 6–3. Yet this, too, failed to hold.[45]

By the time Clark had switched his vote, Whittaker had entered Walter Reed Hospital, where he would stay under observation for seventeen days. He would never return to the bench. Ever since his confirmation to the Supreme Court in 1957, Whittaker had struggled to cope with the demands of the job. He lacked the sort of coherent judicial philosophy that guided someone like Frankfurter, and instead approached each case on its merits. As a former clerk remarked, the justice put himself in the position of casting "the critical vote too often" and "agonized" over each decision. No case proved more difficult for him than *Baker* v. *Carr*. By early 1962, as the pressure from his work intensified, Whittaker fell into a deep depression. At the time, mental illness was poorly understood by medical professionals, much less by laypersons. Whittaker had kept his condition from his colleagues and clerks, and certainly had never disclosed it to the president who had appointed him. In early February, while Warren, Brennan, and Clark were in Puerto Rico, Whittaker retreated to a lodge in rural Wisconsin owned by the *Kansas City Star*. Accompanied only by a former law associate, Whittaker did and said little for days at a time.[46]

Whittaker returned to the Court in the latter part of February and continued to struggle. Warren paid a private visit to his chambers on Saturday, February 24. Whittaker attended the Court's all-day conference on Friday, March 2, and they again met privately the following day. On Monday, Whittaker spent his final day at work as an associate justice, joining his colleagues for a conference that adjourned in midafternoon. On Tuesday, March 6, he admitted himself into Walter Reed. When his son Keith, an air force captain who had just finished medical school, arrived at the hospital several days later, he was shocked by his father's condition. Highly agitated from the drugs prescribed by his doctors to treat the depression, the justice was, according to his son, "making plans for suicide." Keith Whittaker thought "he was ready to do it. . . . I'm sure he would have killed himself if I hadn't been there to stop him." But the son extracted a promise from his father not to take his own life.[47]

Warren visited Whittaker on Thursday, March 15, and, like others who spent time with the justice during his hospitalization, was unnerved by his state. Apparently without consulting his colleagues, Warren prevailed upon hospital officials to convene a medical review board, which certified that Whittaker had become permanently disabled and should "be retired." The chief could have pressured Whittaker to resign, but that would have meant forfeiting a lifetime pension of $17,500, the equivalent of 50 percent of an associate justice's salary. Instead, that same day, March 16, Warren informed President Kennedy of Whittaker's official status and of his intention to retire from active service as of April 1. By signing a certificate of disability on behalf of Whittaker, Warren enabled his troubled colleague to retire with full benefits. Still unwell, Whittaker left Walter Reed on Friday, March 23, his impending retirement not yet public.[48]

On Monday, March 26, 1962, Warren gaveled the Supreme Court into session. With what *Newsweek* described as a "barely perceptible nod," he signaled to Brennan, who sat toward the end of the bench on the chief's left. "I have for announcement No. 6—*Baker* v. *Carr*," Brennan began, as a hushed audience waited with great anticipation. Holding the floor for nearly an hour, Brennan summarized the Court's decision, laid out in six separate opinions: the majority opinion; concurrences from Douglas, Stewart, and Clark; and dissents from Frankfurter and Harlan. The absent Justice Whittaker, Brennan noted without further explanation, took no part in the final disposition of the case. Brennan, who for months barely held together a five-person majority, had ended up with six votes for and only two opposed. As he spoke, Warren scribbled a quick note to his colleague and good friend. "Dear Bill," he playfully wrote, "It is a great day for the Irish." Before passing the note to Brennan, the chief justice crossed out "Irish" and replaced it with "country."[49]

The news spread quickly, making headlines across the nation. *Newsweek* put Earl Warren on the cover and called the decision "truly historic," one that would bring about a "bigger voice for big cities." A somewhat less enthusiastic *Wall Street Journal* speculated that the "historic ruling" had the potential to "alter the political complexion of most or all of the 50 states in years to come." The *New York Times* ran three separate front-page articles the day after the ruling, as well as numerous others in the week that followed, all of which dissected the decision and its probable ramifications. In the estimation of the *Washington Post*, the Supreme Court had performed "Heart Surgery on Our System." Back home, the *Nashville Tennessean* congratulated the local litigants who had worked so hard to bring about meaningful reapportionment and ran a picture of Tom Osborn and Molly Todd, both with wide smiles, on the front page.[50]

Three days after the Supreme Court handed down its decision in *Baker* v. *Carr*, John F. Kennedy addressed the nation's press corps. "It is with extreme regret," he said, "that I announce the retirement of Associate Justice of the Supreme Court Charles Evans Whittaker." (In his own statement released in conjunction with the president's announcement, Whittaker cited the "physical exhaustion" that resulted from "the great volume and continuous stresses of the Court's work" as the reason for his retirement.) Kennedy said nothing more about Whittaker and refused to be drawn into a discussion about potential successors, but he did weigh in on *Baker* v. *Carr*. In response to a reporter's question, he unequivocally endorsed the Court's decision. "Quite obviously," the president stated, "the right to fair representation and to have each vote count equally is, it seems to me, basic to the successful operation of a democracy." Urging elected officials in the states to recognize their obligation to alleviate malapportionment, the president concluded that "if no relief is forthcoming, then of course it would seem to the administration that the judicial branch must meet a responsibility."[51]

Over time, Court watchers speculated about how Whittaker had intended to vote. One Warren biographer claims that just prior to his hospitalization, Whittaker changed his mind and was ready to join the majority. Given Whittaker's comment during the deliberations that he was willing to provide a sixth vote but not the fifth, it is tempting to imagine that he decided to join the majority once Potter Stewart and Tom Clark signed on. But that never happened. Furthermore, Whittaker's own biographer errs when he concludes that his subject never formally gave his vote to Frankfurter or Harlan prior to his decision to step down. He clearly did. On February 14, Whittaker wrote to both of them and admitted to difficulty in deciding *Baker* v. *Carr* but unequivocally joined their opinions. Whittaker's name remained on multiple recirculations of both dissenting opinions as late as March 15. After March 16, however, the day Whittaker notified the president of his intention to retire, his colleagues removed his name from their opinions. His participation in the case ended when the medical review board found him permanently disabled.[52]

On April 4, a week after the Supreme Court handed down its decision in *Baker*, an embittered Felix Frankfurter wrote to Alexander Bickel, a former law clerk then serving on the faculty of Yale Law School. "Am I right in assuming," he asked, "that your headnote for *Baker* v. *Carr* would be, '*Held*, a little judicial pregnancy is permissible.'" He went on to harshly criticize his colleagues in the majority and the process they had followed to achieve their ends. "Your stomach too would have turned," he wrote. The following day, Frankfurter suffered a massive stroke. Although he did not formally retire until August, he never returned to active duty on the Supreme Court. *Baker* v. *Carr* had claimed—at least to a certain extent—its second victim.[53]

Not long after, Irving Brant, a journalist and friend of former justice Wiley Rutledge, paid a visit to the chambers of William Brennan. He wanted to share a story that he had kept to himself ever since the Court's decision in *Colegrove* v. *Green* in 1946. Brant told Brennan that he went to see Rutledge after the decision, because he had not understood why his friend had cast the decisive fourth vote with Black and Douglas on the issue of jurisdiction, but with Frankfurter on the merits. Rutledge explained that his vote had been purely strategic. He was certain that for the foreseeable future a full Court would side with Frankfurter; Justice Robert Jackson, who was at the Nuremberg war crimes trial but was scheduled to return soon to the bench, and Fred Vinson, who had been appointed to replace Harlan Fisk Stone as chief justice and who took his seat ten days after the Court's decision in *Colegrove*, were likely to accept Frankfurter's position with regard to jurisdiction. So Rutledge looked for a way to dispose of the case in such a manner that a full bench would not have an opportunity to rule on the issue of jurisdiction. Believing that the facts of *Colegrove* did warrant federal court intervention, Rutledge signed his name to an opinion to which he agreed only in part in order to enhance the likelihood of more far-reaching and long-lasting reapportionment in the future. For Irving Brant, the Court's decision in *Baker* v. *Carr* was "a vindication for Wiley Rutledge."[54]

As commentators debated the implications of *Baker* v. *Carr*, the Nashville journalist Gene Graham perceived the birth of a movement, as lawyers and litigants in dozens of states, along with political scientists and journalists such as Anthony Lewis (whose seminal *Harvard Law Review* article was cited by William O. Douglas in his concurring opinion), began to demand that federal district court judges across the nation turn their attention to the issue of apportionment standards. Over the course of the next two years, the movement would become a revolution.[55]

Support for the Supreme Court's ruling in *Baker* was broad but far from unanimous. As the movement for reform coalesced, opponents struggled to contain the damage. Gathering in Chicago in December 1962, delegates to the sixteenth biennial convention of the General Assembly of the States—which was sponsored by the Council of State

Governments, an organization whose policy positions and lobbying efforts tended to reflect the views of its disproportionately rural and small-town legislative membership—expressed, as they usually did at this event, their general antipathy toward the federal government. On this occasion, delegates asked Congress to call a convention for the purpose of adopting three constitutional amendments. One proposed amendment, to revise Article V to allow two-thirds of the states to initiate constitutional amendments directly, instead of relying on Congress, passed 37–4 (each state delegation received one vote). The second proposal, a direct assault on *Baker* v. *Carr*, guaranteed every state the right to determine for itself the composition of its legislature and stripped the federal judiciary of the right to intervene in apportionment disputes; it passed 26–10. The final amendment sought to establish a Court of the Union, composed of the chief justices of the highest courts in each state, and to vest it with the power to review certain decisions of the Supreme Court of the United States. The most contentious of the three, the final amendment passed by one vote, 21–20.[56]

William V. Chappell, a member of the Florida legislature and the driving force behind the three amendments, assembled a committee to oversee the campaign and hired George Prentice, a thirty-seven-year-old former newspaperman and legislative aide, to run the campaign's day-to-day operations. According to Prentice, Chappell and other leading sponsors of the amendments were acutely aware that "such a movement would be unsuccessful if it were pinned to the apron of the South." They made a concerted effort to disassociate their campaign from any taint of racial intolerance, political extremism, or pro-South identification, and placed a priority on maintaining distance from organizations such as the John Birch Society and Citizens' Councils. Shunning the term "states' rights," the organization chose to call itself the Dual Sovereignty National Committee, but appeared in press reports as the Volunteer Committee on Dual Sovereignty (VCDS). The group named mostly northerners to its leadership. The Republican speaker of the Pennsylvania house, Stuart Helm, served as chairman, and the six vice chairs—three Republicans and three Democrats, including Chappell—held office in Illinois, Wisconsin, Kansas, Oklahoma, Florida, and New Jersey. Prentice oversaw operations from Tallahassee, but he ensured that all press releases, official announcements, and general information were routed through Helm's office in Harrisburg and carried the dateline of the Pennsylvania capital.[57]

The tactics of the VCDS reflected the clear influence of Virginians David Mays and James Kilpatrick, the chairman and head of the publications department, respectively, of the Virginia Commission on Constitutional Government (VCCG). Chartered by the Commonwealth of Virginia in March 1958, the VCCG served as a vehicle for Mays, who would later defend Virginia's system of apportionment before the Supreme Court, and Kilpatrick, the editor of the *Richmond News Leader* and one of the nation's leading conservative columnists, to put into practice their staunch belief that southern resistance to federal intervention was doomed to fail unless shorn of its sectional identity and openly racist rhetoric. Operating under the auspices of the VCCG, Mays and Kilpatrick published numerous tracts and pamphlets that, in the words of one scholar, "depicted the problems facing southern segregation as but one outgrowth of an assault on national constitutional principles." Their efforts to forge a broader national conservative coalition began to bear fruit in July 1962 when Mays, Kilpatrick, and other conservative Democrats from Virginia met with a group of conservative Republicans from Pennsylvania to discuss common concerns. Stuart Helm led the Pennsylvania contingent.[58]

George Prentice began by reaching out to state legislators across the country and lobbying on behalf of the three proposed amendments. He avoided talking about the Supreme Court's segregation decisions or civil rights issues in general, trying instead to sell a probusiness agenda and arguing that the Court had granted unwarranted power to the federal government to intrude into the economy and influence state matters such as wages, working hours, pensions, and unemployment compensation, among others. Reapportionment, Prentice maintained, represented the latest means by which the Supreme Court had expanded federal power at the expense of the states. With minimal national attention, fifteen states passed at least one of the proposed amendments in the first four months of 1963, and another dozen appeared poised to go along.[59]

The low-key nature of Prentice's campaign caught supporters of reapportionment off guard. In early 1963, few voices appeared in opposition to the proposed amendments. The *Louisville Courier-Journal,* which did devote reporting and editorials to the issue, denounced the proposals as "dangerous and revolutionary" and described the public's general lack of awareness as "disquieting." Arthur Freund, a prominent lawyer in St. Louis, launched what Earl Warren later referred to as a "one-man crusade" to alert the nation to the "miserable" press coverage of the three amendments. Freund shared his concerns with Warren, William O. Douglas, and William J. Brennan, all of whom he knew personally, as well as Archibald Cox. Freund distributed to the justices and the solicitor general copies of a letter from Yale law professor Charles Black, who denounced the proposals as "radical in the extreme." Black concluded that the proposals "aim not at the preservation but at the subversion of that balance in federal-state relations which has . . . enabled us to escape 'the evils of despotism and totalitarianism.' "[60]

Freund's viewpoint finally began to gain traction in April 1963. That month, Black published his concerns in the *Yale Law Journal*, calling the proposals "a threatened disaster." Arthur's cousin Paul Freund—the eminent constitutional scholar at Harvard who had turned down Kennedy's offer of solicitor general and recommended Cox in his stead—derided the proposals as "the greatest threat to the existence of our Republic as we know it in our entire history." Most important, Earl Warren gave an address in Durham, North Carolina, on April 27, to help dedicate a new law school building at Duke University, an address in which he touched on the proposed amendments. Without taking a specific position on any of the three, he noted that the absence of public discussion of them was appalling, given that the amendments "would make profound changes in the judiciary, the relationship between the federal and state Governments, and even the stability of the United States Constitution." He called on the bar to recognize its responsibilities. "If lawyers are not to be the watchmen for the Constitution, on whom are we to rely?" he asked. Less than a month later, Warren repeated the substance of his remarks in Washington to the annual gathering of the American Law Institute.[61]

Warren's attention to the issue resulted in not only a profusion of coverage in newspapers and periodicals but also the recognition by a number of local and state bar associations, as well as powerful political entities such as the AFL-CIO and the ACLU, that the amendments merited their attention. The chief justice's words also had the effect of drawing the Kennedy administration into the debate. Throughout the winter and spring of 1963, White House aides reiterated the president's support for *Baker* v. *Carr*, but otherwise the administration did not comment as the VCDS went about its work. When the administration did decide to join Warren in the fray, the Department of Justice took the lead. In a series of coordinated addresses in early May, Assistant Deputy Attorney General Joseph Dolan and Solicitor General Archibald Cox attacked the proposed constitutional amendments, as did Attorney General Robert Kennedy (in a speech prepared for a visit to the University of Virginia Law School that was ultimately canceled because of worsening racial violence in Birmingham, Alabama). Lawrence Speiser, the director of the Washington office of the ACLU, pushed for the president to comment, but White House aide Lee White explained that the proposals were not serious enough to merit a pronouncement from the president. Speiser, determined to get Kennedy on the record in opposition to the three amendments, arranged for a reporter to raise the issue with the president at a forthcoming presidential news conference. Less than a week later, Speiser's plan succeeded, when Kennedy made clear his opposition.[62]

With the three amendments attracting heightened scrutiny, Felix Frankfurter unleashed a withering verbal assault on Earl Warren. Writing to Potter Stewart, ostensibly to congratulate him for a dissent in a recent case, the retired justice raised "a matter that is not easy for me to deal with, for it implies criticism of the Chief Justice in the way he is talking about the proposed Constitutional Amendments." But criticism of the chief is exactly what Frankfurter intended. He assured his former colleague that "I think of those Amendments as ill as you do, or the Chief." But in a clear reference to *Baker* v. *Carr* and other Warren Court decisions from which he had dissented, Frankfurter concluded that "the Court has brought upon itself these mischievous proposals." He claimed to have warned William Brennan several years earlier that such amendments "would be forthcoming" if the Court continued to ignore precedent and to make decisions on an ad hoc basis. Distraught at the direction in which the Court had headed, Frankfurter took some solace in the knowledge that he could count on Stewart, along with John Marshall Harlan, to "still believe in law."[63]

By mid-July 1963, support for the amendments had stalled; only two additional states passed resolutions, bringing the total to seventeen, a figure that remained unchanged for the rest of the year. But opposition to the Supreme Court's reapportionment decisions had not been quelled. Indeed, it would reignite a year later, when the justices turned to the question of standards.[64]

6 ||| ONE PERSON, ONE VOTE

n 1955, the political scientist Gordon Baker wrote that "'one man, one vote' has been the most concise and effective phrase employed to illustrate the ideal that all citizens should have approximately the same political weight." Nearly fifteen years later, in the aftermath of the reapportionment revolution, Nashville journalist Gene Graham asked Charles Rhyne if he knew where and when the term "one man, one vote" originated. Rhyne confessed that he did not. Writing in the 1980s, Morris Abram, who spent more than a decade challenging Georgia's county-unit system, claimed that he had invented the phrase. Abram, who later served as the president of Brandeis University, explained that as early as 1935, when he was attending the University of Georgia, he began advocating "for the principle for which I later coined a slogan, 'one man, one vote.'"[1] This seems to be a stretch; in his briefs and oral arguments, Abram came close to uttering those four concise and deeply evocative words but, the records show, never actually used the precise phrase.[2]

The phrase, interestingly enough, may have had its roots in the struggle against apartheid and colonial rule in South Africa and its neighbors. As early as June 1953, Nelson Mandela wrote of "one adult, one vote" as the definition of democracy. Two years later, the African National Congress and several like-minded organizations joined together to adopt a Freedom Charter that declared, "Every man and woman shall have the right to vote." The Freedom Charter stopped short of using the phrase "one man, one vote," but in May 1961 Mandela, while in hiding, told a television interviewer that "the Africans require, want, the franchise on the basis of one man, one vote. They want political independence." In fact, as late as the mid-1980s, South African government and business leaders continued to condemn the ANC's insistence on an electoral system based on "one man, one vote."[3]

Events in southern Africa did not go unnoticed in the United States. After the Supreme Court's ruling in *Baker* v. *Carr*, the New York–based Twentieth Century Fund convened a panel of scholars and tasked them with establishing a set of principles to guide legislative apportionment. In its subsequent report, the panel referred specifically to "the cry of 'one man, one vote' heard today in the emerging new lands of Asia and Africa." The following year, John Lewis, the son of Alabama sharecroppers and a Nashville seminarian, drew an explicit link between demands for universal suffrage in Africa and the goals of the American civil rights movement. Preparing to address the March on Washington in August 1963 on behalf of the Student Nonviolent Coordinating Committee, Lewis was moved by a photograph in the *New York Times* of a political demonstration in Rhodesia in which women carried signs that read ONE MAN, ONE VOTE. In his impassioned oration, delivered before Martin Luther King Jr. gave his "I Have a Dream" speech, Lewis declared to the 250,000 people assembled on the Washington Mall that "'One Man, One Vote' is the African cry. It is ours, too. It must be ours." In the following weeks and months, SNCC adopted "One Man, One Vote" as its official slogan, as it worked to register black voters in the most hostile parts of the American South.[4]

While the general concept and exact phrase resonated around the world in the 1950s and early 1960s, "one man, one vote" appears to have first entered the annals of American reapportionment jurisprudence in 1960, in a dissenting opinion in the Michigan supreme court. In 1952, voters in Michigan went to the polls to choose between two competing reapportionment plans: one based on "strict population" and a counterproposal that would have created a "balanced legislature" modeled on a federal system—a house of representatives based on population and a senate based on geography. The counterproposal, supported by the Farm Bureau, Chamber of Commerce, and Manufacturers Association, prevailed and effectively froze senate districts that were already malapportioned when they were first drawn in 1925. In December 1959, Detroit attorney Theodore Sachs filed suit, challenging Michigan's reapportionment on behalf of August Scholle, the president of the Michigan State AFL-CIO and the leading advocate in the state for a population-based legislature. In June 1960, the Michigan supreme court upheld the constitutionality of the 1952 plan by a vote of 5–3. In his dissent, Justice Talbot Smith cited Gordon Baker, writing that "the base upon which our political structure was built, namely, 'one man, one vote,' has been distorted into 'some privileged men, many votes.'"[5]

Heartened by Smith's dissent, Sachs and Scholle appealed to the Supreme Court of the United States in December 1960, just weeks after the Court had accepted probable jurisdiction in *Baker* v. *Carr*. Their case, however, lay dormant, with the Court choosing to take no action until it had decided the Tennessee case. In the more than fifteen months that the Supreme Court took to render a decision in *Baker*, Sachs, who was barely thirty years old, corresponded frequently with attorneys involved in reapportionment litigation in other states. Years later, he recalled that during this period a "remarkable network of plaintiff attorneys evolved" based on the shared conviction that apportionment reform was a necessity. Located across the United States, these attorneys closely followed one another's cases, willingly shared ideas and briefs, and contributed to one another's arguments. After *Baker*, the size of the group expanded, as attorneys filed lawsuits in more than thirty states. "When the landmark decision finally came down," Sachs wrote in reference to *Reynolds* v. *Sims*, "it bore the imprint of many and was in that regard extremely satisfying."[6]

Early on, Sachs himself went to Daniel Magraw and his attorneys in Minnesota, and to Walter Chandler in Tennessee, for advice. Once he filed a suit, attorneys in other states looked to him for guidance. In early 1960, Sachs began an especially fruitful exchange of ideas and strategies with Alfred L. Scanlan, an attorney in Washington who filed the Maryland reapportionment suit that ultimately reached the Supreme Court. On at least two occasions, Sachs traveled to the nation's capital to meet with his expanding network of contacts; he saw Morris Abram prior to the Georgian's January 1963 appearance before the Supreme Court, and he attended the oral arguments of the decisive state reapportionment cases in November 1963.[7]

In formulating his initial strategy in the Tennessee case, Chandler invited Sachs to file an amicus brief in *Baker* v. *Carr*. Sachs demurred, still hopeful that the Supreme Court would decide to hear arguments in his case as well as the Tennessee case; if the Court placed the Michigan case on its calendar, Sachs would have the opportunity to present his argument not as a friend of the court but as a direct participant. But as the months passed and the Court prepared for the second round of arguments in *Baker* in the fall, all without signaling any intention to hear arguments in the Michigan case, national strategists for Walter Reuther's United Auto Workers pressed Sachs to file an amicus brief emphasizing the "political, legislative and economic" effects of malapportionment rather than the narrow legal claims over jurisdiction at the center of the existing briefs. Sachs readily agreed.[8]

Prior to submitting his amicus brief, Sachs wrote to Archibald Cox and "expressed concern at the seeming readiness of the Solicitor to accept under the fourteenth amendment a basis for legislative representation other than population in one house of a bicameral legislature." Cox replied that he "regretted having to make" the argument but thought it necessary to do so in order to prevail on the main point, "to persuade the Supreme Court that such issues are justiciable." Disappointed in Cox's caution, Sachs turned to the dissenting opinion of Talbot Smith for inspiration as he crafted his amicus brief on behalf of August Scholle. The young attorney left no doubt as to his, and his client's, position: he declared that "we believe the doctrine of 'one man–one vote' is the basic principle to be necessarily derived from the Fourteenth Amendment and from the voting rights cases, and necessarily to be applied to all states and to all 'state action.'" His final product, filed in September 1961, marked the first time that the term "one man, one vote" appeared in a brief in a reapportionment case before the Supreme Court. At no other point in the extensive record of *Baker* v. *Carr* did anyone use the term.[9]

Whatever its origins, the term "one man, one vote" had entered the American lexicon as the Supreme Court prepared in January 1963 to hear oral arguments in *Gray* v. *Sanders*, Morris Abram's latest challenge to the Georgia county-unit system. Technically not a reapportionment case, *Gray* v. *Sanders* nevertheless had a profound influence on the ultimate disposition of the numerous state reapportionment cases filed post–*Baker* v. *Carr*. In announcing its majority decision in *Gray*, the Supreme Court not only embraced the essence of the term but, just as important, also redefined subsequent reapportionment jurisprudence with the substitution of a single word: the all-male Supreme Court of the United States envisioned political equality by referring not to "one man, one vote" but to "one person, one vote." Surprising, for a considerable length of time, no other organization or interest group, not even the League of Women Voters, followed suit.

The Georgia County-Unit System

Jimmy Carter, writing about his first campaign for elected office, called *Baker* v. *Carr* a "turning point" that shook "the foundation of the ancient political order" in his native Georgia. Within forty-eight hours of the Supreme Court's decision in *Baker*, attorneys in Georgia filed two lawsuits, one that intended to abolish the state's notorious county-unit system and one that challenged the apportionment of the state legislature. Several weeks later, a third lawsuit took on Georgia's system of congressional apportionment. According to Carter, "political leaders on both sides of the issue were obsessed with the subject." Opponents of reapportionment, in particular, recognized the implications of the pending lawsuits. Whether at work, at church, or at Lions Club meetings, Carter's neighbors expressed a pervasive fear of an Atlanta fairly represented in the state's legislature. Without a doubt, according to Carter, the race of Atlanta's residents accounted for their central concern.[10]

Atlanta attorney Morris Abram, by contrast, eagerly anticipated the Court's ruling in *Baker* v. *Carr*. Born in 1918 in rural Ben Hill County in south-central Georgia to Jewish parents, Abram had resolved as an undergraduate at the University of Georgia to commit himself to challenging minority rule and white supremacy in his native state. He studied at Oxford University on a Rhodes Scholarship and, after returning in 1948, settled in Atlanta, began a law practice, and launched a fifteen-year campaign against Georgia's county-unit system.[11]

One of only three states to provide for some form of a unit plan—Maryland and Mississippi were the others—Georgia adopted its county-unit system in 1917. Known more formally as the Neill Primary Act, the statute technically governed the running of primaries for statewide offices such as governor, lieutenant governor, and U.S. senator. But in practice it ensured that a rural minority maintained almost absolute control of the urbanizing state. Under the terms of the act, the eight most populous counties in the state received six unit votes each; the thirty next most populous counties received four unit votes each; and all remaining counties received two unit votes each. The winner of a county's popular vote received all of that county's unit votes; the candidate who received the most unit votes, not the candidate who won the statewide popular vote, received the nomination of the party. At the time, Georgia had 159 counties; 121 sparsely settled rural counties, home to less than one-third of the state's population, controlled 242 unit votes, nearly 60 percent of the total. By 1960, the eight most populous counties alone contained more than 40 percent of the state's residents but controlled less than 12 percent of the unit votes. More than 550,000 persons, 14 percent of the state's population, resided in Georgia's most populous county, Fulton, but received only 6 of the 410 unit votes, while the 1,876 residents of tiny Echols County controlled 2 unit votes. At the time, winning the Democratic nomination was "tantamount to election" throughout the South, and rural Democrats in Georgia manipulated the county-unit system with brutal efficiency in order to weaken their urban counterparts.[12]

Three times in the 1950s, Abram and his colleagues rode a challenge to Georgia's county-unit system all the way to the Supreme Court, and each time the Court declined to intervene, citing *Colegrove*. In 1950, in *South* v. *Peters*, and again in 1952, in *Cox* v. *Peters*, William O. Douglas and Hugo Black published strongly worded dissents that inspired Abram to believe that he might ultimately prevail. In their brief in *South* v. *Peters*, the appellants had stressed that a strong link existed between the county-unit system and white supremacy. They quoted Georgia governor Herman Talmadge, who had taken to the airwaves and declared, "There is more behind this suit than meets the eye. It is part of a master plan—to disfranchise white people in rural areas and enfranchise the great horde of bloc voters in urban centers," an unsubtle reference to African American voters who had migrated to the state's urban centers in the years after World War II. In their dissent from the Court's per curiam decision in *South* v. *Peters*, Douglas and Black agreed that the county-unit system allowed those in power to circumvent previous Court rulings prohibiting racial discrimination in primary and general elections. But the pair went beyond the question of racial discrimination and wrote that, in and of itself, the obvious "discrimination against citizens in the more populous counties of Georgia" constituted a clear violation of the Equal Protection Clause. Noting that the plaintiffs had sued "as individuals" in order to enforce rights that were "personal and individual," Douglas and Black concluded that the state had created a favored class of voters with "preferred political rights . . . the worst of all discriminations under a democratic system of government." In 1958, when it turned aside *Hartsfield* v. *Sloan*, the Supreme Court refused for the third time in less than a decade to reconsider the merits of the county-unit system. Even so, Abram picked up two additional votes with this latest try: William Brennan and Earl Warren joined Douglas and Black in a procedural vote (the Court never heard arguments in any of the three cases).[13]

Sensing that *Baker* v. *Carr* would be the breakthrough, Abram prepared an up-to-date complaint as the case progressed, and he again named William Hartsfield, who had retired just weeks before after six terms as the mayor of Atlanta, as the plaintiff. Abram had planned to file his suit in the federal district court as soon as the Supreme Court announced a favorable opinion in *Baker*. But when Hartsfield, who had aggressively campaigned against the unit system for years, telephoned in the early afternoon on Monday, March 26, to inform Abram of the Supreme Court's decision in *Baker*, the former mayor added that he would not serve as the plaintiff without the consent of Robert Woodruff, the president emeritus of the Coca-Cola Company, a major powerbroker in Atlanta and a key supporter of Hartsfield. After speaking with "the Cigar," Hartsfield's nickname for Woodruff, he withdrew from formal participation in the case, although he remained a vocal supporter of the lawsuit. By the time Abram named Atlanta businessman James O'Hare Sanders as a replacement, the district court had closed for the evening. The following day, March 27, Abram filed suit on behalf of Sanders against James H. Gray, the chairman of the Georgia State Democratic Executive Committee.[14]

The clerk of the court scheduled the case for oral argument at the end of April, forcing Georgia governor Ernest Vandiver to call the legislature into special session for the sole purpose of amending the Neill Primary Act so that it passed constitutional muster without diluting its usefulness. As Abram presented his case to a three-judge court on the

morning of April 27, a messenger arrived from the state capitol and informed the jurists that the legislature had, indeed, just amended the
law, prompting a lawyer for the state to move for dismissal since the facts
as presented in the complaint no longer matched the law. But Abram,
who had prepared for numerous contingencies, instantly produced an
amended complaint that correctly anticipated the terms of the new
statute. The counsel for the state of Georgia looked on dumbfounded.
After six hours of arguments, the district court adjourned.[15]

The following day, the three-judge court handed Abram a clear victory, asserting jurisdiction on the basis of *Baker* v. *Carr* and ruling that
Georgia's county-unit system violated the Fourteenth Amendment
rights of individual citizens residing in the state's metropolitan areas.
The panel noted that the Supreme Court's majority opinion in *Baker*
embraced the position William O. Douglas and Hugo Black first enunciated in their dissent in *South* v. *Peters*—a measure of the progress that
had been made since Abram saw that case turned away by the Court in
1950. As the judges in *Sanders* v. *Gray* wrote in their decision, "Where
nominations are made in primary elections, there shall be no inequality
in voting power by reason of race, creed, color or other invidious discrimination." The district court did not, however, grant Abram a complete victory. It refused to concede, as Abram had argued, that all unit
systems necessarily violated the Equal Protection Clause. The judges
left open the theoretical possibility that an acceptable unit system might
exist, so long as the disproportionate value assigned to any individual
voter was not excessive.[16]

January 1963

Oral arguments in *Gray* v. *Sanders* were national news, but not solely
because of the substance of the case. Attorney General Robert Kennedy
had decided to argue the federal government's position in place of Archibald Cox. Kennedy had never argued a case in any courtroom, much
less the Supreme Court, and he never did so again. But his immediate
predecessors had made at least one appearance before the nation's highest court, and he wanted to burnish his credentials and silence those
critics who considered him unqualified. Once Kennedy made clear his
determination to appear before the Supreme Court, Cox and Burke

Marshall, the head of the Civil Rights Division, determined that, from a legal standpoint, *Gray* v. *Sanders* was a relatively "easy case" and thus the best one for Kennedy to argue.[17]

Kennedy devoted two weeks over Christmas and New Year's to the preparation of his argument, poring over the full record, the government's amicus brief, and a detailed memorandum from a somewhat nervous Cox. Kennedy spent an additional six hours over two days with Bruce Terris, who had contributed to the drafting of the government's brief, just as he had in *Baker*, and who helped Kennedy refine his approach.[18]

Cox's memo to Kennedy emphasized that the Georgia county-unit system clearly discriminated against urban voters but that the Supreme Court had not yet considered what standard, if any, the Fourteenth Amendment imposed on "the power of States to apportion voting power in State legislatures or the election of officials." Calling the issue of standards "the $64 question" that lay at "the heart of the case," Cox wrote that "one theoretically possible answer is that all votes must be given equal weight, i.e. any discrimination among voters is unconstitutional." But Cox, who worried about putting the Kennedy administration too far in front of where the Supreme Court was prepared to go, predicted that other than Justices Black and Douglas, the Court was "very unlikely" to embrace such a "dogmatic interpretation." Instead, Cox reminded Kennedy that the government had argued in its brief, consistent with its position in *Baker*, that "any departure from equality of voting power must have some rational foundation in terms of permissible State policy." In other words, the federal government, like the district court, allowed for the theoretical possibility that some form of a unit system might pass constitutional scrutiny.[19]

Abram, in contrast, had maintained in the district court that the Fourteenth Amendment forbade any form of vote dilution and thus any unit system whatsoever. He planned to make the same argument in the Supreme Court. Summoned by Cox to a meeting to "coordinate" their arguments, Abram joined the solicitor general, the attorney general, and Burke Marshall in Kennedy's office at the Department of Justice. Recounting the meeting many years later, Abram recalled that in justifying his objection to the government's position, he claimed to "stand squarely on the principle of one man, one vote." "You don't agree," he told Cox, "but grant me this: it's one thing to disenfranchise a man because he is illiterate, or a felon, or even unpropertied, but once you give a man a vote how can you give someone else twice a vote? You can't grade the franchise and give qualified voters varying amounts of voting strength. A man either is a voter or he isn't." Kennedy turned to Cox and expressed sympathy with Abram's position, but the solicitor general reminded his boss that he had an obligation not to deviate during oral argument from the position that the administration had already presented in its brief.[20]

When Earl Warren gaveled the Supreme Court into session on Thursday, January 17, 1963, the presence of a dozen other members of the Kennedy clan in the audience—including Robert's wife, Ethel, his mother, Rose, and his brother Edward, who had been sworn in as a U.S. senator from Massachusetts just days earlier—caused quite a stir. Well into the proceedings, but just minutes before Robert Kennedy began his argument, First Lady Jacqueline Kennedy added to the excitement when she took a seat in the front row. "Bobby's Court Debut Socially Brilliant: Kennedys Outnumber Justices," one headline would read the next day. Not everyone in attendance was there in support of the attorney general, however. "It was a big day," Terris remembered. "Everybody in town wanted to see Robert Kennedy get his teeth knocked out."[21]

Kennedy waited patiently as representatives of the state of Georgia, followed by Abram, preceded him. B. D. Murphy, a deputy assistant attorney general of Georgia, emphasized the deep historical roots of the Neill Primary Act. E. Freeman Leverett, who held the same rank as Murphy, defended the weighting of votes as legitimate and insisted that "the Fourteenth Amendment does not limit a state's choice in allocating its electoral power to . . . equal population representation." Before his time expired, Leverett warned the Court that it lacked the power, or the competence, to establish "judicially manageable standards."[22]

At last, after years of petitioning the Supreme Court to hear his challenge to Georgia's county-unit system, Abram approached the podium. Conceding that his position differed in certain respects from the federal government's, Abram argued that any unit system, not just the one at issue in the case, violated the Constitution. He chose not to dwell on the link between the unit system and racial discrimination, stating instead that "the only purpose" of the unit system was "to see that a minority prevails." Justice Potter Stewart asked a series of questions intended to decouple the issue before the Court from questions about legislative apportionment, but Abram dodged apportionment and refused to make any claims about standards. Although Abram did not utter the term he would later claim as his own, he did insist in his closing that "a qualified voter is a qualified voter is a qualified voter, and a vote is a vote is a vote."[23]

After more than two hours of oral arguments and a break for lunch, Earl Warren called on Robert Kennedy at ten minutes past two o'clock. In "his morning coat and striped trousers," the traditional garb worn by counsel before the high court, the attorney general looked, according to James Clayton, the Supreme Court correspondent for the *Washington Post*, "like a nervous and uncomfortable young bridegroom." Yet Kennedy performed admirably, if not spectacularly, and grew in confidence as he addressed the Court without reading directly from his notes. For ten minutes, the justices refrained from interrupting as Kennedy more or less stuck to the script dictated by Cox. Kennedy stated that the government was "not against a county-unit system as such" and did not claim "that under all circumstances, in every situation, that every vote must be given equal weight." But, he added, any departure from a general commitment to one man, one vote must be "minimal" and must "further some part of the elective process." The government opposed the Georgia system, Kennedy explained, because it departed excessively and unreasonably from population equality. When Warren shrewdly asked if "there is any place in a state system of voting for weighting the votes in a general election" for statewide offices, Kennedy responded, as Cox had instructed him to do, that the Court need not reach that question in this particular case. But then the attorney general unexpectedly (to Cox, at least) veered from the script, saying that although he had given the issue "a great deal of thought, I have difficulty coming up with any system that makes any sense."[24]

Mary McGrory, a respected political reporter for the *Washington Evening Star*, was among the journalists who observed Kennedy's argument. In her column the following afternoon, she noted that John Marshall Harlan, the lone member of the Court to remain faithful to the Frankfurter doctrine, took part in the Court's friendly reception of the attorney general. Harlan even "gently reminded" Kennedy that he had digressed from the government's brief after the latter's response to Warren's question. But according to McGrory, "Bobby was not leaning on it too heavily." When he remarked for a second time that "the ideal is one man, one vote," subject to reasonable limitations, Justice Arthur Goldberg, who had replaced Frankfurter a few months earlier, asked the attorney general why the government lacked "the courage of its convictions" and refused to be forthright about its position. Kennedy answered, "We have the courage of it, Mr. Justice. We just don't think it is necessary to say at the moment." According to Abram, the exchange deeply distressed Cox, who was seated next to him.[25]

A leading constitutional scholar, seconded by at least one Warren biographer, credits Robert Kennedy as the first person "to utter the magic words, 'one man, one vote,'" in the Supreme Court. But in fact Kennedy had been beaten to the punch by more than an hour; ironically, it was not Morris Abram but opposing counsel Freeman Leverett who can claim the distinction. In his opening remarks, Leverett argued that America's Founding Fathers, in conceiving their new nation's political and electoral structure, rejected French thinkers, such as Rousseau, who were committed to the concept of "one man, one vote." Instead, Leverett explained, the Founders embraced the British theory of government, "which saw the necessity for imposing limitations upon majority will at its very source," a description of the logic that made possible the rotten borough. In a subsequent exchange with Leverett, Potter Stewart became the second person to utter the phrase "one man, one vote." Or, rather, he almost did. Leverett, arguing that the Court was not equipped to make policy statements or set standards, slipped into a discussion of legislative apportionment. Stewart interrupted and stated for the fifth time—by his own count—that *Gray* v. *Sanders* had nothing to do with apportionment. He reminded Leverett that the Georgia case concerned nothing more, or less, than the election of candidates for statewide office. Every state in the union except Georgia, Maryland, and Mississippi, explained Stewart, held statewide elections on the basis of "one man, one voter, one vote."[26]

The following day, as newspapers around the nation reported on the attorney general's performance, the nine justices met for conference. The ideological balance of the Court had shifted dramatically in the months since illness had forced Charles Whittaker and then Felix Frankfurter to step down, and the justices disposed of the Georgia county-unit case without a great deal of discussion.

Less than three weeks after Whittaker's resignation, Byron R. White had taken his seat on the Supreme Court at the age of forty-four. White's status as a Kennedy insider raised no objections from the Senate, which confirmed his nomination without recorded dissent just eight days after receiving it from the White House. Certainly the most athletic individual to ever serve on the Supreme Court, White finished at the top of his class and was named an All-American in football while at the University of Colorado. Nicknamed "Whizzer" for his prowess on the college playing fields, White led the National Football League in rushing as a rookie for the Pittsburgh Steelers but gave up his promising athletic career to accept a Rhodes Scholarship to study at Oxford. When World War II broke out, White returned to the United States, entered Yale Law School, and then resumed his football career with the Detroit Lions. After the Japanese invasion of Pearl Harbor, White served in the Pacific with the navy. Returning to Yale after the war, White graduated with honors in 1946 and accepted an offer to serve as a clerk for the Supreme Court's chief justice, Fred Vinson.[27]

After a year in the nation's capital, White moved to Colorado to build a legal career and remained there for more than a decade until the Kennedys invited him back. White chaired the Kennedy presidential campaign in Colorado, earning him the trust and admiration of the future president and his brother. After his narrow victory over Richard Nixon, John F. Kennedy appointed White to the post of deputy attorney general. Only fifteen months later, White replaced Whittaker. When he retired thirty-one years later, White was the Court's most senior justice and perhaps the most difficult to characterize in terms of a judicial philosophy: he voted with conservatives in criminal rights and abortion cases, among others, but consistently sided with the Court's more liberal members in cases that involved equal protection, civil rights, and voting rights claims.[28]

White did not remain the junior justice for long. After suffering a stroke in April 1962, Frankfurter held out hope that he would be able to return to work. By August, however, he had realized that would not be possible and had stepped down from the Court. In his place, President Kennedy nominated Arthur Goldberg, a native of Chicago who finished first in his class at Northwestern Law School before dedicating himself to the practice of labor law. The general counsel of both the United Steelworkers and the Congress of Industrial Organizations, Goldberg played a seminal role in the merger of the CIO with the American Federation of Labor in 1955. His prominence as one of the nation's leading labor lawyers made him an obvious choice for secretary of labor in the Kennedy administration. Kennedy then sent Goldberg to the Supreme Court in the fall of 1962, aware of the debt he owed the labor movement for his election.[29]

Unlike White, Goldberg remained on the bench a mere three years, the odd man out in one of Lyndon Johnson's more arrogant and ultimately self-destructive maneuvers. Early in his presidency, Johnson grew impatient for a vacancy on the Court; he wanted to appoint his friend and confidant Abe Fortas. But no senior justice showed signs of obliging him, and so in 1965, Johnson cajoled Goldberg into accepting an appointment as the American ambassador to the United Nations. Johnson's machinations ultimately cost him dearly; not only did Goldberg's departure deprive the Court and its previously ascendant liberal bloc of a reliable vote, but Fortas resigned in disgrace from his new position only four years later. When Johnson, his influence sapped by the Vietnam War and his decision not to run for reelection, tried to elevate Fortas to chief justice in 1968, the Senate balked, in part because of Fortas's cozy relationship with the president. Furthermore, the confirmation hearings raised questions about financial improprieties, which resulted in Fortas stepping down from his position as an associate justice. Johnson had handed not one, but two appointments to his successor, Richard Nixon.[30]

But even though Goldberg's tenure was short-lived, it proved significant. He quickly allied himself with Warren, Brennan, Douglas, and Black to form the core majority that would expand the scope of individual rights in a host of controversial decisions in the mid-1960s. As one constitutional scholar wrote, Goldberg embraced a "belief that the Court should protect a 'permanent minority' that had been excluded from the political process." Goldberg represented a clear departure from Frankfurter's rigid commitment to judicial restraint. More often than not, he questioned state action and sided instead with individual claims of discrimination.[31]

At conference on the morning of January 18, 1963, eight members of the Court voted to affirm the lower-court ruling in the Georgia county-unit case. Of those eight, three—Warren, Douglas, and Goldberg—expressed their belief that "exact" or "absolute" equality should be the rule. According to notes kept by Douglas, Justices Black, Clark, Brennan, Stewart, and White affirmed the district court without further explanation. Only John Marshall Harlan, who believed that states should enjoy wide latitude in crafting laws and was not willing to concede that the Georgia system was necessarily irrational, voted to reverse the lower court.[32]

Warren assigned the majority opinion to Douglas. A famously fast writer—notoriously so to his critics, who thought him careless and insufficiently deferential to precedent—Douglas produced an initial handwritten draft and then a typed revision in a matter of days. Rather than merely affirming the decision of the lower court, as the justices had appeared to do at conference, Douglas's opinion went one step further. He stated that the majority agreed with most aspects of the district court's ruling and that he and his colleagues concluded that no unit system could pass constitutional scrutiny. "Once the class of voters is chosen and their qualifications specified," read a passage that remained unchanged in the published opinion, "we see no constitutional way by which equality of voting power may be evaded." With those words, the Court had in effect elected to side with Morris Abram, not the federal government as represented by Cox and Robert Kennedy. Douglas ended his initial draft by referring to the amendments that guarantee that the right to vote cannot be abridged on account of race or sex, and that provide for the direct election of senators by popular vote, observing that "the conception of political equality from the Declaration of Independence, to Lincoln's Gettysburg Address, to the Fifteenth, Seventeenth, and Nineteenth Amendments is engrained in our system."[33]

But Douglas soon made a seemingly modest but, as it would turn out, extremely influential edit. Striking the last five words of his initial draft, Douglas wrote the words that transformed the parameters of subsequent reapportionment jurisprudence: "The conception of political equality from the Declaration of Independence, to Lincoln's Gettysburg Address, to the Fifteenth, Seventeenth, and Nineteenth Amendments can mean only one thing—one person, one vote." Just before he shared the new draft with his colleagues, Douglas dismissed the suggestion of a law clerk who recommended replacing "person" with "voter."[34]

As Douglas circulated additional drafts with minor changes in February, the rest of the Court, except Harlan, signed on. In mid-March, Harlan distributed his dissent. In it, he strongly criticized the Court's embrace of "one person, one vote" as "constitutionally untenable" and warned of the implications for the more than thirty legislative reapportionment cases pending in state and federal courts. Harlan's coupling of the ruling in the Georgia county-unit case with apportionment prompted a terse response from Potter Stewart. With Tom Clark, Stewart drafted a short concurrence in which he insisted that, despite Harlan's claim, *Gray* v. *Sanders* "does not involve the validity of a State's reapportionment" or "the basic ground rules implementing *Baker* v. *Carr*." The Georgia county-unit case, Stewart averred, involved nothing more than statewide elections.[35]

The Supreme Court's decision in *Gray* v. *Sanders*, announced March 18, vindicated—and delighted—Morris Abram. That evening and the next morning, newspapers across the nation, and especially those in Atlanta, ran reports and editorials about the significance of the ruling and praised Abram for his perseverance. While some reports adhered to Stewart's distinction that the decision had no bearing on legislative apportionment, others brushed it aside and, as Harlan had foreseen, saw obvious implications for the dozens of reapportionment lawsuits, including several that had already reached the Supreme Court docket. Looking ahead to the disposition of these cases in the Court's next term, the *New York Post* declared that "reapportionment is no panacea for all our troubles. But it is perhaps the most important business of our day."[36]

To the attorneys preparing to argue legislative reapportionment in the Supreme Court the following term, Douglas's language in the Georgia county-unit majority opinion provided a priceless gift: a basic, unassailable assertion of equality and a definition of the essence of American democracy. Even critics of the Court saw the importance of Douglas's opinion. In the late 1960s, Robert Dixon, a leading expert on reapportionment who supported reform but felt the Court had gone too far, pointed to the "many fortuitous events in the course of the 'Reapportionment Revolution.'" He told Archibald Cox, who was back on the Harvard faculty, that "perhaps the most fortuitous of all, and certainly the most advantageous from the plaintiff's standpoint, was the timing of *Gray* v. *Sanders*." "Although a non-'representation' case," he explained, "it nevertheless coined the easily transferable 'one man–one vote' phrase, and conditioned all that followed."[37]

Dixon, of course, misquoted Douglas, who aligned the eight men in the majority behind the principle of "one person, one vote," not "one man, one vote." But in this regard, Dixon enjoyed good company. Well into the 1960s, officials in the League of Women Voters and the Young Women's Christian Association consistently cited their support for "one man, one vote," as did John Lewis and his compatriots in SNCC. Only the all-male Supreme Court seemed truly attuned to the gender-neutral one person, one vote. What, exactly, inspired Douglas to choose "person" rather than "man" or "voter" is impossible to know, but it is interesting to note that Freeman Leverett may once again have earned himself an ironic footnote in history. In his closing rebuttal to Abram and Kennedy, Leverett engaged in an exchange with Stewart, in which the justice remarked, "The basic issue that we end up with, I suppose, is whether a state, under the Constitution, in the election process of statewide officials, can absolutely disregard what we think of as the traditional American system of majority rule." Speaking casually but clearly, Leverett replied by referring to majority rule as "one person, one vote." Leverett probably never imagined that his words would provide inspiration for the justice's opinion and, by extension, dozens of pending litigants preparing to transform the basic meaning of the Constitution of the United States.[38]

7 ||| THE MAKING OF *REYNOLDS* V. *SIMS*

larke Stallworth enjoyed a plum assignment covering the Alabama legislature for the *Birmingham Post-Herald*. A native of Marengo County, in the heart of Alabama's agricultural Black Belt—the traditional home of most of the state's African American population—he understood well the arrangement that political leaders in Black Belt counties had entered into with the Big Mules, the industrial titans in the northern part of the state who controlled the steel mills and other factories in densely populated areas such as Birmingham, Gadsden, and Huntsville. The Big Mules consented to Black Belt control of the state legislature, which the Black Belt considered crucial to the perpetuation of Jim Crow. In exchange, the legislature delivered the antiunion and low-tax legislation coveted by the Big Mules.[1]

The arrangement depended on legislative apportionment that guaranteed the overrepresentation of Black Belt and other rural counties and the underrepresentation of the state's more urban counties. This situation was made possible by the legislature's refusal to reapportion every ten years, as required by the 1901 state constitution. Between 1901 and 1961, members of the house and senate introduced more than 1,000 reapportionment bills; not a single one passed. By the 1960s, Black Belt members of the Alabama house of representatives represented as few as 6,000–7,000 people. By contrast, representatives of the state's most populous area—Jefferson County and the city of Birmingham—spoke for 90,000 constituents. The Gulf Coast county of Mobile, the second most populous region in Alabama, was the state's most underrepresented area in the house, with only one member for each 104,000 residents. In the state senate, malapportionment proved every bit as severe and further ensured Black Belt domination of the legislature.[2]

The initial apportionment of 1901 was based ostensibly on population, but by 1960, Alabama's system of reapportionment had become utterly irrational. Tuscaloosa County, population 109,047, had two representatives in the state house, as did Madison County and its 117,348 residents; Dallas County, a Black Belt stronghold, had 56,667 residents and three representatives. Even within the heart of the Black Belt, no rhyme or reason determined apportionment. Lowndes County with 15,417 residents, Henry County with 15,286, and Bullock County with 13,462 all had two representatives, while Pickens County with 21,882 residents, Monroe County with 22,372, and Macon County with 26,717 each sent one representative to the state house.[3]

Stallworth had attended the University of North Carolina, had lived in Birmingham for the better part of a decade, and had come to resent the stifling effect that malapportionment had on Alabama's economic and social development. He did not understand how the legislature could so clearly violate its constitutional mandate to reapportion every ten years. In the spring of 1961, Stallworth stood in the well of the state house of representatives, near the press table, talking with Sam Nettles, a member of the legislature and an old family acquaintance. A point man for Black Belt legislators, Nettles served as a valuable source of information for Stallworth during the time he covered the legislature, from 1956 to 1961. Stallworth asked Nettles why the legislature did not do its constitutional duty and reapportion itself. With a look of sheer "arrogance," Nettles fixed a stare at Stallworth and replied, "Clarke, you all just keep sending the money down here and we'll keep spending it." Stallworth cursed Nettles under his breath and vowed to get even.[4]

Stallworth did that, and then some. Over a ten-day span in May 1961—at the exact same time that the Freedom Riders arrived in Birmingham to challenge the segregation of the city's interstate bus terminal—he wrote a series of eight columns for the *Post-Herald*. When Stallworth began work on the series, he hoped to focus people's attention on the dire consequences of malapportionment and thereby force the legislature to at least ponder fixing the problem. He never imagined that he was initiating a process that would see the district court in

Montgomery become the first federal court in the nation to propose a remedy to malapportionment post-*Baker*, and that would end with *Reynolds* v. *Sims*, a landmark Supreme Court decision that established the principle of one person, one vote in all state legislative apportionments.[5]

Stallworth based his series on the fact he raised with Nettles: that the 1901 Alabama constitution mandated that it "shall be the duty of the Legislature" to reapportion on a decennial basis, and to do so based on population. Stallworth highlighted the statistical disparities in the Alabama house and senate that effectively gave residents of the Black Belt and other rural counties many times the electoral power of their urban counterparts. He devoted an entire column to the process by which urban residents contributed a disproportionate amount of state revenue in the form of sales, income, gasoline, and liquor taxes, and rural legislators decided how those funds were spent. He cited one study showing that residents of Birmingham alone provided about 25 percent of the state's gasoline tax but received only 1.5 percent of state expenditures on roads. "In effect," Stallworth concluded, "the people of the more populous counties put up the money to run the state, and the legislators from the rural counties decide how to spend it." Possibly with Nettles in mind, Stallworth added that "sometimes the rural legislators appear to be more interested in the tax money coming from the cities than they are in the problems of the cities themselves." Writing just weeks after the Supreme Court heard the first oral argument in *Baker* v. *Carr*, Stallworth noted the movements for reapportionment in other states and observed that the federal courts might have to step in if officials in Alabama did not do their constitutional duty.[6]

Stallworth's series caught the attention of fellow members of the Young Men's Business Club (YMBC), an organization that appealed to a range of young professionals: lawyers, accountants, business executives, architects, and journalists. Founded in 1946, the YMBC conceived of itself as a progressive alternative to the Chamber of Commerce and the Jaycees. Impressed by Atlanta and its mayor, William Hartsfield, members hoped to guide Birmingham along a similar path of economic growth and diversification. George Peach Taylor, known to his friends as "Peaches," a lawyer and YMBC member who would play a central role in the reapportionment lawsuit to come, talked later in his

life about how the YMBC used its regular luncheons and annual ban-
quet to bring in controversial speakers to "stir up interest" in local,
national, and international affairs. Although it was considered "very liberal" and even "radical" by some in Birmingham, the YMBC was actually quite conservative. It had no black or female members and ignored
issues of race for as long as possible. In the early 1960s, as the civil rights
movement was putting Birmingham on the international map and
made it impossible to remain silent, YMBC members urged a gradualist approach to alleviate the worst vestiges of Jim Crow but did not support the complete eradication of racial segregation. The organization,
for instance, passed a resolution criticizing Police Commissioner Eugene "Bull" Connor and the police department for failing to "avert" a
"riot" when the Freedom Riders arrived in May 1961. And members
spearheaded the successful referendum in November 1962 to change
Birmingham's system of government, a shift that diminished Connor's
power. At the same time, the YMBC urged Martin Luther King Jr. and
his lieutenants in the spring of 1963 to end their demonstrations and to
allow the new system of government a chance to respond to their demands. King declined to wait; he was arrested and wrote his legendary
"Letter From Birmingham City Jail."[7]

In the summer of 1961, not long after the publication of his series,
Stallworth addressed fellow members of the YMBC at a luncheon meeting. Toward the end of his remarks, he shared his conclusion that the
intransigence of the legislature and the unwillingness of the state courts
to intervene meant that the federal courts offered the only avenue of
relief. He suggested that the YMBC consider filing a lawsuit and found
a ready audience among a number of members, above all Charles
"Chuck" Morgan and George Taylor.[8]

A graduate of the University of Alabama in 1953 and the university's law school in 1955, Morgan looked more like a southern sheriff in
a three-piece suit than a supporter of civil rights. Morgan had once been
intent on a career in politics and had spurned the chance to go to college
in the North in order to build the necessary relationships to advance a
political career in his home state. According to one biographer, Morgan
showed "signs of political genius" as early as his freshman year at the
University of Alabama, moving easily among "an array of cliques without exactly betraying his own essence." He remained a prominent figure

in campus politics throughout his time in Tuscaloosa. After law school, Morgan moved to Birmingham, where he set up a practice and never passed up an opportunity to shake another hand or greet a passerby on the street. The owner of a lunch spot favored by the city's leading businessmen nicknamed Morgan "Governor."[9]

But Chuck Morgan was different from most white Alabamians: he opposed segregation. At the University of Alabama, Morgan had supported the admission of Autherine Lucy as the first African American student in the school's history. Until 1960, he managed to downplay his racial views enough to hold realistic political ambitions, but the trajectory of his professional life changed radically that year, when he agreed to defend, in separate cases, two white clients involved in interracial activism. For Morgan, who by then had a wife and young son, the decision to accept such clients did not come easily, and it produced a certain amount of anxiety.[10]

In the first case, Morgan defended Tommy Reeves, a ministerial student at Birmingham Southern College, who was arrested for organizing interracial meetings inspired by the sit-in movement then sweeping across the South. Reeves's case never went to trial, and Morgan's involvement remained unknown to most in Birmingham. But several months later, Morgan took on the case of Reeves's mentor, the Reverend Robert Hughes, a Methodist minister and the executive director of the Alabama Council on Human Relations, an organization whose members were committed to alleviating the most basic inequities of racial segregation. Authorities suspected Hughes of providing information to Harrison Salisbury, a Pulitzer Prize–winning reporter for the *New York Times*, who had written a series of scathing indictments of the absence of leadership in Birmingham, especially on matters of race. City officials brought libel charges against Salisbury. As part of the Salisbury investigation, a grand jury ordered Hughes to turn over membership records, lists of donations, and other documentation for the council dating back to 1958. Hughes agreed to testify about his conversations with Salisbury but refused to turn over the records. Cited for contempt of court, Hughes spent several days in jail before the grand jury lifted its order.[11]

For Morgan, threatening late-night phone calls became a regular feature of his life after his involvement in the Hughes case was publicized.

By the time he turned his attention to reapportionment, he had dis-
solved his law partnership and begun practicing on his own, hoping to
protect his former partner from retaliation. In 1963, Chuck Morgan
completed his journey from civil rights sympathizer to activist when he
successfully defended Bob Zellner, a field secretary for the Student
Nonviolent Coordinating Committee, who had been arrested on man-
ufactured charges on suspicion of organizing desegregation demonstrations in conjunction with the inauguration of George Wallace in
January 1963. Even more so than Tommy Reeves or Robert Hughes,
Zellner, who worked for a black-run organization and had a lengthy
civil rights–related arrest record that could also be seen as a record of
SNCC projects throughout the South, posed a more direct threat
to whites in Alabama bent on keeping segregation in place. By the end
of 1963, Morgan, his wife, and their young son were forced into exile
and left the state.[12]

Five years older than Morgan, George Taylor also received his law
degree from the state university, but he and Morgan did not meet until
both moved to Birmingham to launch their legal careers. Looking back
more than forty years later, Taylor remembered Morgan as the only
member of the YMBC who openly opposed segregation prior to the
upheavals of the early 1960s. Taylor initially argued for incremental
changes to the status quo. Toward the end of his life, he credited Morgan with profoundly influencing his thinking. By the time the black
freedom struggle erupted in the early 1960s, Taylor had come around
to the view that a gradualist approach was futile. While never personally threatened to the extent that Morgan was, the racial climate in
Birmingham, and especially the attitudes of the city's elites, convinced
Taylor and his wife to leave Alabama. They joined the Peace Corps in
early 1965 and moved with their four young children to Sierra Leone.[13]

In the summer of 1961, when Stallworth suggested a reapportionment lawsuit at the YMBC luncheon, Morgan was just thirty-one but already, according to Taylor, an "innovative and imaginative" thinker. He
was also confident, domineering, and at times brash, a man who loved
the spotlight. As Taylor reflected many years later, although Stallworth
first raised the idea of a lawsuit, "it was Chuck's case." The unassuming Taylor described his own role as primarily to support Morgan—as
a sounding board for Morgan's ideas, a proofreader of his drafts. So

different in temperament, the two exceptionally close friends made an effective team as they began to research Alabama history and law, pore over census figures, consult with the Tennessee attorneys in *Baker* v. *Carr*, and craft a legal strategy.[14]

Around the same time, the Alabama legislature rebuffed yet another reapportionment bill. Sam Nettles, the Black Belt legislator who so offended Stallworth, showed off his linguistic dexterity when he appeared on a news program with a proponent of reapportionment and publicly denied that the 1901 constitution mandated reapportionment every ten years. Nettles argued that if the framers of the state constitution had indeed intended decennial reapportionment to be mandatory, they would have used the word "must" rather than "shall." When his opponent responded that reapportionment would result in a more democratically governed state, Nettles asserted, without a trace of irony, that "many times minority rule is also true democracy. There are times when minority rule is really important."[15]

Morgan and Taylor found support for a lawsuit from the unlikeliest of places. As a result of the 1960 census, Alabama lost a seat in the U.S. House of Representatives, and it fell to the malapportioned state legislature to decide how to fold nine existing congressional districts into eight new ones. One proposal gaining steam in the summer of 1961 was a plan to "chop up" or "carve up" Birmingham and Jefferson County, which had constituted a single congressional district, into four parts and attach each part to a different neighboring district. Devised by Black Belt legislators to protect the seats of all other incumbents in the state, the chop-up bill infuriated already underrepresented residents of Jefferson County.[16]

The chop-up bill, in Morgan's words, "came as a rude jolt to Birmingham's political and economic powers. They felt betrayed. Their tryst with the Black Belt was over, at least temporarily, and the Big Mules found themselves at war with their traditional allies." Perceiving the direct link between legislative and congressional malapportionment, residents of Birmingham and Jefferson County, who had long opposed reapportionment, began to reconsider. Morgan and Taylor knew that their legislative reapportionment lawsuit would be attractive to these residents only as long as the chop-up bill remained a topic of debate, so they moved quickly. In early August, the pair signed up twelve plaintiffs, all

members of the YMBC, randomly selecting Owens Sims, a Birmingham accountant, as the lead plaintiff. The number rose to fourteen
when Morgan and Taylor formally added their own names to the list of
plaintiffs in the event that "all the others got cold feet." Their caution
proved prescient; two of the original plaintiffs did, in fact, withdraw
under pressure from their employers.[17]

On Saturday, August 12, the Alabama house of representatives
broke a twenty-one-hour filibuster waged by urban representatives and
passed the chop-up bill, sending the measure to Governor John Patterson. Within minutes of the house's action, Morgan and Taylor filed their
reapportionment lawsuit in the United States District Court for the
Middle District of Alabama, based in the state capital of Montgomery.[18]

Although Morgan and Taylor randomly selected Sims as the lead
plaintiff, they deliberately listed Alabama secretary of state Bettye
Frink as the lead defendant. Their decision ensured not only that the
case would be heard in the courtroom of federal district court judge
Frank Johnson, but also that Fifth Circuit Court of Appeals judge Richard Rives would join Johnson on a three-judge panel. Morgan and
Taylor felt confident they would get a fair hearing from Johnson and
Rives. Johnson was a native of Winston County, a Republican stronghold
in northern Alabama, and, at thirty-seven, the youngest federal judge in
the country at the time of his appointment by Eisenhower in 1955. He
spent his first years on the bench issuing a series of civil rights–related
decisions that inflamed segregationists. In the most important cases,
such as the Montgomery Bus Boycott decision, Johnson was joined by
Rives. Twenty-four years older than Johnson, Rives completed only one
year of college and had no formal legal training before embarking on
a prosperous career as a Montgomery lawyer. A traditional southern
Democrat in many respects, Rives came around to a progressive stance
on race due to the influence of his son, Richard Jr., who was educated at
Phillips Exeter and Harvard and served with African Americans in
World War II. While attending law school at the University of Michigan, Richard Jr. was killed in a car accident. Rives had been planning to
practice alongside his son; crestfallen after his death, he accepted an
appointment to the federal bench from Harry Truman in 1951. Daniel
Thomas, a district court judge from Mobile, rounded out the panel.[19]

In their complaint, Morgan and Taylor voiced an argument repeatedly made by Stallworth: that while each county was entitled to at least one representative in the state house, the constitution clearly stated that representation in both branches of the legislature "shall be based upon population" and must be reapportioned after each decennial census. Morgan and Taylor chose the Black Belt stronghold of Lowndes County as representative of the state's failures to meet its own obligations. Home to only 15,417 people according to the 1960 census, Lowndes sent two representatives to the state house and one to the state senate. By contrast, the 634,864 residents of Jefferson County had seven representatives in the state house and just one in the senate. Noting that Alabama's apportionment was already "unconstitutional, obsolete and discriminatory in 1911," Morgan and Taylor asserted that the plaintiffs had a right to a reapportionment based on the 1960 census. Given the legislature's repeated failure to reapportion itself, and the unwillingness of the state judiciary to intervene, the plaintiffs asked the federal court to declare the existing districts null and void, and to order that primary and general elections for all legislative seats be held on an at-large basis in 1962. A statewide at-large election—in which every qualified voter in the state casts a ballot for every member of the legislature, as if the state were a single legislative district—would have favored candidates from the most heavily populated regions of the state. Morgan and Taylor were requesting a drastic measure, albeit one with precedent in other states.[20]

Birmingham's two daily papers, the *Post-Herald* and the *News*, grew more insistent in their support for the lawsuit as the battle over the chop-up bill reached its climax. In a rare front-page editorial, the *Post-Herald* excoriated the "devilishly clever" bill Black Belt legislators had designed to sow animosity between residents of Jefferson County and other urban areas. The paper pleaded with Alabama's urban residents to recognize their common interests as overtaxed and underrepresented citizens being "bled every year to build roads and support schools in counties not willing to support themselves" while the "tax fat politicians from the Black Belt" attempted to "plunge a knife deep under our ribs, to still our voice in Washington." The newspaper called on the governor to find the "wisdom and courage" to veto the bill.[21]

Governor Patterson did, in fact, veto the chop-up bill, though more because of pressure from the Big Mules, not the press. The legislature, unable to override the veto, passed what came to be known as the "9-8" plan, a convoluted scheme that avoided the drawing of new congressional districts by allowing candidates to run initially in each of the nine old districts. Successful candidates from the nine districts then entered a statewide run-off, and the top eight finishers became the nominees of their party and proceeded to run in a statewide at-large general election. Incumbent members of Congress lined up behind the 9-8 option as preferable to a general at-large election that would probably include multiple candidates from Birmingham and other urban centers. Ultimately the 9-8 plan was ruled unconstitutional by a federal district court but not before the state conducted congressional elections in 1962 and 1964 according to its rules.[22]

For the Big Mules and other powerful individuals in Birmingham, the resolution to the chop-up controversy signaled the end of their interest in reapportionment. Taylor remembered a "general consensus" in Birmingham that he and Morgan should withdraw their lawsuit once the "threat of county dismemberment had passed." The city's Business and Professional Men's Association went a step further, publicly denouncing the lawsuit as asking for a "dangerous encroachment by the federal government into state affairs." The young lawyers, however, never considered dropping their lawsuit. Instead, they turned their attention to the Supreme Court of the United States and the resolution of *Baker* v. *Carr*.[23]

In late August 1961, Chuck Morgan received encouragement from Walter Chandler, one of the lead attorneys in the Tennessee case. Chandler thought that "the Alabama legislative mal-apportionment situation is even worse than that in Tennessee" and urged Morgan not to back down. Seven weeks later, Morgan and Taylor traveled to Washington and were present as Chandler's colleagues reargued the merits of *Baker* v. *Carr* in the Supreme Court. On that same day, October 9, Earl Warren formally admitted Taylor and Morgan as members of the Supreme Court Bar.[24]

In the fall and winter of 1961–1962, *Sims* v. *Frink* lay dormant as all involved waited for the Supreme Court to decide *Baker* v. *Carr*. During the interim, the only noteworthy development in the Alabama case occurred in November when Jerome "Buddy" Cooper, a seasoned labor lawyer in Birmingham who had clerked for Justice Hugo Black from 1937 to 1940, intervened in the case on behalf of five members of various Alabama affiliates of the United Steelworkers of America. Cooper recalled running into Morgan in the fall of 1961. When Cooper had asked Morgan how the reapportionment case was going, the latter admitted that he and Taylor had essentially run out of money. It is not clear how much direct financial support, if any, the steelworkers ended up contributing, but the addition of Cooper's plaintiffs to the suit meant the inclusion of residents of urban areas other than Birmingham and, more important, that the two younger attorneys could count on Cooper's counsel.[25]

On March 29, 1962, just three days after the Supreme Court declared in *Baker* v. *Carr* that the federal courts did in fact have jurisdiction in reapportionment disputes, Morgan and Taylor returned to Montgomery and asked the district court to grant their request for at-large primary and general elections. The following day, the panel denied the request, but it did schedule a hearing for April 14. Indicating that it would give the legislature a final chance "to comply with its duty under the Constitution of the State of Alabama," the district court did not say what it intended to do if the legislature failed to meet its obligations.[26]

The April hearing lasted barely an hour and offered no major surprises. Morgan acknowledged at the outset that the judges had a "tremendous responsibility," as they constituted the first court in the nation being asked to address malapportionment post-*Baker*. Morgan said that more than a half century of inaction had created a situation where "the voice of a boll weevil in Barbour, Lowndes, or Wilcox Counties is more strongly heard than that of the builders and bankers, the brokers and butchers, and all of the residents of the urban areas of our State." Morgan knew that the prospect of an at-large primary election frightened many stakeholders in Alabama, and because of this he predicted that no such election would ever take place. Rather than face the uncertainty of an at-large election, he reasoned, the mere possibility of one would compel "those forces which have controlled" the legislature "so effectively for so many years" to reapportion "immediately."[27]

The defendants made no attempt to deny the factual allegations in the complaint. One defense attorney, a former state legislator, even expressed a desire to see reapportionment happen. But the defendants

denied that they had any responsibility for reapportionment and insisted that such power lay only with the legislature.[28]

Just eighteen minutes after the conclusion of oral arguments, the
district court panel reiterated its unwillingness to involve itself in the
May primaries but made clear its understanding that Alabama's system
of apportionment clearly violated the state constitution and that the
plaintiffs were entitled to relief in advance of the November general
election. The district court set a deadline of July 16 and pledged that it
would retain jurisdiction until the legislature adopted an acceptable
plan. Writing in the *Post-Herald*, Stallworth painted the decision as a
final warning.[29]

On June 12, a special session of the Alabama legislature convened to
consider the district court's order. In his opening remarks, Governor
Patterson defiantly declared that "as long as I am governor of Alabama,
no Federal Court will be permitted to set the policies of this state." He
spent most of his speech denouncing the "dictatorial" and "unwarranted" actions of the district court but admitted that "as realists, we
must face up to the ominous fact that the Federal government . . . has
no intention to cease and desist." Ultimately, he implored the legislature to "beat the federals to the draw" by meeting the court-imposed
deadline.[30]

Over the next five weeks, the legislature displayed a willingness to
make, at best, modest adjustments to the state's system of apportionment, not the kind that Morgan, Taylor, and the court had envisioned.
Representatives from the Black Belt pushed from the start of the special
session to protect and reinforce their control of both the house and senate. Confident that the constitution's guarantee of at least one representative per county would preserve rural domination of the house, the
legislature grudgingly assigned additional representation to Birmingham, Mobile, and other large cities. But rather than make adjustments
that enhanced the voice of urban and suburban voters in the state senate, lawmakers adopted a plan that actually strengthened minority rule
in the upper chamber. Since this plan involved explicit alterations
to the constitution that had to be voted upon by the electorate in a November referendum, they also passed a standby bill. The alternative
measure, scheduled to take effect only if the electorate failed to amend
the constitution, did little to address malapportionment. After heated

and at times acrimonious debate, the legislature completed its work just days before the deadline imposed by the district court.[31]

Appearing before the district court on July 16, Morgan denounced the results of the special session as having met "the requirements of nothing but a fight for self preservation on behalf of the men who sit in those legislative halls." He attacked the standby act as a "mere alteration and reshuffling of some of the present seats" and as "totally arbitrary" with "no basis in law." Morgan spoke for all the plaintiffs when he declared, "We accuse the Legislature of deliberately flying in the face of this Court and refusing to do its constitutional duty."[32]

By this time, two additional sets of intervenors had joined the original plaintiffs and Cooper's group. The first consisted of David Vann and Robert Vance, who, like Morgan and Taylor, were young attorneys in Birmingham with a genuine desire to reform the city and a belief that the old racial order stood in the way of such change. To that end, Vann and Vance, along with Morgan, Taylor, and other members of the YMBC, had attempted in a 1961 campaign to unseat a staunch segregationist in the Democratic primary for the city commission. When that effort failed, Vann initiated a successful bid to replace Birmingham's commission form of government with a more typical mayor-council system. Vann's ambition was to abolish the office and thus eradicate the base of power of Bull Connor.[33]

But unlike Morgan, who set aside his dreams of a political career in Alabama in favor of civil rights activism, and unlike Taylor, who chose to leave Alabama rather than raise a family in an environment hostile to his values and politics, Vann and Vance stayed in Birmingham. Vann, who had clerked for Hugo Black and thus joined Jerome Cooper as a member of what author Diane McWhorter has referred to as "Alabama's most controversial fraternity," failed in a run for Congress in 1964 but later served on the city council and then as the city's mayor in the 1970s. Vance would later quip that he was not suited for politics because he couldn't "remember names," but in fact he was a skilled negotiator and able administrator who spent more than a decade as the chairman of the governing body of the Alabama Democratic Party, holding the party together at a time when deep divisions over the future of white supremacy threatened to split the organization. Vance's management of the difficult time was one of the reasons why President Jimmy Carter appointed him to a seat on the U.S. court of appeals in 1977. Twelve years later, less than a fortnight before Christmas, Vance was killed, and his wife gravely injured, by a mail bomb.[34]

Vann and Vance had followed the reapportionment lawsuit from the start. A member of the YMBC, Vann had taken part in early discussions of the issue and had done some research for Morgan and Taylor the previous fall. Vance, although not a member of the YMBC, had expressed interest in reapportionment as early as 1958.[35]

From the beginning to the end of *Sims* v. *Frink* and *Reynolds* v. *Sims*—from the filing of the original complaint in August 1961 through the oral arguments before the Supreme Court in November 1963—Morgan avoided putting forward a specific plan of apportionment to the federal courts. Instead, he stated a number of broad principles and left the particulars to the federal courts. Vann and Vance, on the other hand, drew up a very precise plan in advance of the district court's July 16 deadline. They worried that it would be difficult to mount a successful challenge to the state constitution's guarantee of at least one representative for each of the 67 counties and decided to save that challenge for a later date. In the meantime, they asked the district court to apportion the 39 remaining seats in the 106-member house on a strict population basis, which would raise, for instance, Jefferson County's delegation from seven to seventeen. For more than a half century, no county had been assigned more than one representative in the thirty-five-member senate. But Vann and Vance recognized no statutory or constitutional rules against one county having more than one state senator and proposed that the senate be based solely on population. The rural counties would still dominate the state house, but populous counties would now have the ability to block constitutional amendments in the senate.[36]

The plan put forward by Vann and Vance failed to persuade John McConnell, the lawyer who represented the second set of intervening plaintiffs, a group of voters from Mobile, the second most populous region in the state. McConnell was older than the Birmingham attorneys. He received his bachelor's degree from the University of Alabama and had intended to stay for law school until World War II interrupted. After serving with the occupation forces in Germany until December

1945, he returned to the United States and enrolled in Yale Law School with the help of the G.I. Bill. He found Yale "exhilarating." He not only began his studies in admiralty law, which later became the focus of his practice, but he also developed an interest in reapportionment. The Supreme Court decided *Colegrove* v. *Green* just as he arrived in New Haven in June 1946, prompting McConnell to enroll in a course with Thomas Emerson, a leading expert on reapportionment. While in Emerson's class, McConnell delved into the history of apportionment in his native state.[37]

McConnell, who followed the other plaintiffs in speaking before the district court on July 16, distinguished himself by arguing that the Equal Protection Clause required the apportionment of both branches of a bicameral legislature on a population basis. "If population is the basis of equal protection," he reasoned, "it has to be in both houses, since both houses are necessary in the legislative process." McConnell based his argument on the simple proposition that a bill cannot become law without the assent of both branches of a bicameral legislature, and that, conversely, a single malapportioned branch held a veto over any legislative action. Though his logic gained no traction that day in the district court, it would eventually provide the basis for the Supreme Court's majority opinion in the case.[38]

Addressing the district court on behalf of the defendants, state senator Douglas Webb introduced a twist to the proceedings when he maintained that "personality conflicts between counties" rendered significant reapportionment impossible. Webb had not expected to take part in the hearing; the defense asked him just days before to assess the difficulties the legislature had confronted during the special session. In his remarks, Webb conceded that the legislature was grossly malapportioned and cited his own south Alabama district as a region that deserved increased representation. He contended, however, that "statistical methods and trite mathematical formulas work nicely with inert substances or in chemical solution" but not so well "when the material to be mixed consists of people with firm minds" and "unruly passions." He noted to the court that representatives of certain counties simply refused to be grouped with other counties. In particular, he pointed to the unwillingness of adjacent counties to join with either Lowndes County or Macon County. The defense had hoped that Webb would convince the court that the legislature had done all that could reasonably be expected of it. But in rebuttal, Chuck Morgan offered Webb's comments as evidence that the present legislature was incapable of passing a constitutional plan of apportionment—a position soon echoed by the *Birmingham Post-Herald*.[39]

In his testimony, Webb never explicitly stated why adjacent counties refused to join with Lowndes or Macon, but the following day the *Post-Herald* revealed that "the objection to Lowndes and Macon stemmed from heavy Negro populations," which exceeded 80 percent in both counties. At no point in *Sims* v. *Frink* and *Reynolds* v. *Sims*—or any of the other state reapportionment cases, for that matter—did an attorney for either side ever directly broach the subject of race. Legislative reapportionment was argued in terms of the rights of individual voters, not the rights of groups or in terms of racial discrimination. (By contrast, Morris Abram's brief in *Gray* v. *Sanders*—which, technically, was not a reapportionment case—did explicitly make the connection between minority control and racial discrimination.) But, as Douglas Webb implied before the district court, malapportionment did serve as a cornerstone of white supremacy in the South.[40]

On July 21, 1962, judges Richard Rives, Frank Johnson, and Daniel Thomas unanimously declared Alabama's system of apportionment an unconstitutional violation of the Equal Protection Clause of the Fourteenth Amendment. Noting that all parties to the litigation generally conceded that Alabama's existing apportionment constituted "invidious discrimination," the district court also declared both laws passed by the legislature during its special session "void, invalid and ineffective." The jurists did not hesitate to state that the proposed legislative remedies were unconstitutional, but they did avoid drafting a plan of their own design, deciding instead to accept on an interim basis "such parts of the Acts of the Legislature as have any merit." They had little to choose from. They left intact the guarantee of one representative per county in the house of representatives but, as suggested by Vann and Vance, increased Jefferson County's delegation from seven to seventeen and Mobile County's from three to eight. With regard to the state senate, the district court had no other option but to halfheartedly endorse the provisions of the standby measure, which would have done little to address the most egregious inequalities. The court admitted that this measure would be inadequate over the long term but expressed confidence that such "moderate steps" would allow the newly elected legislature to "break the strangle hold" and enact a constitutional apportionment. If not, the district court vowed to step in again.[41]

Despite its limitations, the district court's decision represented a resounding victory for the plaintiffs and for residents of metropolitan Alabama. No matter that the federal panel had made only incremental changes; the ruling was indeed "historic," as the *Birmingham Post-Herald* proclaimed. The decision marked the first time that a federal court enacted a specific plan for apportioning a legislature. The three-judge panel unambiguously accepted the essential points of the complaint and ordered the state legislature to take actions that would have been incomprehensible prior to *Baker* v. *Carr.*[42]

The final line of the district court's decree called for relief of a more practical kind: it ordered the defendants to pay for the costs of litigation. Unlike their counterparts in Tennessee, the attorneys in Alabama's reapportionment case operated (and would continue to operate) on a minimal budget. None of the plaintiffs' attorneys was ever paid for his time. When the suit was first filed in August 1961, the Young Men's Business Club committed a meager $400 to reimburse Taylor and Morgan for their expenses. Over the next three years, the YMBC and other supporters in Birmingham contributed no more than $5,000, and the actual figure may well have been far less. In a letter thanking Jerome Cooper for his intervention, Morgan wrote that he and Taylor did not know "what we would do if we lost with respect to costs." In Mobile, as McConnell's costs climbed, he wrote to three of the voters on whose behalf he had filed suit and asked whether they might contribute. Decades later, Clarke Stallworth remarked that funds were so low that the plaintiffs would have had to drop the case if, at any point, the court had ordered them to pay costs.[43]

The plaintiffs, though more than pleased with the essence of the ruling, diverged sharply over how best to respond to the district court's remedy. Vann, Vance, and McConnell immediately filed a motion asking the court to require more meaningful reapportionment of the state senate. The court promptly denied the motion. Morgan, Taylor, and Cooper, on the other hand, were willing to overlook the shortcomings of the court order in view of its historic nature and the fact that the court had maintained jurisdiction. Taylor told a Birmingham newspaper that if the legislature did not reapportion, "we'll be right back in Court." Special primary elections would be held in late August to nominate ten additional representatives from Jefferson County to the state house. Morgan acknowledged that the court had not done nearly enough to reapportion the state senate but professed confidence that "the Court will finish the job next year."[44]

In late July, Attorney General MacDonald Gallion announced that he would not appeal the ruling of the district court, having determined that the court had acted with restraint. McLean Pitts, a Selma attorney with deep ties to the state's political leadership, revealed privately that Gallion feared an appeal would lead to an even more adverse decision. Hoping to forestall such an outcome, the attorney general had placed the onus of an appeal, and the attendant costs, on the shoulders of the original plaintiffs and intervenors.[45]

Over the next month, the Birmingham attorneys debated, at times heatedly, whether to pursue a more favorable apportionment of the state senate. On August 10, Vance wrote to McConnell, the only attorney in the case not from Birmingham, and asked for his help, informing him that he found himself in a "distinct minority," with Morgan, Taylor, and Jerome Cooper adamantly opposed to an appeal.[46]

The three, and to a lesser extent, Vann, objected to an appeal for three central reasons. First, according to Vance, they considered it "unlikely that the Supreme Court would reverse the District Court" and saw "no good reason to change our posture from one of victory to one of defeat." Second, those opposed to an appeal worried that continued litigation might lead to the postponement of the special primary to select additional candidates for the state house of representatives from the state's most populous regions; Vance knew that the newspapers in Birmingham would likely oppose an appeal on these grounds. Third, since Gallion had chosen not to appeal the core finding of the district court, filing an appeal entailed costs that the original plaintiffs could not afford.[47]

Vance, by contrast, was certain that the Supreme Court would have to address the issue of standards, and soon. He surveyed the multitude

134 ON DEMOCRACY'S DOORSTEP

of reapportionment cases winding through various state and federal courts, saw the issue of population versus geography as key to most of them, and concluded that the Court could no longer avoid the question. "Unless some reasonably definitive guidelines are set down," he argued in a letter to McConnell, "continued litigation is probably going to be interminable." Vance believed that the Alabama case presented the Supreme Court with "a stronger vehicle" for confronting the issue than other cases and that, therefore, "we should be the ones to go all-out for immediate relief with respect to the Senate." In his letter to McConnell, he shared his belief that the original plaintiffs—Morgan, Taylor, and Cooper—should have the first chance to appeal, but that if they did not, the intervening plaintiffs—Vance, Vann, and McConnell—should seize the opportunity.[48]

By the middle of August, however, Vance and Vann realized that an appeal would simply cost too much money. What they did not know was that a meeting had taken place on Tuesday, August 7, at which Bernard A. Reynolds, the probate judge of Dallas County, a Black Belt stronghold immediately adjacent to Lowndes County, and Frank Pearce, a probate judge in Marion County, resolved to appeal the district court's order. Whites in Dallas County and the county seat of Selma were terrified of the potential consequences of reapportionment, especially the long-term threat of being lumped into a district with Lowndes County and its overwhelming black majority. Attorneys for Reynolds and Pearce, with assurances of additional financial assistance from supporters in Montgomery, filed an appeal on August 17 in which they maintained that the district court had exceeded its authority. As a result of the appeal, Alabama's reapportionment suit went to the U.S. Supreme Court as *Reynolds* v. *Sims*. To Vance and Vann—the latter had decided to join Vance—Reynolds and Pearce's appeal was a godsend: it placed the burden of costs on the appellants, allowing Vance and Vann to proceed with a cross appeal.[49]

Vann and Vance filed their cross appeal—arguing that the district court had not gone far enough in reapportioning the state senate—in the Supreme Court on August 23. Perhaps the most immediate effect was that Chuck Morgan, according to Vance, became "extremely displeased." Vance later reported to McConnell that Morgan considered it "extremely poor personal public relations to take any position which would allow the public to assume that the plaintiffs had won anything less than a complete victory before the district court." In the same letter to McConnell, Vance revealed that Morgan had previously threatened "to attack David and me if we pursued the matter." On August 25, the *Birmingham Post-Herald* ran an editorial critical of the cross appeal, which Vance identified as "quite clearly the result" of Morgan's efforts.[50]

Morgan's intense opposition to the cross appeal stemmed from his feeling that the plaintiffs should back the district court, especially Johnson and Rives, who had been so heavily criticized within the state for their rulings in recent civil rights cases. Morgan recognized the limitations of the court's remedy but thought it "merely a temporary one" and was certain that the court would maintain jurisdiction until appropriate relief was achieved. Years later, Taylor, who had sided with Morgan, reiterated this point, characterizing their position as "pragmatic." He and Morgan were sure that they would win the case and "wipe this thing out," and so they saw no reason to ask more of the court at the time. Taylor admitted that he and Morgan never considered the possibility of a ruling as sweeping as "one person, one vote" for both chambers of the legislature. Among the Alabama attorneys, only John McConnell did.[51]

There were more personal reasons for Morgan's fury. His ego matched his girth, a characteristic noted by admirers and detractors alike, and he undoubtedly considered *Sims* v. *Frink* his case. Although he, Taylor, and Cooper made no effort to block the involvement of Vann, Vance, and McConnell, Morgan reacted with a clear feeling of "resentment," according to Vance, when the latter raised the possibility of a cross appeal. In an interview many years later, Cooper said that after the Supreme Court's decision in *Baker* v. *Carr*, "a lot of other people got in the act. A lot of politicians and folks joined in and intervened, and subsequently gained some credit by working in the Alabama case." Cooper made clear that he did not mean to denigrate the important contributions made by the intervenors, but that primary credit belonged to Morgan, the YMBC, and the steelworkers.[52]

Morgan and Vann had never been close, their distinct personalities seeming to work against the possibility of a strong relationship. "Vann had a basic awkwardness and Morgan was the personification of charm," Diane McWhorter wrote in her Pulitzer Prize–winning study of

Birmingham during the civil rights years. "Vann's ambition seemed to spring from spiritual yearning, transcending his cohort's zeal to make a mark." And yet the pair had a great deal in common and recognized in each other a shared purpose. In fact, it was Vann who unwittingly and indirectly set in motion the chain of events that provoked Morgan to reevaluate his life's ambitions. A close friend of the Reverend Robert Hughes, Vann had no qualms about becoming a member of the Alabama Council on Human Relations, an organization that Morgan never joined. But as a young associate at Birmingham's most prestigious law firm, Vann was forbidden by his senior partners to defend either Tommy Reeves or Hughes (Vann later left the firm as he threw himself even more into political activism). In his stead, he recommended Chuck Morgan to both men.[53]

However much animosity Morgan directed at Vance and Vann, he assumed a completely different tone with McConnell when the Mobile attorney returned from a month-long vacation. Morgan explained to McConnell, who had not received Vann's letter while on vacation and had been unaware of the dispute simmering among his Birmingham counterparts, why he felt the intervenors should not have appealed. But given that Vann and Vance had already filed their cross appeal, Morgan encouraged McConnell to file a separate appeal that would ask the Supreme Court whether or not the Equal Protection Clause required population equality in both houses. On September 22, McConnell did just that.[54]

With three separate appeals pending before the Supreme Court, the parties in Alabama's reapportionment case waited nearly nine months to find out if their case would be heard. In the interim—from September 1962 to June 1963—the world turned its attention to Birmingham as the southern freedom movement launched Project C and precipitated a confrontation that called attention to segregation in the city. Officials in Birmingham initially refused to take the bait. Black leaders, desperate for a reaction that would expose the evil and extent of white supremacy, sent Birmingham's black children into the streets to march downtown and demand service at whites-only establishments. In response, Public Safety Commissioner Bull Connor unleashed the city's police dogs and fire hoses on them. To this day, videos and pictures of young demonstrators in Birmingham, being attacked by police dogs and being rolled across the city park by the pressure of fire hoses, remain among the most iconic images of the American civil rights movement.[55]

On June 10, 1963, exactly one month after the end of the civil rights demonstrations in Birmingham, the clerk of the Supreme Court informed the litigants that the Court had noted probable jurisdiction in *Reynolds* v. *Sims*, *Vann* v. *Frink*, and *McConnell* v. *Frink* but had consolidated the three appeals into one case for the purpose of oral argument. On the same day, the justices noted probable jurisdiction in state reapportionment cases from Maryland, Virginia, and New York, and in a congressional reapportionment case from Georgia. A day later, as George Wallace, who had succeeded John Patterson as governor of Alabama in January 1963, made his infamous stand in the schoolhouse door—a futile gesture intended to prevent the integration of the University of Alabama—the clerk announced that the Court had scheduled oral arguments in all of the reapportionment cases for the week of November 12.[56]

On Sunday, September 15, 1963, Ku Klux Klansmen bombed Birmingham's Sixteenth Street Baptist Church, killing four young girls on their way to Sunday school. The following day, Chuck Morgan arrived for the regular noon luncheon of the Young Men's Business Club and delivered the words that ensured his exile: "Four little girls were killed in Birmingham yesterday. An aroused, remorseful, worried community asks, 'Who did it? Who threw that bomb. Was it a Negro or a white?' The answer . . . is really rather simple. . . . Who is really guilty? Each of us. . . . Every citizen and every school board member and school teacher and principal and businessman and judge and lawyer . . . who has, in any way, contributed during the past several years to the popularity of hatred is at least as guilty, or more so, than the demented fool who threw that bomb."[57]

Morgan's speech elicited a storm of reactions. The Birmingham press and elected officials defended themselves against his charges. More ominously, Morgan began to receive increasingly detailed death threats as word of his speech circulated. Friends feared for his safety and that of his wife and son; some urged him to stop speaking out. Somehow, Morgan and Taylor found time the week after Morgan's speech to complete and submit their brief in *Reynolds* v. *Sims* to the Supreme Court. By mid-October, however, Morgan was telling Tommy Reeves that "the threats have wound around to my wife and son." In a letter to the Right Reverend George M. Murray, the bishop coadjutor of the Episcopal Diocese of Alabama, who had officiated at Chuck and Camille Morgan's wedding, Morgan wrote, "I know of nothing else to do but fight against those things to which our Governor has dedicated himself and I do not believe that it is possible to do this and remain alive for long in Alabama." With no advance warning, Morgan closed his law practice, distributed his books and office furniture to a handful of other attorneys, pulled his son out of school, and put his house on the market. Members of the Ku Klux Klan took credit for forcing him to leave town.[58]

Morgan's sudden departure surprised Jerome Cooper, who had seen him just days earlier but had no idea that Morgan was even thinking of leaving Birmingham. While personally disappointed that his friend was moving away, Cooper recognized the broader significance of Morgan's decision and poignantly called Morgan's flight a "further victory of the forces of darkness." Morgan and his family eventually settled in Atlanta, but not before living for a period in Alexandria, Virginia, just across the Potomac River from Washington, D.C. From Alexandria, Morgan awaited the arrival of the other attorneys in Alabama's reapportionment case. Just weeks later, they joined a host of lawyers from four other states, who gathered at the Supreme Court for a remarkable week of oral arguments.[59]

8 ||| CONVERGING ON WASHINGTON, D.C.

I n October 1963, Chuck Morgan arrived as an exile, but not a stranger, in northern Virginia. Just ten weeks earlier, he had traveled to the area at the behest of Edmund "Ed" Campbell, a resident of Arlington County with a prominent law practice in the nation's capital. The architect of Virginia's reapportionment lawsuit, the sixty-four-year-old Campbell had invited Morgan and the lead attorneys in the New York and Maryland state reapportionment lawsuits to a July strategy session, at which they coordinated the arguments they would present to the Supreme Court in the fall. Interestingly, Campbell chose not to include the attorneys who filed a congressional reapportionment lawsuit in Georgia, which was also before the Court, most likely because that case presented a different set of technical issues than did the state cases. But all five cases were, in fact, related, and, argued one after the other, they dominated the Court's November calendar.[1]

These five cases, as well as cases from Delaware and Colorado that the Court heard later in the term, emerged from among more than seventy legislative and congressional reapportionment lawsuits filed in forty states in the aftermath of *Baker* v. *Carr.* The justices considered reapportionment so important that by the end of the term, they had devoted a staggering twenty-two hours, spread across eight days, to oral arguments on the subject.[2]

Each of the cases presented the Supreme Court with a unique set of facts and circumstances, but, taken together, they raised three fundamental questions. First, what standard did the Equal Protection Clause require when applied to legislative and congressional apportionments? Just how equal did districts have to be to pass constitutional muster? Second, did the Equal Protection Clause allow the states to adopt a modified federal system, with one branch of a bicameral legislature based on population and the second branch based on other factors? More than half of the fifty states used some form of the so-called federal plan, and the attorneys in the various cases disagreed as to how far the Court should go in pronouncing on the matter. Third, did it make any difference if a state's malapportionment was the result of recent action by a majority of the state's voters rather than the product of decades of neglect and inaction on the part of the legislature?[3]

Back in January, in his oral argument in *Gray* v. *Sanders*, Georgia assistant attorney general Freeman Leverett had insisted that any attempt to establish a standard was "judicially insoluble" and advised the Supreme Court to avoid the issue altogether. How, Leverett asked, could the Court establish a standard when it lacked even the ability to decide which statistical method to use? Leverett took aim at a favorite statistical method of political scientists: the theoretical minimum percentage of a state's residents living in districts capable of electing legislative majorities. Citing numerous district court rulings issued after *Baker* v. *Carr*, Leverett noted that the various federal courts had arrived at disparate theoretical minimums, which to him was evidence of the utter confusion and chaos certain to follow the intervention of the Supreme Court. For a majority of justices, by contrast, conflicting decisions in the lower courts signaled that a national standard might be necessary.[4]

By the time he filed Virginia's reapportionment suit just days after the Supreme Court's decision in *Baker* v. *Carr*, Ed Campbell had spent thirty years fighting entrenched interests in the state. Born in 1899, Campbell served on the Arlington County board of supervisors during a period of tremendous demographic change in the 1940s. Drawn to the Washington suburbs as the federal government expanded, the county's new residents demanded better services, better schools above all, a position at odds with the low-tax philosophy of the Byrd Organization, Virginia's oligarchic political machine headed by U.S. Senator Harry F. Byrd Sr. This growing rift between the needs of an emerging metropolis and those of politically powerful traditionalists widened considerably after the Supreme Court's *Brown* decision in 1954. When the Virginia General Assembly passed a series of laws designed to close public schools rather than allow even token integration, Campbell and his wife, Elizabeth, emerged as two of the most effective leaders in the campaign against what became known as "massive resistance." Spearheading a statewide effort, they fought tirelessly to block the closing of the commonwealth's schools, ultimately prevailing when state and federal courts struck down the noxious laws. Intimately aware that malapportionment had allowed a minority of the commonwealth's citizens to impose their will on the rest of the state, Ed Campbell's entry into the reapportionment battles of the 1960s came about naturally.[5]

The constitution of Virginia was amended in the 1920s to mandate reapportionment in 1932 and every ten years thereafter, but it provided no guidelines whatsoever as to how reapportionment should be accomplished. Legislators ostensibly considered population as the main factor in reapportioning both the house of delegates and state senate, but they were bound by no particular standard. Unlike their counterparts in Alabama and Tennessee, who simply ignored mandates to reapportion after each decennial census, members of the Virginia General Assembly regularly fulfilled their constitutional obligation. They did so reluctantly, however, as postwar demographic changes threatened the organization's control of the commonwealth. In addition to the northern Virginia suburbs of Washington, D.C., composed of Arlington and Fairfax Counties and the city of Alexandria, the most substantive population growth in the 1940s and 1950s took place in the sprawling southeastern region of the state known as Hampton Roads (also commonly referred to as the Tidewater), which includes Norfolk, Newport News, Hampton, Portsmouth, Virginia Beach, and Chesapeake. Driven primarily by the rapid enlargement of the American military during World War II and the cold war, the region, with its valuable deep-water harbor, became the site of scores of naval shipyards, defense plants, and bases for all branches of the armed forces.[6]

Their concerns rising, organization insiders ordered the General Assembly to adjourn in 1952 without reapportioning. In response, a legislator from Alexandria put together a handbook that effectively illustrated population disparities in the state's legislative districts. House districts had as few as 14,829 people and as many as 106,092, while senate districts ranged from 41,442 to 193,956. After the same legislator asked the commonwealth's attorney general for a formal opinion, the latter confirmed that the legislature did have a constitutional duty to reapportion. The governor soon called the legislature into special session. Although lawmakers did not come close to drawing districts with equal numbers of persons or voters, they did provide a modicum of relief to the most underrepresented districts.[7]

Yet this relief was only temporary, and the problems that had prompted it only worsened. While the population of the state as a whole grew by 20 percent during the 1950s, the population of Hampton Roads expanded by 33 percent and northern Virginia saw a remarkable 72 percent leap in its number of residents. The population of Fairfax County alone nearly tripled. By 1960, the disparities already evident a decade earlier had become even starker: districts in the house of delegates now had as few as 20,071 residents and as many as 142,597, while senate districts ranged from 51,637 to 285,194.[8]

After the 1960 census, Governor Lindsay Almond appointed a commission of legislators and nonelected officials to consider reapportionment. Working closely with the Bureau of Public Administration at the University of Virginia, the Hoover Commission, named for Chairman Lawrence Hoover, drafted a series of proposals that would have significantly reduced population disparities among districts, but the General Assembly buried them. Instead, on April 7, 1962, less than two weeks after the Supreme Court's decision in *Baker* v. *Carr*, Almond's successor, Albertis Harrison, signed into law a reapportionment plan that addressed a handful of the most glaring inequalities but essentially froze existing districts in place. Two days later, Ed Campbell, joined by Fairfax attorney E. A. Prichard, responded by filing suit in the U.S. district court in Alexandria on behalf of underrepresented voters in northern Virginia. Soon thereafter, the attorney Henry E. Howell Jr. intervened in the lawsuit on behalf of voters in Norfolk, the commonwealth's largest city at the time.[9]

Like Campbell, Howell devoted his life to fighting entrenched power in Virginia. In the process, he so thoroughly vexed the commonwealth's governing elites that they found it necessary to destroy him politically. Born in Richmond in 1920 to a lumber salesman and his wife, Howell came of age in Norfolk, a port city with a vibrant working class, and early on embraced the populist politics that would define his career. A true liberal in a state where both parties remained fundamentally conservative for most of the twentieth century, Howell railed against the corrupting influence of big business and private utilities, pushed hard for civil rights legislation, devoted his prodigious legal skills to overturning the state's poll tax, and persistently challenged, albeit unsuccessfully, antiunion right-to-work laws.[10]

Howell also harbored political ambitions and was elected to the house of delegates in 1959. He lost two years later in a bitter contest and then regained his seat in the General Assembly in November 1963, only days before arguing Virginia's reapportionment case in the Supreme Court. After moving to the state senate two years later, Howell set his sights on the governor's mansion. He failed to secure the Democratic gubernatorial nomination in 1969 but was elected lieutenant governor two years later in a special election called when the popular incumbent, J. Sargeant "Sarge" Reynolds of the Reynolds Metals fortune, died from a brain tumor. By 1971, however, Howell lacked the support of his party's establishment and ran for lieutenant governor as an independent, as he did in 1973, when he ran for governor for the second time. The Democrats, irreconcilably divided between conservatives and progressives, declined to nominate a candidate of their own. No longer in control of their party's nominating machinery, old-guard Democrats turned to the Republican Party in the hope that it could help stop Howell. The Republicans, similarly unsettled by the end of Jim Crow and the passage of national civil rights legislation in the 1960s, nominated Mills Godwin, a former Democratic governor, a stalwart of the recently defunct Byrd Organization, and one of the most ardent leaders of massive resistance against desegregation. Immortalized in Garrett Epps's novel *The Shad Treatment*, the campaign was ultimately decided by a slim margin, with Godwin prevailing by a mere fifteen thousand votes. Running a third time, Howell finally won the Democratic nomination four years later, but he lost decisively in the general election. As with Ed Campbell, Henry Howell's enlistment in the push for reapportionment made perfect sense in the context of his previous endeavors.[11]

Campbell welcomed Howell's participation from the outset, in view of the common grievance that bound them together. They were soon coordinating their briefs and arguments, and met several times in advance of oral arguments for the suit Campbell and Prichard had launched, scheduled for October 1962. Drawing heavily on the nationally recognized work of political scientists Ralph Eisenberg and Paul T. David of the Bureau of Public Administration at the University of Virginia, the same group that had advised the Hoover Commission, Campbell and Howell presented a fairly straightforward argument rooted in statistical evidence and focused on the irrationality of legislative districts in the state. They borrowed the term coined by Justice Tom Clark in his concurring opinion in *Baker*, labeling Virginia's reapportionment a "crazy quilt," in which most, but not all, urban and suburban voters were decidedly underrepresented, while most, but not all, rural voters exercised political muscle beyond their numbers.[12]

Although Campbell and Howell represented voters in the state's largest metropolitan areas, they understood that the issue could not be defined simply as one of urban versus rural. Campbell, in particular, repeatedly distinguished between rapidly growing cities and those "of relatively static or declining population." Furthermore, he averred, the recently signed reapportionment law protected very specific, but not all, rural and urban areas with static populations, and ensured that those areas that supported the state's political leadership would maintain control of the legislature. For instance, a number of sparsely populated counties and independent cities in the southwestern part of the state, the traditional home of Virginia's Republican Party and a primary source of opposition to the Byrd Organization, remained underrepresented, while Southside Virginia, the string of counties that extended from Richmond to the North Carolina border, and from Hampton Roads to the foothills of the Appalachian Mountains, retained more than its fair share of representation, as did the Shenandoah Valley, the home base of Senator Byrd. Within these regions, urban areas such as Danville, Petersburg, and Winchester were overrepresented, while Richmond, the capital and second-largest city in the state, enjoyed representation proportional to its population.[13]

Neither Campbell nor Howell requested that the district court require reapportionment based strictly on population. Without providing any clear parameters to the court in Alexandria, Howell asked the three judges only for a "fair and proportionate representation" for all the state's voters. For his part, Campbell granted that the Virginia constitution provided no guidelines for reapportioning legislative districts but argued that the document did, in fact, offer a path for the court to follow. The constitution, he pointed out, required that congressional districts contain "as nearly as practicable, an equal number of inhabitants." Noting that it was nearly impossible to draw districts with equal numbers of people while adhering to the state's tradition of not dividing its ninety-eight counties and thirty-two independent cities, Campbell did not ask the court to break with the precedent of tradition. Instead, he requested that the court grant the General Assembly a final chance to pass a more equitable reapportionment bill. In the event that it failed to do so, he urged the court to implement a plan, drafted by the Bureau of Public Administration, in which no district deviated from the ideal number by more than 15 percent.[14]

To defend its reapportionment plan, the Commonwealth of Virginia hired Richmond attorney David J. Mays, arguably the most influential nonelected official in the state. Born in 1896, Mays was the antithesis of Ed Campbell and Henry Howell in just about every way imaginable. Where Campbell and Howell persistently challenged the ubiquitous and suffocating power of the Byrd Organization, Mays served as the organization's consigliere. Advising the state's top elected officials most frequently from the shadows, Mays managed to cultivate a persona of moderation and reasonableness despite his own deeply held commitment to racial segregation. A corporate lawyer by trade, Mays liked to think of himself as a constitutional expert with a specialization in the rights of the states under the federal compact. When the General Assembly created a Commission on Constitutional Government at the height of massive resistance, Mays was the obvious choice for chairman. Over the next several years, he and his colleagues on the commission, most notably *Richmond News Leader* editor James Kilpatrick, produced a steady stream of pamphlets that denounced encroachment by the federal government into school prayer, voting rights, and reapportionment, among other areas. In this work, Mays and Kilpatrick directed their ire at the Supreme Court and Chief Justice Earl Warren.[15]

From the outset, Mays crafted his defense of Virginia's 1962 reapportionment act around one central point: his core belief that, despite the Supreme Court's decision in *Baker*, reapportionment remained a state matter and the federal courts could not adjudicate the lawsuit, at least not until state appellate courts had had an opportunity to consider the merits. Consequently, Mays devoted most of his brief to a discussion of the finer points of federal-state relations and only briefly mentioned the facts and evidence that preoccupied Campbell and Howell.[16]

This choice reflected a convergence between Mays's thinking and Kilpatrick's. In June 1962, as Mays began to work on the reapportionment lawsuit, Kilpatrick wrote to him to privately share his concern that "as in the area of racially separate schools, the law is fine but the facts are not so good." Kilpatrick, whose provocative editorials in response to the Supreme Court's *Brown* decision had encouraged the most strident resisters, reasoned that "the South has had trouble defending segregation because most of the country regards segregation as indefensible," and "a great many persons" felt the same way about the most extreme examples of malapportionment. Therefore, Kilpatrick suggested, Mays had little choice but to follow the logic of Felix Frankfurter's dissent in *Baker*. Encouraging Mays to argue that "however serious these evils may be, the American system does not authorize Federal judges to correct them," Kilpatrick admitted that such an argument would be difficult, as it would require the state "to demur on the evidence, concede the inequities, and fight it out on higher grounds." Even so, he believed it offered the only path to success in federal court.[17]

Although it was not a main feature of the argument he made before the district court, Mays did not completely ignore the statistical evidence on which Campbell and Howell had built their case. In an effort to soften the impact of that evidence, Mays and his subordinates devised a series of charts that showed not the disparities and inequities in Virginia's reapportionment scheme but rather Virginia's favorable rank compared to other states. The exhibits suggested that however malapportioned, Virginia was more representative than all but seven other states in the nation. Mays also pointed out that numerous inhabitants of northern Virginia and Hampton Roads were transient military personnel and thus should not be counted for the purposes of reapportionment. Mays concluded that Virginia's system of apportionment was not only rational but also quite fair.[18]

In late November, the three-judge district court ruled in favor of Campbell and Howell. Circuit court judge Albert V. Bryan and district court judge Oren R. Lewis found the plaintiffs' statistical evidence compelling and clear proof that Virginia's system of apportionment resulted in "invidious discrimination." District court judge Walter E. Hoffman, who had played a central role in striking down Virginia's massive resistance laws in January 1959, reached a different conclusion. Ignoring the bulk of Mays's argument, Hoffman seized upon the exhibits the defense had introduced almost as an afterthought and concluded that "proof of disparity in population" alone was not enough to condemn Virginia's reapportionment. Instead, Hoffman stressed that Virginia ranked "eighth in the nation in an index of representativeness among state legislatures." Furthermore, Hoffman noted in his dissent, a three-judge federal district court had recently upheld the reapportionment of New York's legislature, despite "a far greater disparity than that which exists in Virginia."[19]

Immediately after the district court's decision, Governor Albertis Harrison met with David Mays and key legislative leaders to discuss whether or not to appeal. That evening, Mays wrote in his diary that "my advice was to appeal." No doubt pessimistic about his chances in front of a Court led by Earl Warren, a man he had criticized so harshly over the previous several years, Mays "could not see much chance of success." But, he added, "the people of Virginia would expect no less." Earlier that day, before making the final decision to appeal, Harrison had criticized Mays, asking why the state "offered no evidence to justify the present representation." Mays defended his handling of the case and reminded the governor of the exhibits he had introduced. But Harrison's allegation, coming on the heels of Hoffman's dissenting opinion, would influence Mays to take a quite different approach when he argued Virginia's reapportionment case before the Supreme Court. Rather than repeat tired arguments about jurisdiction and federal-state relations, Mays built his case on the assumption that Virginia's rank as the eighth most representative state protected it from judicial interference. Surely, he reasoned, the Supreme Court was not willing to strike down apportionments in forty-three of the fifty states.[20]

Whereas the Virginia case was filed soon after *Baker*, the challenge to New York's reapportionment began a year earlier, at the same time that the Supreme Court decided to put over the Tennessee case for reargument in the fall. Peter Straus, the president of WMCA, a rock-and-roll radio station with a liberal editorial bent that backed issues as varied as the rights of tenants in New York City and those of tenant farmers in the American South, asked the station's attorney, Leonard Sand, to look into the possibility of challenging New York's reapportionment. Sand, who also happened to be Straus's brother-in-law, had attended Harvard Law School and afterward worked in the office of the solicitor general in Washington and as an assistant U.S. attorney. Later in life, Sand served with distinction as a judge on the federal District Court for the Southern District of New York. On May 1, 1961, Sand filed suit in that same court on behalf of Straus and equivalently situated New Yorkers, alleging that the state's system of apportionment violated their Fourteenth Amendment rights to equal protection.[21]

Since at least the late nineteenth century, as Henry Cookingham so colorfully demonstrated in addressing his fellow delegates to the 1894 Constitutional Convention, residents of upstate New York knew how important malapportionment was to their control of the state. More than sixty years later, the apportionment provisions of the 1894 constitution continued to serve their intended purpose with remarkable efficiency. Unlike the constitution of Virginia, which provided no guidance to legislators other than the requirement to reapportion after each decennial census, the New York constitution included a densely complicated series of provisions that left legislators with little leeway in the reapportionment process. On its face, the constitution called for a senate with districts that contained "an equal number of inhabitants," but additional requirements assured that the most populous counties were also the most underrepresented. By 1960, an average or ideal district would have had 289,350 inhabitants, but the fifty-eight members of the New York senate represented as few as 168,398 and as many as 666,784.[22]

The New York constitution guaranteed that sixty-one of the state's sixty-two counties received a representative in the state assembly. (Apparently Cookingham and his colleagues were willing to go only so far in fostering rotten boroughs, as they judged that Hamilton County in the Adirondack Mountains, whose population fluctuated between 4,000 and 5,000, did not merit its own representative. Instead, Hamilton had to share an assemblyman with the adjacent Fulton County.) Another incredibly complex set of provisions dictated the apportionment of the remaining 89 members of the 150-person assembly. As with the senate, the result was that the most populous regions of the state—the boroughs of New York City and, by 1960, the rapidly growing Long Island suburbs—suffered the most severe underrepresentation. With an average or ideal of 111,882 people, assembly districts in 1960 contained anywhere from 15,044 to 222,261 inhabitants. The system of apportionment installed by Cookingham and the other authors of the 1894 constitution proved so effective in allowing upstate Republicans to control the legislature that Al Smith, a former governor and the 1928 Democratic nominee for president, characterized New York's apportionment provisions as "constitutionally Republican."[23]

Appearing in June 1961 before U.S. district court judge Richard H. Levet, and again in November in front of a three-judge panel composed of Levet and two colleagues, Leonard Sand attacked New York's malapportionment as a clear violation of the Fourteenth Amendment. But when pressed, Sand did not propose a precise standard that the state should meet. Crucially, the young attorney did not ask the district court to find that both houses of a bicameral legislature must be apportioned on the basis of population. Rather, Sand expressed a willingness to allow the legislature to apportion one branch of its legislature on factors other than population, as long as the apportionment of the other branch was based substantially on population.[24]

In early January 1962, as the Supreme Court moved closer toward a decision in Baker, the court in New York dismissed Sand's complaint without ruling on the actual merits. Sand appealed to the Supreme Court, and five months later the Court remanded the lawsuit to the district court in the wake of its decision in Baker. This action of the Supreme Court prompted Lee Rankin, Eisenhower's solicitor general, who in one of his final actions in that office had authorized the participation of the government in Baker as amicus curiae, to urge Nelson Rockefeller, the Republican governor of New York, to call a special session of the legislature for the purpose of amending the state's system of apportionment. Stating his belief that "reapportionment need not and should not be a partisan political issue," Rankin told the governor that the Supreme Court preferred to defer to the state legislatures, but that he and lawmakers must act without delay to avoid court intervention.[25]

In August 1962, before the district court, Sand reiterated the position he had argued previously, insisting that the Equal Protection Clause did not permit the state of New York to make "an implicit value judgment that some citizens of the state are worthier of representation, having a right to the disproportionate say in the government than other people." He nevertheless conceded that both branches of the legislature need not be apportioned on a population basis. In response, Irving Galt, an assistant state solicitor general, claimed to be befuddled by Sand's argument. Comparing New York's reapportionment with apportionment in the U.S. Congress, and reminding his opponent that neither the Senate nor House of Representatives was based strictly on population (given that each state was guaranteed at least one representative), Galt mockingly asked, "If it is rational to represent population only in one house and other factors in the second, what is irrational, what is wrong, what is unreasonable, what is invidiously discriminatory about having a composite of those same factors in both houses?" The judges agreed, handing down a unanimous decision only two weeks later that found New York's system of apportionment to be within the bounds of the Fourteenth Amendment. At the end of August, Sand and WMCA appealed to the Supreme Court; more than nine months later, the Court announced probable jurisdiction.[26]

In the same period that a handful of lawyers, representing a small group of plaintiffs, brought suits in Virginia and New York, a broad bipartisan coalition of individuals and organizations from suburban Baltimore and Washington joined together under the umbrella of the Maryland Committee for Fair Representation (MCFR) to challenge the flagrant disparities in that state's system of apportionment. In March 1960, when the Maryland General Assembly declined yet another opportunity to meaningfully reapportion itself, a businessman named Jesse L. Maury called on his colleagues in the Western Suburban Democratic Club of Montgomery County to consider a lawsuit. Maury credited "The Next Election Is Already Rigged," the exposé that ran in *Harper's Magazine* in November 1959, as his inspiration, a clear sign of the national momentum coalescing around the issue at the time.[27]

Early supporters of the MCFR worked diligently throughout the spring of 1960 to win the support of civic, political, and labor leaders in the state's urban and suburban regions. This effort underscored the centrality of the suburbs in reapportionment politics and revealed the truly bipartisan desires of suburban residents. By May, the MCFR's board of directors included a Democratic county executive from Baltimore County, the chair of the Republican Party in Baltimore City, the head of the state AFL-CIO, and leaders in the state's chapter of the League of Women Voters. Branches in Montgomery and Prince George's Counties recruited members from both political parties, finding the most success by going to local civic associations, Parent-Teacher Associations, labor union locals, and county affiliates of the LWV. During the first two years of its existence, the MCFR raised approximately $5,000; only a handful of donations exceeded $100 and none was greater than $200. The printing of legal briefs and documents consumed close to $4,000. No individual received a fee or salary for work done on behalf of the MCFR.[28]

The organization faced a Sisyphean task. Its initial brochure noted, "Maryland is among the four worst apportioned states in the United States!" As in New York, the state constitution dictated reapportionment of the legislature. Each of the state's twenty-three counties constituted a legislative district, while the city of Baltimore was divided into six districts. These twenty-nine districts were each represented by one senator and between two and six delegates in the lower house. The four suburban counties—Montgomery and Prince George's, which border Washington, D.C.; Anne Arundel, which includes the state capital of Annapolis; and Baltimore—were severely underrepresented in both branches of the legislature and, as occurred throughout the United States, the disparities grew every year. As the MCFR emphasized in its literature, a majority of the lower chamber theoretically represented no more than 24 percent of the population, while only 15 percent of the population lived in districts that elected a majority of senators. Exacerbating the situation was the fact that Maryland, like Georgia, employed a county-unit system in statewide primary nominations, meaning that candidates for governor, U.S. senator, and several lesser offices owed their election to voters in less populated regions of the state. By comparison, Virginia and New York appeared enviably democratic.[29]

Unlike the Alabama, Virginia, and New York cases, the Maryland complaint began as a challenge in state court. Originally filed in August 1960 by Alfred Scanlan, a resident of Montgomery County with a law practice in the District of Columbia and a founding member of the MCFR, the suit was clearly intended to prod the legislature to reform itself. In keeping with the MCFR's initial willingness to accept some version of the so-called federal plan as a compromise, Scanlan, who took no fee during the four years that he shepherded the case through the courts, did not ask the state court to institute a precise population-based reapportionment, but rather, and more generally, requested a "formula which reasonably reflects the present population" of all of the counties and the city of Baltimore. The circuit court dismissed the complaint without a trial on the merits.[30]

After *Baker*, Scanlan appealed to the Maryland court of appeals, which reversed the lower court's dismissal and ordered a hearing on the merits of the complaint. Affirming in its order that it was not "possible (or advisable if it were possible) to state a precise, inflexible and intractable formula for constitutional representation" and specifying that the Maryland constitution had no provision mandating that representation follow population, the court nevertheless concluded that "there is a strong implication in the *Baker* decision that there must be some reasonable relationship of population, or eligible voters, to representation in the General Assembly." Meanwhile, the board of the MCFR, emboldened by *Baker*, adopted a "new 'minimum' position requiring that a majority of the population control a majority of seats in both houses," a significant departure from its original stance.[31]

The decision of the appeals court to order a trial on the merits precipitated a series of rapidly unfolding events. After a trial in late May 1962, Circuit Court Judge Bowie Duckett found that while certain counties (though not the city of Baltimore) did indeed suffer invidious discrimination in the apportionment of the lower chamber of the state legislature, he did not strike down the existing system. The most significant aspect of Duckett's opinion, however, was what he declined to state. He deliberately avoided saying anything about the apportionment of the state senate. As soon as he announced his decision, Governor Millard Tawes called the General Assembly into special session; the legislature quickly passed and the governor signed a bill that granted nineteen new delegates to the most underrepresented counties but left the senate untouched.[32]

The court of appeals then ordered Duckett to weigh in on the apportionment of the senate, which moved the Maryland case onto the national stage. Citing the results of the legislature's special session, Duckett contended that reapportionment of the lower chamber now sufficiently reflected population. He then posed a question that would soon preoccupy the Supreme Court: "Does the Fourteenth Amendment . . . require that a State having one House of its Legislature fairly based on population, shall also base its other House on population?" Duckett observed that a three-judge federal district court in Georgia held recently that the Supreme Court had never reached such a determination, and then quoted at length from a speech Solicitor General Archibald Cox gave to the Tennessee Bar Association just weeks earlier, in which Cox appeared to suggest that individual states need apportion only one legislative chamber in direct proportion to population. Arguing that the reapportionment of the Maryland legislature now fell within these parameters, Duckett ruled the Maryland senate constitutional.[33]

The MCFR saw that the reapportionment of the lower house was an improvement for the most underrepresented counties but insisted that it still fell far short of equitable representation. And since the MCFR now took the stance that both houses must be apportioned in direct ratio to population, the organization and Scanlan appealed Duckett's ruling to the Maryland court of appeals. In late July, the state's highest court upheld the lower court's determination, but only four of seven judges concurred. Chief Judge Frederick W. Brune's minority opinion agreed with the MCFR's argument on every point. "Geography simply cannot be divorced from people as a basis for representation," Brune wrote. "We grant that no exact mathematical rule or guide should be attempted by this Court; but it seems to us that when the disparity in population reaches the point where it has no rational justification, the limit of permissible discrimination is passed." Brune reasoned, in closing, that the state's reliance on the "magic phrase 'federal analogy'" was lacking as a justification for such disparities.[34]

Within days of the decision, Scanlan appealed to the Supreme Court on behalf of the MCFR. On June 10, 1963, the Court noted probable jurisdiction in the Maryland case, along with the New York, Alabama, and Virginia cases. Six weeks later, Scanlan walked out of his office building on Fifteenth Street in Washington, just across the street from the White House, headed north for less than one block, and arrived at the office of Ed Campbell. There, Scanlan joined Campbell, Chuck Morgan, Leonard Sand, and Henry Howell, who were comparing notes and beginning to design a strategy for their appearance before the Supreme Court.[35]

The protagonists in the four state reapportionment cases did not think to invite the attorneys in a congressional reapportionment case from Georgia to their summit. But on the same day that it noted probable jurisdiction in the Alabama, Maryland, New York, and Virginia cases, the Supreme Court announced its intention to take up the related, but distinct, issue of congressional reapportionment. One of three cases filed in the federal district court in Atlanta immediately after the resolution of *Baker* (the others challenged the state's county-unit system and the reapportionment of the state legislature), the suit centered on the gross underrepresentation of voters in the city's booming suburbs.[36]

As in most state reapportionment complaints of the period, the numerical facts of the Georgia congressional complaint were never in dispute. As a result of the 1930 census, Georgia's congressional delegation was reduced from twelve to ten members; in response, the state legislature drew districts that had not changed in the intervening years. Since the statewide population was just under four million, the average or ideal size of the ten districts was 394,312 residents. But the Fifth District, which included suburban Fulton and DeKalb Counties, as well as the more rural Rockdale County, was home to 823,680 people. By contrast, the Ninth District, the least populous district in the state, had only 272,154 inhabitants. The only underrepresented congressional district in the state, Georgia's Fifth was the second most populous district in the nation, trailing only the Fifth District of Texas.[37]

Representing Fulton County residents James Wesberry and Candler Crim and all similarly situated persons in the Fifth District, Atlanta attorney Frank Cash condemned Georgia's congressional apportionment as an "arbitrary, capricious, and invidiously discriminatory" system that violated not only Fourteenth Amendment guarantees of due process and equal protection, but also Article I, Section 2, which requires that "the House of Representatives shall be composed of members chosen every second year by the people of the several states." Cash cited guidelines established by the American Political Science Association and asked the three-judge court to require that all congressional districts deviate by no more than 15 percent from the ideal or average.[38]

The state of Georgia made no effort to dispute the facts of the case but responded by essentially shrugging its shoulders: it maintained that the Supreme Court, in *Baker*, did not strike down *Colegrove* v. *Green* but rather went to great pains to distinguish the facts of the former case from those of the latter. Thus *Baker* had no bearing on congressional reapportionment. If the Supreme Court in *Colegrove* had sanctioned congressional districts in Illinois that ranged from 112,116 to 914,000 persons, then less disparate districts in Georgia must stand. Furthermore, the defendants claimed, "The form of congressional districting complained of in Georgia is not exotic, but epitomizes a national practice."[39]

In mid-June, a three-judge district court dismissed the complaint of the appellants. Judge Griffin Bell, who just weeks earlier had written the opinion striking down Georgia's county-unit system, now wrote the majority opinion accepting the state's contentions about congressional apportionment. Bell, who later served as attorney general of the United States under President Jimmy Carter, believed that *Colegrove* v. *Green* was still controlling with regard to congressional reapportionment. He did not challenge the fact that residents of Georgia's Fifth District were underrepresented but concluded that the inequities suffered did not reach the level of invidiousness. Bell stated, just as the defendants had argued, that "the problem here is not peculiar to Georgia." Surveying all 413 congressional districts in the United States—he did not include the 22 that elected representatives statewide—Bell found that 170 did not meet the guidelines established by the American Political Science Association and presented to the Court by the petitioners.[40]

Elbert Tuttle, the chief judge of the Fifth Circuit Court of Appeals, who, like Frank Johnson in Alabama, had issued a series of important civil rights rulings, dissented from the key portions of Bell's opinion. A Republican appointed by Dwight Eisenhower, Tuttle disagreed with his colleague's understanding of *Baker* and argued that the federal courts did have "the power to grant relief in a congressional district case." Tuttle unsuccessfully encouraged his colleagues to maintain jurisdiction and allow the legislature a final chance to come up with a plan of congressional reapportionment. In August 1962, the plaintiffs appealed to the Supreme Court; ten months later, the Court added the Georgia congressional case to the slate of reapportionment arguments scheduled for November 1963.[41]

As soon as Alfred Scanlan returned to his office after meeting with Campbell, Morgan, Sand, and Howell, he placed a call to Harold Greene, the chief of the Appeals and Research Section in the Civil Rights Division in the Department of Justice. According to Greene, who relayed details of the conversation to his boss, Burke Marshall, the head of the Civil Rights Division, the attorneys in all four state reapportionment cases planned to "argue for the strict population principle in both houses of their respective legislatures." Even though they saw the need to "leave some room for maneuver," Scanlan and his colleagues "expressed the strong feeling that they hoped any brief to be filed by the Government would not undercut their 'one man, one vote' position."[42]

In the lower courts, not all the attorneys in the state reapportionment cases had argued for a strict population standard in both houses of a bicameral legislature. But on appeal before the Supreme Court, that single issue came to define the debate. Believing that the federal government's argument would carry great weight with the Court, the attorneys were understandably sensitive to the government's position. Had they known what was transpiring at that very moment just blocks from Scanlan's office, they would have had great cause for concern. Within the nearby halls of the Department of Justice, key officials were locked in intense discussions, struggling to determine just what that all-important position would be.

9 ||| AMICUS CURIAE

T he flood of lawsuits filed across the United States in the immediate wake of *Baker* v. *Carr* compelled officials within the Kennedy administration to consider what role, if any, the Department of Justice should play in subsequent litigation. Assistant Attorney General Burke Marshall, the chief of the Civil Rights Division, requested help from U.S. attorneys and the Federal Bureau of Investigation. In an April 1962 memorandum to FBI director J. Edgar Hoover, Marshall instructed regional field agents to notify his office of any congressional or state legislative reapportionment lawsuit filed in federal or state court within their district (the bureau would do so until Marshall rescinded the request about two years later). At the same time, attorneys from all corners of the nation—including Ed Campbell in Virginia, Alfred Scanlan in Maryland, and Theodore Sachs in Michigan—reached out to Marshall and his staff for support. In view of the sheer volume of reapportionment litigation pending before state and federal judges, Marshall and Solicitor General Archibald Cox decided that the Department of Justice would limit its participation as amicus curiae to cases argued before the Supreme Court.[1]

Senior officials in the Civil Rights Division and in the solicitor general's office also began to consider what positions the DOJ should take when it did intervene as a friend of the court. Attorney General Robert Kennedy and Burke Marshall praised the Supreme Court's decision in the Tennessee case in early May 1962 during commemorations of Law

Day to audiences in Virginia and Connecticut, but they studiously avoided any speculation about the standards the Court would or should dictate. Speaking at Vanderbilt University in Nashville on the same occasion, Deputy Attorney General Nicholas Katzenbach ventured a step further than either Kennedy or Marshall and noted that the Supreme Court had not yet weighed in on the issue of standards, particularly whether or not the Equal Protection Clause "permits sharp or even mild departures from equality of representation in either or both houses of a state legislature." Katzenbach offered no guess as to what the Court might rule and provided no hint as to what position, if any, the Department of Justice had decided to take.[2]

Like Kennedy and Marshall, Cox avoided any discussion of standards in a Law Day speech delivered in Portland, Oregon, in early May. Five weeks later, however, he appeared before the Tennessee Bar Association and, for the first time, publicly offered his thoughts on the matter. Reiterating the position staked out by the Kennedy administration in *Baker*, Cox said that "the starting point in determining the constitutionality of any apportionment should be *per capita* equality of representation and that any serious departure from this standard is invalid unless shown to have a rational justification." Though he was careful to add that he did "not mean to suggest how the question should be decided," Cox hinted at his personal feelings when he speculated that "it would not surprise me greatly if the Supreme Court were ultimately to hold that if seats in one branch of the legislature are apportioned in direct ratio to population, the allocation of seats in the upper branch may recognize historical, political and geographical subdivisions *provided that the departure from equal representation in proportion to the population is not too extreme.*"[3]

Despite such speculation in the immediate aftermath of *Baker*, the Kennedy administration did not have to formulate its position for more than a year, until the Supreme Court noted probable jurisdiction in the four state reapportionment cases and the congressional case from Georgia in the summer of 1963. But when that happened, the DOJ began what would turn out to be extensive internal negotiations. Unlike *Baker* v. *Carr* and *Gray* v. *Sanders*, the state reapportionment cases divided officials within the department. There was much to ponder and decide before the administration filed its briefs as a friend of the court.

No one within the Department of Justice, with the possible exception of Cox, devoted as many hours to the latest reapportionment cases as did Bruce Terris. Terris, having already figured so importantly in *Baker*, would appear alongside Cox on the amicus briefs in each of the ensuing reapportionment cases that came before the Supreme Court during the October 1963 term. No other individual could claim that distinction.[4]

Before the Fourth of July holiday in 1963, Terris sent an audacious eleven-page single-spaced memorandum to Cox. In the document, which would reach the attorney general and the White House, Terris anticipated and, to a certain extent, delineated the terms of the debate over standards that soon occupied the senior leadership within the DOJ. Just as he had in *Baker*, Terris found himself a step ahead of his senior colleagues.[5]

After reviewing the record of the five cases, Terris framed the issues in the strongest possible terms. "The subject of this memorandum is of enormous importance," he began, stating that not even the sit-in cases, in which the Court would consider the constitutionality of the arrests of those agitating for African American rights, would prove more consequential than those he was about to discuss. "I say this," he astutely explained, "because the Negro civil rights movement will almost surely continue regardless how the sit-in cases are decided by the Supreme Court, for it depends essentially on mass action, not approval by the courts. . . . In contrast the issue of reapportionment depends almost entirely on what the courts, and especially the Supreme Court, decide." Given the historical reluctance and inability of state legislatures to reapportion themselves, Terris suggested that "the standard laid down by the Supreme Court will be the one followed in numerous states."[6]

Referencing *Baker*, Terris stressed his belief that the Kennedy administration would play an equally seminal role in guiding the Court toward the establishment of a standard. "I think it is unlikely that the Court will impose a stricter standard on the states than we suggest," he speculated. "However, I think that there is probably a majority for deciding as strict a standard as we are willing to support." Although Terris underestimated the willingness of the Supreme Court to forge a stricter standard than that supported by the administration, he proved prophetic in gauging where the Court was headed. "In my view," he wrote, "the proper standard under the equal protection clause is that both houses must be apportioned on the basis of population." Accepting "minor discrepancies" for "administrative convenience"—so that natural boundaries such as rivers or mountains, or even existing political subdivisions such as cities or counties, could be followed—Terris granted that his proposal "does not mean absolute equality between districts." But he did insist that such variations remain within fixed parameters. Offering two possibilities, he proposed no more than a "10 or 20 percent discrepancy between the largest and smallest districts or requiring that at least 45 percent of the people reside in districts having a majority of the legislative body." In a footnote he addressed congressional reapportionment, arguing that because it involved "the same policy and legal issues," it should be subject to essentially the same standards.[7]

Terris then moved to a critique of the most common justifications for apportionments based on anything but population. Brushing aside "unworkable" and "impractical" claims that "it is reasonable for a State to give minority interests greater weight in at least one house of the legislature in order to protect them from the majority," Terris pointed out that if residents of certain rural areas were entitled to disproportionate representation, "so are Negroes, Catholics, Jews, unionists, businessmen, and the like." Referring to a range of recent Supreme Court decisions that expanded the rights of citizens as individuals, he wrote that "such minority power is inconsistent with the very nature of a democracy . . . giving special representation to minorities on the basis of race or religion is almost surely unconstitutional. It would be strange if the Constitution permitted such special rights for rural interests but not for other minority groups."[8]

Indeed, Terris believed that there were only two logical justifications for reapportionment based on factors other than population: the federal analogy, which he confidently dismissed, and history, which he thought compelling but ultimately insufficient. Voicing the position of most legal scholars at the time, Terris rejected the federal analogy as unconvincing, for two reasons. "The apportionment of the Senate is fixed by the Constitution itself," he wrote. Furthermore, he reasoned, echoing an argument popular with proponents of reapportionment, the compromise that established the bicameral U.S. Congress was the result of a grand bargain made between sovereign states; counties, by contrast, were never sovereign entities but rather mere administrative creations of the states with no inherent right to representation. "There is little reason to give each county separate representation," Terris wrote, "let alone equal representation."[9]

Turning to history, Terris conceded that "apportionment based on population in both houses has been the exception and not the rule" and pithily added that "the stricter the standard we apply the more history will be against it." But Terris was not daunted by the prospect of arguing against historical precedent. In language reviled by strict constructionists, who consider the Constitution a fixed instrument not subject to reinterpretation over time, but that was hardly radical at the time, Terris asserted that "the meaning of equal protection is necessarily a changing concept." He cited the ultimate incorporation of African Americans and women into the body politic: the ratification of the Seventeenth Amendment in 1913, which provided for the direct election of U.S. senators by popular vote, and the ongoing movement to abolish the poll tax (which succeeded with the ratification of the Twenty-fourth Amendment in January 1964). He observed that "the history of this country shows increasing awareness of the requirement that all citizens be permitted to participate equally in our government." He summarized his disquisition on history with a confident assertion: "The equal protection clause today requires that both houses of the state legislature be apportioned on the basis of population."[10]

Terris next took indirect aim at his boss. "We could argue, and the Court could hold," he wrote, summarizing the standard that Cox had suggested in his address to a Nashville audience the year before, "that one house had to be apportioned on the basis of population while other factors could be considered in apportioning the other house as long as the deviation from apportionment based on population was not too extreme." Such a standard, Terris thought, would certainly lead to an improvement in many states from the pre-*Baker* era but "would leave much of the problem untouched" and would encourage other states to become less representative. Aligning himself with the position taken by John McConnell in the Alabama case, Terris argued that allowing deviations in the second chamber made little sense from the perspective of equal protection because a minority could still wield veto power over any piece of legislation. "Arguably, such a standard makes sense as a matter of political wisdom," Terris reasoned, "but it is hard to justify logically from the equal protection clause."[11]

Terris had discussed the issue of standards with Cox on numerous occasions, and the latter had made it "very clear" that he would have difficulty embracing population equality in both houses of a bicameral legislature. Terris also knew that Robert Kennedy typically left the formulation of the government's legal position before the Supreme Court to Cox. So Terris brilliantly redefined the issue as political rather than legal. As he deftly put it, the question of which standard to follow was a "political decision properly made at the highest levels of government" and "largely outside my province." With that bold stroke, Terris appealed to Cox's superiors within the administration and encouraged them to make sure that the formulation of the government's position was not left to the solicitor general alone. Terris ended his letter by writing, "I think it would be a tragedy if the great victory in *Baker* v. *Carr* were thrown away by our persuading the Supreme Court to accept a weak substantive standard."[12]

In December 1960, when Solicitor General Lee Rankin was weighing whether or not to file an amicus brief in *Baker* v. *Carr,* Terris had expressed a belief in the limits of the federal government's role. He felt that the government should intervene on behalf of the plaintiffs, but that "it is not unconstitutional for a state to provide for an upper house of its legislature which gives considerable advantage to rural voters over urban." Yet influenced primarily by the Supreme Court's decisions in *Baker* and *Gray,* but also by the inherent logic of the black freedom movement and its claims on the Fourteenth Amendment, Terris reached a new understanding of what the Equal Protection Clause required in the field of apportionment. He was hardly alone in adopting a more activist position; indeed, his evolution represented a shift taking place across the American political landscape and within the chambers of the Supreme Court.[13]

Soon after delivering his lengthy memorandum to Cox, Terris sent a copy to David Rubin and Howard Glickstein, young attorneys in the Civil Rights Division. In mid-July, the pair forwarded the memo to their boss, Harold Greene, the chief of the Appeals and Research Section. In their cover letter, Rubin and Glickstein gave their unqualified support to Terris's position. "We do not see why such inanimate factors as land or cows should be represented in a legislature," they wrote. "Nor do we see why a minority should have more than that share of representation which is dictated by its numbers. Minorities are protected by bills of rights."[14]

Greene quickly digested the contents of both documents and passed them to his immediate superior, Burke Marshall. In his cover letter to Marshall, Greene agreed with the legal and practical arguments outlined in both memos but recommended that the department move cautiously. Citing Terris's suggestion of a "qualified approach" that allowed certain deviations from strict population equality, Greene thought his superiors should not adopt a "strict population principle—at least not in these cases." Instead, the DOJ should back a standard in which population "should be the exclusive factor in one of the houses of a legislature," while in the other chamber, "population should be given controlling weight, but there perhaps somewhat greater variation, based on geography or districting, might be allowed." In conclusion, he wrote that he was "doubtful that an absolute population standard for both houses can be justified, either now or in the future," as "history and the federal example too strongly militate against such a result." Fortunately, he reasoned, each of the reapportionments before the Court so clearly violated the Constitution that the issue of allowable variations could be left for another day.[15]

More than a month passed before Cox weighed in. Throughout July and August, he dissected the lengthy record as he meticulously prepared his arguments and recommendations for the attorney general. Aware of—and to some extent burdened by—his dual obligation to the administration and to the Court, Cox wrestled with what he described as "extraordinarily difficult questions." Finally, at the end of August, Cox sent Robert Kennedy a thirty-three-page single-spaced analysis of the issues, as well as recommendations about what position the government should take in each case. As the journalist Victor Navasky wrote, Cox's memorandum "precisely reflected his state of mind—a kind of tortured but clear, painful thinking aloud, brilliantly setting forth alternatives, preferences, tactics, law, policy, philosophy and jurisprudence."[16]

Although Cox arrived at a far different conclusion on the substantive issue of standards than Terris and the young attorneys in the Civil Rights Division, he did not hesitate to entangle the administration, and himself, in the political thicket. Despite the later claims of some critics that Cox remained at heart a disciple of Felix Frankfurter, the solicitor general endorsed the administration's participation in the reapportionment cases for reasons that Frankfurter would never have agreed with. In explaining to Robert Kennedy why the administration should file an amicus brief, Cox first noted that the "correction of the malapportionment presently existing in State legislatures . . . is in the public interest." Even if Frankfurter had agreed with the sentiment, he would have denied that the federal courts had any say in the matter. Second, Cox, like Terris, believed that the important role that the United States played in *Baker* and in *Gray*—especially in the former—"imposes upon us a heavy obligation to give the Court all possible assistance in cutting its way through the thorny thicket that we persuaded it to enter."[17]

Cox moved to the much thornier question of standards, presenting to the attorney general the various options available to the administration. He summarized the most salient points put forward by Terris and by Rubin and Glickstein. Determined not to misrepresent his younger colleagues—"against the chance that I fail to do them justice," he wrote—Cox had forwarded the complete text of their memoranda to Kennedy.[18]

He then pivoted toward a full explanation of his personal position: "In a State constitutional convention my vote would go to apportion both houses of a bicameral legislature in accordance with population." Yet he could not agree with Terris, Rubin, and Glickstein that "the Supreme Court should be advised to impose that rule upon all 50 States by judicial decree." For Cox, the weight of history imposed a greater burden than it did for the younger attorneys. Noting that such a standard would invalidate thirty-seven of the fifty state constitutions and forty-six of the fifty legislatures, Cox labeled it "radical" and warned that imposing it would prove "too revolutionary to be a proper exercise of the judicial function."[19]

Cox wanted to insulate the Court, as an institution, from the harsh criticism directed its way ever since the landmark segregation rulings a decade earlier. He considered this particularly important because the Court would soon have to "carry the burden" in difficult debates on issues such as criminal procedure and First Amendment rights. "The Court could not lay down the stricter rule without great damage both to the country and itself," Cox predicted. "Many men believe that the present Court has already gone too far too fast in imposing its ideals upon the States. Some are segregationists but many are not. Some are Birchers, in spirit if not in fact, but many are men of moderation." He assured Kennedy that he did "not share their view." But, he went on, "my appraisal of sentiment within the legal profession—and probably outside—is that while the invalidation of the egregiously malapportioned legislatures would command a consensus of opinion, a 'one man–one vote' decision would precipitate a major constitutional crisis causing an enormous drop in public support for the Court."[20]

The argument Cox wished to present to the Court called for "*per capita* equality of representation" but allowed for the possibility that deviations might be constitutional if "shown to have a relevant and substantial justification." What did or did not constitute a reasonable, relevant, or substantial exception, however, was less than straightforward. Cox offered three corollaries. First, he posited that "the Fourteenth Amendment condemns an apportionment that lacks any rational, i.e. intelligible, foundation." An apportionment that assigned one representative or one senator to each county was not, Cox explained, necessarily unconstitutional. But, embracing the terminology used by Tom Clark in his opinion in *Baker* v. *Carr*, "where the apportionment is a crazy quilt, where some citizens are given several times the representation of others without any rhyme or reason, then the underrepresented citizens are denied the equal protection of the laws." Next, Cox argued that "the Fourteenth Amendment condemns any apportionment based upon hostile or invidious discrimination against any persons or groups." Citing *Gomillion* v. *Lightfoot*, he noted that "the plainest illustration" of this form of discrimination involved districts that were assigned fewer representatives because their population was "predominately Negro, Irish or Italian." To him, such a prohibition clearly extended to condemn any scheme "that selects persons who belong to a particular geographical area, for oppressive, unfavorable treatment."[21]

Conscious that more than a few grossly malapportioned state legislatures would survive his first two tests, Cox put forward a third and final proposition: "An apportionment which makes the principle of popular representation subordinate to the representation of established political subdivisions to such a degree as to give control of the legislature to small minorities of the people constitutes an unreasonable classification of qualified voters." Here Cox clearly intended to make sure that states could not use otherwise rational methods to empower small minorities. For instance, an apportionment that assigned one representative or senator to each county might meet the solicitor general's first test and yet fail on his third point. But unlike Terris, who favored a requirement that a majority of a legislative body represent at least a specifically stated minimum percentage of a state's population—Terris suggested 45 percent—Cox offered no definition of "small minorities."[22]

Cox's belief in the need to avoid a defined standard—a belief voiced throughout his memo to Kennedy—reflected his ambivalence about one particular case: the challenge to New York's apportionment. Cox had absolutely no trouble urging the Supreme Court to strike down existing systems in Alabama, Maryland, and Virginia. Alabama, he explained, not only had created a crazy quilt with no rational basis but also had ensured that a distinct and impermissible minority controlled the legislative process. Similarly, Maryland empowered too few voters at the expense of the majority, and, in addition, discriminated against voters in the state's suburban counties. Although slightly more than 40 percent of Virginia's residents in mid-1963 lived in districts that elected a majority of the legislature—better than all but seven other states— Cox argued that the state's system of apportionment clearly violated the rights of residents of Arlington and Fairfax Counties and the city of Norfolk. In his recommendations to Kennedy, Cox also advised the administration to side with the plaintiffs in the Georgia congressional redistricting case. Though Cox had devoted little time in his lengthy memorandum to the issue of congressional reapportionment, and, unlike Terris, he had avoided altogether the issue of standards in congressional reapportionments, he did maintain that the logic of *Baker* v. *Carr* extended to congressional districting and that the federal courts, therefore, did have jurisdiction.[23]

Only with regard to the New York case did Cox have reservations. "I am unsure what course should be pursued in *WMCA, Inc.* v. *Simon*," he informed Kennedy. Though "minorities control both houses," the percentage of voters in question—36.9 percent in the upper house and 38.2

percent in the lower house—was higher than in most other states. Furthermore, Cox speculated that the Supreme Court would look to uphold the lower federal courts, if at all possible, and in this case the district court had affirmed New York's scheme. Cox did see a tactical advantage in asking the Supreme Court to sanction New York's apportionment. "Our showing that a line can be drawn and our being willing to draw one," he reasoned, "would probably increase the chance of the Court's invalidating the egregiously unfair apportionments" in Alabama, Maryland, and Virginia. On the other hand, Cox believed that it was "undesirable" for the administration "to argue against those who are seeking more representative apportionment." Consequently, he recommended that the Department of Justice file a brief in the New York case in support of the plaintiffs. But in this brief, the government should "make it plain that the New York case is much closer than the others and that the Virginia, Alabama and Maryland apportionments should be invalidated even if that of New York is affirmed."[24]

After reading the Cox and Terris memoranda, Kennedy consulted with Assistant Attorneys General Burke Marshall and Nicholas Katzenbach, and even discussed the issue "briefly" with the president. John F. Kennedy had committed himself as a candidate to reapportionment and had spoken openly and forcefully as president in support of the Supreme Court's decision in *Baker*, but he never made a statement about standards. By his own admission, Robert Kennedy never asked his brother "what his position was." The attorney general, however, did solicit the input of key White House advisers, most notably Larry O'Brien, the president's chief congressional liaison and one of his most trusted aides. O'Brien, who later served as the chairman of the Democratic National Committee and whose office was the target of the Watergate break-in, responded that he and his staff had reached "clear consensus that the recommendations of Archie Cox are sound and make good sense both legally and politically." Commenting that "the one-man one-vote approach . . . is the ultimate in the eyes of our political scientists and liberal friends," O'Brien communicated his understanding that certain members of the attorney general's staff favored such a position "either on moral grounds or as a position for you to take to insure a limited fall back from that position by the Court." But O'Brien reached a different conclusion. "I cannot agree with this approach in the context of this problem," he told the attorney general. "To confront the Court with all or nothing could well mean nothing." Turning to the possible political ramifications of the government's position, O'Brien wrote, "I can think of no state where we can suffer politically from the establishment of the principles as outlined in the Cox memorandum." By contrast, O'Brien worried that too rapid an embrace of "one-man, one-vote" might meet with resistance from Democrats in certain parts of the country. Consequently, O'Brien counseled "moderation" and reiterated his belief that "Archie Cox's approach is the right one."[25]

Although he appreciated O'Brien's political instincts, Robert Kennedy sided in his own mind with Terris and those who wanted to beseech the Supreme Court to move in "the direction of 'one man, one vote.'" But given the concerns expressed by O'Brien and his staff and, especially, the position staked out by Cox, he understood that "we couldn't do it immediately." The attorney general had the deepest respect for Cox, as both a person and a lawyer, and understood that, as the younger brother of the president and an average law student at the University of Virginia, he could not credibly dictate the administration's position to the solicitor general. So Kennedy and his top lieutenants in the Department of Justice began to subtly prepare the ground for Cox to come around to their position.[26]

As August turned into September and the deadline to file amicus briefs in the reapportionment cases rapidly approached, Kennedy scheduled a meeting to discuss the government's position. Set for September 4, it was postponed, as was a second meeting two days later. Finally, on Tuesday, September 10, DOJ and White House staff gathered in the office of the attorney general to discuss the government's position. In addition to Kennedy, those in attendance included Marshall, Cox, and Terris from the DOJ; O'Brien and Ted Sorensen from the White House staff; and Kennedy in-laws Sargent Shriver and Stephen Smith, both valued advisers to the president. It was, Cox recalled years later, the only time during his tenure in which "there was frankly political discussion with the White House about the position that the government would take in the Supreme Court."[27]

Cox, asked by Kennedy to open the discussion, warned against advocating straight population equality and painstakingly went through the stance he had proposed in his memorandum to the attorney general. After listening to what Terris later described as a twenty-minute "dissertation," Kennedy got antsy, stood up, poured himself a glass of juice, and finally interrupted, albeit politely. "Archie," he asked, "isn't the real issue should some people's vote count more than other people's vote?" The solicitor general demurred and ceded the floor as others shared their views. Several years later, Cox remembered that Shriver and Smith "both emotionally wanted to go the whole hog"—to argue for population equality as the standard in both houses of the legislature. O'Brien, according to Cox, was "very pragmatic." He raised the likely political ramifications but "refused to do more than report," and earned the lasting gratitude of the solicitor general "by urging us to frame our brief without regard to political consequences." When all parties had spoken, Kennedy turned to Cox and stressed the necessity of supporting the plaintiffs in all of the cases, but did not advocate a particular position. Instead, the attorney general said, "Archie, I know you can put this issue in a way that will convince the Supreme Court. I have full confidence."[28]

Kennedy's restraint supports the contention of Victor Navasky, who claims that the primary purpose of the meeting was not, in fact, to reach agreement on the government's position, but rather "to make the Solicitor General of the United States feel good, to let him know that his own reservations were not being taken lightly, to let him know by implication that it would be unthinkable to come out *against* one man, one vote—to reaffirm his right to make up his own mind to assure him it was *his* decision to make." In this regard, the meeting was a resounding success. Having received the assurance that he was free "to file the brief I wanted to file," Cox did just that. In each of the reapportionment cases, he wrote the brief himself, seeking input from Terris and others only after he had completed a draft.[29]

Selecting the Maryland case because it involved "a greater variety of issues" than the other state reapportionment cases scheduled for argument in November, the federal government filed its principal amicus brief two weeks later. In the Maryland brief and in a lengthy appendix, Cox exhaustively detailed the government's general position on standards and addressed the substantive issues in each case. Over the next month, the federal government filed additional briefs in the Alabama, New York, and Virginia cases. In each brief, Cox adhered to the language, logic, and core guidelines that he had articulated in his memorandum to Kennedy. In short, the federal government asked the Supreme Court to strike down each of the state legislative reapportionments as unconstitutional but did so without advocating a strict standard. So long as one branch of a bicameral legislature was apportioned on the basis of population, the federal government allowed for the possibility that "the Constitution may leave room for considerable accommodation of competing considerations in the other house."[30]

The briefs, though disappointing to Terris and others at the Department of Justice, as well as to the plaintiffs' attorneys who looked to the Kennedy administration for support, met the immediate needs of the two main protagonists. Robert Kennedy got a brief that supported the plaintiffs in every reapportionment case then before the Supreme Court and that allowed the Court to continue to move in the direction of population equality. For his part, Cox was able to support the plaintiffs in each case without asking the Court to move more quickly than he thought prudent.[31]

In the summer and fall of 1963, the Department of Justice achieved consensus with regard to the reapportionment cases without any demonstrable rancor, for two reasons. Surrounding himself with superb lawyers, Robert Kennedy fostered an atmosphere of open and honest debate and encouraged the nonconfrontational expression of different points of view. Kennedy's leadership and the process he championed allowed Cox to reach, on his own accord, a middle ground acceptable to all the major participants. In addition, the facts of the cases before the Court documented such blatant discrimination that all the major players within the DOJ recognized the need to side with the plaintiffs. Even the New York apportionment—the one that initially troubled Cox the most—proved easy to condemn.[32] Cox's final brief in that case, devoid of the doubt and ambivalence that had pervaded his August memorandum, argued explicitly that "in New York, neither house is apportioned substantially in accordance with population" and dismissed the state's claim that its system protected a variety of interests as "a euphemism for guaranteed minority rule."[33]

As the Supreme Court prepared to hear oral arguments in November, the federal government avoided taking a position on the central substantive question and, indeed, encouraged the Court to avoid the issue altogether. Citing "the settled principle that the Court will not go farther in deciding questions of constitutional law than required by the record before it," Cox's amicus brief called on the Supreme Court to decide all four state reapportionment cases "without ruling upon whether the Fourteenth Amendment always requires substantially equal representation *per capita* in both houses of a State legislature."[34]

10 ||| NOVEMBER 1963

On Tuesday, November 12, 1963, at a few minutes past ten o'clock in the morning, Chief Justice Earl Warren invited New York attorney Leonard Sand to the podium to begin oral arguments in the first of five reapportionment cases on the Supreme Court's November docket. Over the next week, eighteen additional attorneys followed Sand as the justices devoted nearly sixteen hours of oral argument to legislative and congressional reapportionment. Breaking only for lunch, they spent three to four hours on each case, pivoting from one to the next. In summarizing the proceedings for its readership, *United States Law Week* remarked, "Nearly five full days of argument exhausted the issues and, it seemed, the Justices and counsel." Never, before or since, has the Supreme Court devoted so much time to a single issue.[1]

Representing the appellants in the New York case, Sand began by arguing that in the wake of the Court's decision in *Baker*, a clear consensus had emerged in state and lower federal courts: at least one house in a bicameral legislature must be apportioned on a per capita basis. Starting from this position, Sand maintained that reapportionment in both houses of a bicameral legislature must be based "primarily" on population. But in a clear attempt to align himself with the solicitor general and the federal government, Sand conceded that there was room for some deviation in the second house, as long as the first chamber was apportioned according to population.[2]

Alfred Scanlan, the lead attorney in the Maryland case, echoed this position.[3] Chuck Morgan, the exiled Alabamian and lead attorney in that state's case, seemed to do so as well—a sign of the coordination among the various plaintiffs during the summer—describing population as "the most easily judicially maintainable standard of apportionment" yet refraining from lobbying the justices on behalf of a particular standard and asking only that the Supreme Court uphold the ruling of the three-judge district court. However, when pressed by a series of questions from the bench, Morgan stated that "the majority surely should have the right to elect representatives in both houses of the legislature." When one justice asked, in an attempt to clarify Morgan's position, "You conclude, then, that both houses have to be on a population basis?" Morgan strayed from his brief and replied, "Correct."[4]

Archibald Cox appeared before the Supreme Court in all four state legislative cases, the only person other than the justices involved in more than one of the arguments. Not surprising, given the deliberations that had taken place within the Department of Justice, he struck a cautious tone. Insisting that the Court find the reapportionments of the New York, Alabama, Maryland, and Virginia legislatures unconstitutional, Cox nevertheless encouraged the justices not to decide more than was required by the facts of each case and to postpone for the future any ancillary decisions. In his New York argument, Cox outlined the major propositions that the government set forth in its amicus briefs but insisted that not one of the four cases required the Court to address what he referred to as the "ultimate question," namely, whether or not both houses of a bicameral legislature must reflect per capita equality. In each subsequent argument, Cox returned to and stressed this point. During the Alabama argument, he explicitly exhorted the Court not to establish a guideline that would apply to every state. In response to a probing question from Potter Stewart in the Maryland case, the solicitor general said, "I think it has been implicit in everything I have said that the Court should decide these cases, that what guidelines there are should emerge from deciding the minimum required in each of these cases, and that the invitation to set forth general abstract rules is not one I am pressing upon the Court."[5]

Despite a clear preference among the attorneys for the original plaintiffs for the establishment of a sweeping standard, only John McConnell of Alabama argued unequivocally in favor of the position that

Bruce Terris had tried to impress upon Cox in July. "Whatever the Court gives as a minimum apportionment," McConnell predicted, "will be the maximum apportionment that you receive in the legislature." He asked the justices to recognize that the Equal Protection Clause required the apportionment of all legislative chambers on a population basis.[6]

In a nimble, well-crafted, and powerfully argued performance that drew the attention of counsel in the other cases and from third-party observers in the courtroom—who later reached consensus that he had delivered the "ablest and most outstanding" argument in all of the re-apportionment cases—McConnell deftly handled questions from the bench, connected his position to the arguments and questions posed the previous day in the New York case, and never wavered from his core conviction. "Our sole point on appeal," he explained, "is that we think that population must be the initial controlling guide; and that that must be in every stage of the legislative process." Therefore, according to McConnell, every legislative chamber—whether a unicameral, bicameral, or even, theoretically, a six-house legislature, as Potter Stewart had imagined in a question the day before—must be based on population. McConnell contended that in Alabama, as in all states except unicameral Nebraska, the assent of both houses of the legislature was required to pass a bill. "Therefore to give equality in one house, and to deny equality in the second house," he reasoned, "is to deny equality to the entire legislative process."[7]

Throughout his argument, McConnell repeatedly reminded the Court, as did counsel in each of the other cases, that he appeared before it on behalf of individual citizens who wanted the "protection of individual, civil, private rights," and not on behalf of urban voters or any other class of citizens. Pointing out to the Court that the Big Mules and certain other residents of Alabama's more populous counties "are happy with the rural domination of the legislature," McConnell insisted that urban residents were "not unanimous" on the subject of reapportionment.[8]

McConnell, though granting that the Court should allow for some "administrative deviations" from exact per capita equality, argued that such deviations must be minimal. He cited the Court's opinion in *Gray v. Sanders* and called on the justices to begin "with the idea of one man–one vote." His invocation of the Georgia county-unit decision drew a

pointed objection from Stewart, who in every one of the reapportionment arguments attempted to distinguish between the statewide elections at issue in *Gray* and the process of drawing legislative districts
now before the Court. But each time, counsel for the original plaintiffs,
seconded by Cox, pushed back by noting the obvious implications. In
the proceedings in the New York case, Cox reasoned that if a state cannot weight votes in a statewide election, it cannot do so in apportioning
the legislature. For his part, McConnell conceded to Stewart that states
are free to experiment with units of representation. "But once that unit
is determined," he said, "there can be no experimentation in the equality of representation from that unit."[9]

Predictably, attorneys for the various states provided a drastically different assessment. Irving Galt, the assistant solicitor general of New York,
denied that gross inequality defined New York's system of apportionment and mentioned that his state ranked among the top one-third of the
fifty states in various measures of equality of representation. He argued
that responsiveness to popular will and not simple per capita equality
was the appropriate measure by which to judge New York's apportionment, and that, in addition to population, states can rationally consider
county representation, the physical size of districts, and a desire for the
diffusion of political power. Galt's assertion prompted Justice Hugo Black
to ask how much latitude the states had in this regard. For instance, could
New York assign a single senator and representative to New York City
and an additional one hundred representatives to the rest of the state?
Choosing his words carefully, Galt claimed that such an apportionment
would not necessarily be unconstitutional. But he did acknowledge that
a point of absurdity, beyond which the state could not go, did exist.
When Earl Warren asked for help in determining just where that point
of absurdity lay and to what extent population must be considered, Galt
refused to speculate. When he argued that the state had a reasonable
interest in limiting the concentration of political power that would ac-
crue to any one region, Justices Byron White and Arthur Goldberg asked
whether Galt was not, in fact, arguing in favor of the tyranny of the
minority over the tyranny of the majority. Undeterred, Galt finished by
warning the justices that if they accepted the contention of the appellants that population must be the starting point, they must be prepared
to strike down apportionments in virtually every state in the nation.[10]

McLean Pitts, a prominent resident of Selma in the Black Belt stronghold of Dallas County, had appealed the district court's decision in the Alabama case on behalf of Dallas County probate judge Bernard A. Reynolds and his counterpart in Marion County. Given the appalling disparities that resulted from decades of legislative inaction in Alabama, Pitts had little room to maneuver, and he knew it. At one point, Stewart, who favored granting wide latitude to the states in crafting reapportionment plans, directed Pitts to remember that both sides had accepted in the district court that Alabama's apportionment constituted "invidious discrimination." Consequently, unlike counsel representing New York, Maryland, and Virginia, Pitts could not credibly defend Alabama's system as rational. But he tried nevertheless. He claimed that the state's plan was rational, even if the legislature "had, for 60 years, failed to follow its own constitution," and blasted *Baker* as a "radical departure," after which he exhorted the Court to reconsider its decision in that case. Pitts asserted that as a result of *Baker*, the district court had exceeded its authority and had threatened the sovereignty of the state.[11]

Taking a similar position, Maryland assistant attorney general Robert S. Bourbon cited history and geography to defend his state's system of apportionment, and to argue that Maryland had a right to base representation, at least to some degree, on political units rather than on population. In response, Hugo Black noted that Bourbon was, in effect, "arguing that you have a right to deprive people in a particular area of their full right of suffrage because you want to strip them of some of their power."[12]

By prior arrangement, Bourbon ceded the final fifteen minutes of his time to New Jersey assistant attorney general Theodore I. Botter, who had filed an amicus brief on behalf of New Jersey and fourteen other states that subscribed to some version of the so-called federal arrangement. Invoking the decision of a lower court that Illinois's 1954 reapportionment plan fairly balanced the interests of Chicago and Cook County with the rest of the state, Botter insisted that "Equal Protection means more than mathematical equality; it also means protection. Our argument is that majority rule in both houses does not afford adequate protection for minority interests. . . . We think the minority in one branch of the legislative government should have some bargaining power." In rebuttal, Alfred Scanlan scoffed at the claims of Bourbon and Botter, and warned the justices that *Baker* v. *Carr* would "mean nothing at all" if the Court allowed Maryland's system to stand.[13]

Richmond attorney David Mays was the first to speak in defense of Virginia's system of reapportionment, and he wasted no time in attacking the brief of the federal government in general, and Cox in particular. In a tone far more harsh, bordering on disrespectful, than anything directed at opposing counsel, both Mays and Robert D. McIlwaine, III, the assistant attorney general of Virginia, lambasted Cox for concluding that Virginia, which ranked eighth in the nation in its degree of representativeness, somehow violated the Equal Protection Clause. Virginia, Mays stated, was "not Tennessee"; the gross disparities that defined apportionment in other states, he argued, did not exist in his state, which was perfectly justified in not counting transient military personnel as residents for the purpose of apportionment. Mays did not ask the Court to overturn *Baker*, as Pitts had done, but he did tell the justices that the consequences of siding with the plaintiffs would be enormously problematic: "You are in grave danger of breaking down state government . . . because when you change apportionment . . . you have put your hand on the whole system of legislation, which to my mind is the very heart of state government." For his part, McIlwaine attacked Cox as "less than kind, less than objective, and less than accurate" for using the state's refusal to count military personnel as evidence that the state did not consider such persons "worthy of representation" in the General Assembly.[14]

Partway through McIlwaine's argument, Earl Warren pounded his gavel and brought an end to the day's, and the week's, oral arguments. In the first three days, the justices had engaged frequently with counsel but also exhibited a general willingness to allow advocates on both sides to develop their points. An antiquated taping system makes it difficult to identify each justice's voice with perfect accuracy, but most members of the Court appear to have participated. Potter Stewart, who had been at the center of the Court in *Baker* and remained ambivalent about reapportionment, asked far more questions than any other justice. Occupying the two ends of the bench reserved for the most junior justices, Byron White and Arthur Goldberg, neither of whom had participated in *Baker*, interjected regularly, as did John Marshall Harlan. The chief justice, along with Black, Brennan, and occasionally Clark, chimed in as well, albeit not as often. William O. Douglas rarely spoke. With the exception of Harlan, who had made it clear in *Baker* and in *Gray* that the federal courts had no business getting involved in reapportionment, the other justices appeared to accept that some level of intervention was necessary but were not at all settled as to what that intervention should entail. The nuances of each case worried Stewart and contributed to his feeling that the Court should not set a specific standard; other justices, in contrast, looked at the same circumstances and concluded that a uniform standard was precisely what was needed.

Like all the other attorneys involved in the four state reapportionment cases, David Mays attended the arguments in every case. Unlike the other attorneys, however, the Richmond native kept a detailed diary, which was sealed for a quarter century after his death in 1971 and now offers a unique and uncensored perspective on the events. Each evening, after cocktails and dinner, Mays recorded a few observations and thoughts about what had taken place that day. The first day of proceedings did not inspire much confidence in him. The questions of John Marshall Harlan and Potter Stewart "showed much sympathy" for the state of New York, he wrote, but "the majority I judge to be adverse." Mays saved his most critical remarks for Cox, writing that he approached his argument "like a classroom lecture at Harvard" and left him "unimpressed."[15]

Twenty-four hours later, Mays's mood had not improved. Limiting his diary entry to a few sentences—he was also making final preparations for his own appearance before the Court—Mays was annoyed that the Court would not sit on Friday and that, therefore, he would have to return to Washington to finish his case on Monday. He renewed his critique of the solicitor general, blasting his "sorry appearance" in the Alabama case, and lamented that "New York may lose its case; Alabama certainly has."[16]

Mays and his cocounsel left Washington immediately upon adjournment on Thursday afternoon and made it home to Richmond in time for dinner. That night, Mays devoted five single-spaced pages to an account of his appearance before the Court. He wrote that the "press boxes were full and running over" and that the courtroom had been "packed and hushed." His cocounsel had tried to dissuade him from citing the Court's decision to allow school integration to proceed with "all deliberate speed" as precedent for arguing that the Court should delay imposing a remedy in the reapportionment cases. "How much effect this will have upon the Court I do not know," Mays wrote. Betraying no lack of confidence, he went on: "I do know that they sat bolt upright on the edges of their chairs and listened with very serious faces, and Potter Stewart, who I took to be into me, kept peering down the line of chairs to see how his brethren were reacting."[17]

Near the end of the entry, Mays offered a few "random observations" about the first three days of reapportionment arguments. "Stewart, Harlan and Goldberg were constant questioners," he noted. "The others said little. Douglas never once opened his mouth except to make one brief whispered observation to Warren." Harlan and Stewart "seemed anxious to help the states," but each time Harlan tried to "get counsel to say that the 14th Amendment was not the real basis for *Baker* . . . Brennan would be ruffled and insist that it was." Mays recounted that "finally, Harlan gave up trying to make headway in that direction."[18]

This time, Mays spared Cox and instead saved his most caustic remarks for William O. Douglas, the Court's most unabashed civil libertarian and a frequent target of conservatives. "Douglas looked like the devil," the Richmond attorney wrote. Referring to the justice's increasingly controversial personal life—in August, the sixty-four-year-old Douglas had married for the third time, to a twenty-three-year-old, and just five days after the finalization of his divorce from his second wife— Mays wrote that "his extremely florid face and white eyebrows make him no prize at any time, but he seemed especially unpromising after the most recent of his honeymoons." Mays criticized Douglas's courtroom demeanor. "He was late in taking his seat on Tuesday and absented himself for a few minutes every hour, I assume to go to the toilet. He gave every appearance of extreme boredom and that his mind was closed before coming into the courtroom." Mays wrote, almost with glee, "It is strongly rumored that this little sexual gymnast will soon retire. Hasten the day!" Douglas retired twelve years later and remains the longest-serving justice in American history.[19]

The following morning, November 15, the chief justice and eight associate justices gathered for their weekly conference. As dictated by tradition, each member of the Court shook hands with the others, a practice that served as a reminder that significant philosophical differences need not infringe on basic rules of civility and decency. After working their way through an extensive list of motions and other orders for their review, the justices turned their attention to the cases argued that week. The New York, Alabama, and Maryland reapportionment cases dominated their deliberations. Given where the Court eventually ended up, it is remarkable that not one justice, in the beginning, took the position that all legislative chambers must be based strictly on per capita equality.[20]

According to William O. Douglas, Earl Warren said that the "principle of equality is the starting point" but nevertheless offered an initial assessment that there could be "no rigid rule." Speaking in general terms, the chief granted that a state "can divide its political units any way it wants, but the end result cannot be discriminatory." Turning to the specifics of the New York case, Warren stated his belief that the state's reapportionment was not a "crazy quilt," but that, over time, it had come to constitute "invidious discrimination." Referring to the New York, Alabama, and Maryland lawsuits, Warren accepted the contention of Archibald Cox and others when he enigmatically said, "We do not reach the question whether a state can have a federal plan." John Marshall Harlan, however, interpreted Warren's comments as an indication that the chief justice was "ok" with some form of a federal system.[21]

According to Harlan, Hugo Black told his brethren that he was "not ready to express his views." Douglas characterized Black's position as "unsettled." Black expressed a desire to go along with the majority and to avoid multiple opinions. Sensitive to the fact that the Court was entering a "new field" and that many folks were anxious, Black looked ahead to the Georgia congressional reapportionment case, which would be argued the following week, and hypothesized that there was "far more support" throughout the nation for the Court's intervention in congressional apportionment than in state legislative apportionment. Nevertheless, the former senator from Alabama reiterated his support for Baker v. Carr. In reaching any standard, Black explained that he would put "great weight on the sheer force of numbers." At some point, he saw,

13 REASONS WHY

YOU SHOULD VOTE
"YES" #13
SENATE REAPPORTIONMENT

Is This Representative Government, California?

6,000,000 CALIFORNIANS = 5 SENATORS

4,000,000 CALIFORNIANS = 35 SENATORS

No county may have more than one senator, so five counties, Los Angeles, San Francisco, San Diego, Alameda and Contra Costa, with a total of 6,000,000 people in 1948, have five senators. The area system of apportionment gives 4,000,000 others 35 senators.

CITIZENS' COMMITTEE FOR EQUAL REPRESENTATION
in the California State Senate

411 Flood Bldg.
San Francisco 2, California

149 East 14th Street
Oakland 16, California

205 Hayward Hotel
Los Angeles 14, California

In the 1920s, California voters limited the political power of the state's most populous regions, particularly Los Angeles. Proponents of reapportionment, led by the state's labor unions, qualified Proposition 13 for the ballot in 1948 in an attempt to increase urban representation. (Whitaker & Baxter Campaigns, Inc., Papers, California State Archives)

A broad coalition of business and trade groups joined rural-based interests and the state's political elite to defeat Proposition 13 by an overwhelming margin. (Whitaker & Baxter Campaigns, Inc., Papers, California State Archives)

Considered the first professional political campaign consultants in the
United States, the husband and wife team of Clem Whitaker and Leone
Baxter dominated California politics in the 1930s, '40s, and '50s. Whitaker
and Baxter oversaw every aspect of the campaign to defeat Proposition 13
in 1948. (Jon Brenneis Photograph Archive, Bancroft Library, University of
California, Berkeley)

The Supreme Court, 1961: (seated, left to right) William O. Douglas, Hugo L. Black, Earl
Warren, Felix Frankfurter, Tom C. Clark; (standing, left to right) Charles E. Whittaker,
John Marshall Harlan, William J. Brennan, Potter Stewart (Collection of the Supreme
Court of the United States)

A popular three-term governor of California, Earl Warren served as chief justice of the United States from 1953 to 1969. (© Henry Burroughs / AP / AP / CORBIS)

Throughout the 1960s, as the Supreme Court rendered controversial decisions involving school prayer, birth control, the rights of criminals, and reapportionment, billboards such as this one appeared on roads and highways across the United States. (Collection of the Supreme Court of the United States)

"If You Don't Like This Situation, You Can Cast Your Twentieth Of A Vote Against It"

HERBLOCK
© 1961 THE WASHINGTON POST Co.

Throughout the 1960s, the *Washington Post* political cartoonist Herb Block repeatedly turned his attention to the issue of malapportionment. The Pulitzer Prize winner, who signed his work "Herblock," drew this cartoon in October 1961 as the Supreme Court heard the second round of arguments in *Baker* v. *Carr*. (A 1961 Herblock Cartoon, © The Herb Block Foundation)

- 9 -

But once the class of voters is chosen and their qualifications (es)pecified, we see no constitutional way by which equality of voting power may be evaded. The conception of political equality from the Declaration of Independence, to Lincoln's Gettysburg Address, to the Fifteenth, Seventeenth, and Nineteenth Amendments ~~is engrained in our system.~~ can mean only one thing — one person, one vote.

In this early draft of his opinion in *Gray* v. *Sanders* (1963), William O. Douglas edits his original language to include the phrase "one person, one vote" for the first time in a Supreme Court opinion. In a later draft, Douglas rejected the suggestion of a law clerk to substitute "voter" for "person." (Library of Congress, Manuscript Division, William O. Douglas Papers)

During his speech at the March on Washington in August 1963, Student Nonviolent Coordinating Committee (SNCC) president John Lewis declared, "'One Man, One Vote' is the African cry. It is ours, too. It must be ours." Subsequently, SNCC adopted the phrase as it attempted to register African American voters in the most hostile corners of the South. (Photograph © Danny Lyon, Magnum Photos. Reproduction from Joseph and Nancy Ellin Freedom Summer Collection, McCain Library and Archives, the University of Southern Mississippi)

The combative, feisty Chuck Morgan (seated, front row, in dark suit) and the unassuming George Taylor (standing and speaking) were exceptionally close friends who filed the lawsuit that reached the Supreme Court as *Reynolds* v. *Sims*. (Courtesy of Jarred O. Taylor II)

Attorney General Robert F. Kennedy oversaw the federal government's involvement in each of the reapportionment cases that reached the Supreme Court in the early 1960s. From the outset, Kennedy favored an expansive view of equality, but he knew that he had to carefully manage the concerns of the solicitor general. (Photograph © Henri Cartier-Bresson, Magnum Photos)

Widely considered an outstanding solicitor general, Archibald Cox opposed asking the Supreme Court to adopt a standard of "population equality" in both houses of a bicameral legislature. Ultimately, Cox moderated his position. A professor of labor law at Harvard, Cox later served as the special prosecutor for the Watergate scandal, a position from which he was fired during the infamous Saturday Night Massacre. (Library of Congress, Prints & Photographs Division, *U.S. News & World Report* Collection [reproduction number LC-U9-27830 #14])

Burke Marshall, the head of the Civil Rights Division in the Department of Justice, played a key role, along with Nicholas Katzenbach, in reaching the compromise that allowed Archibald Cox to moderate his position. (Library of Congress, Prints & Photographs Division, *New York World-Telegram* and the *Sun* Newspaper Collection [reproduction number LC-USZ62-135502])

Nicholas Katzenbach, the deputy attorney general at the time of the reapportionment debates, later succeeded Robert Kennedy as attorney general when Kennedy was elected to the U.S. Senate. (Library of Congress, Prints & Photographs Division, *New York World-Telegram* and the *Sun* Newspaper Collection [reproduction number LC-USZ62-121115])

A young assistant to the solicitor general, Bruce Terris emerged as the most vociferous advocate within the Department of Justice for the "one person, one vote" standard. (Courtesy of Bruce J. Terris)

On November 20, 1963, the president and Mrs. Kennedy hosted the justices and their wives at the White House. At one point in the evening, the chief justice and several of his colleagues jokingly warned the president to be careful during his upcoming trip to Texas. Thirty-six hours later, the president was shot in Dallas. (© Bettmann / CORBIS)

In 1962, Byron White (standing, far left) and Arthur J. Goldberg (standing, far right) replaced Charles E. Whittaker and Felix Frankfurter, respectively. Without White and Goldberg, the Court would not have had the votes to adopt so sweeping a standard as "one person, one vote" in the state reapportionment cases. (Collection of the Supreme Court of the United States)

In this cartoon, which first appeared in the *Chicago Sun-Times* on June 18, 1964, the Pulitzer Prize–winner Bill Mauldin perfectly captured the importance of the Supreme Court's reapportionment decisions. (Copyright by Bill Mauldin [1964]. Courtesy of Bill Mauldin Estate, LLC. Reproduction from Bill Mauldin Cartoon Collection, Archives Center, National Museum of American History, Smithsonian Institution)

As the Republican minority leader in the Senate, Everett Dirksen of Illinois championed a constitutional amendment that would have gutted the Supreme Court's reapportionment decisions. (© CORBIS)

The senior U.S. senator from Illinois and one of the chamber's most liberal members, Paul Douglas (shown here with Robert Kennedy in October 1966 during a failed bid for a fourth term) led a small band of senators who launched an unlikely filibuster and successfully stymied Dirksen's efforts. (© Bettmann / CORBIS)

As Everett Dirksen persisted in his efforts to modify the Supreme Court's reapportionment decisions, (left to right) Philip Hart of Michigan, Edward Kennedy of Massachusetts, Birch Bayh of Indiana, and Joseph Tydings of Maryland ably assisted Paul Douglas. (Copyright by Estate of Stanley Tretick. Library of Congress, Prints & Photographs Division, *Look* Magazine Photograph Collection [reproduction number LC-L9-65-2320-U # 21A])

"My Dear Chaps, Have You No Refinement, No Finesse?"

As debate over the Voting Rights Act intensified in Congress in June 1965, Herblock suggested that Everett Dirksen's campaign against the Supreme Court's reapportionment decisions might influence southerners' willingness to use violence to deny equal voting rights to all American citizens. (A 1965 Herblock Cartoon, © The Herb Block Foundation)

In this July 1965 cartoon, Herblock lampooned Dirksen for an audacious parliamentary sleight of hand. The senator forced his constitutional amendment onto the floor of the Senate by substituting his bill for an innocuous resolution proclaiming the first week of September "National American Legion Baseball Week." (A 1965 Herblock Cartoon, © The Herb Block Foundation)

"I Ask Only That Certain Players Be Given A Few Extra Turns At Bat And A Few Extra Strikes"

LET THE
PEOPLE
DECIDE

The nationwide public effort in support of the Dirksen Reapportionment Amendment (SJR103)—to restore to the people of each state the right to determine the composition of their State Legislatures—stems from the mainstream of American democratic beliefs in the principles of self-government

★ WHAT THE EFFORT IS ABOUT

★ HOW YOU CAN HELP

COMMITTEE FOR GOVERNMENT OF THE PEOPLE
★

Whitaker & Baxter, now run by Clem Whitaker Jr., devised "Let the People Decide" as a pithy, appealing alternative to the increasingly popular "one person, one vote." Whitaker & Baxter distributed tens of thousands of these flyers on behalf of the Committee for the Government of the People, an organization devoted solely to pushing Dirksen's amendment through Congress. (Whitaker & Baxter Campaigns, Inc., Papers, California State Archives)

THE BIG CITY
GERRYMANDER
GRAB

IT'S THE POLITICAL PATTERN OF THE FUTURE UNDER FORCED "ONE-MAN-ONE-VOTE"

Millions of suburban and non-urban Americans will be effectively disfranchised by the Supreme Court's forced reapportionment, UNLESS . . .

In this flyer produced for the Committee for the Government of the People, Whitaker & Baxter attempted to align increasingly important suburban voters with rural residents by predicting that reapportionment would lead to domination by labor-backed urban political machines. (Whitaker & Baxter Campaigns, Inc., Papers, California State Archives)

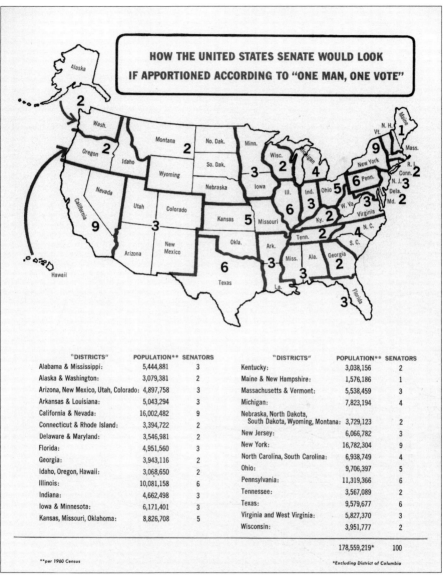

HOW THE UNITED STATES SENATE WOULD LOOK IF APPORTIONED ACCORDING TO "ONE MAN, ONE VOTE"

"DISTRICTS"	POPULATION**	SENATORS
Alabama & Mississippi:	5,444,881	3
Alaska & Washington:	3,079,381	2
Arizona, New Mexico, Utah, Colorado:	4,897,758	3
Arkansas & Louisiana:	5,043,294	3
California & Nevada:	16,002,482	9
Connecticut & Rhode Island:	3,394,722	2
Delaware & Maryland:	3,546,981	2
Florida:	4,951,560	3
Georgia:	3,943,116	2
Idaho, Oregon, Hawaii:	3,068,650	2
Illinois:	10,081,158	6
Indiana:	4,662,498	3
Iowa & Minnesota:	6,171,401	3
Kansas, Missouri, Oklahoma:	8,826,708	5

"DISTRICTS"	POPULATION**	SENATORS
Kentucky:	3,038,156	2
Maine & New Hampshire:	1,576,186	1
Massachusetts & Vermont:	5,538,459	3
Michigan:	7,823,194	4
Nebraska, North Dakota, South Dakota, Wyoming, Montana:	3,729,123	2
New Jersey:	6,066,782	3
New York:	16,782,304	9
North Carolina, South Carolina:	6,938,749	4
Ohio:	9,706,397	5
Pennsylvania:	11,319,366	6
Tennessee:	3,567,089	2
Texas:	9,579,677	6
Virginia and West Virginia:	5,827,370	3
Wisconsin:	3,951,777	2
	178,559,219*	100

**per 1960 Census

*Excluding District of Columbia

Opponents of the Supreme Court's reapportionment rulings warned that the decisions would lead to the reapportionment of the U.S. Senate, a possibility never remotely considered by the justices or by any of the litigants who argued in favor of reapportionment. This map suggests what the U.S. Senate would have looked like in the mid-1960s if it had been reapportioned according to population. (Whitaker & Baxter Campaigns, Inc., Papers, California State Archives)

"By The Way, What Are We In Line For?"

This cartoon, which Herblock drew in May 1967, caricatures the obliviousness of those who supported the call for a constitutional convention to overturn the Court's reapportionment decisions. (A 1967 Herblock Cartoon, © The Herb Block Foundation)

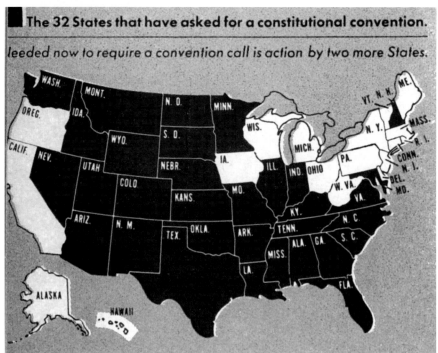

The 32 States that have asked for a constitutional convention.

Needed now to require a convention call is action by two more States.

As illustrated by this map, which appeared in *U.S. News & World Report*, by June 1967 thirty-two states had petitioned Congress to call a constitutional convention in order to modify or overturn the Court's reapportionment decisions. In April 1969, Iowa became the thirty-third state to call for such a convention, just one shy of the constitutional threshold. (*U.S. News & World Report*, June 1967. Copyright by *U.S. News & World Report*. Reproduced with permission) the Court would have to address whether or not states were free to apportion one chamber on factors other than population. "Logically it would seem a state can," he said, but for the time being, he tentatively argued that it was enough to strike down the existing apportionments. According to Douglas, his colleague was clear that "he would not sanction any device that put control of the legislature in any minority group."[22]

By his own recollection, Douglas agreed with Warren and Black. He had insisted in his concurring opinion in *Baker* v. *Carr* that apportionments must adhere closely to population, and he now said that "the question of a federal system for the states will have to be faced." But, like Warren and Black, he saw no need to reach the question in the cases now before the Court. Even so, he predicted that the Court would not be able to dodge the question—the "ultimate question," according to Cox—in perpetuity, especially given that it was "squarely presented" in a case from Colorado that awaited the Court's consideration. Douglas's comments led Harlan to write that he did not know how Douglas would "come out on that question."[23]

Tom Clark expressed general satisfaction with the positions staked out by Warren, Black, and Douglas, but he made it clear that he would support some form of a federal arrangement. He found it "difficult . . . to set up guidelines" and said that the Court "can't be too specific," maintaining that "our system is based on compromises, even in decisions of courts, certainly in legislatures." He felt that it "makes sense in our tradition" to allow one branch of a bicameral legislature to be based on geographical units where the other house was responsive to population. This did not mean, however, that he accepted the apportionments before the Court. Since neither house of the New York legislature was based on population, he voted to reverse the lower-court decision in that case.[24]

The only active justice to have dissented in *Baker* v. *Carr,* John Marshall Harlan continued to take a contrary view and rejected all claims that the Fourteenth Amendment had any bearing on apportionment. Even a "crazy quilt" apportionment, he insisted, did not run afoul of the Equal Protection Clause. Increasingly isolated from the rest of the Court, Harlan retreated to his chambers at the end of the conference and wrote to Felix Frankfurter on the occasion of the retired justice's eighty-first birthday. After conveying good wishes, Harlan confessed to a feeling of "despondency that I no longer have you as an active colleague—this being particularly accented today by the constitutional convention into which the Court convened itself at the Conference today in the first reapportionment cases!"[25]

Following Harlan, William Brennan agreed with the chief justice and Associate Justices Black, Douglas, and Clark that "the standard is equality" and that "population is the basis." Unlike Clark, though, Brennan questioned how much latitude the Court might allow in the second house of a bicameral legislature, even where the first branch was based squarely on population. Pointing to New Jersey, his home state, where approximately 19 percent of the populace lived in districts represented by a majority of the state senate, he argued that such an arrangement could not "stand the test of equal protection." Although he did not propose where the line should be drawn, he did echo a number of his colleagues when he concluded that the Court might not be able to "avoid" ruling on the question.[26]

Potter Stewart expressed his customary ambivalence over questions of apportionment. "He has not reached a settled conclusion," Douglas recorded. "He agrees in part with what everyone has said but not wholly with anyone." Although Stewart rejected Harlan's contention that reapportionment did not fall within the purview of the Fourteenth Amendment, he was far more circumspect than his colleagues about intervening. In fact, he worried that overturning the Virginia or New York plan would require the Court to void apportionments in almost every state in the nation, an unthinkable step. Stewart made clear that "guidelines should not be established." Believing firmly that "the value of our federal system is that each state is unique" and had the freedom to "experiment," he said that a republican form of government "does not necessarily mean equality. It never has meant that in practice." Instead, Stewart supported "any system that is rational," as Douglas put it. In Stewart's mind, the New York and Maryland schemes were completely reasonable, and though the original Alabama plan was "irrational and a crazy quilt," the state's revised plan was, he believed, based on rational considerations.[27]

Following Stewart, Byron White agreed that states should be free to organize their legislative chambers along different lines, but he balked at sanctioning minority rule. The New York, Alabama, and Maryland apportionments, he felt, clearly violated the Equal Protection Clause. "A state should have power to have one house one way and one another," Douglas had him as saying, but "when both houses are in the iron grip of minority interests then the people have no chance even to compromise. A majority can vote an unequal system but they can't violate the Constitution." Citing the case from his native Colorado that Douglas had brought up, and that would soon force the Court to confront the "ultimate question" head-on, White argued that voters in the state had been given a real choice and had elected to set up an "unequal system of two houses." Harlan concluded that White "probably would agree to bicameral differences." Clark interpreted White's remarks the same way but added that White was suspicious of the backers of the plan, who wanted, quite simply, "to control the legislature politically." Douglas provided a more direct assessment of White's remark. "A handful of cattlemen run Colorado," White said, according to Douglas, "and will continue to do so no matter what system is adopted."[28]

Arthur Goldberg, as the junior member of the Court, had the last word. Declaring not only that he accepted *Baker* v. *Carr* but also that he "heartily approves it," he had "no difficulty" declaring all four of the state legislative apportionments unconstitutional. To him, not one of them could be considered rational. The only justice to substantively address the still unfinished Virginia case, Goldberg dismissed the state's argument about military personnel as a "not very important," after-the-fact excuse designed to disguise the real purpose of the state's apportionment. He drew an explicit connection between malapportionment and civil rights, as the latter had lingered beneath the surface of the reapportionment debates and been absent from the briefs and oral arguments. Virginia's apportionment "gives Richmond more senators" than similarly sized counties in northern Virginia, he said, according to Douglas, because "the northern counties are 'enlightened' on civil rights and Virginia is bent on keeping them down."[29]

On Monday morning, November 18, in the final day of arguments in the Virginia case, Robert McIlwaine once again went after the solicitor general. After listing federal district and state court rulings that had upheld nine separate state reapportionment plans considered less representative than Virginia's, he condescendingly asked how the principles enunciated by Cox could be so clear if they went unrecognized in the lower courts. He claimed that Virginia had achieved a fair and reasonable balance in the apportionment of its legislature, and dared the Supreme Court to consider annulling apportionments in Virginia and the forty-two states ranked below it. Just before the assistant attorney general finished, Byron White asked, "Your proposition really is that the state may decide to vest legislative control in a minority portion of the population?" Attempting to draw a distinction between a "check" on the majority and the "tyranny of the minority," McIlwaine responded, "Yes, your honor, to keep the majority from controlling both the executive and the legislative branch."[30]

Next to the podium was Ed Campbell, who proceeded to shred his adversary's argument. He praised the "magnificent classic brief" filed by John McConnell in the Alabama case, calling on the Court to adopt the principles set forth in that "outstanding document." Paraphrasing McConnell, he maintained that minorities are protected by bills of rights and other such restrictions as the courts may impose, but that affirmative government must be government by the majority—and the people and the courts "must always choose tyranny of majority over tyranny of minority." Since "acres don't vote, it's only persons that vote," any legislative classification must be "rational" and cannot favor any group by race, color, residence, occupation, sex, or wealth. Campbell then ran through a litany of examples from across Virginia that demonstrated the discriminatory nature of the state's system of apportionment.[31]

Representing voters in Norfolk, Henry Howell took particular offense at the commonwealth's effort to justify malapportionment as a by-product of a rational decision not to count military personnel. He informed the Court that military employees do not live on ships in the harbor but rather are stationed in Virginia for three years at a time. Even when the sailors were at sea, their spouses remained in the commonwealth and paid taxes, enrolled their children in the public schools, and used state and county roads. Claiming that the "entire history and tradition" of the state has been to count military personnel, Howell told the Court that it "appalls me" to hear the assistant attorney general claim otherwise. Howell then delivered the coup de grâce: "Virginia is a crazy quilt when measured by legal criteria, but it is a skillfully, closely woven, and almost invisible net when measured by the intent of a political machine born a half-century ago to maintain power." Howell discussed the hold that Senator Harry Byrd and his organization had on the commonwealth since the 1920s and added that "there can be found rhyme or reason for this crazy quilt. Those communities that are politically manageable in Virginia were favored, and those who had shown some sort of independence were disfavored."[32]

Cox ignored the vitriol directed his way by Mays and McIlwaine and spent his twenty minutes addressing the merits of the Virginia case. He argued that the issue was not whether the legislature as a whole was representative but that clear discrimination existed against residents of Arlington and Fairfax Counties and the city of Norfolk. The fact that Virginia ranked higher than most states in its overall level of representation mattered little, for as long as "capricious or invidious discrimination" existed against residents of certain areas, the Court must find the commonwealth's plan of apportionment unconstitutional. After a brief rebuttal from the appellants, arguments in the Virginia case came to an end, just in time for the lunch recess.[33]

That night in his diary, David Mays wrote with reference to Ed Campbell, Henry Howell, and Archibald Cox that "none of the three was very good and each left wide openings." He had considered it "much more important to reply to Cox" in the few minutes of rebuttal left to his side, and had quoted to the justices portions of a speech that the solicitor general had delivered in early July in Seattle to a gathering of state attorneys general from across the United States. In the address, which Cox delivered just prior to receiving Bruce Terris's memorandum recommending that the Department of Justice embrace population equality in both houses of a bicameral legislature, the solicitor general expressed his own doubts about what he referred to as "the purist's view." "It would assert that well over half the States have been violating the Fourteenth Amendment continuously since its enactment," Cox had said. "It would require the total reconstitution of at least two-thirds of the State legislatures. It would leave no room for local autonomy in matters of representation. Perhaps I shall later find myself arguing for the principle but I must confess that at least today I wonder whether in the face of these considerations, the Fourteenth Amendment could fairly be held to lay down so rigid a rule."[34]

Mays believed that he had exposed Cox as a hypocrite for now taking a position that would, in effect, require the Court to invalidate more than two-thirds of the state legislatures, and credited himself in his diary with creating a "sensation" that was "bound to hurt, not only Cox's argument, but Cox himself in the eyes of the Court." He wrote that "the Justices were obviously amazed at the contrast with his arguments of last week and today." Nevertheless, Mays knew that defeat was likely. "I still don't see where I am going to get five votes," he wrote.[35]

The conclusion of the Virginia case marked the end, for the time being, of the Court's review of state legislative apportionments. The justices next turned their attention to the congressional reapportionment case from Georgia. Only twenty-six years old, Emmet Bondurant opened the oral argument for the appellants from Georgia's Fifth Congressional District. The youngest of the nineteen attorneys to appear before the Supreme Court in the five reapportionment cases argued in November 1963, Bondurant had played no part in the district court proceedings, but he was brought on board to spearhead the appeal to the Supreme Court. Bondurant, a native of Athens, Georgia, earned undergraduate and law degrees from the University of Georgia, spent a year clerking on the Fourth Circuit Court of Appeals, and then pursued a master's degree in law at Harvard, where a class in constitutional law, taught by Paul Freund, was especially influential in his intellectual and professional development.[36]

The timing of Bondurant's graduate work meant that he was absent from Georgia during the 1961–1962 school year, the critical period during which the *Baker* decision came down and a wave of lawsuits was filed in response. From his temporary home in Massachusetts, Bondurant kept close tabs on his native state and wrote an amicus brief in *Gray v. Sanders* in which he entreated the Court to recognize one man, one vote as the only standard compatible with the Fourteenth Amendment. By the time Bondurant returned to Atlanta, Morris Abram was in firm control of the challenge to Georgia's county-unit system, after having won in the district court. The attorneys who had filed a challenge to the malapportionment of Georgia's congressional districts, on the other hand, had failed to convince the three-judge district court of the merits of their cause. Lacking expertise on the subject, they asked Bondurant, who had only recently been hired by an Atlanta firm, to join their team.[37]

In November 1963, in his appearance before the Supreme Court, Bondurant drew a sharp distinction for the justices between his case and the state legislative cases. He agreed that the malapportionment of Georgia's Fifth District violated the Equal Protection Clause of the Fourteenth Amendment but emphasized that in his case, the Equal Protection Clause "merely reinforced" Article I, Section 2 of the Constitution and its mandate that the House of Representatives be chosen "by the people." Furthermore, the Constitution clearly intended that members of the House of Representatives be elected by "the people of the state" and "not the 'city people,' not the 'country people,' not those in power, not those not in power." The young attorney encouraged the justices to see that Article I, Section 2 allows "no permissible deviation" from population.[38]

In response to an exchange that had taken place during one of the state cases the previous week, Bondurant insisted that "the principle of democratic government does not entitle you to prevail, but only to have an equal opportunity to elect a representative. It's the equal participation which it secures, and not the right to prevail." In order to protect that right to equal participation, Bondurant asked the Court to find Georgia's congressional reapportionment scheme unconstitutional and to enjoin the state from holding additional elections on the basis of the existing system. He then urged the Court to adopt a "uniform federal standard which will govern all states equally." The next day, the *Washington Post* commended Bondurant for his performance.[39]

When Bondurant finished, Bruce Terris, not Archibald Cox, approached the podium to present the position of the federal government. A seasoned veteran compared to Bondurant, Terris had argued before the Court at least a half dozen times previously. From the outset, he adhered closely to the federal government's amicus brief, as Cox had no doubt instructed him to do, and that meant asking the Court not to go any further than necessary. Agreeing with Bondurant that the power of the federal courts to intervene in congressional malapportionment cases was even "more clear" than in state legislative cases, Terris suggested that the Court decide only the issues of jurisdiction and justiciability and not consider standards. Whether or not Georgia's system of congressional apportionment actually violated Article I, Section 2 should be left to the district court and a trial on the merits, he said. In effect, the federal government advocated an incremental approach, similar to its position when first confronted with legislative malapportionment in *Baker* v. *Carr*.[40]

Terris was not pleased to be voicing this argument. Bondurant had complained privately to a friend in September that he was "quite disappointed" with the government's narrow brief and did not understand how the Court could avoid the issue of standards. Several of the justices apparently agreed and repeatedly criticized Terris for the questionable logic behind avoiding a decision on the merits. Given the constraints imposed by the government's brief, the assistant to the solicitor general had little choice but to maintain his composure and reiterate, "We think only that the substantive standards need not be decided here for essentially the same reasons that they were not required to be decided in *Baker* v. *Carr*." Even John Marshall Harlan believed by this point that the Court should go ahead and decide the issue of standards. "We're in it as much as we are," Harlan declared, "and I cannot see any reason for not deciding this aspect of the matter now."[41]

The narrowness of the federal government's position prompted Paul Rodgers, the assistant attorney general of Georgia, to quip during his argument before the Court, "Frankly, I'm somewhat surprised that the Solicitor General is not our *amicus* instead of theirs." He tried to blur substantive differences between the state of Georgia's position and that taken by the federal government, conceding the jurisdiction and justiciability of the federal courts and adopting Terris's position that the question of standards "should be reserved for future consideration." But unlike the federal government, which asked the Supreme Court to remand the case to the district court for a trial on the merits, Rodgers argued that the complaint should be dismissed because adequate state remedies already existed. Pointing to the abolition of the county-unit system (a direct result of *Gray* v. *Sanders*) and the recent reapportionment of the state senate on a strict population basis (a by-product of *Baker* v. *Carr*), Rodgers claimed that Georgia had met its constitutional obligations and taken steps recently to ensure that adequate power resided in the hands of a majority of the state's voters. Unless and until the Supreme Court ruled in the legislative reapportionment cases that both houses of a bicameral legislature must be based on per capita equality, Rodgers reasoned, the Georgia legislature was constitutionally valid and should be given a chance to redraw the state's congressional districts without judicial interference.[42]

After addressing the Court for nearly an hour on Monday afternoon, Rodgers returned to the podium for an additional thirty minutes on Tuesday morning, November 19. The sense of fatigue felt by all parties was evident. The justices asked few questions as Rodgers repeated the points he had raised the day before, though now he dared the Supreme Court to adopt a uniform standard, as Bondurant had requested. Such a ruling, Rodgers predicted, would "create a traumatic shock upon Congress unparalleled in history." Frank Cash, who initially filed Georgia's congressional reapportionment lawsuit before turning the case over to Bondurant, followed Rodgers for a brief rebuttal. Malapportionment, he stated, did constitute a national problem. Unlike the state of Georgia, Cash asked the Court to recognize that the magnitude of the problem required "an immediate, uniform, and final solution, which only this Court is capable of granting."[43]

Three days later, at precisely ten o'clock in the morning, Earl Warren and the brethren again gathered for their regularly scheduled conference to discuss the case. With the exception of Harlan, who continued to believe that the Georgia case presented "no constitutionally protected right," the entire Court agreed to reverse the decision of the district court, which had leaned on *Colegrove* v. *Green*.[44]

Yet the justices were less certain about how far, and how fast, to go. Warren and Tom Clark felt the district court should allow the legislature no longer than one year to reapportion, with the chief justice specifying that the district court should fashion a remedy of its own if the legislature did not act in time for the 1964 elections. Potter Stewart, by contrast, recommended that the Court "go slow and not act too fast." Conceding, according to William O. Douglas, that "if Congress acted to set up this lopsided districting, that act would be unconstitutional," Stewart implored his colleagues, "We are hitting Congress where it lives. Their jobs are involved. . . . I would plead not for abstention, but for delay." The last to speak, Arthur Goldberg agreed that "this is biting off a big chew" but concluded that "time should be a factor."[45]

Interestingly, only Warren and William Brennan had directly addressed the issue of standards during the conference. Warren had asserted that "the Constitution compels the apportionment of Congress by population. This one is grossly out of proportion." For his part, Brennan argued that "there must be substantial equality. This one is way out of line." But beyond those two observations, the justices initially appeared content to allow the district court to determine the standards that would guide congressional reapportionment.[46]

At approximately one thirty in the afternoon, just as the justices wrapped up their discussion, an unexpected knock at the door broke the solitude of the conference. Interruptions were rare, and this one, coming so soon after a break for lunch, seemed even more unusual than others. The room fell silent; Goldberg answered the door. Alvin Wright, a Court staffer tasked with guarding the entrance to the conference room, handed Goldberg a note that had been sent by Margaret McHugh, the chief justice's executive secretary. Without reading the note's contents, Goldberg walked across the room and handed it to the chief. Nothing in his three decades of public service—as a district attorney, state attorney general, governor, or chief justice—had prepared Earl Warren for what came next. Fighting back tears, the chief justice relayed stunning news to his colleagues: the president had been shot in Dallas.[47]

By all accounts, the death of John F. Kennedy hit Warren hard. Although a lifelong Republican, he had come to greatly admire the young president. "It was like losing one of my own sons," he confided years later. "He was just a little older than my oldest boy." On the evening of Wednesday, November 20, less than forty-eight hours earlier, the president and Mrs. Kennedy had hosted an annual reception for the justices and their wives at the White House. In what turned out to be his last personal conversation with the president, Warren and several of his colleagues had advised him, in jest, to be careful during his upcoming trip to Texas. Now, the conference having broken up, Warren sat in his office, following the breaking news on the radio and struggling with the magnitude of the loss.[48]

After the death of the president was confirmed and Lyndon Johnson was sworn in as the thirty-sixth president, official Washington joined most of the nation in a long weekend of mourning. On Saturday evening, Warren answered his telephone to find Jacqueline Kennedy on the other end; she was calling to ask the chief justice, who in this moment was "almost speechless," to deliver a eulogy the next day, when her husband's body would lie in state in the Capitol Rotunda. With only a few hours to prepare, Warren drafted deeply personal and uncharacteristically critical remarks in which he blamed the "forces of hatred and malevolence . . . eating their way into the bloodstream of American life." The chief justice, who had been a target of right-wing political threats for many years, declared, "If we really love this country; if we truly love justice and mercy; if we fervently want to make this Nation better for those who are to follow us, we can at least abjure the hatred that consumes people, the false accusations that divide us and the bitterness that begets violence." He asked: Is it "too much to hope that the martyrdom of our beloved President might even soften the hearts of those who would themselves recoil from assassination, but who do not shrink from spreading the venom which kindles thoughts of it in others?" The following day, Warren and his wife, Nina, took their places in the official funeral procession as John F. Kennedy was buried in Arlington National Cemetery.[49]

11 ||| LEGISLATORS REPRESENT PEOPLE, NOT TREES OR ACRES

L aw clerks occupy a unique place in the American legal system. After earning degrees from the nation's finest law schools, they spend a year—as chronicled by Bob Woodward and Scott Armstrong at a time when clerkships remained primarily the domain of young men—serving as "confidential assistants, ghost writers, extra sons, and intimates" to the nation's most important jurists. Earl Warren's clerks revered the chief, and no wonder. He trusted them with significant responsibilities. Warren was not thought to be "an abstract thinker" or a "gifted scholar," but a jurist who endeavored to achieve a fair and just solution in every case, rather than adhering to an identifiable judicial philosophy. Once he decided the result he favored in a case, he granted his clerks great latitude as they delved into the legal research and drafted opinions.[1]

Among Warren's many talented clerks, few had as remarkable an experience as Frank Beytagh. Several years older than his fellow clerks—Beytagh spent nearly four years on active duty in the navy prior to law school—the native of Savannah, Georgia, had the added privilege of serving as Warren's head clerk, a distinction that included a slightly higher salary and additional administrative responsibilities.[2]

The process by which clerks are assigned to cases varies from chamber to chamber, but there was never much doubt that Beytagh would end up working on the reapportionment cases. As editor in chief of the *Michigan Law Review*, he had devoted an issue to a symposium on *Baker* v. *Carr* and maintained a deep interest in the subject. By the time he went to work for Warren in the summer of 1963, the Court had placed the five reapportionment cases on the November calendar. Beytagh prepared lengthy bench memoranda in advance of the oral arguments and became intimately familiar with the nuances of each case. As much as if not more than any other clerk, he eagerly awaited the results of the Court's deliberations on November 22.[3]

But then came reports from Dallas, and all thoughts of the conference evaporated. Like most of the clerks and other Court personnel, Beytagh had learned of the shooting before his boss. In fact, it was Beytagh who had encouraged the chief's executive assistant, Margaret McHugh, to interrupt the conference with the news. When Warren received word later that day that Air Force One was heading back to Washington with the body of the slain president, his widow, and his successor, he decided to meet the plane. But Warren's regular driver was stuck in traffic in suburban Maryland with his wife, so Warren drafted Beytagh to drive him to Andrews Air Force Base. Navigating the streets of Washington on that solemn afternoon, Beytagh did not utter a word as the chief shared his grief.[4]

Discussing the events with precision nearly a half century later, Beytagh remembered that it was not until Tuesday, November 26, four days after the president's assassination, that Warren had a chance to tell his law clerks what had transpired during the conference on November 22. Only moments before learning that the president had been shot, Warren had assigned the Georgia congressional case to Hugo Black but kept the legislative cases from New York, Alabama, Maryland, and Virginia for himself. Beytagh now had the task—the opportunity—of drafting the chief's opinion. But what exactly had Warren and the majority decided?[5]

Neither Warren nor anyone else in the majority had reached a definitive conclusion on the issue of standards. As governor of California, Warren had wholeheartedly supported a system that based the apportionment of the lower house, but not the state senate, on population. Given his boss's own indeterminate views, Beytagh initially suggested a series of rulings that stopped well short of a one person, one vote standard, and drafted an eight-page summary of the New York, Virginia, Alabama, and Maryland cases, recommending that the Court strike down reapportionments in the latter two.[6]

When it came to the New York and Virginia cases, Beytagh believed that "both of these states' apportionment schemes, considered as a whole, make the legislatures reasonably responsive to the popular will." Citing numerous other cases pending on the Court's docket, he worried that the Court could not strike down these reapportionments without "effectively holding that all but seven or so of the 50 states are legislatively malapportioned," a proposition that initially alarmed him. "I just don't think that is, or should be, so," he wrote.[7] Beytagh was not alone among the clerks in this view. Notably, Stephen Barnett, a clerk to William Brennan, took a similar stance in a 350-page memorandum devoted solely to the issue of standards that he prepared in advance of the oral arguments. After advising Brennan to "reject the absolutist insistence upon strict population equality in both houses," he did concede that "the question remains whether there are any limits on the extent to which the second house may deviate from population equality in pursuance of such a countervailing policy." As he succinctly summarized, "This is the great 'federal plan' controversy."[8]

After taking off Thanksgiving, Beytagh returned to work on Friday, November 29. That afternoon, as the clerk discussed the reapportionment cases and other Court business with his boss, Warren received a call from the White House. He had already informed Beytagh that Nicholas Katzenbach and Archibald Cox had approached him earlier in the afternoon and asked him to chair a presidential commission on the assassination. He had politely refused them in the firm belief that the constitutional separation of powers dictated that judges should abstain from such assignments. But Lyndon Johnson summoned Warren to the White House and made a successful appeal to the chief's patriotism and sense of duty. When Warren returned to the Court that evening, Beytagh noticed that he "looked almost ashen."[9]

Warren quickly assumed his new duties despite his reservations and fell into a rigorous schedule that dominated his life, and that of his staff, for the next ten months. In order to facilitate his dual responsibilities, the President's Commission on the Assassination of President Kennedy, as it was formally known, set up shop across the street from the Supreme Court. Walking back and forth between the two offices, Warren attended oral arguments and most conferences but came to rely on his clerks and colleagues more than ever. During the first few weeks of the commission's existence, prior to the hiring of an executive director and staff, Beytagh and his fellow clerks did double duty. On one memorable day, Beytagh escorted Lee Harvey Oswald's rifle from the commission's office to the Department of Justice.[10]

Even with this workload—prodigious for an able-bodied young man, astonishing for a man in his seventies—Warren never considered giving up the reapportionment cases. He understood their importance to American democracy and was determined to shape the Court's final opinion. The chief justice huddled at the Court with Beytagh in the early mornings, late afternoons, or on Saturdays, and they spoke by phone in the evenings; the rest of his time was devoted to the commission. Throughout the process, Warren provided guidance but largely left his head clerk to flesh out his ideas and turn those ideas into an opinion. Beytagh spent most of his time during the next six months on the reapportionment opinions.[11]

On December 9, before Beytagh had begun to write, the justices heard oral arguments in yet another legislative reapportionment case, this one from Delaware. Launched by Republicans in Wilmington, the state's lone metropolitan center, the challenge to Delaware's apportionment had little bearing on the Court's ultimate disposition of the issues. In fact, Beytagh considered Delaware's apportionment scheme "so patently bad" that he did not understand why the case had been set for argument at all. The federal government agreed, saying in its brief that the Delaware case was "by far the easiest of the reapportionment cases now before the Court on the merits." The justices reached the same conclusion. Coming so soon after the exhaustive arguments of the previous month, the Delaware case elicited little discussion in conference. Referring to it as a "clear case," Warren led eight members of the Court who voted to strike down Delaware's system; John Marshall Harlan provided the lone dissenting voice.[12]

On the same day that the Court sat through three hours of arguments in the Delaware case, the justices noted probable jurisdiction in another apportionment case, this one from Colorado. Arguments in *Lucas* v. *Forty-Fourth General Assembly of Colorado*, however, would not take place until the end of March. In the meantime, Beytagh began the process of drafting an opinion in the other cases. When the Supreme Court hears arguments in multiple cases that address related issues, the justices typically select one case through which to announce the Court's central ruling, and then issue separate, shorter opinions applying their findings to the specific facts of each case. During conference, Brennan had suggested *Reynolds* v. *Sims* as the lead case. Beytagh concurred. Among the state cases, the challenge to Alabama's apportionment presented the issues in the most straightforward manner; initially apportioned primarily on the basis of population, the Alabama legislature had simply refused, for sixty years, to reconstitute itself in a manner that reflected subsequent demographic shifts. After a brief discussion with his head clerk—Warren wanted to make sure that the Court would not appear to have "a vendetta against the Southern states"—the chief accepted Beytagh's recommendation.[13]

In early January 1964, the Court formally selected a date in late March for arguments in *Lucas* v. *Colorado*. At that point, Beytagh wrote to Warren that he had become "increasingly concerned about the problem of uncertainty which might result . . . if this Court announces its decisions in the five argued cases prior to announcing its decision in the Colorado case." Earl Warren had favored a quick resolution to each case—New York, Alabama, Maryland, and Virginia argued in November, and Delaware argued in December—so that any rulings would cause minimal disruption to primaries and general elections in the fall. But Beytagh imagined a scenario in which the Court took the advice of the solicitor general and found the apportionments of those five states unconstitutional without establishing a clear population standard in both houses. State legislatures and lower courts would then begin reapportioning under the assumption that only one branch of a bicameral legislature must be based on population equality. If the Court then instituted a more stringent standard in both houses several months later in the Colorado case, confusion would reign. So Beytagh suggested that Warren consider "withholding announcement of the decisions in the five cases argued until after the Colorado case has been argued and decided." His boss readily agreed.[14]

While Frank Beytagh toiled to give shape to the chief's opinion, Hugo Black and his clerks worked on an opinion for the congressional reapportionment case from Georgia. Circulating a first draft to the conference in mid-January, Black recommended that the Supreme Court reverse the decision of the lower court and remand the case for a consideration on the merits. Within a fortnight, he learned of Warren's decision to hold his opinion in the state reapportionment challenges until after arguments in the Colorado case. But since that case—and the other state reapportionment cases—had no direct legal bearing on the Georgia congressional case, Black exhorted his brethren to hand down a decision "without waiting for the others."[15]

The Court complied. On February 17, 1964, the Supreme Court announced its decision in *Wesberry* v. *Sanders*. Writing for a six-person majority, Black decisively rejected *Colegrove* v. *Green* and held that congressional reapportionment cases were, indeed, justiciable. Choosing not to address the secondary claim of the appellants that Georgia's system of congressional apportionment violated the Fourteenth Amendment, the majority instead based its ruling on Article I, Section 2. "Construed in its historical context," Black wrote, "the command of Art. I, § 2, that Representatives be chosen 'by the People of the several states' means that as nearly as is practicable one man's vote in a congressional election is to be worth as much as another's." Referencing the Court's decision the previous year in the Georgia county-unit case that votes could not be weighted in a statewide election, the majority concluded that the framers of the Constitution did not intend "to permit the same vote-diluting discrimination to be accomplished through the device of districts containing widely varied numbers of inhabitants. To say that a vote is worth more in one district than in another would not only run counter to our fundamental ideas of democratic government, it would cast aside the principle of a House of Representatives elected 'by the People.' "[16]

In an impassioned dissent, John Marshall Harlan excoriated the majority. "I had not expected to witness the day," he began, "when the Supreme Court of the United States would render a decision which casts grave doubt on the constitutionality of the composition of the House of Representatives. It is not an exaggeration to say that such is the effect of today's decision." In a two-sentence concurrence to Harlan's dissent, Stewart agreed, but he added one critical qualification in rejecting Harlan's contention that the issue was not justiciable. Concurring in part and dissenting in part, Clark objected to the majority's reliance on Article I, Section 2, and argued that Harlan had "clearly demonstrated" that a proper reading of the historical background of that section of the Constitution could not possibly be read to require "'one person, one vote' in congressional elections." On the other hand, Clark agreed with the majority's determination that "congressional districting is subject to judicial scrutiny" and that, therefore, the district court had erred in dismissing the case. Given his conclusion that Article I, Section 2, did not require what the majority claimed, Clark expressed his belief that the trial court must "examine" Georgia's congressional districts "against the requirements of the Equal Protection Clause of the Fourteenth Amendment."[17]

Not surprising, Emmet Bondurant was pleased with the decision in *Wesberry*. He wrote to Fourth Circuit Court of Appeals judge Clement Haynsworth, for whom he had clerked, that the majority "seems to have established an even higher standard" than he and his cocounsel had initially called for. In view of the Georgia legislature's most recent plan, which included districts that ranged from 330,000 to 455,000 people, Bondurant praised the plan devised by a seventh-grade civics class in which the most populous of Georgia's ten congressional districts contained only 26,000 more residents than the least populous. If seventh graders could draw up such a plan, Bondurant told Haynsworth, it was "difficult to envision a case in which it will be impractical to achieve close numerical equality in drafting congressional districts." To Bondurant, "The implications of the standard set forth by the Court [in *Wesberry*] are indeed broad."[18]

Simultaneous with the Court's discussions of *Wesberry* v. *Sanders*, a potentially divisive debate was taking place within the Department of Justice about the federal government's position in the last of the reapportionment cases to come before the Supreme Court during the October 1963 term. Among the cases decided on June 15, 1964, *Reynolds* v. *Sims* is most frequently mentioned in history books and law school lectures, but the decision rendered by the Court in *Lucas* v. *Forty-Fourth General Assembly of Colorado* was the most influential. Unlike the legislative reapportionment cases argued in November and December 1963, *Lucas* v. *Colorado* forced all involved—litigants on both sides of the issue, key officials in the Johnson administration, Supreme Court justices, the press, the public, and politicians from both parties—to confront what Archibald Cox had referred to as the "ultimate question": Does the Equal Protection Clause require population equality in the apportionment of districts in both houses of a bicameral legislature?

Reapportionment had been a contentious topic in Colorado for decades. Both houses of the legislature were ostensibly based on population, but they in fact had become increasingly malapportioned as a result of a scheme known as the "differential ratio of population." When first established in 1881, the scheme granted one seat in the state house for the first 1,000 persons in a district, plus one more representative for each additional 5,000 persons. In the state senate, the first 5,000 persons in a district elected one representative, with an extra seat for each additional 9,000 persons. In order to maintain a lower house of sixty-five members and a senate of thirty-five representatives, both constitutional requirements, the legislature adjusted the ratios as the population of the state increased. By 1961, 32 percent of the population had the capacity to control the lower house, where districts ranged from 7,867 to 63,760 people, while just under 30 percent of the populace resided in districts that elected a majority of senators, whose voting populations ranged from 17,481 to 127,520. As the Colorado League of Women Voters put it, the state's scheme served "to maintain the status quo in the face of increased population."[19]

As in many other states, the nonpartisan LWV took the lead in bringing malapportionment to the attention of the citizens of Colorado. The league, not satisfied with the findings of a study commission appointed by the governor in the late 1950s, intensified its efforts after the 1960 census confirmed the extent of the problem. Aware that any chance of success "required an enlightened and aroused public," the Colorado LWV commissioned studies, distributed pamphlets, and launched a radio and television campaign. As the legislature prepared to meet in January 1962, the LWV announced its support for the abolition of the differential ratio system. But in an effort to assuage the concerns of "geographic and economic interests" in the sparsely settled regions of the state west of the Rocky Mountains, it agreed to accept deviations from straight population of as much as 33⅓ percent above or below the average. Despite this significant concession, the LWV found itself unable to support a single one of the nine bills and three constitutional amendments proposed by lawmakers during the session that concerned reapportionment.[20]

Frustrated, the Colorado LWV began to contemplate the possibility of putting reapportionment before the voters in the form of a ballot initiative. But before committing itself, the league joined talks with representatives from a diverse set of interest groups that had traditionally not agreed on reapportionment, including the state Chamber of Commerce, the Cattlemen's Association, the Farm Bureau, the state Labor Council (an affiliate of the AFL-CIO), and the Education Association. Meeting in February and early March 1962, the group attempted to find common ground, but within three weeks the LWV concluded that "any further continuation of the meetings could only lead to a perpetual stall." In collaboration with the Colorado Labor Council and the Colorado Education Association, it soon formed the Voters' Organization to Effect Reapportionment (VOTER) and announced plans to put a ballot initiative before the electorate in November. On March 20, the Colorado Chamber of Commerce, the Colorado Farm Bureau, and the Colorado Cattlemen's Association responded with the establishment of Federal Plan for Apportionment, Inc., and pledged to put a competing measure before the voters.[21]

A week after the formation of Federal Plan for Apportionment, Inc., residents of metropolitan Denver filed suit in federal district court, alleging that Colorado's system of apportionment violated the Equal Protection Clause of the Fourteenth Amendment. Four months later, attorneys representing a second set of metropolitan voters refined the challenge. As the consolidated lawsuits awaited a trial on the merits, backers of the federal plan qualified Amendment No. 7, dubbed the "Colorado plan" by its supporters, for the November ballot. The amendment proposed to establish a lower house with districts "nearly equal in population as may be." It not only provided for a senate based on area but also froze senate districts into place. Meanwhile, the Colorado LWV and its allies in VOTER procured the requisite number of signatures to place on the ballot an alternative measure, Amendment No. 8, that would have required the apportionment of the house and senate on a population basis. In August, a three-judge court agreed with the plaintiffs that Colorado's existing system of apportionment constituted "invidious discrimination" and stated that "the defendants had shown no rational basis for the disparities." But rather than ordering the legislature to reapportion, the district court postponed a final ruling until after the election and the votes on the competing amendments.[22]

The people behind VOTER understood that they faced an uphill task. Led by former governor and U.S. senator Edwin C. Johnson, proponents of the Colorado plan outspent their adversaries by more than ten to one. They hired professional campaign managers, placed full-page advertisements in major newspapers, and saturated the airwaves. Business groups and other backers of Amendment No. 7 stoked fears and appealed to prejudices as they warned that the labor unions and their permissive, liberal allies in the big city threatened to dominate the rest of the state. Although the state Republican Party never officially endorsed Amendment No. 7, individual candidates and precinct workers openly campaigned on its behalf.[23]

In the November election, Amendment No. 7 received the support of more than two-thirds of Colorado's electorate. Voters in every county rejected the alternative initiative supported by VOTER. What accounts for the landslide? For one, supporters of the VOTER-backed initiative struggled to convince many metropolitan residents of the need for reapportionment, especially during an election campaign in which Republican candidates for the state legislature and for Congress, most of whom opposed reapportionment, ran exceedingly well in Denver and other urban precincts. But without a doubt, metropolitan voters in Colorado in 1962, just as in California in 1948 and in Illinois in 1954, elected to disenfranchise themselves rather than risk empowering labor unions, big-city politicians, and other seemingly unsavory elements lurking in the cities. Looking to the model of the U.S. Congress, these voters believed minority control of one branch of the legislature to be a reasonable arrangement.[24]

With the passage of Amendment No. 7, the debate over Colorado's system of apportionment returned to the federal district court. In July 1963, a divided three-judge panel rejected the claims of the plaintiffs, upholding the constitutionality of the Colorado plan on the grounds that the unmistakable will of the people had been expressed at the polls the previous November. Unlike in so many other states, including Alabama, reapportionment in Colorado did not reflect decades of legislative inaction. Unlike any other legislative reapportionment plan that reached the Supreme Court, *Lucas* v. *Colorado* presented the "ultimate question" in clear, nearly unavoidable terms.[25]

As soon as the Supreme Court noted probable jurisdiction in *Lucas* v. *Colorado* on December 9, 1963, Denver attorney Stephen H. Hart wrote to Archibald Cox and asked for a meeting to discuss the government's position. A leading figure in Denver's legal community, Hart had intervened in the Colorado litigation on behalf of prominent backers of Amendment No. 7; although the state attorney general and his staff were ostensibly responsible for the defense of Colorado's reapportionment scheme, Hart assumed actual control of the case once it headed to the Supreme Court. Cox replied that he was "not sufficiently familiar with the Colorado case to know how it measures up" with the other cases but indicated that he would welcome the opportunity to meet with Hart in the New Year.[26]

Prior to filing any briefs, Hart and his team tried time and again to convince the solicitor general of the merits of their position. Nearly a half century later, an associate in Hart's firm assigned to the case remembered the dramatic weight loss he suffered as a result of long and intense hours of preparation. Hart and the other defenders of the Colorado plan tied their position to the history of apportionment in Colorado and the overwhelming support for Amendment No. 7, arguing that the state's unique geography and varied economy necessitated some form of a federal system. Without the Colorado plan, they claimed that residents of the eastern slope would dominate the other regions of the state both politically and economically.[27]

In late January, Hart met with Cox in the solicitor general's office. Cox refused to commit himself one way or the other but promised to keep an open mind. Within two weeks of Hart's visit, discussions within the Department of Justice intensified as Cox received separate memoranda from Burke Marshall and Bruce Terris. Aware that Cox had serious misgivings about a strict standard in the reapportionment cases, Marshall attempted to alleviate Cox's concerns by presenting four options.[28]

First, the government could argue that the trial court had clearly erred in recognizing the rights of certain economic interests and in allowing the state to dilute the weight of metropolitan voters. "We have already said in other briefs," Marshall wrote, "that the 'interests' of bankers, farmers, Negroes, or Protestants cannot be considered." Therefore, he reasoned, economic interests such as water, mining, and agriculture could not receive special treatment, either. Marshall believed that this option would provide the Supreme Court with a rationale to skirt the issue of standards, at least for the time being. Second, the federal government could take the position that even if the trial court had not erred in recognizing such interests, the malapportionment of the state senate under Amendment No. 7 remained too extreme "to satisfy equal protection standards." Third, the federal government could argue that population equality in both houses of a bicameral legislature was required by the Constitution. Finally, the Johnson administration could decide that the Colorado plan was, in fact, constitutional. Such an argument would be founded on the fact that Amendment No. 7 had been "adopted by a majority of the people" and the notion that "the departures from equality are not too extreme when the other house is apportioned on a per capita basis." Still, Marshall doubted that the courts would view overwhelming popular support as determinative. "It would seem," he explained, "that whether or not a man's neighbors vote to settle for less than per capita representation has little bearing upon the rights involved."[29]

Not surprising, given the position he took in the other apportionment cases, Bruce Terris recommended that the federal government support the broadest possible standard: "that all Americans were entitled to equal representation in their state legislatures." Though the Colorado plan was far more equitable than reapportionment schemes in most other states, Terris argued that it continued "to give a veto to a quite small minority of the people." Like Marshall, Terris regarded the November 1962 referendum as effectively "irrelevant."[30]

The day after receiving Terris's memorandum, Cox presented Robert Kennedy with a strikingly different recommendation. Describing the Colorado plan as "much the fairest State apportionment to be challenged in the Supreme Court," Cox unequivocally advocated not supporting the plaintiffs. To him, the Colorado plan not only satisfied the various tests that the federal government had developed to condemn the New York, Alabama, Maryland, Virginia, and Delaware schemes, but "it is

204 ||| ON DEMOCRACY'S DOORSTEP

unquestionably one of the half dozen most equitable apportionments in the entire United States." Rejecting the first two options outlined by Marshall, Cox argued that "the only honest option for attacking the Colorado Apportionment is that the Equal Protection Clause of the Fourteenth Amendment requires every State to apportion both houses of its legislature strictly *per capita*." Ironically, given the position that Cox would eventually argue before the Supreme Court, he added, "To say that there is some room for variation but that the Colorado apportionment is to be condemned as excessive is, in my judgment, to be confused by arithmetic."[31]

For Cox, the federal government coming out in favor of population equality in both houses of a bicameral legislature was simply not an option in 1964. "Such a position," he wrote to Kennedy, "would be at variance with our entire constitutional history" and "would be contrary to the basic philosophy that ours is a federal system of government in which the people of the States have a large measure of local self-government." Optimistic that the country would support a gradual process of "reasonable" court-ordered reapportionment, Cox worried that an "absolutist position" could bring about "a severe constitutional crisis." He said, no doubt thinking about southern resistance to racial integration, that "some states might be encouraged to defy the Court" and asked Kennedy, "Are we then to use troops to remake the State legislature, or will we ignore the defiance because the country supports it?"[32]

Nevertheless, Cox did not, in fact, think the Colorado plan was constitutional. "For the Supreme Court to hold that the Colorado apportionment is constitutional," he explained, "would have the unfortunate consequence of tending to freeze a situation that ought to be kept fluid." Emphatic in his belief that "reading the principle 'one man, one vote' into the Equal Protection Clause" constituted a "major blunder *today*," Cox looked forward to a point in the future when the nation would be ready to accept such an expansive view of the Fourteenth Amendment. He thought that might require twenty or thirty years. In order not to foreclose the possibility of eventual success, he recommended that the federal government file an amicus brief asking the Supreme Court to dismiss *Lucas* v. *Colorado* for want of equity, a technical maneuver that would have allowed the Supreme Court to let the district court decision stand without actually ruling on the substantive issue of standards.[33]

Cox's recommendation did not arise out of a strict devotion to the judicial philosophy of Felix Frankfurter, as some critics have alleged; rather, it was an attempt to define to his own satisfaction the appropriate role for the federal courts. "A strong liberal in objectives," as Arthur Schlesinger Jr. wrote of the solicitor general, "he was conservative about the role courts should play in attaining them." Yet no matter how cautious an approach he took, Cox never argued that the federal courts should not join the debate. He understood the severity of malapportionment and did not hesitate to enter the political thicket. In later years, Cox granted that his "gloomy predictions" and dire warnings about a constitutional crisis had "proved unwarranted." But he was not being entirely unreasonable when he dug in his heels in February 1964. "Another substantial risk," he predicted, this time more prophetically, "would be a constitutional amendment denying the Court jurisdiction to pass upon the constitutionality of any legislative apportionment." Within six months, the House of Representatives would pass precisely such an amendment.[34]

Cox's memo set off a tense seven days within the Department of Justice. Robert Kennedy chafed at the solicitor general's recommendation and, as the deadline approached for the administration to file its amicus brief, solicited the input of senior officials and trusted advisers in the DOJ and in the White House, including Ted Sorensen, who had served as his brother's primary speechwriter, Deputy Attorney General Nicholas Katzenbach, and John W. Douglas, the assistant attorney general in charge of the Civil Division. Sorensen drafted a one-page memorandum in which he argued that the federal government must not ask the Supreme Court to dismiss the suit, as Cox recommended, lest such a position be misinterpreted as signaling approval of the district court's ruling. But he also thought that the time had not yet arrived "for the Administration to press for 'one man, one vote' in both houses of every state legislature," and so he favored remanding the case to the district court for reconsideration, the first option raised by Marshall and a position rejected by Cox.[35]

After discussing Cox's objections privately with Terris and Marshall, Katzenbach wrote to Kennedy that "the government need not decide between supporting the State in this case or arguing for 'one man, one vote.'" In doing so, he threw his weight behind the second option proposed by Marshall, also dismissed previously by Cox. Katzenbach acknowledged that the Colorado plan apportioned the lower house of the state legislature on a population basis, but he argued that it still empowered an unconstitutional minority in the apportionment of the state senate.[36] In his memo, Douglas rejected Katzenbach's recommendation as based on a distinction without meaning and characterized it as a disguised call for "one man, one vote." Given the overall makeup of the Colorado legislature, Douglas, like Cox, considered it disingenuous to accept a standard short of population equality but then reject the Colorado plan as excessive. He wholeheartedly agreed that the administration "should take a position which will keep pressure on for fair apportionment," but he, too, opposed "advancing the 'one man, one vote' theory at this time." Like Sorensen, Douglas was for remanding the case.[37]

These memos did not influence the personal views of the attorney general, but they did contribute to the final resolution of the dispute within the DOJ. Kennedy already knew precisely where everyone stood. He had discussed the Colorado case with his principal lieutenants, especially Marshall and Katzenbach, and had held two or three informal conversations with the solicitor general. For his part, Kennedy believed it was imperative not to take a position adverse to the plaintiffs. He was willing to postpone active support of one person, one vote, but he wanted to make sure that the Supreme Court would continue to move in that direction. Having supported the plaintiffs in each of the other legislative reapportionment cases, he worried that withholding support in the Colorado case threatened that momentum. But he still needed Cox to come around to his position.[38]

Kennedy scheduled two meetings for Tuesday, February 11, 1964, to hammer out the administration's position. As ten inches of snow fell on Washington, the attorney general huddled in the early afternoon with a handful of advisers, but the group reached no consensus. After a trip to the White House with Katzenbach and Marshall, presumably to discuss the strategy for maneuvering the Civil Rights Act through Congress, Kennedy prepared to convene a second and larger meeting at five thirty that afternoon. On his way to the attorney general's office, Marshall stopped in to see Cox. Marshall pleaded with Cox to end the impasse as they made their way to Kennedy's office together. "Bob will never file a brief that you won't sign," Marshall said, "but you ought to realize that he really can't turn around now and oppose all those who are arguing for the 'one person, one vote' rule. We've stood together too long. You've got to think of some solution." As Cox remembered the conversation years later, he replied, "Maybe I have an answer. I won't go for 'one person, one vote,' but we can argue that the Colorado apportionment fails to satisfy the standards we've already proposed. That's a stretch and not likely to win, but I'm willing to make the argument." Satisfied with this compromise, Marshall informed Kennedy, who called off the meeting.[39]

The immediacy of Cox's response to Marshall indicates that the solicitor general was attuned to the attorney general's political inclinations and obligations. In an interview ten months later, Kennedy credited Cox for his willingness to carve out a middle ground that "didn't violate his own conscience." But however much credit Cox deserves for ending the impasse, the resolution is also a testament to the skill with which Kennedy and his top aides, especially Marshall and Katzenbach, managed the situation. Marshall first proposed the outlines of the eventual compromise, was seconded by Katzenbach in his memo to the attorney general, and then Kennedy allowed Cox the time and space to come around to a position that he had dismissed in forceful terms just a week earlier.[40]

Cox and Terris began drafting the federal government's amicus brief in the Colorado case at the same time that Frank Beytagh put the finishing touches on the opinion in *Reynolds* v. *Sims*. Given the profound importance of the reapportionment cases, Earl Warren very much wanted to avoid a 5–4 ruling. At the very least, he wanted a majority of six, which would likely require the vote of either Potter Stewart or Byron White, both of whom appeared initially to be "on the fence." Even as Warren himself inched toward a full embrace of the Equal Protection Clause—and thus a ruling that population must serve as the basis for the apportionment of both branches of a bicameral legislature—he "consciously explored alternatives" that would allow a sixth justice to join the majority. To that end, Beytagh made the decision to draft two distinct opinions. In the first, he provided the rationale for the Court to rule that the Equal Protection Clause required only a single branch of a bicameral legislature to be based on population. In the second, he laid out the argument for the standard applied to both houses. Throughout the winter, Beytagh consulted with his boss whenever he could catch him, typically just a few minutes at the start or end of the day. The chief read his clerk's drafts and offered suggestions; Beytagh wrote and rewrote, drafted and redrafted.[41]

In late January, Beytagh completed the first version for the chief justice. Emphasizing that no state could "provide that the votes of citizens in one part of the State should be given two times, or five times, or ten times the weight of votes of citizens in another part of the State," the draft opinion reasoned that "the effect of State legislative districting schemes which give the same number of representatives to unequal numbers of constituents is identical." Nevertheless, the draft allowed that, if reasonable, "minimal deviations from the equal-population principle are constitutionally permissible with respect to the apportionment of seats in one of the two houses of a bicameral State legislature." The first draft of *Reynolds* v. *Sims*, therefore, went no further than holding that "as a minimal and threshold constitutional standard, the Equal Protection Clause requires that at least one house of a bicameral State legislature must be apportioned on a population basis."[42]

Over the next four weeks, Beytagh turned his attention to the alternative draft, which would provide Warren the rationale to reach a far more sweeping, and historic, conclusion. While the chief justice remained preoccupied with his duties chairing the Warren Commission, Beytagh worked throughout February and consulted regularly with William Brennan, who "helped edit" the second draft. Beytagh retained much of the language from his first version but concluded that the Court could not strike down the federal analogy without requiring population equality in both houses of a bicameral legislature.[43]

During the first week of March, just days after Beytagh delivered the second version to his boss, Warren met at least three times with his head clerk. Together they had explored a range of alternatives over the previous three months, and Warren had decided that the Equal Protection Clause left no room for a federal system at the state level. According to one biographer, the chief "burst without ceremony into Brennan's chambers" and announced, with reference to the federal system, "It can't be. It can't be." But Warren's epiphany did not occur in an instant. It evolved over time, the result of a thoroughly deliberative process. Aided most ably and faithfully by Beytagh, the chief justice untangled the causes and implications of minority rule throughout the United States. As Warren later confided to Jesse Choper, who had clerked for him several years earlier, "After a while I just couldn't see any other way, any other principle that would handle the situation." In embracing population equality as the standard in all legislative bodies, Warren was forced to reconsider the position he had taken on the issue as governor of California. "As a political matter," he explained to Beytagh while discussing California's system of apportionment, "it seemed to me to be a sensible arrangement. But now, as a constitutional matter, with the point of view of the responsibilities of a Justice, I . . . look at it differently." Warren would be pilloried for his apparent hypocrisy, yet he never shied away from allowing that he "was just wrong as Governor."[44]

As soon as Warren made his decision, he instructed Beytagh to send the second version of his opinion to the Supreme Court's printing shop. Warren circulated the draft on March 11 to Hugo Black, and then on the following day to Justices William O. Douglas, William Brennan, and Arthur Goldberg. Over the course of the next thirty-six hours, Warren met privately with Douglas and Brennan, and three times with Goldberg. On March 12, the same day that he received the draft, Douglas cast his vote. "I think you have written a splendid opinion and I agree with all of it," he confided. "I did not want to agree to less than this." The following day, Goldberg added his assent. "My congratulations on an historic opinion which will take its place with *Brown*," the Court's most junior justice, who had taken no part in *Baker* v. *Carr*, wrote. Black informed the chief that he was "very happy to agree to your very fine treatment of this difficult case." Brennan, Earl Warren's most reliable ally on the Court, had already made clear his stance—he had assisted Beytagh in drafting the opinion.[45]

Confident that he had already secured a narrow majority for a far-reaching ruling, Earl Warren circulated his opinion in *Reynolds* v. *Sims* to the entire Court for the first time on March 16.[46]

Although Warren had a slim majority for his far-reaching opinion, he still wanted—as he had from the outset—a sixth vote for a decision with such tremendous, and potentially divisive, implications. By now he was doubtful that he would get Potter Stewart's vote, and so turned his attention to Byron White. White's views on the constitutionality of the Colorado legislature, because he was a native of the state, mattered to Warren and, he suspected, to others on the Court as well.[47]

On March 31 and April 1, 1964, the Supreme Court devoted a final three hours and twenty minutes of the term to legislative reapportionment. Appearing on behalf of the appellants, Denver attorney George Creamer provided the most notable performance. Creamer struggled throughout his life with a variety of health issues and would die in 1973 at age forty-seven. His physical fragility, however, in no way diminished his abilities; he was deemed "unique, odd, and brilliant" by both friends and opposing counsel in the Denver bar.[48]

Addressing the Court in a reedy voice, Creamer pulled no punches during a largely uninterrupted hour as he likened his adversaries to a "Greek chorus" that defended the Colorado plan with nothing more substantive than the cry of "topography, geography, and history." He dismissed the relevance of all three to equal protection, denounced the overrepresentation of formerly populated mining areas as "precisely parallel to the rotten borough," and then said that "once population has gone away, there is, we submit, nothing left to represent." He derided as "mythology" the claim of the appellees that the isolation of the state's more remote regions required disproportionate representation in the state senate. As his time drew to a close, Creamer leveled his most potent criticism. Condemning state officials and proponents of Amendment No. 7 for devising a system whose true purpose was to protect certain economic interests over others, Creamer told the Court, "We cannot have a senator for beef or a senator for sheep, or a senator for water, or a senator for wheat barley, or sugar beets. That is impossible." Representatives, he insisted, must represent people.[49]

Archibald Cox followed Creamer and adhered to the line of attack that he had worked out with Burke Marshall. Cox distanced himself from Creamer's position, informing the Court that the federal government was not arguing that both chambers of a bicameral legislature must be based on population. But Cox did second Creamer's contention that the state cannot favor rural voters or certain economic interests. In response to a question from Byron White, the solicitor general answered that "a man because he is a farmer cannot be given twice or five times the vote of another man." Cox ended by maintaining that the Colorado plan arbitrarily and capriciously violated the constitutional rights of individuals living in certain metropolitan regions.[50]

Anthony Zarlengo then stepped before the justices on behalf of the state of Colorado. A special assistant attorney general, he faced a steady barrage of questions that clearly rattled him. Between long pauses, he attempted to justify the Colorado plan as a clear expression of the will of the people that was designed not to favor special economic interests but rather to ensure that all interests were adequately represented in the state legislature. As Zarlengo spoke about how urban residents would dominate the state without the Colorado plan, the chief justice interrupted and asked, "Isn't the basic issue whether these appellants, and all other people in the state of Colorado, have proper representation, *as individuals*, regardless of whether they live in the city, or whether they live in the country, regardless of whether they are so-called liberals or so-called conservatives, regardless of whether they are working people or business people? Isn't that the basic question in the case?"[51]

Representing the sponsors of Amendment No. 7, Stephen Hart followed Zarlengo to the podium and did his best to resuscitate the fortunes of the Colorado plan. He acknowledged gross inequalities in Colorado's previous systems of apportionment but argued that Amendment No. 7 must be understood as a rational response to the Supreme Court's decision in *Baker* v. *Carr*. Striking down the amendment, Hart stated, would require the Court to establish a standard of "absolutely arithmetical equality" in all legislative apportionments, a threshold not contemplated in *Baker*. Referring to his own recently announced opinion in the Georgia congressional reapportionment case, Hugo Black responded that no one had suggested that the Court adopt such a rigid standard but only that population equality be "as nearly as practicable." Black's comment prompted Potter Stewart to tell Hart that even if the Court "requires that, you lose."[52]

That Friday, April 3, the justices gathered for their weekly conference. Earl Warren, Hugo Black, and William O. Douglas each cited the chief justice's opinion in the Alabama case as they voted to reverse the decision of the district court. Tom Clark had told Warren three weeks earlier, in response to the chief's opinion in *Reynolds* v. *Sims*, that he was "not yet ready to join a holding striking down the federal analogy." Arguments in the Colorado case did not change his mind; he voted to affirm the lower court, seeing no evidence that the Colorado plan constituted a "crazy quilt" or that it resulted in "invidious discrimination." As he had done in every reapportionment case to date, John Marshall Harlan sided with the state and provided a second vote to affirm the lower court. After William Brennan agreed that the Supreme Court should reverse the lower court, a confident Warren interjected, in a moment of levity, that as governor of California he had supported the federal system, but that as a result of the impending reapportionment decisions, he "won't dare go home."[53]

Potter Stewart joined Clark and Harlan and voted to uphold Amendment No. 7. Byron White then provided a fourth vote to sustain the Colorado plan, albeit "tentatively" according to Stewart and "with a question mark" in the words of Douglas. White said that he might "ultimately reverse" on the grounds that minority control of the state senate by 30 percent of the population could violate the Equal Protection Clause, but he also disagreed with Warren on the basic issue before the Court. In a clear indication of his own uncertainty, White described the Colorado plan as "slick political gerrymandering" and conceded that the chief's opinion in the Alabama case "will make political gerrymandering more difficult." Arthur Goldberg had already signed on to the chief's opinion in the Alabama case and he reiterated his support in the Colorado case. The vote stood at 5–4. Only one question remained: What would White ultimately decide?[54]

In April and early May, Frank Beytagh drafted and circulated separate opinions in each of the legislative reapportionment cases. The chief's majority held firm, but as the term headed toward adjournment, White gave no indication of how he planned to vote. Finally, on June 10, White wrote to Warren a one-line note: "Please join me in all of your reapportionment opinions," he requested, without elaboration, giving the chief the sixth vote that he so desired on the ultimate question. Like Black, White made the decision toward the end of his career to destroy his most significant Court papers in an effort to protect the sanctity of the Court's deliberations, so there is no way to know what exactly led

White to cast his vote with Warren. But there is no question that Warren, who never personally lobbied his junior colleague, was delighted. The reapportionment cases were finally ready for announcement.[55]

On Monday morning, June 15, 1964, at ten o'clock, Earl Warren and the brethren entered the majestic chamber of the nation's highest court. Those in attendance waited anxiously. The Supreme Court's summer recess was scheduled to begin the following week, and thus few opportunities remained to announce decisions in a handful of important cases still on the docket. For the seventy-three-year-old Warren in particular, the coming recess would mean the end of a physically demanding term during which he juggled his duties on the Court and his leadership of the Warren Commission. The chief justice took his seat in the center of the bench. Then, in a calm, measured voice, he cut straight to the central finding of the majority: "We hold today that the Equal Protection Clause of the Fourteenth Amendment to the Federal Constitution requires that seats in both houses of a bicameral state legislature must be apportioned substantially on a population basis." With that single sentence, the chief justice and the majority struck down existing political arrangements in Alabama, Colorado, Delaware, Maryland, New York, and Virginia and, by implication, in almost every state in the Union.[56]

Warren, speaking for a core majority of six justices, declared the reapportionment schemes in all six states unconstitutional, rejected the federal analogy as inapplicable to the states, and extended the principle of one person, one vote to all state legislative apportionments. In summary remarks from the bench and in the Court's published opinions, Warren repeatedly affirmed the right of all citizens, as individuals, to cast ballots that have been neither debased nor diluted, and insisted that "the weight of a citizen's vote cannot be made to depend on where he lives." Borrowing an example first put forth by Cox during oral arguments in *Baker* v. *Carr*, Warren wrote that no state could allow some residents to vote five or ten times in a given election, while others voted only once. Malapportionment, he reasoned, produced an identical result.[57]

Six months earlier, Warren had asked Frank Beytagh to explain the

Court's reapportionment rulings in a "graphic way" that would be accessible to the general public. Beytagh responded by crafting the lead opinion's most frequently quoted passage. In clear yet deeply eloquent language that perfectly articulated the essence of the majority opinion, the Court declared, "Legislators represent people, not trees or acres. Legislators are elected by voters, not farms or cities or economic interests. As long as ours is a representative form of government, and our legislatures are those instruments of government elected directly by and directly representative of the people, the right to elect legislators in a free and unimpaired fashion is a bedrock of our political system." Those three sentences at the heart of the Court's published opinion appeared precisely, word for word, as in Beytagh's first complete draft.[58]

From the bench, Warren explained that neither *Gray* v. *Sanders* nor *Wesberry* v. *Sanders* could be considered controlling in a case involving state legislative apportionment, but that the Court had extended the findings and logic in both cases to reach a decision in *Reynolds* v. *Sims*. Affirming its commitment to "one person, one vote," first articulated in the Georgia county-unit case, as well as its determination that congressional districts must be based on "substantial equality of population," the Court's opinion in *Reynolds* stated that "the Equal Protection Clause demands no less than substantially equal state legislative representation for all citizens, of all places as well as of all races."[59]

The Court's determination in *Reynolds* that all legislative apportionments must reflect "substantially equal" numbers of people momentarily left open the possibility of some room, however small, for states with more equitable systems to set their own standards. Warren's announcement of the Court's opinion in *Lucas* v. *Colorado*, however, drove home the unprecedented nature of the rulings and made clear that henceforth the states would enjoy no such flexibility in devising systems of apportionment. He told a hushed audience that the six-person majority recognized profound differences between the situations in Colorado and Alabama but nevertheless had concluded that the Colorado plan violated the Equal Protection Clause of the Fourteenth Amendment because it empowered an unconstitutional minority in the apportionment of the state senate. The Court held that neither the timing of the adoption of Amendment No. 7 nor the overwhelming support for it made any difference. "An individual's constitutionally protected right to cast an equally weighted vote cannot be denied even by a vote of a majority of the State's electorate," the majority declared in the published opinion, using language that the chief justice had come up with. "A citizen's constitutional rights can hardly be infringed simply because a majority of the people choose that it be."[60]

Potter Stewart and Tom Clark joined the core majority in striking down the manifestly irrational apportionments in Alabama, Virginia, and Delaware but rejected such an expansive interpretation of the Fourteenth Amendment. Instead, they argued in a series of dissenting and concurring opinions that a state's system of apportionment satisfies the requirements of the Equal Protection Clause if it is rational and does not systematically frustrate the will of the people. Stewart, in particular, criticized the majority's favoring of "the uncritical, simplistic, and heavy-handed application of eighth-grade arithmetic." Based on their formula, Stewart and Clark voted to uphold the Colorado and New York apportionments. In the Maryland case, Clark provided Warren a seventh vote, while Stewart voted to remand the case for reconsideration. Speaking from the bench "with great emotion and considerable anger," as the *Washington Post* reported, John Marshall Harlan dissented in all six cases, just as he had done in *Baker* v. *Carr*, *Gray* v. *Sanders*, and *Wesberry* v. *Sanders*.[61]

The effect of the justices' announcements on June 15 was immediate. The majority's ruling stunned many observers and surprised even fervent advocates of reapportionment who had not expected so sweeping a decision. Word of Warren's announcement spread quickly through the nation's capital and newsrooms across the country, eliciting reactions ranging from delight to incredulity and bewilderment. Within hours, members of Congress and others throughout the United States embarked on a crusade to eviscerate the substance of the Court's rulings. A week later, the Court cited its opinion in *Reynolds* and struck down apportionment schemes in nine additional states: Connecticut, Florida, Idaho, Illinois, Iowa, Michigan, Ohio, Oklahoma, and Washington. No region of the country was unaffected.[62]

As Potter Stewart listened to Earl Warren announce the Court's rulings in the state reapportionment cases, he asked himself what, if anything, he might have done differently to save the Colorado and New York plans. An opportunity had fleetingly presented itself two years earlier, and ironically it was Stewart who had failed to perceive it. That he did not speaks not to a lack of foresight on his part but rather to the astonishing speed with which reapportionment jurisprudence evolved and a once unthinkable notion became the law of the land.[63]

In March 1962, as he was preparing his dissent in *Baker* v. *Carr*, Tom Clark had suddenly switched his vote and joined the majority. He made clear that he would rule not only that the federal courts had jurisdiction in reapportionment lawsuits but also that he was prepared to establish a minimum standard the states must meet in apportioning their legislatures. Warren, Black, Douglas, and Brennan also favored addressing the issue of standards. But after months spent cultivating the fifth vote of Potter Stewart, who would not go beyond the narrow issues of jurisdiction and justiciability, the majority decided not to alter its opinion. Had Clark joined the majority weeks earlier, Stewart's vote would not have been decisive and the majority would have been free to establish a minimum standard. Or if Stewart had foreseen what lay ahead— perhaps an unfair expectation, yet precisely what Wiley Rutledge had done in *Colegrove* v. *Green*—he himself might have agreed to a broader decision in *Baker*. For if the Court had reached a decision on the merits in *Baker*, the justices most certainly would have required that only one branch of a bicameral legislature be based on population. Five votes for the more sweeping standard did not exist prior to the confirmation of Byron White and Arthur Goldberg.[64]

As late as 1962, almost no one involved in reapportionment litigation even contemplated population equality in both houses of a bicameral legislature. Across the United States, members of the League of Women Voters and other citizens working on behalf of reapportionment desired no more than the apportionment of one branch of the legislature on a population basis. Even Bruce Terris, who by the summer of 1963 had become the most passionate advocate within the Department of Justice on behalf of population equality in all legislative chambers, came to that position slowly. The force and logic of each opinion—first in *Baker* v. *Carr* and then in *Gray* v. *Sanders*—pointed in the direction of population equality. Terris may have discerned the implication of these opinions sooner than most. But even Archibald Cox, who later told an interviewer that "everybody's thinking developed quite sharply at each stage," eventually reached a similar understanding. More important, so, too, did Earl Warren, Hugo Black, William O. Douglas, William Brennan, Byron White, and Arthur Goldberg.[65]

12 ||| THE LITTLE FILIBUSTER

C ity newspapers and the national press for the most part welcomed the Supreme Court's reapportionment decisions. The
New York Times declared the rulings a "constitutional revolution," among the "most far-reaching decisions since *Marbury* v. *Madison*," and speculated that history would judge the decisions more
important than the school desegregation decisions of the 1950s. The
Washington Daily News proclaimed a "smashing victory" for urban
voters, while *Newsweek* opined that the decisions "cut away the last vestiges of rural power in American politics" and reported that a survey by
its correspondents found that forty-eight states would have to reapportion their legislatures (Oregon and Kentucky were the only exceptions).
Syndicated columnists Walter Lippmann and Roscoe Drummond
added their voices to the acclaim, arguing that recalcitrant legislatures
left the Court with no choice but to enact such a sweeping remedy.[1]

Of course, not all newspapers or columnists were pleased with the
Court's decisions. The business-friendly *Wall Street Journal* grudgingly
admitted that "many states had been exercising their legislative power
in an undesirable way" but rejected the Court's logic and the scope of
the rulings in going so far. Drawing on the dissenting opinions by Justices
Harlan, Stewart, and Clark, the *Journal* said that as opposed to a pure
democracy, "a republican form of government does not proceed from a
one-man, one-vote premise." The *Chicago Tribune* also focused on the
dissenting opinions in drafting its editorial opposition, while the *Dallas
Morning News* more generally criticized the Court for "trampling on the

rights of the states." Conservative columnists David Lawrence and William S. White deplored what they saw as the destructive tendencies of the six-person majority; William F. Buckley Jr. pithily condemned the "ideological fanaticism of Earl Warren and his quintet."[2]

Opponents of the decisions soon turned their attention, as Warren surely anticipated, to what they believed to be evidence of his hypocrisy. In a July 6 column, *U.S. News & World Report* ran an excerpt from a 1948 speech in which the governor of California defended the state's system of apportionment. "Many California counties are far more important in the life of the State than their population bears to the entire population of the State," Warren had said in opposing Proposition 13, the ballot item that would amend California's system. "It is for this reason that I have never been in favor of restricting representation in the senate to a strictly population basis." Critics of the Court pounced. From Richmond, Virginia, to Jackson, Mississippi, to Reading, California, editorial pages incredulously denounced the chief justice.[3]

The most unexpectedly hostile attack on the Court came not from an editorial board or columnist, but from Edwin Johnson, an appellee in Colorado's reapportionment suit. Dubbed "Mr. Colorado" for his eighteen years' service in the U.S. Senate and his three terms as governor of the state, Johnson, a Democrat, led the successful campaign in 1962 to adopt the plan that the Court struck down in *Lucas* v. *Colorado*. Johnson, after explaining in an agricultural publication that the Colorado plan was the product of a long, thoughtful, and respectful debate between parties on both sides of the issue, and that it had the support of overwhelming majorities in the state, equated the Court's reapportionment decisions with the assassination of John F. Kennedy. "On November 22, 1963, our revered and beloved President was assassinated, in cold blood without warning by a madman," Johnson wrote. "And on June 15, 1964, government by the people in the state of Colorado was assassinated by six justices of the United States Supreme Court." Johnson deemed the day "evil."[4]

Though most lawyers and expert witnesses on the other side of the issue exulted in their triumph, all were not so enthusiastic. The *New York Times* reported that a number of self-described liberals wondered if the Court was moving too quickly. James Larson, a political scientist who had assisted the Alabama attorneys, told John McConnell that the decisions would prove beneficial in their "general result," but he believed that "state sovereignty was trampled a bit unnecessarily" in the Colorado and New York cases. In response, McConnell reaffirmed his belief that the Court properly concluded that certain rights "cannot be taken away from any individual by a majority." He added that reapportionment would not provide a panacea for all the problems that plagued the states, nor would it usher in a utopian age, but that, if properly implemented, it would help foster "a better political and economic climate."[5]

McConnell, like the Court majority, focused on individual rather than group rights, but most commentators turned immediately to the effect the decisions would have on the two major political parties. Despite rampant speculation, no one really knew what that effect would be. The chairmen of both parties approved of the Court's rulings, at least in the beginning. John Bailey, the chairman of the Democratic National Committee, hailed the Court action as "something the Democratic Party had long advocated, and fought for, and certainly welcomes." His Republican counterpart, William B. Miller, although less enthusiastic, thought the Court's rulings were "in the national interest and in the Party's interest."[6] Pundits, meanwhile, noted that Republican fortunes looked promising in the South and in other parts of the country where rural Democrats disproportionately controlled state legislatures, while Democrats would pick up seats in areas where rural Republicans held similar sway. Republicans worried that Democrats would make irreversible gains in states with large urban centers, and about higher taxes and the passage of other legislation hostile to business. Newsweek predicted gains for the Democrats in twenty states and the Republicans in eleven, and thought it likely that state legislatures would spend more freely on housing, transportation, education, and welfare, and perhaps introduce new civil rights bills.[7]

The more astute observers understood that the Supreme Court's reapportionment decisions would empower all metropolitan residents, not just city dwellers. By 1960, 70 percent of Americans lived in areas that were technically metropolitan—large population centers and adjacent communities that share a "high degree of social and economic integration"—and no one disputed that the Supreme Court's decisions would enhance the political power of these areas at the expense of rural regions. But as the director of the Bureau of the Census put it at the time,

"Metropolitan areas are complex entities." Between 1950 and 1960, city-center populations actually declined in fourteen of the twenty-one largest metropolitan regions in the United States, while the suburban populations in all twenty-one increased, in many cases dramatically. Such developments did not escape the attention of Warren and the Court majority, who noted in the *Reynolds* opinion that "although legislative reapportionment controversies are generally viewed as involving urban-rural conflicts, much evidence indicates that it is the fast-growing suburban areas which are probably the most seriously underrepresented." In metropolitan Detroit, to cite one example, a post-*Reynolds* increase in representation accrued entirely to the surrounding suburbs, which was more encouraging at the time to Republicans than Democrats. William Boyd, the National Municipal League's reapportionment expert, summed up the situation succinctly: "The suburbs, and in the long run, only the suburbs, will gain in the upheaval resulting from reapportionment of state legislatures on the basis of population. Rather than being dominated by the big cities, as is commonly supposed, the new legislatures will see suburban representation increase the most in number."[8]

Politicians responded immediately to the Court's decisions. Over the weeks and months after June 15, members of Congress from every region of the country introduced more than 140 bills and resolutions aimed at nullifying, modifying, or postponing implementation of the Court's decisions. Representative William Tuck of Virginia and Senator Strom Thurmond of South Carolina, both ardent supporters of segregation and opponents of civil rights, took the most extreme position, introducing legislation on June 16 to strip the federal courts of jurisdiction in all matters pertaining to apportionment. Another group of lawmakers backed measures that granted each state the "exclusive power to determine the composition of its legislature." Most of the new bills and resolutions proposed to amend the rulings to allow the states to apportion one branch of a bicameral legislature on factors other than population. Others would have delayed implementation if they had passed; the representatives who sponsored them apparently hoped that the Court would change its mind.[9]

Congressional opposition soon coalesced around Everett McKinley Dirksen, the Senate minority leader from Illinois. In the words of a biographer, at that moment Dirksen "stood at the peak of his power in the United States Senate, at a peak where few men have ever stood in the Senate's history." The Republicans held just thirty-three seats in the Senate, but Dirksen wielded unusual clout because of deep fault lines among the sixty-seven Democrats and because of his close relationship with Lyndon Johnson. Nowhere was Dirksen's power more evident than in the debate over the landmark civil rights bill. Throughout the spring of 1964, Dirksen played the seminal role in bringing an end to the filibuster of southern Democrats. Working closely with Majority Leader Mike Mansfield of Montana and negotiating daily with Johnson administration officials, including Nicholas Katzenbach and Burke Marshall, Dirksen forced the administration to make key concessions that allowed him to secure the votes of a handful of conservative, pro-business Republicans. On June 10, just days before the state reapportionment rulings, Dirksen and twenty-six other Republicans joined forty-four Democrats in invoking cloture and bringing an end to the seventy-five-day filibuster, the first time in American history that the Senate ended a filibuster against a civil rights measure (at the time, invoking cloture required a two-thirds majority; in 1975, the number was reduced to three-fifths). On June 19, the Senate formally passed the Civil Rights Act. The House accepted the Senate version without change on June 30, and the president signed it into law two days later. *Time* magazine put Dirksen on its cover twice within four weeks in June and July 1964.[10]

Dirksen's achievement, however, came at a significant cost to his health and to the cohesiveness of his caucus. Sixty-eight years old in the spring of 1964, he was a workaholic who started each day before six and remained at his desk until nine or ten at night. He kept a drawer full of medicines in his office to treat a range of ailments, most notably a stomach ulcer that led to his hospitalization just prior to the call for cloture. In an effort to cope with enormous stress, Dirksen smoked too many cigarettes, as many as three packs a day, and drank too many glasses of bourbon each evening. Katzenbach once said, partially in jest, that he "almost became an alcoholic" as a result of nightly negotiating sessions with Dirksen over the civil rights bill. Katzenbach and Burke Marshall came to realize that the key to negotiating with Dirksen was "to get agreement before too much bourbon had dulled the senator's recollection of what he had okayed."[11]

An increasingly disgruntled Republican caucus also marred Dirksen's triumph. Although the minority leader persuaded all but six Republican senators to support cloture in the civil rights debate, the final tally papered over divisions within Dirksen's own party. Conservative members of the caucus and many of their constituents complained bitterly that Dirksen was doing too much lifting for the Johnson administration rather than leading the opposition. Most embarrassing to Dirksen—and most potentially damaging in his estimation to the future of his party—the handful of Republican opponents to the civil rights bill included Barry Goldwater, the senator from Arizona who was poised to accept the Republican nomination for president at the party convention in July.[12]

Dirksen's inability to secure Goldwater's vote on civil rights threatened to open another rift among the Republicans. Dirksen hoped that an attack on the reapportionment decisions would unify moderates and conservatives in his party. On June 21, just two days after Senate passage of the Civil Rights Act, he had his staff begin to look into the possibility of introducing a constitutional amendment to "nullify" the Court's rulings. Minutes from a June 23 meeting of the Senate Republican Policy Committee reveal that Dirksen raised the idea that opposition to the decisions "might well be used as a campaign issue by the Republicans during the forthcoming elections." Committee chair Bourke Hickenlooper of Iowa and several colleagues in attendance agreed. Three days later, Dirksen and his counterpart in the House of Representatives, Charles Halleck of Indiana, issued a joint leadership statement that pushed the idea of a constitutional amendment. Halleck blamed the Court for the "constitutional crisis" at hand, and Dirksen ominously predicted that the Court might next threaten to abolish the electoral college or even order that the U.S. Senate be apportioned according to population. (The Supreme Court, of course, never entertained either possibility.)[13]

Dirksen's proposal undoubtedly contained a strong dose of cynical election-year politicking, but his opposition to the Court's rulings stemmed primarily from his long-held concerns. Lampooned by critics as a "chameleon" and a "political opportunist" for frequently shifting his position on certain issues, Dirksen had supported a number of New Deal programs at the start of his sixteen years in the House of Representatives.

By the time he was elected to the Senate in 1950, though, he had renounced the New Deal, and throughout his tenure in the upper house he was a faithful ally of national business groups—in the words of one journalist, he "reliably represented the concerns of the U.S. Chamber of Commerce and the National Association of Manufacturers."[14]

At the same time, Dirksen remained at his core a native of Pekin, a small town across the Illinois River from Peoria. He graduated from the local high school and spent three years at the University of Minnesota, dropping out to enlist in the army during World War I. After service in Europe, Dirksen returned to Pekin and worked at a variety of jobs, including dredge boat operator and wholesale grocer, a job that entailed delivering bread in central Illinois, which eventually became his political base. Throughout his political career, he championed the interests of rural and small-town Illinoisans who saw the world changing in ways they did not like or understand. He channeled the anxieties of these Downstate residents, who feared nothing more than the corrupting influences of the big city, especially Chicago, its dominant political machines, labor unions, and increasingly multiethnic and multiracial populations. (Into the 1970s, Pekin's high school athletic teams were known as the Chinks.) Dirksen very much saw the Supreme Court's reapportionment rulings as threatening the autonomy and political power of individuals residing in towns like Pekin.[15]

Towns like Pekin could be found all over Illinois, and all over the United States. In some parts of the country, residents of small towns preferred Democrats; in other regions they voted primarily for Republicans. As a result, opposition to the Supreme Court's decisions brought together what the *Wall Street Journal* called "an almost implausible coalition of Republicans, Southern Democrats and a significant sprinkling of liberal Democrats from the hinterlands of such states as California, Pennsylvania, and Ohio." Whatever their party, whatever their region, lawmakers from rural and small-town America worried that the decisions would dilute the disproportionate influence enjoyed by their constituents and, by extension, their own political clout.[16]

By the time Republicans gathered in San Francisco in mid-July to nominate Goldwater for president, they had come a long way in their thinking about reapportionment since their chairman's initial, if tepid, acceptance of the Court's rulings as in the best interests of the party. Indeed, delegates to the 1964 Republican National Convention added a plank into the party platform that called for a constitutional amendment to allow states with "bicameral legislatures to apportion one House on bases of their choosing, including factors other than population." In the run-up to the ensuing general election, Goldwater repeatedly went after the Supreme Court in his speeches, focusing his energies on the reapportionment rulings and a 1962 decision that banned prayer in the public schools (delegates at the RNC also called for the passage of a constitutional amendment to overturn that decision). Blaming the pro–civil rights agenda of Democratic mayors for an increase in urban crime, Goldwater warned that reapportionment would exacerbate the ills of crime-ridden cities.[17]

After the Republican convention, Thomas Graham, the speaker of the Missouri house of representatives, wrote to Lyndon Johnson to request that the Democrats include a similar plank at their nominating convention in August. Graham, who also served as the executive vice president of the National Commission on Constitutional Government, a consortium of state legislators committed to nullifying the decisions of June 15, 1964, observed that President Johnson had not publicly commented on the Court's rulings and asked where he stood. Determined to defuse the issue, White House aides drafted but did not release a statement defending the Supreme Court decisions and avoided a response to an agitated Graham.[18]

Shortly after Congress returned to work following the Republican convention, Dirksen and twenty-three cosponsors in the Senate introduced a constitutional amendment along the lines suggested in the Republican platform. In the House, Representative William McCullough of Ohio proposed a similar measure. But Dirksen doubted that there was enough time in the current Congress to pass a constitutional amendment, so he introduced a bill—soon dubbed the "Dirksen breather"— that would have postponed state compliance with the Supreme Court's reapportionment rulings for at least two, and up to four, years, a delay intended to buy sufficient time to overturn the Court.[19]

Dirksen and others in his loose coalition had good reason to be concerned. The Supreme Court's decisions had established guidelines that the states must meet in apportioning legislative and congressional districts but had left it to the lower courts to enforce those guidelines. In effect, the Supreme Court empowered federal district courts and state appellate courts to order new apportionment plans if state lawmakers did not comply with the new mandate. Almost immediately, lower-court orders or the threat of such orders began to transform state legislatures in fundamental ways, and those legislatures drew the boundaries for congressional districts. In Michigan, the Republican Party had openly—and brazenly—relied on malapportionment for decades, maintaining a firm grip on two-thirds of the seats in the state senate and eleven of eighteen congressional districts despite receiving less than 50 percent of the statewide vote. Just days after the rulings of June 15, 1964, Michigan became the first state to reapportion in compliance with the Supreme Court's new standard. The consequences were staggering: fourteen incumbents in the thirty-eight-member senate chose to retire, while nine of the twenty-four incumbents who did seek reelection lost in the subsequent primary. In July, a federal district court invalidated the composition of Oklahoma's Democratic-controlled legislature. Among those most concerned by these events was Carl Albert, the Democratic majority leader in the House of Representatives and the congressman from the seventh least populous district in the United States.[20]

Dirksen witnessed the elimination of rural-dominated legislatures in Michigan and Oklahoma, and was acutely aware that a federal district court was considering what to do in Illinois, where voters in 1954 adopted a so-called balanced plan of apportionment that had ensured Downstate Republican control of the state senate. Dirksen devised a strategy that one political analyst deemed "shortsighted." Chalmers Roberts, a staff reporter for the *Washington Post*, chided Dirksen and like-minded Republicans for being stuck in a rural-urban dichotomy and for failing to understand the political importance of the rapidly growing and diverse suburbs. Roberts pointed out that suburbanites had overwhelmingly voted for Dwight Eisenhower in 1952 and 1956 but split evenly between John F. Kennedy and Richard Nixon in 1960, which to Roberts was a sign that the political allegiance of suburban residents remained up for grabs. He had no doubt that Dirksen's preoccupation with rural control, and in particular with preserving rural

Republican control of the state senate in Illinois, was at odds with the long-term national interests of the party.[21]

In many ways, but most obviously in his dress, appearance, and voice, Everett Dirksen represented a throwback to a political era in which great orators dominated the stage. David Halberstam judged Dirksen ill equipped to lead his caucus in the age of television, describing the senator as "marvelously overblown, like a huge and rich vegetable that has become slightly overripe; watching him, one had a sense that he was always winking at the audience, winking at the role that he had chosen to play, the stereotype of a slightly corrupt old-fashioned senator." However unkind, Halberstam's assessment was right about Dirksen's overly theatrical style, a theme picked up by *New York Times* theater critic Brooks Atkinson, who saw more to admire in Dirksen but recognized many of the same qualities. Observing the senator at work and onstage during the 1964 Republican Convention, Atkinson wrote that Dirksen exhibited "the poised eloquence of the 19th century thespian. He practices the pregnant pause perfectly. His voice is like the froth on a warm pail of milk just extracted from a fat Jersey cow."[22]

But Dirksen, who had been born in the nineteenth century, *was* old-fashioned, even if Halberstam saw much of his persona as an act. And Dirksen was, unquestionably, a master of parliamentary procedure and stagecraft. On Thursday, July 30, he made a nighttime visit to the White House to inform Lyndon Johnson that he planned to attach his delaying measure to a piece of legislation that was guaranteed to "land right in the middle of that big desk of yours" before the end of the session. Dirksen formally introduced his bill on August 3. The following day, the Senate Judiciary Committee approved the measure by a margin of 10–2 without a public hearing. Immediately after the vote, a confident Dirksen publicly announced his intention to attach his "breather" as a rider to the foreign aid bill, a measure he knew the president would not veto. The *New York Times* opined that Dirksen's "prospects of success may depend on whether President Johnson actively opposes him." The *Washington Post* saw an impending crisis if Dirksen succeeded, and called on the president to intervene. Johnson clearly did not like the rider—he was concerned that Dirksen's maneuvers would delay ultimate passage of the foreign aid bill—but made no public effort to oppose Dirksen at this point. Nor would he make the effort at any other point over the several years that Dirksen kept the issue alive. Dirksen did not suggest any specific quid pro quo during this opening skirmish, but he later managed to extract from Johnson a pledge of silence on reapportionment in exchange for help in passing major legislation.[23]

Legal experts and law professors who endorsed reapportionment denounced Dirksen's rider as unconstitutional. More troubling for congressional leaders, a band of sixty-three liberals in the House of Representatives, all of whom had consistently advocated foreign assistance, pledged to oppose the foreign aid bill if it came back to the House with the reapportionment rider intact. Thomas E. Morgan of Pennsylvania, the chairman of the House Foreign Affairs Committee, called the rider "the craziest thing I ever heard" and promised to bottle up the bill in conference until Christmas rather than accept Dirksen's language.[24]

Aware that Dirksen probably had the votes to push his rider through the Senate, but also anxious that the bill was unconstitutional, Senate Majority Leader Mike Mansfield asked Dirksen to consult with officials in the Department of Justice. Beginning on August 8, staff lawyers for Dirksen, Mansfield, and House Republican leader William McCullough huddled with Solicitor General Archibald Cox in an attempt to come up with language acceptable to all parties. Dirksen rejected the group's first proposal—a resolution that merely expressed the sense of Congress that the federal courts should move slowly in reapportionment cases—on the grounds that it had "no teeth," as well as a second option to "empower" but not "require" the district courts to delay reapportionment proceedings for a limited time. According to news reports, conferees found a precedent for this approach in the Supreme Court's segregation decision, in which the Court had told the lower courts to move with "all deliberate speed."[25]

Dirksen then pledged to take his unchanged proposal to the floor of the Senate, causing Democratic leaders in the Senate and officials in the Johnson administration to panic. They desperately wanted the Eighty-eighth Congress to finish its work—which included passage of the foreign aid bill—and adjourn in advance of the Democratic National Convention, scheduled to begin on August 24 in Atlantic City, so that lawmakers could return to their home districts and begin campaigning for reelection immediately after the convention. Democratic leaders, now joined by Deputy Attorney General Nicholas Katzenbach as well as Cox, renewed negotiations with Dirksen.[26]

Finally, on August 12, at the end of a five-day marathon of talks, Dirksen and Mansfield announced a settlement that required federal district courts to allow current reapportionment schemes to remain in effect, except in "highly unusual circumstances," until after January 1, 1966, and to allow state legislatures "a reasonable opportunity in regular session" to adopt new apportionment plans. Dirksen introduced the compromise rider that evening, saying that it was "99 and $2/3$ percent mandatory." A dejected Mansfield, by contrast, conceded that he was "unhappy" with the compromise he pledged to cosponsor but was "just facing up to realities." Katzenbach and Cox signed off on the constitutionality of the measure, emphasizing that the agreement recognized the legitimacy of the Court's rulings and that the undefined exception for unusual circumstances would allow the district courts the necessary leeway to proceed with meaningful reapportionment. Despite the administration's efforts to spin the compromise, the *New York Herald Tribune* concluded that "the deal amounted to virtually a total victory" for Dirksen and the forces he represented.[27]

The compromise, however, failed to placate the most vociferous critics of the Supreme Court in the House of Representatives, where the reapportionment issue had "exploded with sudden fury." Howard W. Smith of Virginia, the eighty-one-year-old Democratic chairman of the powerful Rules Committee and a passionate segregationist, called the Dirksen breather "worthless" and advanced a rival plan instead. The Tuck bill, introduced on July 2 by Democrat William Tuck, a former governor of Virginia and an architect of that state's massive resistance to school integration, would have removed all reapportionment disputes from the jurisdiction of the federal courts. The chairman of the House Judiciary Committee, Democrat Emanuel Celler of New York, had made sure that the Tuck bill and similar measures had languished in his committee. In mid-August, Smith used all of his legislative sleight-of-hand to convince a group of southern Democrats and Republicans on the Rules Committee to employ a rarely used parliamentary device that had the effect of discharging the Tuck bill to the floor for a vote by the full membership of the House. One newspaper labeled the maneuver "literally subversive," while another reported that Smith's actions led to a "confused and angry struggle."[28]

Amid this deepening rancor, the Senate began debate on the Dirksen rider on August 13. Paul Douglas, a Democrat from Illinois, led the opposition, exhorting his colleagues to see the issue as "perhaps the most serious that has come before the Senate this year," no small claim in view of the ambitious agenda—from civil rights to Medicare and poverty relief—congressional leaders and the Johnson administration had undertaken. Joseph Clark, a Democrat from Pennsylvania, condemned the compromise as a "rotten borough amendment" designed to guarantee minority control of state government. Both promised to do all they could to defeat the rider, a pledge that heightened speculation about a possible filibuster. Many observers, however, doubted the debate would last more than a few days, with the *Washington Post* lamenting that "a small group of liberals appeared determined to talk as long as they could, but ultimate passage seemed assured."[29]

But no one told the small band of liberals—above all Douglas, Clark, William Proxmire of Wisconsin, and Philip Hart of Michigan—that passage of the Dirksen rider was inevitable. They set aside their general antipathy to the filibuster—a device used more frequently to block civil rights legislation—and showed that liberals could effectively wield that weapon, too. Just two months after Dirksen helped end the filibuster against the Civil Rights Act, he watched his senior colleague from Illinois launch what one newspaper soon dubbed the "little filibuster."[30]

It was fitting that Douglas and Dirksen emerged as the leading congressional opponents in the reapportionment debate. Always cordial on the surface and normally faithful to the demands of senatorial deference, the two senators from Illinois had a prickly relationship defined by substantial personal and policy differences. In many respects, the pair mirrored divisions throughout their state and the nation on a range of issues, including reapportionment.

In contrast to Dirksen, who was a product of small-town Illinois, the son of a close-knit, thoroughly Republican family of German immigrants, Paul Douglas—at seventy-two, four years Dirksen's senior—was shaped politically by a troubled childhood. Born in Massachusetts, Douglas was four when his mother died. His father remarried but drank too much and became abusive, forcing his stepmother to flee to backwoods Maine, where she raised Douglas and his brother in virtual isolation and near poverty. Douglas earned a bachelor's degree at Bowdoin College and a doctorate in economics at Columbia, settling in Chicago in 1920 when he joined the faculty of the University of Chicago. A prolific author and committed social activist who involved himself in progressive reform and anticorruption efforts throughout the 1920s and 1930s, in 1939 Douglas was elected an alderman to the Chicago city council as an independent. In 1942, he failed to win the Democratic nomination for U.S. Senate in Illinois. The morning after his defeat, Douglas, a Quaker whose pacifism was no match for the threats posed by totalitarianism, enlisted in the Marine Corps at age fifty. After receiving a waiver for his age and poor eyes and teeth, he survived basic training with teenagers and young men less than half his age. He chafed at a series of desk jobs and repeatedly worked his political connections until he was finally sent to the front lines of the war in the Pacific. Wounded at Peleliu and Okinawa, Douglas lost the use of his left arm, which from that point forward he considered "only a good paperweight."[31]

In the 1920s and 1930s, both as a scholar and as a citizen, Douglas had worked for greater representation for urban and suburban areas, and even started a book on the subject (he never finished it). While recuperating from his war wounds, he threw himself once again into debates over reapportionment. He provided financial assistance to the legal team in *Colegrove* v. *Green*, which had originated in Illinois, and attended the oral argument at the Supreme Court in March 1946. He later contributed money to Morris Abram's challenge to Georgia's county-unit system that culminated in *Gray* v. *Sanders*. In 1948, Democrats who wanted to clean up Illinois politics promoted Douglas and Adlai Stevenson as candidates for governor and the U.S. Senate, albeit without specifying who should run for which office. Seeing that it would be difficult to block the nomination of the pair, the Chicago machine decided to make the best of a bad situation. Preferring Stevenson in the governor's office, it endorsed Douglas for the Senate, betting that a junior senator in Washington could not do much damage back in Illinois. As it turned out, during his three terms in the Senate, Douglas was widely viewed as one of the chamber's most liberal members—an early champion of civil rights for African Americans, a friend of labor, and a leading proponent of financial regulations and environmental legislation.[32]

In the summer of 1964, Douglas and his cohort did indeed face long odds as they launched their filibuster. Few supporters of reapportionment took seriously the threat posed by the Dirksen rider, perhaps swayed in part by the president's silence and the administration's role in negotiating the compromise. Other members of Congress were ambivalent, generally in favor of greater representation for urban and suburban voters but inclined to think that the Supreme Court had gone too far. Douglas's first priority was to stall for time as he attempted to enlarge his ranks. On the second day of debate, Friday, August 14, William Proxmire held the floor for four and a half hours, providing the much older Douglas a needed respite. "My strength was ebbing," Douglas later wrote, rather melodramatically. "Barely able to stand, I did not know how much longer I could hold the floor. A vote might be called at any moment, and I knew we would be beaten. To my great relief, Bill Proxmire bravely stepped forward in the nick of time. He argued ably and at length, giving me a chance to catch my breath." The filibuster continued through a third day, but few had joined Douglas's cause. One newspaper counted eight, and predicted that "this group, unless it is reinforced, cannot continue talking . . . beyond Monday or Tuesday." But by Monday, August 17, the group had grown to fifteen, large enough to map out a "talking schedule" that would enable its members to hold the floor until Friday, August 21, the day Congress had to recess for the Democratic National Convention.[33]

This led to an "angry impasse" that irritated members of both parties, who were eager to begin campaigning for the November elections. President Johnson remained silent on the substance of the issue, but in an attempt to avoid having the Senate return after the convention, the administration once again dispatched Nicholas Katzenbach and Archibald Cox to Capitol Hill. This time, they met with the Douglas bloc and tried to assure the liberals that the language in the compromise, as drafted, "would not be an affront to the Supreme Court." They failed. Proxmire and Wayne Morse of Oregon rejected the claim, and Morse went so far as to contend that a resuscitation of Franklin Roosevelt's court-packing plan would be less meddlesome to the Court's independence. John Pastore of Rhode Island, the scheduled keynote speaker at the Democratic Convention, and Hubert Humphrey of Minnesota, the leading candidate for vice president, took a less confrontational approach but expressed apprehension that the Dirksen rider would threaten gains made in states such as Michigan and Delaware that had already completed reapportionment following the June 15 rulings. Attorneys who litigated the state reapportionment cases on behalf of the plaintiffs in Virginia and Colorado had the same fears about proceedings then under way in their states. Given Dirksen's stated intent to stall for time until he could secure passage of a constitutional amendment, these concerns were eminently sensible, and Cox and Katzenbach were unable to relieve them.[34]

As the Senate remained at a standstill as a result of the filibuster, southern Democrats and rural Republicans in the House of Representatives joined together and passed the Tuck bill, 218 to 175, on Wednesday, August 19. One journalist referred to this as the "broadest Congressional attack on the U.S. courts in the nation's history." But on the same day, supporters of reapportionment awoke to some welcome news. George Gallup reported that by a margin of two to one, Americans approved of the Supreme Court's reapportionment decisions, evidence to one pundit that it was the politicians intent on preserving their own power, and not the general public, who were driving the opposition to the rulings. Simultaneously, big-city mayors from across the country stepped into the fray. Annoyed that the White House had directed officials in the Department of Justice to help draft the compromise over the Dirksen rider, Democratic mayors in Chicago, Philadelphia, Pittsburgh, St. Louis, Boston, Detroit, and St. Petersburg, Florida, questioned why the administration had taken steps so clearly at odds with the needs of their cities and their constituents, the very same people whose votes the Democrats would need in November. Over the next several weeks, the mayors of Los Angeles, Minneapolis, New York City, and Wilmington, Delaware, voiced similar sentiments about the rider and the administration's sanction of it.[35]

The entrance of so many key Democratic mayors into the divisive reapportionment debate could not have come at a worse time for the White House. Lyndon Johnson imagined the Democratic Convention as a coronation of sorts, a bestowal of legitimacy after the difficult circumstances of his elevation to the presidency. Johnson prized a unified convention as an important step in achieving that legitimacy. But even before it officially opened on August 24, officials in the administration and the Democratic Party were confronted with the possibility of an open revolt over the seating of the Mississippi delegation. An interracial group of delegates representing the Mississippi Freedom Democratic Party (MFDP) appealed to the national Democratic Party to seat its delegates at the convention rather than representatives from the all-white Mississippi Democratic Party. Waving banners that proclaimed ONE MAN, ONE VOTE, the MFDP pledged its loyalty to Johnson and the national Democratic Party, something the all-white regulars, who objected in particular to Johnson's support of the Civil Rights Act, refused to do. To this day, the defining image of the Atlantic City convention remains that of Fannie Lou Hamer, a forty-six-year-old sharecropper, the youngest of twenty children, who left school in eighth grade to work full-time in the cotton fields, testifying about the horrors she endured in her attempts to exercise her right to vote and calling on the national Democratic Party to recognize the undeniable moral rightness of the MFDP's request. But despite his own central role in passing the landmark Civil Rights Act, Johnson worried that siding with the MFDP would result in the delegations of other southern states walking out of the convention and thereby threatening the unity he so desperately craved. He and his lieutenants offered the MFDP two at-large seats, a gesture that the MFDP rejected as an insult.[36]

Although not as visible as the dispute over the seating of the MFDP, reapportionment emerged as another contentious issue in Atlantic City. Urban mayors and civil rights leaders pushed for a plank endorsing the Supreme Court's decisions, which would have put the Democratic Party officially at odds with their Republican opponents in the matter. Mayors Raymond Tucker of St. Louis, Robert Wagner of New York, and John Collins of Boston told the convention's Platform Committee that population-based reapportionment was necessary in order to address education and social services needs, among others, in their cities.[37]

Also appearing before the Platform Committee, James Farmer, the director of the Congress of Racial Equality, drew an explicit connection between civil rights and reapportionment. He declared that a successful effort to limit or overturn the Supreme Court's decisions would particularly harm African Americans, given their large numbers in northern cities. "Should the reapportionment cases be overruled or impaired," he testified, "the further disfranchisement of Negroes will result. Racial tension, cynicism and alienation, especially in Northern cities will mount in response to this evidence of hypocrisy."[38]

Robert Kennedy did not come out for or against the proposed plank, but he caused a bit of a stir—and no shortage of embarrassment for the Johnson administration—when he appeared before the Platform Committee. Still the attorney general, Kennedy had been away from Washington campaigning for one of New York's seats in the Senate and his chief deputy, Nicholas Katzenbach, had been running the Department of Justice. It was during Kennedy's absence that the White House sent Katzenbach and Cox to negotiate a compromise with Dirksen. In his testimony, Kennedy did not criticize his deputy or the solicitor general, but he did make clear that he was "strongly against" any attempt to weaken or limit the Supreme Court's decisions. In subsequent years, Senator Robert Kennedy would become one of Paul Douglas's most stalwart allies in turning back Dirksen's attacks on the reapportionment decisions.[39]

The testimony of the mayors, Farmer, and Kennedy swayed rank-and-file members of the Platform Committee, who, perceiving the importance of urban and suburban voters in the upcoming elections, threw their weight behind the plank. But White House aides moved swiftly to quell further action. Informing delegates of the president's desire to maintain party unity, they pointed to the complicated allegiances of Carl Albert, the Democratic majority leader in the House. A representative of a rural district in Oklahoma, Albert had voted in favor of the Tuck bill. He also chaired the Platform Committee. A sustained attempt to add a plank in favor of the Supreme Court's decisions, over strenuous objections from Albert, threatened intense discord. According to one source, the president promised to help defeat the Dirksen rider after the recess if the Platform Committee agreed to leave out the plank.[40]

As the Democrats debated in Atlantic City, Everett Dirksen prepared his next series of moves. Just prior to the recess, he had appeared unconcerned by the little filibuster. "They think they can last," he remarked. "I don't. I'm going to get a vote on this, no matter how long it takes." During the recess, he decided to test Douglas's influence and will by calling for cloture when lawmakers returned to Washington. Dirksen believed that his "hard-core" opponents numbered only five—Douglas, Proxmire, Clark, Hart, and Maurine Neuberger of Oregon. He calculated that ten additional Democrats and three Republicans would support them. Dirksen knew that some supporters of his rider, especially southern Democrats, opposed cloture on principle, but he was nevertheless confident that he could turn out the necessary two-thirds vote to bring an end to the debate.[41]

In an exchange with a reporter from the *New York Herald Tribune*, Dirksen explained why circumstances and timing worked in his favor. He conceded that the Tuck bill was unconstitutional but felt that its passage had been useful in building support for his rider as a more reasonable alternative. Using an unbeatable hand of cards in a poker game as an analogy, Dirksen offered five additional reasons for his confidence. His ten of spades, he claimed, was the foreign aid bill that the president could not veto. His jack was the Department of Justice, and in particular Cox and Katzenbach's affirmation that the language was constitutional. Dirksen's queen was his Democratic counterpart, Mike Mansfield, with whom he had an excellent relationship and who (reluctantly) cosponsored the legislation. The king, of course, was Lyndon Johnson, who had maintained a "judicious silence" in the face of competing pressures within his party. Dirksen's ace of spades was the "overwhelming desire of men and women of the 88th Congress to disband, take a brief rest and try to get reelected."[42]

On the last point, if no other, the Douglas group agreed with Dirksen, though they of course had a different end in mind. Just as Dirksen depended on his ace of spades to produce a vote for cloture, Douglas and those with him were hopeful that if they could turn back such a vote, the same desire of members to go home and campaign would compel Dirksen to withdraw his rider.

The debate over the rider headed toward a showdown after a short recess for the Labor Day weekend. On September 8, Dirksen filed for cloture, with a vote scheduled two days later. On the eve of the vote, Lyndon Johnson was still maintaining his silence. When a reporter asked him if he had any comment on the Dirksen rider, the president responded, "No, sir."[43]

Dirksen's petition for cloture failed by a margin that surprised both sides, but the vote did not accurately reflect where the Senate stood on the rider itself. Richard Russell of Georgia spoke for more than a dozen southern Democrats who vehemently opposed the Supreme Court's reapportionment decisions, but who, despite Dirksen's attempts to convince them otherwise, could not bring themselves to vote for cloture. Only six southern Democrats had joined Dirksen. A subsequent motion to table Dirksen's amendment failed, showing that the Senate on the whole approved of it. Still, liberals, who had expected no more than thirty votes, were delighted to pick up thirty-eight.[44]

Though the Douglas coalition had won a crucial victory, the Senate remained at an impasse. The majority supported Dirksen but could not force a vote. The minority leader refused to allow a vote on an Appalachia aid bill, a top administration priority. The president himself stayed in the background, but his aides and closest allies worked to derail the Dirksen rider by building support for an alternative measure. Yet it, too, failed, prompting the Washington Post to declare it "one of the rare defeats dealt the Johnson Administration during this session of Congress."[45]

As time slipped away and tempers flared, Democrats John Pastore of Rhode Island and Clinton Anderson of New Mexico stepped into the breach and helped bring the impasse to an end. Like many of their colleagues, they were moderates who opposed the Dirksen rider and had voted against cloture, but by the last week of September, their main goal was to get Congress to finish its business and adjourn. Pastore and Anderson, according to White House congressional liaison Larry O'Brien, "told the liberals that either they agree to a compromise which would enable Congress to go home or they would lead a fight to invoke cloture." Whether or not the pair would have followed through on their threat is impossible to know, but on September 23 Douglas reached an agreement with Mansfield on a resolution that refrained from any direct criticism of the Supreme Court and, most significantly for the liberals, lacked any binding legal authority. Before he could make public his agreement with Douglas, Mansfield had to extricate himself from his commitment to Dirksen. The latter, knowing full well that he could not get a vote on his rider, freed Mansfield from any further commitment. Mansfield raced to the floor of the Senate to announce the latest developments; he pleaded with his colleagues, saying that the impasse, if it dragged on, would consign the Senate to "a gross impotence and to a demeaning futility."[46]

The following day, September 24, the Senate passed the Mansfield substitute, 44 to 38. Newspapers across the political spectrum interpreted the vote as a resounding victory for the Douglas forces. During the final debate, Dirksen derided the substitute bill as "not worth the paper it is printed on." Douglas preferred no resolution at all, but he called for its acceptance on the grounds that it would have no practical effect. Among the liberals, only Wayne Morse remained defiant, refusing to vote for any resolution, no matter how weak, that criticized the Supreme Court's reapportionment decisions. Right after the Senate adopted the Mansfield substitute, it passed the foreign aid bill. The following week, a House-Senate conference committee removed the Mansfield substitute from the final version of the bill. The liberals had won the reapportionment battle. But they had consumed so much time that administration and Senate leaders were not able to push through poverty relief for Appalachia or the final version of a Medicare bill, which was stalled in a House-Senate conference. Rather than keep members in Washington a day longer than necessary, the White House and Mansfield agreed to postpone Medicare and aid to Appalachia, thus preserving the president's "untarnished record of legislative accomplishment" and providing him with two issues to take on the campaign trail. Lyndon Johnson reintroduced both bills the following year as part of his Great Society legislation.[47]

The *Wall Street Journal* reporter Dan Cordtz, in a cogent postmortem, noted the irony in a group of liberals using the filibuster, which they had long wished to eliminate, and asked how this particular filibuster had succeeded when other recent ones, those to stop civil rights legislation above all, had failed. Cordtz concluded that Douglas's "little filibuster" was able to achieve its goal not because of "a clearly conceived, smoothly executed master plan" but in spite of a series of missteps and miscalculations on the part of the administration and the Democratic leadership. Cordtz argued that Johnson and Mansfield misjudged the "relative potential strength on both sides of the issue." Convinced that Dirksen had the power to force through an even tougher bill, Johnson had sent Cox and Katzenbach to negotiate the compromise that Dirksen first introduced on August 12. Mansfield also overestimated Dirksen's strength, lent his name to the rider, and pledged to back it. "A rigidly honorable man," in Cordtz's words, Mansfield stuck to this commitment until released from it by Dirksen at the very end. The Douglas bloc was convinced that they could have killed the Dirksen rider much sooner if Mansfield had come to their aid.[48]

The administration's missteps may have been less a misjudgment than a product of the tensions between liberal Democrats in the Senate, who generally believed that Johnson enjoyed too "solicitous" a relationship with Dirksen, and the president, who condescended to many of them, especially Douglas, whom he held in "contempt" and referred to as a "boy scout."[49] Furthermore, unrelated events had probably distracted the administration from taking in the situation in full. Not only had Johnson been eager to unify his party before the convention in Atlantic City, but he also was at that time monitoring the search for three civil rights workers who had been missing in Mississippi since June. And halfway around the world, a pair of incidents in Vietnam's Gulf of Tonkin on August 2 and 4 preoccupied him just as Dirksen first introduced his rider.

Douglas, Proxmire, Hart, and Clark had not necessarily expected to win. As one member of the group, probably Proxmire, recalled, "The best we hoped for, initially anyway, was that we could hold things up long enough for the White House to reverse itself." The administration never did reverse itself, at least not publicly, but as one senatorial aide put it, the White House did shift "from active cooperation with Dirksen to benevolent neutrality toward us."[50]

Even without support from the administration, the Douglas faction succeeded in holding things up long enough to bolster its ranks. According to Philip Hart, a handful of senators, including several who were unsympathetic to the Supreme Court's reapportionment decisions, came to understand that the Dirksen rider could "completely undermine" the constitutional relationship between the Congress and federal courts. Another group responded to the importance of metropolitan residents to their electoral fortunes. Senators on both sides of the issue pointed to events at the Democratic National Convention as key to the fate of the Dirksen rider. The core Democratic constituencies encountered by senators at the convention—big-city mayors, labor leaders, and active members of organizations such as the League of Women Voters who had been working for reapportionment for years—communicated the importance of reapportionment. After such "sobering" interactions, according to Cordtz, "more than one Democratic Senator reassessed his own position."[51]

Dirksen lost in his attempt to break the little filibuster waged by Paul Douglas and his allies, but he was no less determined to preserve, on principle, minority control of state legislatures across the nation. Dirksen and Douglas would renew their battle the following year, though by that time the congressional opposition to the Supreme Court's reapportionment decisions would be just one part of a much larger, more intense, and well-financed national campaign.

13 ||| SCARED STIFF

The failure of the Dirksen breather and the adjournment of the Eighty-eighth Congress brought an end to the frenetic opening skirmish over the decisions of June 15, 1964. Over the summer, Dirksen and Douglas had acted and reacted rapidly without a great deal of time to consider long-term strategy or consequences. The three months prior to the January opening of the next Congress, by contrast, provided leaders on both sides of the debate an opportunity to pause and reexamine their ultimate goals and how best to achieve them.

After the Gallup poll revealed that a majority of Americans welcomed the Supreme Court's affirmation of majority rule, all but the most extreme opponents of reapportionment came to see the futility of an all-out assault on the Court. The goal became to limit the scope and effectiveness of the June 15, 1964, decisions. By the fall, critics shifted away from broad denunciations of the decisions and instead focused more narrowly on overturning *Lucas* v. *Colorado*. Even Virginia attorney David Mays, an unapologetic defender of state sovereignty, came to see the pragmatic nature of this approach. According to a local newspaper, Mays told an audience in Arizona in October that "the present drastic court ruling never would have been made had not some of the states abused and refused to comply with their own laws." In a clear reference to the Colorado case, Mays went on to say not only that the Court had gone too far in correcting such malfeasance by the states but also that he expected the Court to "go along with some formula other than the 'one man, one vote' plan now proposed, if it is reasonable."[1]

Just weeks after the Republican Party suffered crushing losses in the November 1964 elections, Everett Dirksen relaunched his effort to limit the effect of the Court's one person, one vote standard. The Senate minority leader now looked beyond the nation's capital in order to broaden his base of support. On November 30, he called a meeting in Chicago with the intention of opening a second front in his campaign. Joined by Congressmen William McCullough of Ohio and Robert Ichord of Missouri, both members of a bipartisan House Steering Committee intent on overturning the reapportionment rulings, Dirksen gathered twenty-five state legislators from across the country and the heads of two dozen national trade associations. Ernest Tupper, a Washington-based political consultant, outlined a plan to invoke a never-used clause in Article V of the Constitution to petition Congress to convene a constitutional convention, upon the application of two-thirds of the states.[2]

Dirksen chose the timing and setting of the meeting to coincide with the seventeenth biennial convention of the General Assembly of the States. It was at the same meeting two years earlier that, in response to Baker v. Carr, delegates had petitioned Congress to call a constitutional convention for the purpose of passing three separate amendments that would undermine the power of the federal courts. That effort played out in relative anonymity, until prominent figures in the legal community sounded the alarm. When Earl Warren and officials in the Kennedy administration publicly expressed concerns about the amendments in mid-1963, the effort lost steam, although it did not fizzle out entirely.

On December 3, 1964, delegates to the assembly adopted a resolution that proposed a single constitutional amendment that would allow states to apportion one house of a bicameral legislature "on factors other than population." In an attempt to minimize opposition, a provision was added that required any such plan to be "submitted to and approved by a vote of the electorate of that state" prior to taking effect. Enacting a two-pronged strategy devised by Dirksen and his allies, the General Assembly called on Congress to pass its proposed amendment, and in the meantime asked state legislatures "to take immediate, uniform action, in accordance with Article V of the Constitution, to apply to Congress to convene a constitutional convention for the purpose of proposing the amendment." The resolution proposing the amendment included explicit instructions about the form and language that state petitions should follow.[3]

The main sponsors of the resolution designated the National Commission on Constitutional Government (NCCG) to oversee efforts in each of the states. A successor to the Volunteer Commission on Dual Sovereignty (VCDS), the NCCG had formed ten months earlier when more than four dozen legislators from across the country met in Lincoln, Nebraska, and selected Nebraska state senator Hal Bridenbaugh as president. George Prentice, previously the executive director of the VCDS, ran daily operations for the NCCG, a sign of the strong link between the two groups. Prentice insisted that the NCCG chose Lincoln because of its location in the center of the country, but the group clearly wanted to distance itself, both literally and figuratively, from the perception that it pursued a narrow pro-South agenda. Headquartered initially in Lincoln and later in Jefferson City, Missouri, the NCCG's leadership represented states as geographically far-flung as Vermont, Ohio, Wisconsin, Iowa, Nebraska, Colorado, Wyoming, New Mexico, Texas, Oklahoma, Missouri, Florida, and South Carolina.[4]

The NCCG reacted with alarm to the decisions of June 15, 1964. The failure of Congress to pass the Dirksen breather, coupled with the ongoing reapportionment of some state legislatures, only heightened the organization's sense of urgency. Further complicating matters, the NCCG asked George Prentice to resign in late September in the wake of concerns about the financial management of the organization. Thomas Graham, the Democratic speaker of the Missouri house of representatives and a founding board member of the NCCG, took over the duties of the executive director and hired Ernest Tupper to assume much of Prentice's day-to-day work.[5]

In late 1964, despite various missteps over the previous twelve months, the NCCG appeared, at least to Dirksen, to be the logical choice to lead a national campaign against the Supreme Court's reapportionment decisions. Armed with Dirksen's support and the resolution from the General Assembly of the States, Tupper set in motion the plan he had presented to the legislators and business representatives assembled by Dirksen in Chicago. Tupper concentrated on one goal: pushing the single resolution through at least two-thirds of the state legislatures. His first step was to line up sponsors in each of the states. Only six days after the Chicago convention, Tupper reported that "we are well under-way on the project" and noted that the Virginia General Assembly, meeting in special session, had already passed the resolution. From the outset, Tupper made it a priority to "keep out of the papers, and make the effort appear to be completely 'grass roots'" rather than a broad operation orchestrated from the top down. By the end of the month, he had sponsors in forty states.[6]

As Tupper began searching for sponsors, astute political observers raised the possibility that the attempt to call a constitutional convention was in fact designed primarily to compel Congress to pass a constitutional amendment itself. The *New York Times* observed that members of Congress were "leery of the convention method" because they could not control the specific language of a given amendment, nor could they guarantee that a "runaway convention" would not offer other amendments on a host of issues. The *Times* surmised that Dirksen and the NCCG had looked to the passage of the Seventeenth Amendment, which provided for the direct election of U.S. senators, for a model. In 1913, thirty-one states petitioned for a convention before Congress finally relented and drafted the amendment, thereby heading off the uncertainty a convention represented.[7]

Such observations proved prescient. The campaign moved ahead with astonishing speed. Graham and Tupper sent out materials and requests for money to sympathetic parties, publicized work being done by other organizations opposed to the Court's reapportionment decisions, and monitored developments in the individual states. By the end of January 1965, six states had passed resolutions to the satisfaction of the NCCG and the General Assembly of the States. By the end of February, the number had risen to fifteen. Three more states added their support in March, followed by an additional seven in subsequent months. By October, twenty-five states had passed resolutions asking Congress to call a convention to modify the reapportionment decisions. The NCCG and its allies in the Council of State Governments, which sponsored the General Assembly of the States, included in their tally an additional three states that adopted petitions that would be later seen as inconsistent with the other twenty-five. So, depending on who was counting, between twenty-five and twenty-eight of the necessary thirty-four states were on board. In February 1965, Graham expressed confidence that the required number of states would adopt the resolution, but privately he hoped that Congress would act first, "thus obviating the necessity for a Convention." Many others could also foresee Congress stepping in to avoid what one reporter termed "a Pandora's box of Constitution gutting."[8]

In a 1965 profile of the NCCG, the journalist Peter Irons identified the organization as the "spearhead" of a "massive rural counter-revolution." Summing up the group's guiding philosophy in the *Progressive*, Irons quoted its president, Hal Bridenbaugh, who reportedly said, "We fear urban domination." The piece seemed to revive the crude, charged dichotomies put to great rhetorical use by Henry Cookingham in the 1890s and by H. L. Mencken in the 1920s.[9]

There is no doubt that many rural and small-town residents did fear the pervasive and growing cultural, economic, and political influence of cities and metropolitan areas, but in reality a broader series of intertwined divisions defined the debate. In addition to the divide between urban and rural residents, none was more critical than that between business and labor. American businesses, including many based in urban and metropolitan areas, were among the most passionate opponents of the Supreme Court's reapportionment rulings and thus among the most committed supporters of Dirksen's campaign.[10]

In December 1964, just as the NCCG was gearing up to approach the states about a constitutional convention, the U.S. Chamber of Commerce began to throw its considerable weight behind the constitutional amendment Dirksen planned to introduce in the new Congress. In an article titled "How Reapportionment Threatens Business" that appeared in its flagship journal, *Nation's Business*, the chamber summarized its position in stark terms. Gwyn Thomas, an official with the New York branch of Associated Industries who was interviewed for the article, provided a particularly blunt assessment of the potential consequences of reapportionment: "We're scared stiff of the damn thing."[11]

Defining business as a minority interest group with clear rights and protections akin to those held by citizens, Thomas argued that the

246 QLQ ON DEMOCRACY'S DOORSTEP

question at the heart of the reapportionment battles was not one of majority versus minority rule but rather "effective representation of minority interests versus 'winner-take-all' domination." He warned of a "radical shift" in political power that compromised "traditional checks and balances which protect minority interests—business included." Thomas and the chamber believed that "experienced, economically conservative rural representatives" best protected their interests, and were fearful that, as a result of reapportionment, this constituency would "lose out to big-city forces dedicated to restrictive regulation and social welfare programs." Pointing to Michigan and New York, states with powerful unions, *Nation's Business* predicted that reapportionment would result in higher minimum wages, the implementation of new payroll and corporate income taxes, greater unemployment and workmen's compensation benefits, and additional state regulation that might go so far as to empower a state agency to look through corporate files.[12]

That rural legislators protected the interests of business was an article of faith among both proponents and opponents of reapportionment. The former claimed that rural legislators were rarely farmers but rather small-town lawyers in the employ of companies doing business in the state, while among the latter could be found a range of industrial, agricultural, manufacturing, petroleum and mining, financial services, and public utility interests. The NCCG did nothing to fight this perception of the allegiances of rural legislators. For his part, Dirksen seconded the views of the Chamber of Commerce and explained often the many reasons why reapportionment threatened business.[13]

On January 6, 1965, Dirksen introduced Senate Joint Resolution 2, a proposed constitutional amendment that adhered to the language adopted by the General Assembly of the States a month earlier. S.J. Res. 2 allowed one branch of a bicameral state legislature to be apportioned according to factors other than population, but only after such a measure received voter, and not just legislative, approval. The bill was assigned to the Senate Judiciary Committee and the Subcommittee on Constitutional Amendments, chaired by Democrat Birch Bayh of Indiana.[14]

Prior to Senate hearings, the Chamber of Commerce sponsored a panel discussion among four members of Congress who represented a range of views on reapportionment and who provided a snapshot of the debate to come. Congressman Paul Findlay, a Republican from Illinois, sided with the most vocal opponents of the Supreme Court's decisions. Referring repeatedly to "Chicagoland" as if it were a foreign nation, Findlay spoke to the audience of more than one thousand of the "tyranny of the unbridled majority" and the inevitable loss of minority rights once "the grip of Chicago machine politics" extended to both houses of the state legislature. Senator William Proxmire, one of Dirksen's leading opponents, tried to undercut Findlay's remarks by emphasizing that "it's the suburban areas, where the people, by and large, are the best educated, pay the most taxes and by and large, are responsible, informed citizens, have the least representation. I don't argue they should have more representation, but I do argue that they should have no less representation than anybody else." Proxmire reminded the audience that reapportionment, at its root, was a question of individual rights, and he defended the Supreme Court as a necessary guarantor of such rights. Senator John Tower, a Republican from Texas, agreed that rural areas were grossly overrepresented but felt the Court had overstepped its mandate in the decisions. Representative Leo O'Brien, a Democrat from New York, was less certain than the others. He understood that as many as 90 percent of Americans agreed with the principle of one person, one vote, but worried about the unforeseeable consequences of the Court's decisions.[15]

On March 3, Bayh's subcommittee held the first of seventeen days of hearings that would be spread across three months. In total, 74 individuals appeared in person before the committee and an additional 119 people or groups submitted written statements for the record. Members of Congress and a number of governors appeared on both sides of the issue. Municipal and state officials, such as Thomas Graham of the NCCG, testified in support of Dirksen's amendment. Though he had strong liberal credentials and his state was overwhelmingly urban, California governor Edmund "Pat" Brown, a Democrat, took the same position that Earl Warren had taken as governor fifteen years earlier, backing "a reasonable modification of the one man, one vote rule." The Chamber of Commerce, the American Farm Bureau Federation and its state affiliates, the Independent Bankers Association of America, the Cattlemen's Association, the National Association of Manufacturers, and the National Association of Real Estate Boards, among others, argued for the adoption of S.J. Res. 2.[16]

Outside the halls of Congress, business groups mobilized their lobbying and public relations machines. The Bell Telephone Company of Pennsylvania, a public utility, sent out what one critic referred to as a "very subtle" but "strongly conservative" political newsletter to all its employees, prodding them to support Dirksen's efforts. Standard Oil of California (SoCal), one of the leading contributors to anti-reapportionment efforts in California in 1960 and 1962, called on Congress to "Let the People Decide." In maintaining that a majority of people in a given state should be able to choose how best to apportion their own legislature, the petroleum giant ignored the key determination of the Supreme Court that a majority cannot deny constitutional rights to a minority.[17]

The people who ran SoCal stood out as particularly influential among the business, financial, legal, and political elites in California who had fought hard against reapportionment for years and had been wrestling with how best to respond to the Supreme Court decisions of June 15, 1964. These elites enjoyed direct access to Governor Brown and undoubtedly swayed his decision to declare himself in favor of rethinking one person, one vote. By the early spring of 1965, this consortium of California-based interests, with SoCal at its nexus, had begun to raise considerable sums of money and implement a plan that was potentially much more effective than the NCCG's. By the fall, the Californians had emerged at the front of the nationwide attack on reapportionment, while the NCCG had withered and disbanded. Soon thereafter, Dirksen handed the reins of his congressional endeavor to the Californians and began to use their slogan "Let the People Decide" as his own.

Following the reapportionment decisions, most political and business leaders in California rushed to oppose the Court's rulings. State senator Edwin J. Regan, a Democrat and the powerful chairman of the Judiciary Committee, joined elected officials from around the country who flocked to Washington to testify before Emanuel Celler's House Judiciary Committee. Claiming to "have been authorized to represent the entire California State Senate in seeking equitable alternatives to the Supreme Court rulings," Regan defended his state's status quo. He argued, based on a study completed by the League of California Cities—a lobbying group that represented the state's midsize urban areas but not, significantly, the largest cities—that the California senate had been attentive to the state's metropolitan areas, and that strict population equality would prove disastrous for agricultural, agribusiness, timber, and water interests, as well as educational and tax policy.[18]

When Dirksen called for a constitutional amendment, Regan was one of the first to join the cause. Writing in response to a column in the *Saturday Evening Post* in which Dirksen accused the Supreme Court of ignoring "the will of the people" in favor of an "alluring" and "beautifully democratic" but abstract slogan, Regan praised Dirksen's remarks. Notably, he steered clear of the harsh language used by many opponents of the reapportionment decisions and instead soundly endorsed California's "little federal system," which he thought functioned "to the advantage of all." He pointed out that the state's electorate had reaffirmed its support for the federal plan many times. Shrewdly, he refrained from going after the Supreme Court directly. He was willing to grant that the Court had been forced to intervene by the abject failure of some states to reapportion even one legislative body along the lines of population, but he nevertheless felt that the Court went too far in its rejection of the federal analogy.[19]

When Congress adjourned in the fall of 1964 without passing the Dirksen breather, Regan and his allies in the legislature joined with corporate and business leaders to build support for a revised constitutional amendment that Dirksen promised to sponsor in 1965. To that end, they turned to Clem Whitaker Jr. and his political consulting firm. Whitaker & Baxter had managed victorious battles against reapportionment ballot initiatives in California in 1960 and 1962. In those campaigns, as in the one to come, Whitaker oversaw every aspect of the statewide operation, but on the most important issues he reported to Sigvald "Sig" Nielson, a partner in the blue-chip San Francisco law firm Pillsbury, Madison & Sutro, who personally represented his firm's most important client, Standard Oil of California. (Nearly a half century later, SoCal's progeny, Chevron, is still the firm's top source of income.) In turn, Nielson consulted with William F. Bramstedt, a SoCal vice president who headed the fund-raising drive for the campaign.[20]

In January 1965, Whitaker and Nielson drew up a blueprint for the establishment of a citizens' committee that would first "mount over-whelming support" in California for Dirksen's amendment and then try to influence the debate in other states. In a letter to Nielson, Whita-ker summarized the key points of their proposal, sounding like Edwin Regan when he wrote that "strategically, the effort cannot be an 'anti–Los Angeles' or 'anti–Supreme Court' crusade," but instead must fea-ture the "soundness and fairness" of California's plan, which the "voters have repeatedly approved." With respect to the state legislative petitions calling for a constitutional convention, Whitaker saw their "value in ex-erting pressure on Congress" to pass the Dirksen measure but warned that a convention "must be recognized as dangerous" because, if called, it could not be limited to the issue of apportionment. In the most reveal-ing passage of his letter, Whitaker wrote that it was "extremely impor-tant to the business community to have a powerful voice in redrawing [state] Senate districts," yet "it would be unwise to focus public atten-tion" on this community's role. When informed of the proposal, the California Chamber of Commerce concurred in all respects, including that its public role should be limited.[21]

In mid-February, Nielson invited dozens of the most important and best-connected business and civic leaders in California to SoCal's headquarters in San Francisco to discuss the idea of a citizens' commit-tee with key members of the state senate. After that meeting and on the strength of the financial commitments that resulted from it, Whitaker & Baxter started its statewide push. It mailed hundreds of informational packets to a wide range of trade, industrial, and agricultural associa-tions, elected officials, especially members of town councils and county boards of supervisors, and other citizens likely to be sympathetic. On March 8, 1965, only days after Birch Bayh's Subcommittee on Constitu-tional Amendments opened hearings on the Dirksen amendment, Whitaker & Baxter officially announced the formation of the Citizens Committee for Balanced Legislative Representation (CCBLR). James Mussatti, a self-styled constitutional expert who had spent thirty-five years in the employ of the California Taxpayers Association and the state Chamber of Commerce, was named chairman. In a press release and in testimony before the Bayh subcommittee, he referred to reap-portionment as the "gravest governmental crisis in the United States since the Civil War."[22]

Over the ensuing months, Whitaker & Baxter organized a prodigious letter-writing campaign. After receiving signed membership cards from close to one thousand leading businessmen, elected officials, and civic leaders in California, the firm named an executive committee that included the presidents and other top officials of the state Agricultural Council, the Farm Bureau Federation, the Chamber of Commerce, the Manufacturers Association, the Bankers Association, the Real Estate Association, the League of California Cities, the County Supervisors Association, and the Manufacturing Association, among other trade organizations and lobbying groups. Working primarily through this "citizens" executive committee, Whitaker & Baxter then began to look beyond California. By late April, Californians had signed and mailed thousands of letters across the country. Simultaneously, the firm helped California legislators contact, and in some cases visit, elected officials in thirty states. In late June, Clem Whitaker sent Dirksen a summary of the CCBLR's activities. Three days later, the *Washington Post* reported on Whitaker & Baxter's work on behalf of S.J. Res. 2, the first time the firm's involvement received national attention.[23]

To fund their campaign, Whitaker and Nielson knew just where to turn. CCBLR letterhead included the names of the executive committee as well as more than 350 prominent members from around the state, but the major financiers of the operation preferred to remain in the background. In 1962, Whitaker & Baxter solicited $250,000 from opponents of Proposition 23, the initiative to reapportion the state senate, including $25,000 from Standard Oil of California and the same from Pacific Gas & Electric. Between January and August 1965, Californians contributed at least as much to the CCBLR. Standard Oil of California and PG&E gave $30,000 and $25,000, respectively. Southern Pacific added $15,000, while Southern California Edison and the Pacific Lighting Corporation contributed $10,000 each. William Bramstedt, the SoCal vice president who was the chief fund-raiser, claimed that 95 percent of the money came from firms and corporations headquartered in Northern California. Although that figure was probably inflated, it is indisputable that Northern Californians did contribute the bulk of the total. As had happened in previous instances when the specter of reapportionment arose in California, urban corporate interests—and not the rural residents who would supposedly be most affected—proved most willing to open their wallets.[24]

The fortunes of the CCBLR stood in sharp contrast with those of the National Commission on Constitutional Government. By March 1965, the two groups were headed in opposite directions. The sudden emergence and financial success of the CCBLR caught Ernest Tupper and the NCCG off guard. After the March announcement of the founding of the CCBLR, Tupper told Bramstedt that the NCCG could not hope to match the California group's fund-raising prowess, but that he and the NCCG retained advantages, above all contacts and a presence in Washington. Within a few months, however, Clem Whitaker and not Ernest Tupper had the ear of Everett Dirksen.[25]

In the winter of 1964–1965, Paul Douglas and his allies tracked the maneuverings of Dirksen and his network of supporters but moved with decidedly less haste. In December, Douglas assembled representatives from the industrial unions, the American Civil Liberties Union, Americans for Democratic Action (ADA), and the United States Conference of Mayors, as well as key senators and individuals who had been involved in the various reapportionment lawsuits. But this group, which created the National Committee for Fair Representation (NCFR), originally conceived of the NCFR as an information clearinghouse for people and organizations opposed to a constitutional amendment, and not a membership group in the mold of the NCCG or CCBLR.[26]

When Dirksen introduced S.J. Res. 2 in early January, Douglas and his lieutenants in the Senate estimated that sixty senators approved of the bill as drafted, and feared that Dirksen could reach the two-thirds hurdle needed to break a filibuster with a few modifications that he had thus far resisted. The Douglas group settled on a simple strategy: they would delay action on the Dirksen amendment as long as possible, in the hope that support for Dirksen would wane as individual state legislatures complied with the Supreme Court's mandate. Meanwhile, the NCFR produced a pamphlet, "The Vote Shrinkers Are On the Move Again," which blasted the special interests that were then attempting to overturn *Lucas* v. *Colorado*. The NCFR sent one letter to sympathetic parties to alert them to Dirksen's intentions but otherwise left it to individual organizations such as the ADA to mobilize public opposition to Dirksen's efforts.[27]

The Douglas camp was pleased when Birch Bayh's Subcommittee on Constitutional Amendments pushed back the start of hearings on the Dirksen amendment to focus on presidential and vice presidential disability. (Ultimately ratified as the Twenty-fifth Amendment to the Constitution, the disability amendment, among other things, allowed the president, with the consent of Congress, to fill the office of vice president in case of a vacancy. Prior to the ratification of the amendment, for instance, there had been no means to replace Lyndon Johnson after he was elevated to president.) But once the hearings on the Dirksen amendment began in the first week of March, supporters of reapportionment were less sanguine. The first set of witnesses, dominated by members of Congress and state legislators, by and large supported the measure, and it seemed that Dirksen had a real chance of succeeding. Meanwhile, as many as nineteen states petitioned Congress to call a constitutional convention.[28]

Dirksen attempted to define the parameters of the hearings by professing that unlike the amendment he had proposed the previous summer, the revised amendment did not seek to reverse the Supreme Court's reapportionment decisions. Rather, it would "simply" allow a majority of the people in a state to base one branch of their legislature on "factors other than population." He averred that the amendment adhered to the "principle of one man, one vote" because it required that any such plan be approved by a majority of voters, and he claimed to be protecting the "right of the people to determine for themselves the manner in which they will be governed." In Dirksen's formulation— and, he calculated, in the view of two-thirds of the Senate—the Supreme Court had exceeded its authority in rejecting Colorado's reapportionment plan, which had been adopted by voters in that state by a large margin in 1962. As the lead questioner for the Dirksen supporters, Republican Roman Hruska of Nebraska repeatedly led witnesses to state this point and to denounce the Court's ruling in *Lucas v. Colorado* as a violation of popular sovereignty.[29]

Paul Douglas and his lieutenants—William Proxmire and freshman senator Joseph Tydings of Maryland—maintained that the central issue was not majority versus minority rule but rather the fundamental right to representation guaranteed to every individual. For Douglas, *Lucas* v. *Colorado* did not ignore popular sovereignty; it upheld a right that was every bit as sacrosanct as the right to free speech or freedom of religion. Rejecting Dirksen's claim that his amendment did not reverse the Court's reapportionment decisions, the trio foresaw that "factors other than population" might lead to all sorts of mischief. Tydings wondered if these might include wealth, race, or religion. On balance, the arguments of Douglas, Proxmire, and Tydings appeared to have little effect. An early tally counted only ten certain votes, and at most twenty-five potential votes, against the amendment.[30]

The unfavorable start to the hearings woke up the pro-reapportionment forces. On March 8, 1965, the same day that Clem Whitaker announced the formation of the CCBLR from his office in San Francisco, opponents of the Dirksen amendment held a meeting of a far different sort in Washington. In the offices of the AFL-CIO, representatives of national labor, religious, civil rights, and civil liberties organizations joined Senate staff members in an attempt to mold the National Committee for Fair Representation into an organization that could effectively counter Dirksen, the CCBLR, and other opponents. Those in attendance included representatives of the AFL-CIO, the United Steelworkers, the United Auto Workers, the International Ladies' Garment Workers' Union, the NAACP, the ACLU, and the ADA. Officials with the National Council of Churches, the National Urban League, and the American Jewish Congress attended subsequent meetings. The leaders of these organizations knew one another well from earlier political battles in the Washington trenches, and most had been closely involved the previous year in the debates over the Civil Rights Act.[31]

The NCFR's first priority was to round up favorable witnesses to appear before the Bayh subcommittee: big-city mayors, members of Congress, and expert witnesses, including law school deans and the lawyers who had argued the state reapportionment cases before the Supreme Court. No member of the Senate other than Douglas, Proxmire, and Tydings had testified in opposition to the amendment during the initial round of hearings. The NCFR prevailed upon three additional senators—Daniel Brewster of Maryland; Joseph Clark of Pennsylvania;

and Clifford Case of New Jersey, one of only two Republican senators who did not back the amendment—to submit written statements for the record, but no one else appeared in person.[32]

After two organizational meetings, the NCFR announced the appointment of Lawrence Speiser, the director of the Washington office of the ACLU, as chairman. But the NCFR remained a lean organization. Backers of the Dirksen amendment had raised significant sums; the NCFR planned for a budget of only $5,000, almost all of which was used to print and mail newsletters. A check for $200 from the ACLU constituted the first donation. The Religious Action Center, the lobbying arm of Reform Judaism and a strong supporter of progressive causes in the United States, lent the NCFR office space. With no paid staff or public relations personnel, lobbying was handled by the affiliated organizations. The AFL-CIO, for instance, worked through its local and state bureaus to pressure state legislators to oppose the passage of petitions calling for a constitutional convention. Andy Biemiller, the chief lobbyist for the AFL-CIO, consulted with Senators Douglas, Proxmire, and Tydings, and oversaw the lobbying of individual senators.[33]

During the first meeting of the NCFR on March 8, participants discussed injecting civil rights into the debate on the amendment, and they eventually agreed to do so. They could not have known it at the time, but the decision would be instrumental in the defeat of the amendment.

Very few times in years of litigation, thousands of pages of briefs and exhibits, and hours of oral testimony and arguments had lawyers drawn explicit connections between reapportionment and civil rights for African Americans. In *Gray* v. *Sanders*, the Georgia county-unit case, the plaintiffs argued that the county-unit system guaranteed the disfranchisement of black voters, and so served as a linchpin of white supremacy. And under questioning in federal district court, a witness for the state of Alabama conceded that the state legislature was incapable of drafting a plan of equitable, population-based reapportionment because whites in certain counties feared being placed in districts with too many black voters. But otherwise the lawyers, most of whom understood the interconnection between reapportionment and civil rights and several who openly advocated an end to segregation, avoided pointing to racial discrimination in their challenges.[34]

After the Supreme Court handed down its decisions of June 15, 1964, and after Lyndon Johnson signed the Civil Rights Act less than three weeks later, supporters of reapportionment felt less constrained in invoking civil rights. Indeed, some perceived political opportunities where before they had not. At the NCFR's first meeting, Bill Welsh, an aide to Senator Philip Hart of Michigan, broached the idea that the NCFR should connect fair representation to civil rights in order to peel away votes from the Dirksen forces. Clarence Mitchell, the director of the Washington bureau of the NAACP, cautioned against assuming too direct a link between reapportionment and civil rights. Jacob Clayman of the Industrial Union Department of the AFL-CIO questioned the significance of any such link, but Evelyn Dubrow of the International Ladies' Garment Workers' Union argued that malapportionment had hindered the passage of fair housing and other progressive legislation that would have benefited African Americans. After a short debate, the NCFR decided to determine "the full implications of the Dirksen amendment's effect on civil rights."[35]

The climactic battles over voting rights then taking place in Selma, Dallas County, Alabama, helped the NCFR in this regard. On March 7, the day before the NCFR met, Alabama state troopers savagely attacked marchers with billy clubs and tear gas as they attempted to cross the Edmund Pettus Bridge; the marchers had started in Selma and were on their way to the state capital in Montgomery to demand their right to cast ballots without obstruction. Images of the violent clash, dubbed Bloody Sunday, galvanized public support for voting rights and convinced Lyndon Johnson to call on Congress to pass legislation that would become the Voting Rights Act of 1965. From the NCFR's point of view, the violence in Alabama was evidence of their contention that fair representation was necessary for the protection of civil rights. But perhaps more important, the subsequent hearings and debate on the voting rights bill dominated the attention of Congress, the House and Senate Judiciary Committees in particular, temporarily shunting the Dirksen amendment off the calendar.[36]

By the time the Bayh subcommittee resumed hearings on the Dirksen amendment in late April, the NCFR still had no overall strategy, but it had identified the witnesses whose testimony would prove decisive. None had a greater effect than Robert Kennedy and Burke Marshall. During the opening round of hearings in March 1965, the NCFR faced the official neutrality of the White House. Despite its sponsorship of civil rights and voting rights legislation, the Johnson administration did not want to alienate a number of prominent rural Democrats who opposed reapportionment and was perhaps even more determined to hold on to Dirksen's support for a host of domestic and foreign policy priorities. The administration prevented officials in the Department of Justice from testifying before the Bayh subcommittee and from submitting statements for the record. But it had no control over former DOJ employees.[37]

When Robert Kennedy testified, he had been a U.S. senator a mere four months. Yet as a former attorney general who had presided over the Department of Justice when it intervened in the reapportionment cases, Kennedy carried more clout than most other witnesses. And he unambiguously sided with Douglas. Referring to *Lucas* v. *Colorado*, Kennedy stated that, in his judgment, "there really is no federal analogy." He pointed to the fact that 70 percent of the American population resided in metropolitan areas and expressed his conviction that the Court's reapportionment decisions "offered new hope that State governments would at last be truly representative and therefore responsive to the needs of the cities."[38]

Burke Marshall reprised Kennedy's central theme and argued that the Dirksen amendment would curtail the ability of cities to address massive problems "in education, health, welfare, housing, and poverty." But the former head of the Civil Rights Division, who had returned to private practice in January 1965, placed an even stronger emphasis on the link between reapportionment and civil rights. To him, the Dirksen amendment was "specifically dangerous" to African Americans and could very well deprive them of "an effective political voice." Whatever the stated intentions of the sponsors, Marshall noted, nothing in the Dirksen amendment explicitly prohibited the use of racial considerations in reapportioning the second branch of a state legislature that, by definition, would have veto power over the entire legislative process. In a nod to the voting rights bill then working its way through Congress, Marshall said that until such legislation had a certain amount of time to take effect, "it would ignore reality to believe that race would not be a major factor, if not the controlling factor, in any referendum on the apportionment question in several of our States." Americans for Democratic Action called Marshall's testimony "a turning point in the defeat of the Dirksen Amendment."[39]

The case against the Dirksen amendment received an additional boost from Lee Rankin, the solicitor general in the Eisenhower administration, who followed Marshall to the witness table. Because he was a Republican, and because he had first sanctioned the involvement of the Department of Justice in *Baker* v. *Carr*, Rankin gave the anti-Dirksen camp an aura of bipartisanship. In his testimony, Rankin roundly rejected the Dirksen amendment and similar proposals, warning that they would cause "a constitutional crisis of major importance." Rankin reminded his audience that the effect of malapportionment goes well beyond the election of a particular representative and "pervades every part of the legislative process." Consequently, he concluded, "malapportionment does much more far-reaching damage than the violation of other constitutional rights."[40]

On May 20, the next-to-last day of hearings before the Bayh subcommittee, the Detroit attorney Theodore Sachs cogently summarized the argument of those opposed to the Dirksen amendment. The general counsel for the Michigan AFL-CIO, who had argued Michigan's reapportionment case in state court, Sachs provided an overview of the history of malapportionment in Michigan and of its negative effect on the state's social and economic development. He argued that the Dirksen amendment and other attempts to set back reapportionment were merely "smokescreens" for vested interests that wanted to preserve the status quo. Perhaps the most eloquent moment of his eloquent testimony came when he said that "it is tragically ironic, therefore, that while Congress anticipates adoption of the Voting Rights Act, Congress should also be considering its effective repeal. And I mean just that."[41]

The Senate passed the Voting Rights Act on May 26, 1965, and in early June, Joseph Tydings delivered his maiden speech on the Senate floor. The freshman senator from Maryland characterized the Dirksen amendment as a veiled attempt to establish rotten boroughs akin to those found in nineteenth-century Britain and claimed that his "principal fear" was that the amendment would undermine hard-won gains in civil and voting rights. The text of the speech was widely circulated; Clem Whitaker called it "the opposition's first full-blown dissertation on our favorite subject" and even complimented Tydings for "a smooth job which will be effective with many of the northern liberals." Soon after the speech, the National Council of Churches and the Leadership Conference on Civil Rights, among others, formally declared their opposition to the amendment.[42]

Later that month, the Senate Subcommittee on Constitutional Amendments reported S.J. Res. 2 to the full Judiciary Committee by a vote of 6–2, with only Birch Bayh and Joseph Tydings dissenting. The full Judiciary Committee was more evenly divided. Opponents of the amendment tried to delay a vote and went so far as to raise the possibility of another filibuster. But on July 19, Jacob Javits, a liberal Republican from New York, announced that he would not back the amendment, deadlocking the committee 8 to 8. Given that a tie vote in committee would effectively kill the measure, an optimistic Joseph Tydings called for a vote by the full committee on July 20. Dirksen now found himself in the position of needing to delay further action.[43]

Dirksen knew that he lacked the votes to report his amendment to the full Senate, but he promised reporters that he would use every parliamentary device at his disposal to advance his measure. "I'm playing for keeps," he declared. "I may get licked. But it's going to be a fight." Dirksen's closest ally in the fight against reapportionment, Roman Hruska of Nebraska, repaired to the Senate floor and delivered a lengthy address whose title, "Let the People Decide Fair Apportionment," reflected the influence of Clem Whitaker and would become the rallying cry of the Dirksen camp. Two days later, on July 22, Dirksen caught his adversaries off guard when he moved to substitute his entire amendment for an innocuous resolution that designated the first week in September "National American Legion Baseball Week." Final passage of the amendment would still require a two-thirds vote, but Dirksen needed only a majority of votes to place the substitute before the full Senate and thus bypass the deadlocked Judiciary Committee. Dirksen's audacious maneuver, according to one reporter, "dazzled even his most bitter opponents." Douglas labeled Dirksen's latest effort the "foul ball" amendment, swore to fight all summer, fall, and winter, if necessary, and said a filibuster would be the result if his side mustered fewer than the thirty-four votes needed to block final passage of a constitutional amendment. Dirksen's unexpected ploy provided fodder for editorial cartoonists.[44]

As both sides prepared for the climactic vote on the Senate floor, the Douglas bloc was still struggling to force Lyndon Johnson into the debate. The president, however, refused to renounce his neutrality. In mid-March, as the Bayh subcommittee began its hearings, a White House official had stated that the administration had taken no position on any of the reapportionment amendments. In mid-May, as the hearings wound down, conservative columnists Rowland Evans and Robert Novak reported that Douglas and his lieutenants had determined that they needed the president's help to defeat Dirksen. White House aide Bill Moyers privately expressed support for Douglas around this time, but he and other administration officials publicly adhered to the president's position. When a reporter brought up the matter at a press conference, Johnson expressed general sympathy for the need for reapportionment but insisted that "the President does not take action in connection with constitutional amendments."[45]

In late June and early July, leading senators opposed to the Dirksen amendment made one last attempt to pressure the White House. William Proxmire and Joseph Clark organized committees of leading Democrats in Wisconsin and Pennsylvania, respectively, to write to the president and reached out to other senators to do the same. Tydings sent copies of his "Rotten Borough" speech to the mayor of every city in the United States with more than one hundred thousand residents and asked his colleagues to follow up with municipal officials in their states. Mayors from across the country answered the call. In late July, delegates to the annual meeting of the National League of Cities voted by a tally of 429 to 116 to oppose the amendment.[46]

Unlike his boss, Vice President Hubert Humphrey waded into the reapportionment debate. A former mayor of Minneapolis with a long record of support for civil rights and urban issues, Humphrey was a natural ally for Douglas. Humphrey told a reporter for his hometown newspaper—and made clear that he spoke for himself, not the administration—that "the decisions being made now in reapportionment will determine the course of social progress in America for the next 100 years." As the vice president stepped up his lobbying, reporters wondered whether Humphrey, despite his clear disavowal, was indeed conveying the president's opinion. Lyndon Johnson maintained his public silence, leading *Washington Star* political reporter Mary McGrory to quip that "legislative reapportionment, apparently, is the one subject on which Johnson has no opinions." Fed up with Humphrey's meddling, Dirksen asked the president in late July to "call him up and give him hell." Meanwhile, the mayor of Savannah, Georgia, wired the White House and implored Johnson to "unleash Humphrey to fight unnecessary, iniquitous Dirksen amendment."[47]

As the final vote inexorably approached, Hubert Humphrey did, indeed, retreat into the background, but by then Douglas and his allies knew that they had the necessary votes to defeat the Dirksen amendment outright. They would not, in other words, have to resort to a filibuster. Late in the afternoon of Wednesday, August 4, 1965, mere hours after adopting the final conference report on the Voting Rights Act and sending that historic measure to the president for his signature, the Senate turned to what the front page of the *Washington Post* had described as "Douglas vs. Dirksen in the Big Debate." The Senate defeated by a large margin a modified version of the Dirksen amendment devised by Jacob Javits and then voted 59 to 39 to substitute Dirksen's amendment, word for word, for the National American Legion Baseball Week resolution.[48]

As the final speaker in support of the amendment, Dirksen entertained his colleagues for nearly an hour as he recounted the legislative history of his proposal and the many times he had been "lampooned" and "cartooned." Every few minutes, he reminded his audience that he only wanted to ensure that the people of each state could decide for themselves how to structure their political institutions. In response, Douglas began with a humorous nod to the "charming irrelevancies" of Dirksen's address, then quickly served notice that he had no intention of heeding the conventions of senatorial deference. Douglas lashed out at the Dirksen amendment as a "great deception . . . an awesome and, in my judgment, an abominable proposal" created by special interests to "revoke an inalienable right which is now guaranteed by the Constitution of the United States."[49]

When the two principals had finished, the Senate voted in favor of the Dirksen measure, 57 to 39. Dirksen had fallen nine votes short of the two-thirds majority he needed. Commentators agreed that "the defeat ended any hope of Congressional approval," but only one week later, Dirksen served notice that he was not yet done.[50]

14 ||| LET THE PEOPLE DECIDE

The summer of 1965 marked the high point of Lyndon Johnson's Great Society. By early August, the Eighty-ninth Congress had passed an astonishing array of legislation, including Medicare, Medicaid, and the Voting Rights Act. Arguably the most important achievement of Johnson's presidency, and certainly one of the most consequential pieces of domestic legislation in the twentieth century, the Voting Rights Act became law on August 6, two days after the Senate had turned aside Everett Dirksen's second attempt at undermining the Supreme Court's reapportionment decisions.[1]

Even so, Johnson did not see his great endeavor as finished. Most irritating to him was that bills to reform the nation's antiquated immigration system and to repeal section 14(b) of the Taft-Hartley Act languished on the calendar. Again, Dirksen perceived the president's desire to pass legislation unrelated to reapportionment as an opportunity to limit the impact of the Court's decisions. Dirksen and Clem Whitaker launched yet another national campaign, larger and better funded than previous ones. Aware of the need to attract votes as well as money, Dirksen and his advisers offered the American public, and thus their elected representatives, an alternative notion of popular sovereignty, one that proposed the California-born slogan "Let the People Decide" in place of "one person, one vote."[2]

On August 11, 1965, Dirksen introduced Senate Joint Resolution 103, his third attempt to fight the Supreme Court's decisions of June 15,

1964. Declaring that he had taken into consideration every reasonable objection to his previous efforts, he made several key changes that targeted the concerns of a handful of senators who generally supported reapportionment but believed that the Court had gone too far in striking down the plan passed by Colorado voters in 1962.[3]

Dirksen's opponents were quick to criticize his adjusted proposal. Joseph Tydings correctly pointed out that Dirksen's new measure would have sanctioned the 1962 Colorado plan and said that the revised language in the new resolution could not hide "its tired old purpose . . . to perpetuate a minority stranglehold over our state legislatures." Paul Douglas thought it was a trap. In his view, Dirksen had settled for a less drastic measure in the Senate because he expected the House to pass a more draconian version, and he knew that pro-Dirksen senators would dominate any subsequent House-Senate conference proceedings. By this route, Dirksen could possibly bring something close to the House's version to the Senate floor.[4]

Dirksen was confident that his revisions would attract sufficient backing in the Senate, but once again he faced an evenly divided Judiciary Committee, which kept the resolution bottled up through August. Then, in September, Dirksen played his trump card: he threatened to tie up the administration's immigration bill in the Judiciary Committee. With this, Dirksen extracted a commitment from Democratic leaders to report the reapportionment amendment to the full Senate without recommendation. In return, Dirksen agreed to let the immigration bill proceed to the floor at once (where it passed with his support) and promised not to bring up his reapportionment amendment for debate until January 1966. To fulfill the terms of the compromise, Thomas Dodd of Connecticut switched his vote in committee, but only "with the greatest reluctance." Dodd saw no alternative that would not compromise passage of the immigration bill, and he vowed to oppose the Dirksen amendment on the floor.[5]

In the four months before the Senate considered his amendment, Dirksen entered into a formal alliance with Whitaker & Baxter out of which came an ambitious national publicity and lobbying campaign on behalf of S.J. Res. 103. Clem Whitaker sent a proposal to Dirksen for a "Committee for Government of the People (CGOP)," a fund-raising and lobbying organization devoted solely to the passage of Dirksen's amendment. The proposal stated that failure would be "extremely pain-ful and dangerous to the interests of millions of citizens" and identified twenty-one states, including several that had already petitioned Con-gress for a convention, as critical battlegrounds, and ten that merited full-time staff.[6]

Dirksen planned to publicly introduce the CGOP right before the amendment went to the Senate for consideration. In the interim, he and Whitaker & Baxter had much to do. In mid-September, Dirksen and a bipartisan group of senators hosted a dinner in Washington with rep-resentatives of more than three dozen corporations identified by Whita-ker & Baxter as sympathetic to the cause. In the wake of that meeting, Dirksen appealed to prominent businessmen and industrialists to serve on a finance committee. Gabriel Hauge, the president of Manufacturers Hanover Trust Company and a former economic adviser to President Dwight Eisenhower, and George Champion, the chairman of Chase Manhattan Bank, accepted Dirksen's invitation. They were joined on the committee by J. Edwin Warren, the president of petroleum giant Cities Service Company, later CITGO, and Gordon W. Reed, a senior consultant at American Metal Climax, Inc.[7]

Whitaker & Baxter prepared a script for members of the finance com-mittee as they approached the three hundred potential donors the firm had identified as being sympathetic to their cause. Members of the committee were instructed to invoke the bogeymen feared most by big business: labor unions and urban political bosses. The script overstated the involvement of the AFL-CIO in the initial reapportionment law-suits and issued dire predictions about the consequences that would result from a failure to pass the latest Dirksen amendment. Most notably, the script warned that "a labor-city boss dominated legislature would go into the field of wages and hours, unemployment compensation, work-men's compensation, and pension and welfare funds." In soliciting the oil industry, J. Ed. Warren went off script but voiced its essential grievance when he referred to one person, one vote as "the single most portentous and harmful change in the course of government to occur in the past century."[8]

Whitaker & Baxter made a special point of linking reapportionment with the potential repeal of Section 14(b) of the 1947 Taft-Hartley Act. Section 14(b) allowed states to adopt so-called right-to-work laws, which prohibited agreements between employers and employees that mandated union membership as a precondition of employment. At the time, nineteen states, many of them in the South, had such laws on their books. After years of lobbying by organized labor, in July 1965 Section 14(b) was repealed in a close vote in the House of Representatives. The repeal appeared to have enough votes to get through the Senate. Lyndon Johnson, who owed enormous debts to the labor movement for the passage of his signature domestic achievements, had sworn to sign the bill.[9]

Dirksen originally declined to actively oppose repeal of Section 14(b), but after S.J. Res. 2 went down to defeat and he introduced S.J. Res. 103, he reversed himself, much to the dismay of the White House. In October 1965, at the same time that the CGOP was ramping up its fundraising campaign, he led a filibuster that killed the repeal. In February 1966, he again scuttled a bid to repeal Section 14(b) with a filibuster. One Washington insider believed that Dirksen's about-face was the result of criticism from his caucus for working too closely with the White House on the Voting Rights Act and other liberal legislation. Dirksen, in this view, became an active supporter of Section 14(b) as a means of reasserting his party credentials.[10]

George Meany, the powerful president of the AFL-CIO, and his chief lobbyist, Andy Biemiller, arrived at a decidedly different assessment. According to Meany, Dirksen did not have "a damn bit of interest in repeal" of Section 14(b) but saw that he could not win on reapportionment as long as labor continued to work against him. Dirksen had employed the filibuster only to back labor into a corner; in Biemiller's words, Dirksen offered to "call off his dogs on the 14(b) fight" if labor ended its opposition to his amendment. Meany rejected the offer without hesitating, saying that "as badly as I want 14(b) repealed, I do not want it that badly. And the Senate Minority Leader and all his anti-labor stooges can filibuster until hell freezes over before I will agree to sell the people short for that kind of a deal." As important as repealing Section 14(b) was, Meany considered one person, one vote the single most vital component to advancing the agenda of the labor movement.[11]

Whether or not Dirksen felt strongly about Section 14(b), people whom he tried to recruit to his side in the reapportionment battle undoubtedly cared deeply about it. Days after attending the CGOP's first fund-raising dinner in September 1965, W. C. Schade, the president of Ball Brothers Company in Muncie, Indiana, lauded Dirksen's efforts to delay action on the repeal of Section 14(b) and expressed his hope that repeal "can be avoided altogether." William Bramstedt, the vice president at Standard Oil of California and leading fund-raiser for the CCBLR, called Dirksen's performance in blocking repeal "a source of extreme satisfaction" and "an example of the old man's guts and political skills." Nearly a half century later, Section 14(b) remains on the books.[12]

Understandably, business leaders wanted some assurance that Dirksen's latest campaign had a reasonable chance of succeeding before committing financial resources. To this end, Dirksen circulated among potential donors a legislative history of his efforts and insisted to them that the vote on S.J. Res. 2 was actually much closer than the final tally had indicated. He claimed, in fact, that he was just two votes shy of the necessary two-thirds. By contrast, Bramstedt had serious doubts, but he told Ralph B. Johnson, the president of the Hawaiian Electric Company, that "nevertheless, I do think we have to go on making the fight."[13]

Perhaps convinced by Dirksen's assurances, major industrial corporations began to donate to the CGOP. Lammot du Pont Copeland, the president of Du Pont, sent the organization its first check, for $28,500. (The CGOP had set quotas for each firm it approached; Du Pont had contributed $1,500 to the CCBLR and so fulfilled its assigned quota with this latter contribution, as the CGOP thought of itself as the successor to the CCBLR.) General Electric also met the $30,000 ask, Procter & Gamble gave $25,000, and General Motors and the Ford Motor Company each contributed $20,000. United States Steel sent a check for $15,000, as did Minnesota Mining & Manufacturing, Olin Mathieson Chemical Co., R. J. Reynolds Tobacco, and the Winn-Dixie grocery chain.[14] No sector of the American economy contributed more money to the CGOP than the oil industry. J. Ed. Warren, who personally gave $10,000, solicited each of the oil companies on Whitaker & Baxter's list, securing $25,000 from Standard Oil of Indiana and $15,000 each from Phillips Petroleum, Shell, Socony Mobil, and Gulf. His own firm, Cities Service Company, sent the same amount. The total from the oil industry surpassed $175,000, well over one-quarter of the $620,000 raised by the CGOP in support of S.J. Res. 103.[15]

Yet as Dirksen and Whitaker made final preparations for the public debut of the CGOP, a number of press accounts raised the possibility that they were running out of time. Late in 1965, the *New York Times* reported that the drive to secure petitions in state legislatures had stalled. The *Wall Street Journal* and the *Washington Post* remarked on the rapidity with which at least thirty states, whether driven by legislative action or court order, had already met the Supreme Court's one person, one vote standard—and on the fact that most of the remaining states appeared headed in the same direction. The *Journal* lamented that Dirksen's outlook was "dim."[16]

Dirksen, who was adamant that he could get his amendment passed, announced the formation of the CGOP at a Capitol Hill press conference on January 19, 1966. He insisted that his fundamental purpose was "to let the people of each state decide the manner of apportionment of their state legislatures." First envisioned by Whitaker & Baxter as a counterweight to the pithy, popular, and highly effective "one person, one vote," the phrase "Let the People Decide" thereafter became the rallying cry of pro-Dirksen forces.[17]

By this point, the CGOP was more than an appendage of Dirksen's political party; it was a thoroughly bipartisan entity. In December 1965, as the corporate donations flowed in, Dirksen had prevailed upon five senators and five representatives—six Democrats and four Republicans—to join him on an official advisory committee, while Clem Whitaker staffed his newly opened Washington office with people close to both the Democratic and Republican National Committees.[18]

In conjunction with Dirksen's January announcement, Whitaker & Baxter began to reach out to the news media and national organizations. Over the next ninety days, the firm sent out forty-five press releases, each announcing that it had won the support of a member of Congress or a prominent local official. Whitaker & Baxter distributed more than 1.6 million copies of its primary pamphlet, "Let the People Decide," to members of trade and business groups, real estate and manufacturing associations, state and local chambers of commerce, political committees, and professional societies. Although corporations contributed more than 95 percent of the funds raised by the firm, a number of individuals—perhaps these were the "people" who would "decide" the fate of reapportionment—did send small donations to defray the cost of the pamphlets. Miss Loyola T. Haenel, the vice chair of the Republican County Committee of Dormont, a suburb of Pittsburgh, sent $2 to pay for two thousand copies of "Let the People Decide," while Mrs. John F. Hector of Narrowsburg, New York, sent $1 for enough copies to distribute to her 150-person mailing list. "There is so much to be done," Hector wrote in her request. "The average citizen has no idea whatever about this Supreme Court decision. Please keep heart, and remember there are many of us scattered throughout the country who will do their best." Nearly a half century later, these and other small donations, one for as little as 50¢, remained unspent in the surviving papers of Whitaker & Baxter.[19]

Also during this time, Clem Whitaker recruited prominent individuals in each of the fifty states to be official members of the CGOP. More than 2,500 people returned signed pledge cards proclaiming that "the best solution to the reapportionment crisis is corrective action in the form of an amendment to the United States Constitution." Among those who returned a signed card was George Bush of 5525 Briar Drive, Houston, Texas.[20]

Even with the support of the future forty-first president of the United States, the debate over Everett Dirksen's reapportionment amendment differed little from the debate over the previous one. Given the extensive record accumulated in support of S.J. Res. 2, Birch Bayh's Subcommittee on Constitutional Amendments held no additional hearings. Paul Douglas, William Proxmire, and Joseph Tydings once again found themselves the primary opposition. Proxmire and Tydings made a point of chiding Dirksen for refusing to reveal who was financing Whitaker & Baxter's operations. Proxmire, vastly underestimating the resources at the public relations firm's disposal, guessed that thousands, perhaps tens of thousands of dollars, had been spent on behalf of Dirksen's amendment.[21]

On April 20, 1966, the Senate defeated the new Dirksen amendment, 58–41. Lee Metcalf, a Democrat from Montana who voted against the amendment, was the only senator to switch his vote from the previous year. The lack of movement within the chamber gave credence to the assertion made by the *New York Times* that the debate over S.J. Res. 103 offered little more than a "tired rerun of arguments used the last three years."[22]

Ever defiant, Dirksen vowed to press on and introduce his amendment the following year, but reality intervened. By the summer of 1966, forty-six of the fifty states had substantially complied with the Supreme Court's mandate, and the remaining four—Louisiana, Mississippi, Maine, and Hawaii—were expected to do so within two years. Even in California, lawmakers avoided the intervention of the courts by reapportioning both branches of the state legislature on a strict population basis. Overnight, residents of Los Angeles County saw their representation in the forty-member senate increase from one to fourteen and a half (they shared one senator with a neighboring county). As the *Washington Post* editorial page saw it, though many citizens and legislators believed that the Supreme Court had exceeded its authority, they recognized that "it would be impossible to put Humpty-Dumpty together again."[23]

Dirksen had one remaining option: to secure sufficient state petitions to call a constitutional convention. With an eye toward the early months of 1967, when most state legislatures were scheduled to convene, Clem Whitaker canvassed the country, consulted with legislators and lobbyists—especially those with ties to state chambers of commerce, manufacturers' associations, farm bureaus, and petroleum interests—and evaluated the prospects for success. Dirksen needed at least six additional petitions to reach the constitutional threshold of thirty-four; Whitaker identified nine states that he believed were most likely to call for a convention, plus several others that presented an outside chance of doing the same. The California political consultant then began intense lobbying in each of the targeted states.[24]

The results of the 1966 midterm elections, in which Republicans made notable gains in Congress and in state legislatures across the country, figured prominently in Whitaker's analysis, but they defied the easy categorization he applied to them. Although reapportionment had always been a bipartisan issue, varying from place to place depending on which party benefited the most from the status quo, Whitaker interpreted all Republican victories as favorable for Dirksen. In states such as Illinois, Indiana, Iowa, and Colorado, this was the correct assumption. In other states, however, Republican legislators turned out to be less enamored of Dirksen's crusade. The executive vice president of Associated Industries of Vermont told Whitaker that most of the Republicans in the Vermont legislature were "left of center" and had no appetite for a convention. In Oregon, a state that Whitaker rated as likely to call for a convention, party leaders balked, mindful that their gains had been primarily in suburban areas, while Democrats continued to enjoy strength in less populated parts of the state. Meanwhile, Republican legislators in Delaware owed their electoral gains to metropolitan voters in the Wilmington area, and urban Republicans had filed the state's reapportionment lawsuit, which was among the six decided on June 15, 1964, in response to rural Democrats stifling control of the state's government.[25]

Throughout the early months of 1967, Whitaker and his staff monitored, and attempted to influence, the proceedings in various state capitals. Their efforts paid off in Indiana, North Dakota, Illinois, and Colorado, which all adopted resolutions calling on Congress to convene a constitutional convention. Now claiming that thirty-two states had petitioned Congress to call a convention, the CGOP needed just two more to complete its unlikely mission. Clem Whitaker had good reason to feel optimistic. At least ten states that had not yet taken a position on the Dirksen amendment were in session. In two of them, Iowa and Alaska, the lower chamber of the legislature had adopted the Dirksen resolution in February, and support in the respective state senates appeared sufficient for passage. Whitaker saw victory within reach.[26]

The news that Indiana, North Dakota, Illinois, and Colorado had lent their support to a constitutional convention caught proponents of reapportionment, along with "official Washington," unawares. The non-partisan League of Women Voters, for instance, had stepped back from the issue after the defeat of S.J. Res. 103 the previous April. But within days of news reports that thirty-two states had adopted petitions, the national LWV mobilized its state affiliates. Mrs. Robert J. Stuart, the president of the LWV, reiterated her organization's commitment to reapportionment and challenged the legitimacy of most of the petitions.

She placed the number of states in Dirksen's pocket at thirty, not thirty-two, pointing out that Wyoming and Washington, although they had passed petition resolutions in 1963 to strip the federal courts of jurisdiction in all apportionment disputes, did not subsequently embrace the language proposed by the General Assembly of the States and championed by Dirksen. Another of her arguments would shape the coming debate in a more important way: in Stuart's view, twenty-four of the other thirty petitions were invalid because the state legislatures that adopted them were, at the time, constituted on a nonpopulation basis. Only six states, she claimed, had first reapportioned both houses on a population basis and then called for a convention to allow one house to be based on other factors.[27]

On Capitol Hill, Proxmire and Tydings echoed Stuart. The senators reasoned that Congress was under no obligation to accept flawed petitions and, therefore, was unlikely to call a convention. Dirksen dismissed their claims and predicted that Congress would, in fact, call a convention upon the application of two more states. At the same time, he attempted to quell mounting concern that a convention could not be limited to a single issue, asserting unequivocally that a convention would confine itself to reapportionment. Tydings and Proxmire wasted no time before they began stressing the dangers of what the newspapers soon labeled a "runaway convention."[28]

After the Colorado, Illinois, Indiana, and North Dakota legislatures called for a convention, the *New York Times* and the *Washington Post* noted the stealth manner in which Dirksen's campaign had progressed. The *Times* went so far as to remark that "most of the nation has been completely unaware of this effort or any need for it." Over the next two months, a riveted, even startled, national and regional press corps kept the possibility of the first constitutional convention since 1787 very much in the news.[29]

As opponents of the Dirksen amendment honed a two-part argument—the first challenged the legitimacy of many of the state petitions, and the second tapped into fears of what might transpire in a constitutional convention—supporters of the senator launched a counteroffensive. Conservative commentators David Lawrence and James Kilpatrick mocked the technical objections and the claims that Congress had some say in deciding whether or not to call a convention.

Both columnists expressed incredulity that Proxmire and Tydings could so easily misconstrue the meaning of Article V, which states that Congress "shall" call a convention upon application of two-thirds of the states, not that it "may" do so. For their part, Dirksen and his primary confidant, Roman Hruska, raised the possibility, perhaps unaware of the irony, that aggrieved states might turn to the Supreme Court to force Congress to call a convention.[30]

Aided by sympathetic publications such as *U.S. News & World Report*, Dirksen and Hruska argued against the idea that a convention might do great harm. Sidestepping the question of whether a convention could be limited to a single issue—no one really knew the answer—Dirksen and Hruska maintained publicly that no one should fear the wisdom of the American people as the ultimate arbiters of the democratic process. Dirksen accused his opponents of being "completely devoid of any faith in the process of democracy and the capacity of the people to render judgments in a crisis of this character and magnitude." Hruska added that a convention itself, like the Congress, had the power only to suggest amendments, not make changes to the Constitution without ratification by the people of the individual states. He professed his belief that opponents of the Dirksen amendment greatly exaggerated what might transpire.[31]

Even so, Dirksen and Hruska understood that many of their own supporters, especially in Congress and the business community, feared a runaway convention. Dirksen and his closest advisers, including Clem Whitaker, had long envisioned the threat of a convention as no more than a prod to push an amendment through Congress. Whitaker, who owed his livelihood to various corporations, knew that an actual convention had to be avoided at all costs. In the spring of 1967, Dirksen was publicly stumping for a convention but still had not abandoned his original strategy. In early April, he contacted legislative leaders in states still considering a convention petition and asked for their help. He needed only two more states to sign on, he claimed, and then two-thirds of the members of both houses of Congress would pass an amendment and send it to the states, thus obviating the need for a convention. The following month, Dirksen assured former president Dwight Eisenhower that Congress would pass an amendment rather than allow a convention to assemble.[32]

Ted Sorensen, the former special counsel to Presidents Kennedy and Johnson, wrote an article in which he criticized both sides in the debate. The author of John F. Kennedy's finest speeches chided Tydings and Proxmire for their "strict and rigid" attack on the legitimacy of the petitions, which he felt "contradicted the very spirit of the Constitution." Like his ideological opposites Kilpatrick and Lawrence, Sorensen argued that the Constitution was perfectly clear in mandating that Congress "shall call a convention" upon application of two-thirds of the states. In Sorensen's mind, the Founders had intended that the convention method be as accessible an avenue to amending the Constitution as the congressional route. In this regard, Sorensen believed Dirksen's "quiet campaign to rewrite the Constitution" was justifiable. On the other hand, Sorensen saw that this campaign could lead to "a constitutional nightmare"—one that had the potential to do nothing less than "tinker with the Bill of Rights, to halt supposed pampering of the criminally accused, to stop so-called abuses of the Fifth Amendment, to limit free speech for the disloyal, to reopen the wars between church and state, to limit the Supreme Court's jurisdiction or the President's veto power or the Congress's war-making authority."[33]

As the possibility of a convention became national news, attention focused most intensely on two states, Alaska and Iowa. In 1965, the Alaska legislature, dominated by Democrats, had voted for a resolution asking Congress to pass Dirksen's amendment in the form it then took but declined to request that Congress call a convention. Following the 1966 elections, in which Republicans in the state stunned observers and won control of the governorship and both houses of the legislature for the first time, Dirksen dispatched Whitaker to Juneau, where the latter found a generally favorable, but complicated, situation. Informed by an aide to Governor Walter J. Hickel that the newly elected chief executive intended to remain neutral, Whitaker reported that Hickel was "philosophically inclined" to support Dirksen's efforts, but that he did not want to compromise his party's momentum. Ted Stevens, the Republican majority leader in the state house of representatives, expressed no such reservations. Just two weeks after Whitaker's visit, he led a bipartisan coalition that passed the convention resolution 34 to 4.[34]

In Alaska's upper chamber, eleven of twenty state senators backed the Dirksen proposal, but Majority Leader Brad Phillips made sure the measure did not escape committee. National leaders on both sides of the issue attempted to influence the debate. Tydings conveyed to Phillips that a convention might open up the entire Constitution. Dirksen and his staff in Washington also spoke to Phillips and sent a telegram rebutting Tydings's claims. As the pressure intensified on Phillips to allow the full chamber to vote on the measure, he publicly declared that he found Tydings's argument persuasive, or at least persuasive enough, to give him pause. Privately, however, Clyde Flynn, a Dirksen staff member and the senator's point man on reapportionment, confided in a memo to his boss that Phillips was motivated by a personal grudge against Ted Stevens. According to Flynn, Stevens and Phillips both intended to vie for one of Alaska's U.S. Senate seats in 1968, and to that end both wanted credit for shepherding the convention petition through the legislature. (As it turned out, neither Stevens nor Phillips won the Republican nomination in 1968. But in December 1968, weeks after the elections, Alaska's other U.S. senator, E. L. Bartlett, died unexpectedly. Walter Hickel appointed Stevens to finish Bartlett's term, and Stevens held the seat for forty years.)[35]

On the final evening of the 1967 legislative session, Phillips relented and let the measure out of his committee. But as Stevens later explained to Whitaker, Phillips did so with the knowledge that three of the eleven supporters of the Dirksen position, unaware that the senate would have a chance to consider the resolution, had left Juneau for a trip to Japan. Phillips's canny timing proved decisive: the resolution was defeated nine to eight. Afterward, Stevens reported that the president of the senate was "furious" with Phillips. "I am hopeful that you get to 34 without us," Stevens wrote in a letter to Whitaker. "If we are needed next year, we will succeed!"[36]

Meanwhile, in Iowa, the results of the 1966 elections appeared to guarantee that the legislature would petition for a convention. In 1965, a bipartisan coalition in the Democrat-controlled senate had voted for a convention resolution, but the lower chamber, which had an even higher proportion of Democrats, did not follow suit. Two years later, Republicans held more than two-thirds of the seats in the house. They passed a convention resolution in mid-February and sent the measure to the senate. Democrats remained in charge of the upper chamber but now only by a slim margin.[37]

Whitaker & Baxter's contact in Iowa believed that the senate would pass the resolution, as enough Democrats in that body were in favor of it. Opponents of the measure made the same calculation and knew that their only chance was to prevent a vote by the full senate. Aided by a lingering concern that a convention could not be limited to reapportionment, and by a Republican senator who wanted the resolution amended to ensure that southern states could not deny African Americans the right to vote, opponents buried the resolution in committee throughout March, April, and May. Not one Democratic opponent of the resolution broke ranks. In late June, after nearly four months of debate, the measure died when the legislature adjourned.[38]

Six state legislatures that had not yet acted on the Dirksen resolution remained in session at this point, but not one of them seemed as likely to pass it as Alaska and Iowa had. Running low on funds, Dirksen and Whitaker decided to shutter the Washington office of the Committee for Government of the People at the end of July. Whitaker continued to work on behalf of the CGOP from California, but on a more limited basis.[39]

By the time the Alaska legislature reconvened in January 1968, Ted Stevens's enthusiasm had dampened considerably. Stung by his senate counterpart the previous year, Stevens informed Dirksen that, heading into an election year, his caucus would not take up a convention resolution unless the senate moved first. He informed Dirksen that his primary objective "to re-elect a Republican Legislature in 1968" would not "be achieved if Republicans in the House battle with Republicans in the Senate over whether we should support National Republican goals." Stevens's rebuke no doubt served as a telling reminder to Dirksen that the demands of local and state politics more often than not trumped his own national agenda. Dirksen, whose anti-reapportionment stance was based on the belief that each state had a right to determine its own system, should have understood this better than just about anyone else.[40]

Whitaker struggled to make inroads in Juneau as Brad Phillips tied up the new convention resolution in his senate committee. With the help of an Alaska attorney and lobbyist for Standard Oil of California, Whitaker managed to cobble together commitments from fourteen of twenty senators, an increase of three from the previous year. Facing a consensus among his peers, Phillips again gave in on the last night of the legislative session. But this time, as word of the impending vote spread through the capitol, Hickel broke his own pledge of neutrality and prevailed upon the Republican caucus to withdraw the measure. Hickel's reasons for interceding remain ambiguous but very likely reflected his concern, as disclosed to Clem Whitaker, that reapportionment had proved beneficial to Republicans in Alaska.[41]

In December 1968, the *Los Angeles Times* reported that Dirksen was "quietly reviving" his anti-reapportionment endeavor. The Senate minority leader believed that he had come very close to victory, and evidently thought that his goal was still within reach. Refusing to tip his hand and name the states he thought would come to his side, Dirksen referred to the general results of the recent elections, in which Republicans across the country expanded on gains made two years earlier. But Dirksen appeared not to fully comprehend that the Supreme Court's reapportionment decisions had empowered Republican voters in the suburbs every bit as much as they had Democrats in the shrinking cities. As the *Times* wrote, "Republicans generally have profited more than the Democrats from reapportionment."[42]

Dirksen's son-in-law, Senator Howard Baker of Tennessee, understood what Dirksen did not. After the 1966 elections, the newly elected Baker covertly shared with his colleagues a survey revealing that Republicans in the House stood to gain anywhere from ten to twenty-five seats once all congressional districts were reapportioned on a strict population basis. Armed with this information, Baker teamed up with Democrat Edward Kennedy of Massachusetts to deal his father-in-law what one newspaper called "an astonishing licking on the Senate floor." Always on the lookout for ways to undermine the reapportionment decisions, Dirksen backed a congressional redistricting bill that would have allowed districts to deviate by as much as 30 percent until 1972, at which time the population of the largest district in a state could not exceed the smallest by more than 10 percent. When the House bill reached the floor of the Senate, Baker and Kennedy had it amended so that the 10 percent limit would be imposed immediately.[43]

Everett Dirksen, however, was not entirely wrong in his reaction to the 1968 elections. In Iowa, Republicans had taken firm control of the state house and senate, and the following April, both branches of the state's legislature petitioned for a constitutional convention. Iowa became the thirty-third state to do so, just one short of the required two-thirds.[44]

In response to the Iowa action, Senator Sam Ervin of North Carolina introduced a bill in Congress that he thought was necessary "to avoid the threat of a major constitutional crisis in the very near future." A Democrat and an unyielding critic of the Warren Court, Ervin had voted in favor of the Dirksen amendment at every opportunity. Yet he had worried for some time that the Constitution contained no clear parameters for the calling of a convention or the recognition of petitions. Fearing chaos, he had convened hearings in October 1967. According to a member of the LWV, legal experts and senators who participated all became "horrified at the idea of a wide-open convention." Ervin's subcommittee of the Judiciary Committee determined that the Founding Fathers had never contemplated a wholesale revision of the Constitution, and he crafted a bill that would have limited a convention to the particular issue or issues named in a petition, and that mandated that petitions remain valid for seven years from the date they were first passed, a length of time deemed "traditional" and consistent with most proposed constitutional amendments up until that time. If signed into law, the Ervin bill would have nullified the contested reapportionment petitions from Wyoming and Washington as of the spring of 1970.[45]

Still short one petition, Dirksen and his supporters shifted their attention to Delaware and Wisconsin. In Delaware, the state senate pushed through a convention resolution amid the chaos typical of the final days of a legislative session. The LWV, however, was monitoring the situation closely and quickly mobilized its supporters. The Republican majority leader of the state house of representatives responded to the LWV and made sure that his chamber never voted on the resolution. In Wisconsin, parliamentary maneuvering in both the senate and assembly postponed votes until the fall.[46] Meanwhile, Dirksen's opponents, again led by the LWV, began to make modest headway as they lobbied legislatures to rescind petitions. In 1969, the Texas senate and the Illinois house voted to withdraw their petitions, while a judge in Utah considered a lawsuit aimed at forcing officials to withdraw that state's petition. The attorney general of Oklahoma ruled in early August that his state's convention resolution, passed in 1965, had not been signed by the governor and therefore had "no binding effect" on subsequent sessions of the legislature. On August 18, the president pro tempore of the Oklahoma state senate informed Dirksen that his state should no longer be counted among those that had petitioned for a convention.[47]

On Sunday, August 31, 1969, Everett Dirksen checked into Walter Reed Hospital for a surgical procedure scheduled two days later. Intent on keeping up with his massive workload, he had packed a full briefcase, whose contents included correspondence related to the Oklahoma matter. On Tuesday, September 2, doctors removed a cancerous tumor and the surrounding upper lobe of Dirksen's right lung. In the immediate aftermath of the surgery, Dirksen's prognosis appeared excellent and doctors expected a full recovery. The optimism, however, was premature. On Sunday, September 7, Everett Dirksen died at age seventy-three from postsurgical complications. Political friends and foes, along with members of the press corps, rushed to eulogize a man they remembered for his almost unparalleled legislative skill and distinctive oratorical style.[48]

In the wake of Dirksen's death, his campaign for a constitutional convention met its own demise. Despite the ruling in Oklahoma in August, newspapers continued to report that Wisconsin had the potential to provide the thirty-fourth petition. But in October, as the Ervin bill languished in committee, where it eventually died, the Wisconsin assembly defeated the petition. During final debate, a member of the state's legislature pleaded with his colleagues "to let this resolution go to rest as Senator Dirksen did." Several months later, in February 1970, Kansas became the first state to officially rescind its resolution. Single chambers in North Carolina, Maryland, and Washington followed suit. By June 1970, Arthur Freund, the St. Louis attorney who had worked tirelessly to defeat the original reapportionment amendments sponsored by the Council of State Governments, told a retired Earl Warren, "I am satisfied the proposal is a dead issue but one can never be sure." A year later, Idaho became the second state to rescind its resolution. Dirksen's campaign to overturn the Supreme Court's reapportionment decisions had finally come to an end.[49]

EPILOGUE

I n retrospect, it is tempting to conclude that Everett Dirksen and his supporters came closest to victory in the spring of 1967, when Alaska and Iowa appeared ready to file the final two petitions for a constitutional convention that would have gutted the Supreme Court's reapportionment decisions. Or perhaps the turning point came as early as August 1964—once Senators Paul Douglas and William Proxmire launched their "little filibuster" against Dirksen's efforts and forced Congress into recess for the Democratic National Convention, the campaign to reverse the Court never truly recovered. But history does not unfold in retrospect. For five years—from June 1964 until the fall of 1969—an intense battle was waged in the United States over the legitimacy of the Supreme Court and its interpretation of the rights of the individual voter in a representative democracy. The stakes were high. Entrenched interests—among them the most powerful people and corporate entities in America—were dug in. The outcome was not inevitable.[1]

Ultimately, time was the great ally of those who supported the Supreme Court's decisions. By the end of 1968, legislative action and judicial intervention had reapportioned forty-nine of fifty states, or ninety-three of the ninety-nine state legislative chambers in the United States (Nebraska has a unicameral legislature), and redrawn 395 out of 435 congressional districts. In addition to the Oregon house and senate—which had been reapportioned in 1961—only the lower chambers in Alaska, Hawaii, and South Carolina, and the upper chamber in Massachusetts, escaped reapportionment in the six and a half years after

Baker v. *Carr*. Despite the many dire predictions, reapportionment pro-ceeded with relative ease. As legal scholar Robert Dixon wrote at the time, "In the space of five years reapportionment virtually remade the political map of America."[2]

Had Dirksen lived longer, he would have seen that the political con-sequences of reapportionment did not turn out quite as he had expected. Throughout the 1940s and 1950s, reapportionment was commonly understood as a means to correct urban underrepresentation and rural and small-town overrepresentation. Opponents of reapportionment worried that big-city political machines and labor unions would come to dominate state legislatures. And they did, but not everywhere, and not always as expected. By the 1960s, the United States had become a metro-politan nation with a suburban plurality, a shift largely ignored by the key players who litigated the reapportionment battles. As the 1960 cen-sus revealed, the majority of major American cities lost population between 1950 and 1960. Meanwhile, suburban populations in every major metropolitan area grew by extraordinary leaps. In 1950, one-quarter of the nation's population lived in the suburbs; by 1960 the number had risen to one-third; by 1990 one of every two Americans resided in a residential neighborhood defined as suburban.[3]

The importance of this trend was not lost on William Boyd, who monitored reapportionment litigation for the National Municipal League. In the wake of the *Reynolds* decision, as opponents denounced the Supreme Court, Boyd examined the results of the 1960 census and concluded, "The United States is an urban nation, but it is not a big-city nation. The suburbs own the future."[4]

Reapportionment freed suburbanites from urban control just as ef-fectively as it ended rural and small-town domination. Prior to *Reyn-olds* and *Lucas*, metropolitan residents had been lumped together into districts. As long as residents of Memphis, Tennessee, outnumbered sub-urbanites in neighboring Shelby County, for instance, suburban candi-dates needed the backing of city political leaders and residents to win elections. But once they were apportioned their own seats in the legisla-ture, newly elected suburban representatives were free to pursue their own agendas. William James, the president of the Maryland senate in the late 1960s, said that "reapportionment changed the whole complex-ion of my Legislature. Of course, I couldn't honestly say that this has been a great help for Baltimore. The new, younger men come mostly from Baltimore suburbs, and they ran away from the city in the first place. They seem to scorn it as much as the old Eastern Shore farmers used to." These suburban representatives, like their constituents, had fled the cities for a reason and felt no inclination to appropriate taxpayer funds for sewer construction, public housing, school lunch assistance for urban schoolchildren, and other items on the municipal agenda. Most prevalent in the South and in parts of the West—both regions previously controlled by rural Democrats—they soon formed the nucleus of a resurgent national Republican Party as they promoted a "new brand of conservatism" built on the supposedly race-neutral politics of homeowner and property rights and a firm commitment to individualism.[5]

Meanwhile, the rulings' larger promise of a more representative democracy was frustrated in important ways. Nearly a half century ago, an analyst with the Library of Congress's Legislative Reference Service prophetically commented that "we may be passing from the age of the grossly malapportioned district to that of the strangely gerrymandered one." Identified by the New York Times as the "twin evil" of malapportionment, gerrymandering had, of course, been used since the founding of the republic by parties in power to draw favorable legislative districts. After June 1964, both political parties, no longer able to gain an advantage simply by designing districts made up of wildly divergent numbers of people, came to rely on gerrymandering more than they had before. After the 1970 census and every ten years thereafter, legislators across the nation turned to gerrymandering with gusto. In October 2012, the Atlantic referred to gerrymandering as "the dark art and modern science of making democracy a lot less democratic."[6]

In fact, gerrymandering became such a prominent tactic that many scholars dismissed the importance of the Supreme Court's reapportionment decisions, on the ground that gerrymandering negated their effect. In the early 1970s, the political scientist Ward Elliott mocked the "conventional wisdom among the cognoscenti" that "malapportionment was to blame for the worst problems of government at every level." In his view, "the reapportionment cases have revitalized representative government only in the sense that amputating someone's leg and replacing it with a wooden leg 'revitalizes' the leg." Yale law professor Alexander Bickel, a former clerk and confidant to Felix Frankfurter and a critic of the Warren Court, echoed Elliott when he called the decisions of June 15, 1964, "at best a triviality, the movement of mountains and the birth of mice."[7]

Without a doubt, gerrymandering remains a massive stumbling block to the realization of American democracy. As demonstrated during the 2012 congressional elections, when Republican candidates held on to a solid majority in the House of Representatives while receiving 1.4 million fewer votes nationwide, gerrymandering continues to protect minority rule in the United States, just as malapportionment once did. So far the Supreme Court has refused to enter the thicket of political gerrymandering; to do so will require a Court as courageous as Earl Warren's.[8]

At the same time, the Court's historic embrace of one person, one vote comports uneasily with fears that its more recent actions may have enabled "one dollar, one vote" to become a more accurate description of American democracy. Today, corporate interests and antitax groups continue to push a probusiness, antilabor agenda of low taxes, limited government spending, and minimal regulation. The Chamber of Commerce, once Dirksen's primary ally, has led the way as business groups, freed from spending limits by the 2010 Supreme Court decision in *Citizens United* v. *Federal Election Commission*, now spend tens of millions of dollars per election cycle in an effort to influence public policy.[9]

Despite all the skepticism that gerrymandering and other ongoing counterdemocratic practices may provoke, a new generation of political scientists has persuasively argued that the reapportionment decisions did fundamentally remake the American system of government as well as advance progressive political aspirations. The expansion of the suburbs may have resulted in cities in certain regions of the United States missing out on the long-awaited representation they so desperately required. But in other regions of the country, reapportionment had as profound an effect as Everett Dirksen and his supporters had feared. Throughout the Northeast and Midwest in particular, but also in parts of the West, liberal and progressive Democrats won elections they had lost pre-*Baker*, took control of many state legislatures for the first time in decades, and then voted to appropriate public resources for education, roads, hospitals, and other programs anathema to the rural Republicans who had benefited most from malapportionment. In Michigan, the reapportioned state legislature expanded workmen's compensation and unemployment relief, and established a mental-health program. Lawmakers in Delaware established a minimum wage, while the Colorado legislature passed a fair-housing act. In general, reapportionment aligned the policy preferences of voters with the politics of their representatives and redistributed public resources in a more equitable manner. The Supreme Court's decisions not only "transformed American politics," according to Stephen Ansolabehere and James Snyder, but also constituted "the greatest peace-time change in representation in the history of the United States, perhaps in the history of democracy."[10]

In 2005, reflecting back on the idealism of his colleagues in the Young Men's Business Club of Birmingham who challenged malapportionment in Alabama, Clarke Stallworth declared, "We changed the fucking world. On a shoestring, we changed the world." In light of ongoing subversions of majority rule, this claim may seem exaggerated, but in his enthusiasm for altering the course of a nation Stallworth touched on the seminal importance of the Supreme Court's reapportionment decisions. In doing so, he echoed Earl Warren. Interviewed after his retirement by Abram Sachar, the chancellor of Brandeis University, Warren attempted to account for the importance of the decisions. "If we believe in our institutions, if we believe that we're all supposed to be equal," he said, "every man's vote should be worth the same as every other man's vote." Having led the Court and the nation to "the threshold of real democracy," as the Detroit labor lawyer Theodore Sachs put it, Warren understood all too well that the journey remained unfinished—and that the struggle to affirm and reaffirm the rights of individuals to a truly equal voice in a representative system of government must go on.[11]

APPENDIX

State Legislative Apportionment

(Population figures based on 1960 census)

STATE	SENATE Population of Average or "Ideal" District	SENATE Population of Largest District	SENATE Population of Smallest District	SENATE % to Control[a]	LOWER HOUSE Population of Average or "Ideal" District	LOWER HOUSE Population of Largest District	LOWER HOUSE Population of Smallest District	LOWER HOUSE % to Control[a]
AL	93,278	634,864	15,417	25.1	30,818	104,767	6,731	25.7
AK	11,308	57,431	4,603	35.0	5,654	6,605	2,945	49.0
AZ	46,506	331,755	3,868	12.8	16,277	30,438	5,754	b
AR	51,036	80,993	35,983	43.8	17,863	31,686	4,927	33.3
CA	392,930	6,038,771	14,294	10.7	196,465	306,191	72,105	44.7
CO	50,113	127,520	17,481	29.8	26,984	63,760	7,867	32.1
CT	70,423	175,940	26,297	33.4	8,623	81,089	191	12.0
DE	26,193	70,000	4,177	22.0	12,751	58,228	1,643	18.5
FL	130,304	935,047	9,543	12.0	52,122	311,682	2,868	12.0
GA	73,021	556,326	13,050	22.6	19,235	185,422	1,876	22.2
HI	8,082	14,796	3,397	23.4	3,962	4,679	2,257	47.8
ID	15,163	93,460	915	16.6	10,590	15,576	915	32.7
IL	173,812	565,300	53,500	28.7	170,865	160,200	34,433	39.9
IN	93,250	171,089	39,011	40.4	46,625	79,538	14,804	34.8
IA	55,110	266,314	29,696	35.2	25,532	133,157	7,910	26.9
KS	54,465	343,231	16,083	26.8	17,428	68,646	2,069	18.5
KY	79,951	131,906	45,122	42.0	30,382	67,789	11,364	34.1
LA	83,513	248,427	31,175	33.0	31,019	120,205	6,909	34.1
ME	28,508	45,687	16,146	46.9	6,418	13,102	2,394	39.7
MD	106,920	492,428	15,481	14.2	29,290	82,071	6,541	25.3
MA	128,714	199,017	86,355	44.6	21,452	49,478	3,559	45.3
MI	200,682	690,259	55,806	29.0	71,120	135,268	34,006	44.0
MN	50,953	99,446	26,458	40.1	26,060	99,446	8,343	34.5
MS	44,452	126,502	14,314	34.6	15,558	59,542	3,576	29.1
MO	127,053	155,683	96,477	47.7	26,502	52,970	3,960	20.3
MT	12,049	79,016	894	16.1	7,178	12,537	894	36.6
NE	32,822	51,757	18,824	36.6	c	c	c	c
NV	16,781	127,016	568	8.0	7,710	12,525	568	35.0

(*continued*)

STATE	SENATE Population of Average or "Ideal" District	SENATE Population of Largest District	SENATE Population of Smallest District	SENATE % to Control[a]	LOWER HOUSE Population of Average or "Ideal" District	LOWER HOUSE Population of Largest District	LOWER HOUSE Population of Smallest District	LOWER HOUSE % to Control[a]
NH	25,288	41,457	15,829	45.3	1,517	822	1,644	43.9
NJ	288,894	923,545	48,555	19.0	101,113	143,913	48,555	46.5
NM	29,719	262,199	1,874	14.0	14,394	29,133	1,874	27.0
NY	287,626	425,276	190,343	36.9	111,882	190,343	14,974	38.2
NC	91,123	272,111	45,031	36.9	37,968	82,059	4,520	27.1
ND	12,907	42,041	4,698	31.9	5,499	8,408	2,665	40.2
OH	288,073	439,000	228,000	41.0	70,850	97,064	10,274	30.3
OK	52,916	346,038	13,125	24.5	19,242	62,787	4,496	29.5
OR	58,956	69,634	29,917	47.8	29,478	39,660	18,955	48.1
PA	226,387	553,154	51,793	33.1	53,902	139,293	4,485	37.7
RI	18,684	47,080	486	18.1	8,594	18,977	486	46.5
SC	51,796	216,382	8,629	23.6	19,214	29,490	8,629	46.2
SD	19,443	43,287	10,039	38.3	9,074	16,688	3,531	38.5
TN	108,093	237,905	39,727	26.9	36,031	79,301	3,454	28.7
TX	309,022	1,243,158	147,454	30.3	62,864	105,725	33,987	38.6
UT	35,625	64,760	9,408	21.3	13,916	32,380	1,164	33.3
VT	12,996	18,606	2,927	47.0	1,585	33,155	38	11.6
VA	99,174	285,194	51,637	37.7	39,669	142,597	20,071	36.8
WA	58,229	145,180	20,023	33.9	28,820	57,648	12,399	35.3
WV	58,138	252,925	74,384	46.7	18,604	252,925	4,391	40.0
WI	119,780	208,343	74,293	45.0	39,528	87,486	19,651	40.0
WY	12,225	30,074	3,062	26.9	5,894	10,024	2,930	35.8

Source: National Municipal League, *Compendium on Legislative Apportionment* (New York: National Municipal League, January 1962), pp. iii–iv and section on New Hampshire.

[a]"Percentage to control" refers to the theoretical minimum percentage of a state's population living in districts capable of electing a majority of a legislative body.

[b]Figure not available.

[c]Unicameral legislature.

Congressional Apportionment

(Population figures based on 1960 census)

State	Number of Members of Congress	Population of Average or "Ideal" District	Population of Largest District	Population of Smallest District	Ratio of Largest to Smallest
AL	8	408,383	634,864[a]	236,216[a]	2.69
AK	1	226,167	—	—	—
AZ	3	434,054	663,510	198,236	3.35
AR	4	446,568	575,385	332,784	1.73
CA	38	413,611	591,822	301,172	1.97
CO	4	438,487	653,954	195,551	3.34
CT	6	422,540	689,555	317,953	2.17
DE	1	446,292	—	—	—
FL	12	412,630	660,345	237,235	2.78
GA	10	394,312	823,680	272,154	3.03
HI[b]	2	316,386	—	—	—
ID	2	333,595	409,949	257,242	1.59
IL	24	420,048	557,221	277,169	2.01
IN	11	423,863	697,567	290,596	2.40
IA	7	393,938	442,406	366,119	1.21
KS	5	435,722	539,592	373,583	1.44
KY	7	434,022	610,947	350,839	1.74
LA	8	407,128	530,264	263,850	2.01
ME	2	484,633	505,465	463,800	1.09
MD	8	387,586	722,018	223,395	3.23
MA	12	429,048	474,691	281,202	1.69
MI	19	411,747	802,994	117,431	6.84
MN	8	426,733	477,884	363,731	1.31
MS	5	435,628	460,100	237,887	1.93
MO	10	431,981	506,000	390,240	1.30
MT	2	337,384	400,573	274,194	1.46
NE	3	470,443	530,507	404,695	1.31
NV	1	285,278	—	—	—
NH	2	303,460	331,818	275,103	1.21
NJ	15	404,452	585,586	255,165	2.29
NM[b]	2	475,511	—	—	N/A
NY	41	409,325	460,000	351,000	1.31
NC	11	414,196	491,461	277,861	1.77
ND	2	316,223	333,290	299,156	1.11
OH	24	404,433	726,156	274,441	2.65
OK	6	388,047	552,863	227,692	2.43
OR	4	442,172	522,813	265,164	1.97

(*continued*)

State	Number of Members of Congress	Population of Average or "Ideal" District	Population of Largest District	Population of Smallest District	Ratio of Largest to Smallest
PA	27	419,236	553,154	260,767	2.12
RI	2	429,744	459,706	399,782	1.15
SC	6	397,099	531,555	272,220	1.95
SD	2	340,257	497,669	182,845	2.72
TN	9	396,343	627,019	223,387	2.81
TX	23	416,507	951,527	216,371	4.40
UT	2	445,314	572,654	317,973	1.80
VT	1	389,881	—	—	—
VA	10	396,695	539,618	312,890	1.72
WA	7	407,602	510,512	342,540	1.49
WV	5	372,084	422,046	303,098	1.39
WI	10	395,277	530,316	236,870	2.24
WY	1	330,066	—	—	—

Source: National Municipal League, *Compendium on Legislative Apportionment* (New York: National Municipal League, January 1962), pp. v–vi.

[a]As discussed in chapter 7, Alabama held at-large elections for its eight members of Congress in 1962 and 1964. The figures for Alabama, therefore, reflect districts in place at the time of the 1960 congressional elections. See *Moore* v. *Moore*, 229 F. Supp. 435 (1964), esp. note 2.

[b]Hawaii and New Mexico elected both representatives at-large.

NOTES

ABBREVIATIONS

AC	Archibald Cox
ADA	Americans for Democratic Action
AJF	Arthur J. Freund
ASC	August Scholle Collection, Archives of Labor and Urban Affairs, Walther P. Reuther Library, Wayne State University, Detroit, Michigan
Bayh Report	U.S. Senate, Subcommittee on Constitutional Amendments of the Committee on the Judiciary, *Reapportionment of State Legislatures, Hearings on S.J. Res. 2*, 89th Congress, First Session, March 3–May 21, 1965 (Washington, D.C.: Government Printing Office, 1965)
BJT	Bruce J. Terris
BM	Burke Marshall
BPH	*Birmingham Post-Herald*
BPL	Birmingham Public Library
CEW	Charles E. Whittaker
CGOP	Committee for the Government of the People
CJS	Clarke J. Stallworth
CM	Charles Morgan
CMP	Charles Morgan Papers, Alabama Department of Archives and History, Montgomery, Alabama
CR	*Congressional Record*
CRDP	Papers of the Civil Rights Division, Department of Justice, Kennedy Administration (on microfilm), JFKL
CSA	California State Archives, Sacramento
CSM	*Christian Science Monitor*
CW	Clem Whitaker Jr.

DJM	David J. Mays
DWP	Dirksen Working Papers, Dirksen Congressional Center, Pekin, IL
ECP	Emanuel Celler Papers, Manuscript Division, Library of Congress
EDC	Edmund D. Campbell
EJB	Emmet J. Bondurant, II
EJBP	Emmet J. Bondurant, II, Papers, in possession of the author
EMD	Everett M. Dirksen
EW	Earl Warren
EWP	Earl Warren Papers, Manuscript Division, Library of Congress
FF	Felix Frankfurter
FFP	Felix Frankfurter Papers, Manuscript Division, Library of Congress
FFP-H	Felix Frankfurter Papers, Law School Library, Harvard University (on microfilm)
FXB	Francis X. "Frank" Beytagh
GGP	Gene Graham Papers, University of Illinois Urbana-Champaign
GPT	George Peach Taylor
HEH	Henry E. Howell
HEHP	Henry E. Howell Papers, Patricia W. & J. Douglas Perry Library, Old Dominion University, Norfolk, Virginia
HLB	Hugo L. Black
JFKL	John F. Kennedy Presidential Library, Boston, Massachusetts
JMH	John Marshall Harlan
JMHP	John Marshall Harlan Papers, Seely G. Mudd Manuscript Library, Princeton University
JWM	John W. McConnell Jr.
JWMP	John W. McConnell Jr. Papers, in possession of author
KGP	Ken Gormley Papers, Law School Library, Harvard University
LAT	*Los Angeles Times*
LBJL	Lyndon Baines Johnson Presidential Library, Austin, Texas
LOC	Library of Congress, Washington, D.C.
LWV	League of Women Voters
LWVP	League of Women Voters of the United States Papers, Manuscript Division, Library of Congress
MBA	Morris B. Abram
MBAP	Morris B. Abram Papers, Manuscript, Archives, and Rare Book Library, Emory University, Atlanta
NARA-SE	National Archives and Records Administration Southeast Region, Atlanta
NML	National Municipal League
NYHT	*New York Herald Tribune*
NYT	*New York Times*
OA	oral argument
PHDP	Paul H. Douglas Papers, Chicago Historical Society, Chicago

PS	Potter Stewart
RG 60	Record Group 60, Department of Justice General Records, Straight Numerical Files #233542, National Archives and Records Administration, College Park, Maryland
SCUS	Supreme Court of the United States
TCC	Tom C. Clark
TCCP	Tom C. Clark Papers, Tarlton Law Library, University of Texas, Austin
TDG	Thomas D. Graham
TN-LWVP	League of Women Voters of Tennessee Papers, Tennessee State Library and Archives, Nashville (on microfilm)
TOR	Transcript of Record
USDC	United States District Court
W&BP	Whitaker & Baxter Campaigns, Inc. Papers, California State Archives, Sacramento
WC	Walter Chandler
WES	Washington Evening Star
WHCF	White House Central Files
WJB	William J. Brennan
WJBP	William J. Brennan Papers, Manuscript Division, Library of Congress
WOD	William O. Douglas
WODP	William O. Douglas Papers, Manuscript Division, Library of Congress
WP	Washington Post
ZTO	Z. Thomas Osborn

EPIGRAPHS

1. Charles Francis Adams, "Address to the People of Quincy, Delivered, At Their Invitation, November 5, 1853," *Boston Daily Advertiser*, reprinted in *Discussions on the Constitution Proposed to the People of Massachusetts by the Convention of 1853* (Boston: Little, Brown & Co., 1854), pp. 233–57 (quotation on p. 251).
2. Telephone interview with author, October 14, 2005.

PROLOGUE

1. "Warren-Johnson Letters," *NYT*, June 27, 1968, p. 30; "Warren Defends Johnson's Naming of a Successor," *NYT*, July 6, 1968, pp. 1, 42 (quotation on p. 1); "Reviews 15 Years of Court: Warren Puts One-Man, One-Vote Ruling 1st," *LAT*, July 6, 1968, pp. 1, 5.
2. "A Conversation with Chief Justice Earl Warren," transcript of interview conducted by Morrie Landsberg, pp. 5–6, 10, broadcast June 25, 1969, McClatchy Broadcasting, Sacramento, CA, box 846, "Interview McClatchy Broadcasting Co., 1969," EWP; Gene S. Graham, interview with EW, March 30, 1970, Washington, D.C., EW to Graham, April 14, 1970, box 3, "Earl Warren," GGP; "A Conversation

with Earl Warren," transcript of interview with Dr. Abram L. Sachar, Chancellor, Brandeis University, *Brandeis Television Recollections*, May 3, 1972, pp. 15–17, box 846, "Misc. Interviews, Brandeis University, 1972," EWP; EW, *The Memoirs of Chief Justice Earl Warren* (New York: Doubleday, 1977), pp. 306–12.

3. Richard White, *Railroaded: The Transcontinentals and the Making of Modern America* (New York: Norton, 2012); Kim Phillips-Fein, *Invisible Hands: The Businessmen's Crusade Against the New Deal* (New York: Norton, 2010); James Bennet, "The New Price of American Politics," *Atlantic* 310 (Oct. 2012): 66–80.

4. *Colegrove* v. *Green*, 328 U.S. 549 (1946).

5. *Baker* v. *Carr*, 369 U.S. 186 (1962).

6. *Wesberry* v. *Sanders*, 376 U.S. 1 (1964); *Reynolds* v. *Sims*, 377 U.S. 533 (1964); *WMCA* v. *Lomenzo*, 377 U.S. 633 (1964); *Maryland* v. *Tawes*, 377 U.S. 656 (1964); *Davis* v. *Mann*, 377 U.S. 678 (1964); *Roman* v. *Sincock*, 377 U.S. 695 (1964); *Lucas* v. *Forty-Fourth General Assembly of Colorado*, 377 U.S. 713 (1964); *Avery* v. *Midland County, Texas*, 390 U.S. 474 (1968). In addition, the Court heard arguments and issued an important ruling in 1963 in a related case, *Gray* v. *Sanders*, 372 U.S. 368 (1963), which challenged the constitutionality of Georgia's county-unit system. The principle of one person, one vote was, in fact, first enunciated in *Gray* v. *Sanders* and then extended to cover the reapportionment cases the following year.

7. "Popular Sovereignty," *WP*, June 17, 1964, p. A18 (first and second quotations); David Lawrence, "Apportionment Ruling Deplored," *NYHT*, June 17, 1964, p. 24 (third quotation); William S. White, "Historic Balance Being Destroyed by Highest Court," *BPH*, June 18, 1964, p. 6 (fourth quotation).

8. Jim Newton, *Earl Warren and the Nation He Made* (New York: Riverhead Books, 2006), esp. pp. 385–87.

1. ROTTEN BOROUGHS

1. Alexander Keyssar, *The Right to Vote: The Contested History of Democracy in the United States*, rev. ed. (New York: Basic Books, 2009); Henry J. Cookingham, *Revised Record of the Constitutional Convention of the State of New York, May 8, 1894, to September 29, 1894* (Albany, NY: Argus Company, 1900), 4:10–11.

2. H. L. Mencken, "Real Issues at Last," July 23, 1928, in Malcolm Moos, ed., *H. L. Mencken on Politics: A Carnival of Buncombe* (Baltimore: Johns Hopkins University Press, 1956), pp. 162–64.

3. *The Speeches in Both Houses of Parliament on the Question of Reform* . . . (London, 1832), p. 27 (quotation); John A. Phillips and Charles Wetherell, "The Great Reform Bill of 1832 and the Rise of Partisanship," *Journal of Modern History* 63 (Dec. 1991): 621–46; Gordon E. Baker, *Rural Versus Urban Political Power: The Nature and Consequences of Unbalanced Representation* (Garden City, NY: Doubleday, 1955), pp. 6–8.

4. Gordon E. Baker, "One Vote, One Value," *National Municipal Review* 47 (Jan.

1958): 16–20, 50 (first and second quotations on p. 17); Baker, *Rural Versus Urban Political Power*, pp. 7–8 (third quotation on p. 7; fourth quotation on p. 8).

5. Baker, *Rural Versus Urban Political Power*, pp. 8–10; Sean Wilentz, *The Rise of American Democracy* (New York: Norton, 2005); Keyssar, *The Right to Vote*.

6. Baker, *Rural Versus Urban Political Power*, pp. 8–10; NML, *Apportionment in the Nineteen Sixties* (New York: NML, Aug. 1967), section on Massachusetts.

7. George B. Merry, "Minority Rule: Challenge to Democracy," *CSM*, Oct. 2, 1958, p. 13.

8. Ibid.; "Constitutional Provisions Governing Legislative Representation," Exhibit G, Brief of Defendant James M. Hare, *Scholle* v. *Hare*, Michigan Supreme Court, pp. 67b–75b; NML, *Compendium on Legislative Apportionment* (New York: NML, Jan. 1962).

9. Merry, "Minority Rule"; John Creecy, "Inflation in Your Ballot Box," *Harper's* 207 (Aug. 1953): 66–69; Gus Tyler, "The House of Un-Representatives," part 2, *New Republic* 130 (June 28, 1954): 14–15; Richard Lee Strout, "The Next Election Is Already Rigged," *Harper's* 219 (Nov. 1959): 35–40; NML, *Compendium on Legislative Apportionment*, Jan. 1962.

10. NML, *Compendium on Legislative Apportionment*, Jan. 1962, pp. iii–iv.

11. Ibid.

12. Gus Tyler, "The House of Un-Representatives," part 1, *New Republic* 130 (June 21, 1954): 8–11 (first quotation on p. 8; second quotation on p. 9); Tyler, "The House of Un-Representatives," part 3, *New Republic* 131 (July 5, 1954): 13–14 (third quotation on p. 13); Charles W. Eagles, *Democracy Delayed: Congressional Reapportionment and Urban-Rural Conflict in the 1920s* (Athens: University of Georgia Press, 1990), pp. 23–31.

13. Eagles, *Democracy Delayed*, pp. 32–84.

14. George B. Merry, "How Minorities Help Shape Congress," *CSM*, June 2, 1959, p. 9; NML, *Compendium on Legislative Apportionment*, Jan. 1962, pp. v–vi; Tyler, "House of Un-Representatives," part 1, pp. 9–10. The American Political Science Association, a leading supporter of reapportionment, advocated a variance of no more than 15 percent from the average or ideal.

15. Tyler, "House of Un-Representatives," part 1, pp. 9–10; George B. Merry, "Overrepresentation in Congress: 'Rotten Boroughs' Elect Party Chiefs," *CSM*, June 4, 1959, p. 3; Strout, "The Next Election Is Already Rigged."

16. J. Morgan Kousser, *Shaping of Southern Politics* (New Haven: Yale University Press, 1974); J. Douglas Smith, *Managing White Supremacy: Race, Politics, and Citizenship in Jim Crow Virginia* (Chapel Hill: University of North Carolina Press, 2002), pp. 295–96.

17. Strout, "The Next Election Is Already Rigged" (first quotation on p. 37; second quotation on p. 38).

18. Gary W. Cox and Jonathan N. Katz, *Elbridge Gerry's Salamander* (New York: Cambridge University Press, 2002), p. 3.

19. George B. Merry, "Gerrymandering Lingers Across U.S.," *CSM*, June 13, 1959, p. 10.

20. Tyler, "The House of Un-Representatives," part 1, pp. 8–11 (quotation on p. 10).
21. Anthony Lewis, "On the Trail of the Fierce Gerrymander," *NYT Magazine*, Feb. 19, 1961, pp. 17, 74, 78, 90 (quotations on p. 74).
22. Senator Mossback McKinley to All Republican Party Workers, "Confidential Bulletin No. 1," box 1, folder "Reapportionment and Related Issues and Problems," "Confidential Bulletin No. 2," box 1, folder "Reapportionment #2," ASC.
23. McKinley, "Confidential Bulletin No. 2." "Mossback McKinley" is clearly a fictitious name, but it is not clear if this memorandum was authored by a Republican operative expressing genuine sentiments about the need to maintain minority control or, more likely, a Democratic operative intent on highlighting the very real effect of minority rule in Michigan.

2. CALIFORNIA, 1948

1. Don A. Allen, Sr., *Legislative Sourcebook: The California Legislature and Reapportionment, 1849–1965* (Sacramento: Assembly of the State of California, 1965), pp. 6–10.
2. Dean E. McHenry, "Urban vs. Rural in California," *National Municipal Review* 35 (July 1946): 350–54; Allen, *Legislative Sourcebook*, pp. 6–10 (quotation on p. 9).
3. Arguments For and Against Proposition 20, "Reapportionment Commission," 1926, Arguments For and Against Proposition 28, "Legislative Reapportionment," 1926, California Ballot Propositions Database, Hastings College of the Law, University of California, http://library.uchastings.edu/library/california-research/ca-ballot-measures.html. This database includes a complete list of arguments in favor of and opposed to all propositions from 1911 to the present. Allen, *Legislative Sourcebook*, pp. 11–13.
4. Allen, *Legislative Sourcebook*, pp. 11–13.
5. U.S. Bureau of the Census, "Table 1. Urban and Rural Population: 1900 to 1990," released Oct. 1995, www.census.gov/population/censusdata/urpop0090.txt.
6. Thomas S. Barclay, "The Reapportionment Struggle in California in 1948," *Western Political Quarterly* 4 (June 1951): 313–24; full text of "Argument in Favor of Initiative Proposition No. 13 (1948)" (quotations), California Ballot Propositions Database, Hastings College of the Law.
7. "Argument Against Initiative Proposition No. 13 (1948)," California Ballot Propositions Database.
8. "Here's the New Threat to Our Balanced Legislature," *California: Magazine of the Pacific* 38 (Feb. 1948): 1–4 (first quotation on p. 4; second quotation on p. 1); Northern California Committee Against Reapportionment, "Don't Be a Legislative Beggar," box 6, folder 33, W&BP; "CMA News," box 6, folder 27, W&BP; Committee Against Senate Reapportionment, "Here's Why You Should Vote No," "Organizations Against Proposed Reapportionment," LP 229:331, Senator Randolph Collier Papers, CSA; "Unions Finance Proposition 13," *LAT*, Oct. 14, 1948, p. A3; "The Money Behind Proposition 13," *LAT*, Oct. 22, 1948, p. A4;

"Anti-Redistricting Group Issues Warning," *LAT*, Oct. 29, 1948, p. 7; "13 Reasons Why You Should Vote 'Yes' #13 Senate Reapportionment," box 6, folder 32, W&BP; Northern California Committee Against Reapportionment, "Release: Tuesday, October 19," "Release Immediate," Sept. 21, 1948 (third quotation), box 6, folder 34, W&BP; "Proposition No. 13, Vote 'No,'" *California: Magazine of the Pacific* 38 (Oct. 1948): 3 (fourth quotation).

 9. Northern California Committee Against Reapportionment, "Release: Tuesday, October 19" (second quotation), box 6, folder 34, W&BP; "CMA News," Arthur Caylor column, "San Francisco," no date, box 6, folder 27, W&BP; "Proposition No. 14," *California: Magazine of the Pacific* 38 (Oct. 1948): 3 (first quotation); Newton, *Justice for All*, pp. 185–97 (third quotation on p. 191).

10. Los Angeles Chamber of Commerce, Stenographer's Reports, March 11, 1926, p. 18, April 8, 1926, pp. 21–23, July 1, 1926, pp. 17–19, Oct. 21, 1926, pp. 19–20, carton 11, LACC Papers, Doheny Library, University of Southern California; LACC, Minutes of the Board of Directors Meetings, April 8, 1948, p. 2, Aug. 12, 1948, p. 2, carton 29, LACCP; Board of Directors, LACC, "Statement of Policy on Proposed Initiative Constitutional Amendment to Reapportion the California Senate," April 21, 1948, box 58, folder 39, W&BP.

11. Lashley G. Harvey, "Some Problems of Representation in State Legislatures," *Political Research Quarterly* 2 (June 1949): 265–71; Tyler, "House of Un-Representatives," part 2, p. 15; Carey McWilliams, *California: The Great Exception* (New York: A. A. Wyn, 1949), pp. 210–12; George Merry, "Rural-Urban Imbalance Aired in Legislatures," *CSM*, Oct. 9, 1958, p. 5; McHenry, "Urban vs. Rural in California" (first quotation on pp. 353–54); Bill Boyarsky, "Why They Fight Against Reapportionment," *Frontier* 16 (March 1965): 11–13 (second quotation on p. 12).

12. Joseph A. Beek to EW, Nov. 1, 1948, folder F3640:2140, "Governor's Office Statements, Oct.–Dec. 1948," EW Gubernatorial Papers, CSA; "Warren Opposes Reapportionment," *LAT*, Oct. 30, 1948, p. 1 (first quotation); "Warren Stresses Legislative Role of Rural Counties," *Sacramento Bee*, Nov. 21, 1947, p. 13 (second quotation); McWilliams, *California*, p. 212.

13. Carey McWilliams, *Factories in the Field: The Story of Migratory Farm Labor in California* (Boston: Little, Brown, 1939); McWilliams, *California*, pp. 210–13 (first quotation on p. 212; second and third quotations on p. 213).

14. Newton, *Justice for All*, pp. 174–77 (quotation on p. 174); McWilliams, *The Education of Carey McWilliams* (New York: Simon & Schuster, 1978), pp. 107–108. For more on McWilliams, see Peter Richardson, *American Prophet: The Life and Work of Carey McWilliams* (Ann Arbor: University of Michigan Press, 2005).

15. Irwin Ross, "The Supersalesmen of California Politics: Whitaker and Baxter," *Harper's* 219 (July 1959): 55–61; Carey McWilliams, "Government by Whitaker and Baxter," *Nation* 172 (April 14, 1951): 346–48.

16. Ross, "Supersalesmen of California Politics"; McWilliams, "Government by Whitaker and Baxter," pp. 346–48; McWilliams, "Government by Whitaker and Baxter, III," *Nation* 172 (May 5, 1951): 418–21 (quotation on p. 419). On the 1934

election, see Greg Mitchell, *The Campaign of the Century: Upton Sinclair's Race for Governor and the Birth of Media Politics* (New York: Random House, 1992).

17. Ross, "Supersalesmen of California Politics" (first quotation on p. 57; fourth and fifth quotations on p. 61); McWilliams, "Government by Whitaker and Baxter, III"; "California: The Partners," *Time* 66 (Dec. 26, 1955): 11–12 (second and third quotations on p. 11).

18. Ross, "Supersalesmen of California Politics"; McWilliams, "Government by Whitaker and Baxter" and "Government by Whitaker and Baxter, III"; "California: The Partners," p. 12.

19. Newton, *Justice for All*, pp. 152–65; "California: The Partners," p. 11; McWilliams, "Government by Whitaker and Baxter," p. 348.

20. Newton, *Justice for All*, pp. 185–92; Carey McWilliams, "Government by Whitaker and Baxter, II," *Nation* 172 (April 21, 1951): 366–68.

21. McWilliams, "Government by Whitaker and Baxter, II," pp. 366–69; "Medicine: Which Weapon?" *Time* 53 (Feb. 21, 1949): 48; "Medicine: Expensive Operation," *Time* 54 (Dec. 19, 1949): 77–78 (quotation on p. 77); "National Affairs: The Price of Health: Two Ways to Pay It," *Time* 55 (Feb. 20, 1950): 19–21; "Milestones," *Time* 78 (Nov. 10, 1961): 78.

22. Box 6, folders 20–36, W&BP.

23. "Milestones," p. 78.

3. THE SHAME OF THE STATES

1. George B. Merry, "Battles Waged to Reapportion State Legislatures," *CSM*, Oct. 13, 1958, p. 7; "Inventory of Work on Reapportionment by State Leagues of Women Voters," Feb. 1959, box 886, "Government-Reapportionment," part III, LWVP.

2. Louise M. Young, *In the Public Interest: The League of Women Voters, 1920–1970* (Westport, CT: Greenwood Press, 1989), pp. 153–70 (quotation on p. 162).

3. "Inventory of Work on Reapportionment by State Leagues of Women Voters," Feb. 1959, "Reapportionment in Minnesota: Democracy Denied," box 678, "Government-Reapportionment-Redistricting," part III, LWVP; *Inventory of Work on Reapportionment by State Leagues of Women Voters* (Washington, D.C.: LWV-US, Jan. 1963).

4. Merry, "Battles Waged to Reapportion State Legislatures," p. 7 (first quotation); Theodore Sachs, "*Scholle* v. *Hare*—The Beginnings of 'One Person, One Vote,'" *Wayne Law Review* 33 (1987): 1607 (second quotation).

5. "Inventory of Work on Reapportionment by State Leagues of Women Voters," Feb. 1959, pp. 1–10, LWV of Washington, "Reapportionment and Redistricting: A Study for the State of Washington," State Memo No. 2, Oct. 1954, box 678, "Government-Reapportionment-Redistricting," LWV of Washington, "A Representative Legislature," State Memo No. R3, Dec. 1957, box 887, "Government-Redistricting," LWV of Washington, "Press Release," June 29, 1962, box 1041,

"Government Redistricting," part III, LWVP; Merry, "Battles Waged to Reapportion State Legislatures."

6. "Inventory of Work on Reapportionment by State Leagues of Women Voters," Feb. 1959, pp. 1–10 (quotation on p. 1).

7. Sachs, "Scholle v. Hare," pp. 1606–607; Merry, "Minority Rule," p. 13.

8. Sachs, "Scholle v. Hare," pp. 1606–607.

9. Ibid., pp. 1607–608.

10. LWV-US, "Michigan," Inventory of Work on Reapportionment, pp. 25–26.

11. C. Herman Pritchett, "Equal Protection and the Urban Majority," American Political Science Review 58 (Dec. 1964): 873; Trevor Armbrister, "The Octopus in the State House," Saturday Evening Post 239 (Feb. 12, 1966): 76–79; John E. Juergensmeyer, "The Campaign for the Illinois Reapportionment Amendment" (Institute of Government and Public Affairs, University of Illinois, Sept. 1957), Appendix A, p. 48, and Appendix E, p. 60; LWV of Illinois, "How Will You Be Represented?" April 1965, "Apportionment," Nov. 1969, part IV, box 259, "Government Apportionment, State and Local, Illinois-Indiana, 1963–1972," LWVP.

12. LWV of Illinois, "Legislative Apportionment," Oct. 1962, pp. 1–3 (quotations on p. 1), part IV, box 258, "Government Apportionment Miscellany 1960–1965," LWVP; LWV-US, "Illinois," Inventory of Work on Reapportionment, Jan. 1963, pp. 15–16.

13. Juergensmeyer, "Campaign for the Illinois Reapportionment Amendment," Appendix B, pp. 49–51.

14. Illinois Committee for Constitutional Revision, "Reapportionment Amendment Is a Fair Compromise," campaign flyer (first quotation), part III, box 678, "Government-Reapportionment-Redistricting," LWVP; Juergensmeyer, "Campaign for the Illinois Reapportionment Amendment," esp. pp. 1–13 (second and third quotations on p. 8).

15. Juergensmeyer, "Campaign for the Illinois Reapportionment Amendment," esp. pp. 14–21 (quotation on p. 21).

16. Mrs. H. B. Hoesly, State Reapportionment Chairman, to Local Reapportionment Chairman, Dec. 20, 1954, box 678, "Government-Reapportionment-Redistricting," part III, LWVP; Mrs. Stanley Kane, "Testimony on Reapportionment," Feb. 20, 1957, pp. 1–3 (first and third quotations on p. 1), box 676, "Government-Reapportionment-Redistricting," part III, LWVP; NML, Compendium on Legislative Apportionment, Sept. 1960, pp. Minnesota 1–2 (second quotation on p. 1).

17. Kane, "Testimony on Reapportionment," p. 1, box 676, "Government-Reapportionment-Redistricting," part III, LWVP.

18. "Report of the Citizen-Legislator Committee on Reapportionment" [file copy Jan. 26, 1959], box 886, "Government-Reapportionment," part III, LWVP; LWV of Minnesota, "Apportionment in Minnesota," 1964, esp. Appendixes I–II, pp. 16–18, box 260, "Michigan-Minnesota," part IV, LWVP; George B. Merry, "More States Face Up to Responsibilities," CSM, Oct. 16, 1958, p. 3.

19. Magraw v. Donovan, Civil No. 2981, 177 F. Supp. 803 (1959); Kane, "Testimony on Reapportionment," p. 1.

20. Commission on Intergovernmental Relations, *A Report to the President for Transmittal to the Congress* (Washington, D.C., June 1955).
21. Ibid., esp. pp. 38–40, 221–32 (first quotation on p. 38; remaining quotations on p. 39).
22. John F. Kennedy, "The Shame of the States," *NYT Magazine*, May 18, 1958, pp. 12, 37–38, 40.
23. Anthony Lewis, "Legislative Apportionment and the Federal Courts," *Harvard Law Review* 71 (April 1958): 1057–98.
24. *Colegrove v. Green*, 328 U.S. 549 (1946), appendix I.
25. *Colegrove v. Green*, 328 U.S. 549, 556 (1946); Lewis, "Legislative Apportionment," pp. 1078–86.
26. Lewis, "Legislative Apportionment," pp. 1087–98 (first quotation on p. 1096; second quotation on p. 1097; third quotation on p. 1098).
27. Ibid., pp. 1077–86 (first and second quotations on p. 1083; third quotation on p. 1077).
28. George B. Merry, "Minority Rule," p. 13, "Inequities Exposed in State Voting Scales," *CSM*, Oct. 6, 1958, p. 15, "Rural-Urban Imbalance Aired in Legislatures," p. 5, "Battles Waged to Reapportion State Legislatures," p. 7, "More States Face Up to Reapportionment Responsibilities," *CSM*, Oct. 16, 1958, p. 3, "How Minorities Help Shape Congress," p. 9, "'Rotten Boroughs' Elect Party Chiefs," p. 3, "Gerrymandering Lingers Across U.S.," p. 10, and "Population Shifts Hint Redistricting," *CSM*, June 16, 1959, p. 10.
29. Strout, "The Next Election Is Already Rigged," p. 40; Henry M. Christman, "How Much Does Your Vote Count?" *Redbook* 112 (Nov. 1958): 41, 130–32.
30. "Remarks of Senator John F. Kennedy," June 16, 1959, box 1032, "Urban Problems," 1960 Campaign Files, Pre-Presidential Papers, JFKL; Bureau of the Census, "Table 1. Urban and Rural Population: 1900 to 1990"; NML, *Compendium on Legislative Apportionment*, Sept. 1960, p. California 1; NML, "Comparative Data on the Composition of State Legislative Districts," April 15, 1964, copy in JWMP.
31. Frank G. Bonelli, "Analysis and Argument in Support of Plan for Senate Reapportionment," Nov. 10, 1959, box 58, folder 14, W&BP; Argument in Favor of Proposition 15, 1960 (quotation), California Ballot Propositions Database, Hastings College of the Law; Los Angeles City Council, Resolution No. 90313 (Sup #1), May 3, 1960, Los Angeles City Council Files, Los Angeles City Archives; NML, *Compendium on Legislative Apportionment*, Sept. 1960, pp. California 2–4.
32. Los Angeles Chamber of Commerce, Stenographer's Report, May 26, 1960, pp. 1–9, and June 2, 1960, pp. 1–9 (first quotation on p. 2), LACC Papers, Doheny Library, University of Southern California; LACC, Minutes of the Board of Directors Meetings, May 26, 1960, p. 2, carton 35, p. 57, and June 2, 1960, pp. 1–2, carton 35, pp. 58–59, LACC Papers; Report of the State and Local Government Committee, LACC, "Senate Reapportionment, Proposition No. 15," May 24, 1960, pp. 1–14 (second quotation on p. 9), LP 229:333, Senator Randolph Collier Papers, CSA. On the political implications of suburban growth in Southern California, see Kevin

Starr, *Golden Dreams: California in an Age of Abundance, 1950–1963* (New York: Oxford University Press, 2009), esp. pp. 191–216.

33. Whitaker & Baxter, "Summary of the Campaign Against Proposition No. 15," box 58, folder 50, "Californians Against Proposition 15," p. 59, box 58, folder 9, "JD's Finance File," W&BP; NML, *Compendium on Legislative Apportionment*, Sept. 1960, pp. California 3–4; "Contributors" to Proposition 15, "You Are in Danger: California Must Defeat State Senate Reapportionment," "Why Proposition 15 Must Be Defeated: Don't Split California in Two," "Don't Be Squeezed Off the Map! Vote No on Proposition No. 15, The Senate Packing Reapportionment Scheme," Whitaker & Baxter, "Report on No. 23," LP 229:334, Senator Randolph Collier Papers, CSA; Proposition No. 23, Senate Reapportionment, 1962, California Ballot Propositions Database, Hastings College of the Law.

34. "Democrats Stage an L.I. 'Tea Party,'" *NYT*, Sept. 25, 1960, p. 34; Columbia Broadcasting System, *Our Election Day Illusions: The Beat Majority*, broadcast Thursday, Jan. 5, 1961.

35. Lewis, "Legislative Apportionment," pp. 1057–98; U.S. Commission on Intergovernmental Relations, *A Report to the President for Transmittal to the Congress* (Washington, D.C., June 1955); Kennedy, "The Shame of the States"; Merry, "How Minorities Help Shape Congress," p. 9.

36. Paul T. David and Ralph Eisenberg, *Devaluation of the Urban & Suburban Vote* (Charlottesville: Bureau of Public Administration, University of Virginia, 1961), esp. pp. 11–14; "1960 Population—23 Largest Metropolitan Areas," in Congressional Quarterly, *Representation and Apportionment* (Washington, D.C., 1966), p. 43.

37. J. Anthony Lukas, "Barnyard Government in Maryland," *Reporter* 26 (April 12, 1962): 31–34 (quotation on p. 31). Lukas was not alone in noting the heightened importance of the suburbs in the early 1960s. See also "Washington," *Atlantic* 208 (Dec. 1961): 4, 8; Lewis, "On the Trail of the Fierce Gerrymander," p. 211.

38. CBS, *Our Election Day Illusions: The Beat Majority*; "Democrats Stage an L.I. 'Tea Party'"; telegram from Mrs. Edward Reisman Jr., Jan. 4, 1961, frame 959, reel 22, TN-LWVP.

4. IT HAS LOTS TO DO WITH THE PRICE OF EGGS: THE MAKING OF *BAKER* V. *CARR*

1. "Annual Report of the Current Agenda Item, Reapportionment, 3/15/59," p. 2 (quotation), box 57, folder 2, reel 22, frame 920, TN-LWVP; *Baker* v. *Carr*, SCUS, No. 103, OT 1960 (renumbered No. 6, OT 1961), *TOR*, pp. 7–8. Among the states that reapportioned both chambers on the basis of population, Tennessee and Massachusetts counted qualified voters rather than all citizens. See *Scholle* v. *Hare*, State of Michigan in the Supreme Court, Mandamus Original Jurisdiction No. 48,580, 1960, Brief of Defendant James M. Hare, Exhibit G, "Constitutional Provisions Governing Legislative Representation," pp. 67b–75b.

2. TN-LWVP, "Study of Tennessee's State Government: Introduction," Sept. 1953, box 969, part III, LWVP; Molly Todd, "Reapportionment," *Tennessee Voter*, Oct. 1957, p. 1, box 59, folder 1, reel 23, frame 69, TN-LWVP; Elena Harap Dodd to the author, Oct. 19, 2011 (quotation); Eileen Harap Drath to the author, Oct. 19, 2011; "Contributors to This Issue: Otto Billig, M.D.," *Psychiatric Quarterly* 44 (April 1970): 378; Anita S. Goodstein, "Mary 'Molly' Hart Todd," *Tennessee Encyclopedia of History and Culture*, version 2.0, last updated Feb. 28, 2011, http://tennessee encyclopedia.net/. On the Nashville sit-in movement, see Andrew B. Lewis, *The Shadows of Youth: The Remarkable Journey of the Civil Rights Generation* (New York: Hill & Wang, 2009).

3. Ann Diamond, "Housewife Agrees, It Has Lots to Do with the Price of Eggs," *Tennessee Oak Ridger*, Dec. 1960, box 1040, "Government Reapportionment," part III, LWVP.

4. Jane Anne Nielsen, State Reapportionment Chairman to New Local Reapportionment Chairmen, "Resume of the League's interest in, and efforts toward, Tennessee Legislative Reapportionment," Aug. 1961, p. 1, box 886, "Government-Reapportionment," part III, LWVP; TN-LWVP, "Once Upon a Time," box 53, folder 19, reel 21, frames 282–83, TN-LWVP.

5. George Barker, "The Unholy Trinity: Trials of a Country Lawyer," *Nashville Tennessean Magazine*, April 5, 1964, pp. 8–9, 11 (first quotation on p. 8; second quotation on p. 9); Gene Graham, *One Man, One Vote* (Boston: Atlantic Monthly Press, 1972), pp. 27–39 (third quotation on p. 29).

6. *Kidd v. McCanless*, 200 Tenn. 282, 292 S.W.2d 40 (1956); Graham, *One Man, One Vote*, pp. 11–91 (first quotation on p. 56; second quotation on p. 81).

7. *Kidd v. McCanless*, 200 Tenn. 273 (1956); *Kidd v. McCanless*, 352 U.S. 920 (1956).

8. Graham, *One Man, One Vote*, pp. 11–91; ZTO to WC, Feb. 4, 1959 (quotations), box 1, "Walter Chandler Letters," GGP.

9. Graham, *One Man, One Vote*, pp. 95–119.

10. "Order Deferring Final Decision," *Magraw v. Donovan*, Civil No. 2981, United States District Court for the District of Minnesota, July 10, 1958, 163 F. Supp. 184 (1958) (quotations on p. 187); Merry, "More States Face Up to Responsibilities," p. 3.

11. *Magraw v. Donovan*, 163 F. Supp. 184 (1958) (quotation on p. 187); Graham, *One Man, One Vote*, pp. 95–119; David Newby Harsh to Gene Graham, Feb. 27, 1971, box 1, "Walter Chandler," GGP.

12. "Ex-Rep. Walter Chandler Dies; Won One-Man, One-Vote Case," *NYT*, Oct. 2, 1967, p. 47; Graham, *One Man, One Vote*, pp. 117–29.

13. WC to Jesse Vineyard, Jan. 5, 1959, Vineyard to WC, Jan. 12, 1959, WC to ZTO, Jan. 29, 1959, WC to Hobart Atkins, Feb. 12, 1959, box 1, "Walter Chandler Letters," GGP; Graham, *One Man, One Vote*, pp. 117–32.

14. ZTO to WC, Feb. 4, 1959, box 1, "Walter Chandler Letters," GGP; Graham, *One Man, One Vote*, pp. 46–49, 129–32, 323–28.

15. WC to Jesse Vineyard, Feb. 25, 1959, WC to ZTO, Feb. 26, 1959, WC and Hobart Atkins to Charles T. Lambert, March 2, 1959, WC to Robert L. Peters, Jr., March 5, 1959, box 1, "Walter Chandler Letters," GGP; Graham, *One Man, One Vote*, pp. 133–37.

16. *Baker* v. *Carr*, USDC for the Nashville Division of the Middle District of Tennessee, Civil Action No. 2724, "Complaint," May 18, 1959, pp. 1–5; Graham, *One Man, One Vote*, pp. 137–42.

17. WC to Frank Farrell, May 11, 1959, ZTO to WC, May 19, 1959, WC to ZTO, May 25, 1959, WC to ZTO and Hobart F. Atkins, June 15, 1959, Daniel B. Magraw to Richard S. Childs, June 23, 1959 (first quotation), Magraw to WC, July 2, 1959, Farrell to WC, Aug. 12, 1959, box 1, "Walter Chandler Letters," GGP; *Magraw* v. *Donovan*, 177 F. Supp. 803 (1959); Graham, *One Man, One Vote*, pp. 153–54.

18. United States Code, Title 28, Part VI, Chapter 155, § 2284; WC to ZTO and Hobart F. Atkins, June 24, 1959, WC to ZTO, July 15, 1959, ZTO to WC, July 20, 1959, ZTO to WC, July 31, 1959, WC to David N. Harsh and Edmund Orgill, Aug. 4, 1959, WC to ZTO, Aug. 6, 1959, box 1, "Walter Chandler Letters," GGP; *Baker* v. *Carr*, "Memorandum Opinion on Convening Three-Judge Court," July 31, 1959, *TOR*, pp. 88–94; Graham, *One Man, One Vote*, pp. 155–58.

19. WC to ZTO, Aug. 6, 1959, WC to ZTO and Hobart Atkins, Oct. 7, 1959, WC to ZTO, Nov. 2, 1959 (quotation), box 1, "Walter Chandler Letters," GGP; Graham, *One Man, One Vote*, pp. 161–63.

20. WC to ZTO, Aug. 6, 1959, ZTO to WC and Hobart Atkins, Oct. 5, 1959, WC to ZTO and Atkins, Oct. 7, 1959, box 1, "Walter Chandler Letters," GGP; Graham, *One Man, One Vote*, pp. 158–62.

21. WC to ZTO, Aug. 6, 1959, John C. Anderson to ZTO, Sept. 15, 1959, WC to ZTO and Hobart F. Atkins, Sept. 16, 1959, ZTO to WC, Sept. 21, 1959, box 1, "Walter Chandler Letters," GGP.

22. Graham, *One Man, One Vote*, pp. 171–83; photograph, "Mayor Ben West With Reapportionment Chart," April 17, 1961, Metropolitan Government Archives, Nashville and Davidson County.

23. ZTO to WC and Hobart F. Atkins, Oct. 5, 1959 (quotation), WC to Edmund Orgill and David N. Harsh, Oct. 9, 1959, ZTO to WC, Oct. 26, 1959, box 1, "Walter Chandler Letters," GGP; Advance Planning Division, Nashville City Planning Commission, "Legislative Apportionment in Tennessee, 1901–1961," Aug. 1961; Graham, *One Man, One Vote*, pp. 172–76.

24. *Baker* v. *Carr*, Motions and Orders Related to Interventions of Ben West and City of Chattanooga, *TOR*, pp. 95–123, "City Council Resolution 59-198," Exhibit 1 to Intervening Complaint, *TOR*, pp. 123–26 (first and second quotations on p. 125); Graham, *One Man, One Vote*, pp. 179–80 (third quotation on p. 179); WC to ZTO and Hobart F. Atkins, Nov. 9, 1959, Atkins to WC, Nov. 13, 1959, Atkins to WC, Nov. 24, 1959, box 1, "Walter Chandler Letters," GGP; "Vouchers from 'Special Legal Counsel,'" box 4, "Ben West," GGP.

25. Jane Anne Nielsen to State Board of Tennessee LWV et al., Oct. 1959, Nielsen to Reapportionment State Committee and Local Chairmen, Dec. 2, 1959, box 57, folder 2, reel 22, frames 924–31, TN-LWVP; Graham, *One Man, One Vote*, pp. 163–70.

26. Graham, *One Man, One Vote*, pp. 163–70; *Baker* v. *Carr*, Per Curiam Opinion, Dec. 21, 1959, *TOR*, pp. 214–20 (first, second, and third quotations on p. 219); WC to Richard S. Childs, Dec. 30, 1959 (fourth quotation), box 1138, folder 10, ACLU Papers, Seely G. Mudd Manuscript Library, Princeton University.

27. *Baker* v. *Carr*, "Order Allowing Ben West Permission to File Intervening Complaint," "Intervening Complaint of Ben West," and "Amendment and Supplement to the Intervening Petition Filed by the Plaintiff, Ben West . . . Filed March 22, 1960," *TOR*, pp. 99–100, 100–208, 223–57; Graham, *One Man, One Vote*, pp. 171–82.

28. Graham, *One Man, One Vote*, pp. 182–91; Gene Graham interview with Charles Rhyne, July 25, 1969, pp. 1–3, 17, box 4, "Charles Rhyne," GGP.

29. Graham interview with Rhyne, p. 9; Graham, *One Man, One Vote*, pp. 191–92; Stephen L. Wasby, "Amicus Brief," in Kermit L. Hall, ed., *The Oxford Companion to the Supreme Court of the United States* (New York: Oxford University Press, 1992), pp. 31–32.

30. Lincoln Caplan, *The Tenth Justice: The Solicitor General and the Rule of Law* (New York: Knopf, 1987), pp. 3–4 (quotations on p. 3).

31. *Hartsfield* v. *Sloan*, 357 U.S. 916 (1958); *South* v. *Peters*, 339 U.S. 276 (1950); *Cox* v. *Peters*, 342 U.S. 936 (1952); J. Lee Rankin, "Memorandum for the Attorney General," April 22, 1958, W. Wilson White, "Memorandum for the Attorney General," April 29, 1958 (quotation), Rankin to the Attorney General, May 1, 1958, DOJ file 72-19-24, reel 99, CRDP.

32. *Baker* v. *Carr*, No. 103, OT 1960, "Jurisdictional Statement," filed May 26, 1960, "Statement in Opposition to Appellants' Statement of Jurisdiction and Motion to Dismiss," filed June 23, 1960, in Philip B. Kurland and Gerhard Casper, eds., *Landmark Briefs and Arguments of the Supreme Court of the United States: Constitutional Law* (Arlington: University Publications of America, 1975), 56:3–32, 33–61; Graham, *One Man, One Vote*, p. 192.

33. TCC, Docket Sheet, *Baker* v. *Carr*, No. 6, OT 1961, box C77, folder 5, TCCP.

34. *Gomillion* v. *Lightfoot*, 364 U.S. 339 (1960); Sachs, "*Scholle* v. *Hare*," p. 1617; Bernard Taper, *Gomillion versus Lightfoot: The Tuskegee Gerrymander Case* (New York: McGraw-Hill, 1962), pp. 78–82.

35. Sachs, "*Scholle* v. *Hare*," p. 1617; Taper, *Gomillion versus Lightfoot*, pp. 91–108.

36. Sachs, "*Scholle* v. *Hare*," p. 1617; Taper, *Gomillion versus Lightfoot*, pp. 91–108 (first quotation on p. 93; second quotation on p. 108).

37. *Gomillion* v. *Lightfoot*, 364 U.S. 339 (1960); "Conference of October 21, 1960," in Del Dickson, ed., *The Supreme Court in Conference (1940–1985)* (New York: Oxford University Press, 2001), pp. 842–44 (quotation on p. 843); FF note to PS accompanying draft of *Gomillion* v. *Lightfoot*, box 176, folder 1631, Potter Stewart Papers, Yale University Library; Taper, *Gomillion versus Lightfoot*, pp. 111–15.

38. TCC, Docket Sheet, *Baker* v. *Carr,* box C77, folder 5, TCCP; WOD, Docket Sheet, *Baker* v. *Carr,* box 1258, folder "Docket Book, OT 1961 No. 1–199," WODP; *Baker* v. *Carr,* "Order Noting Probable Jurisdiction, Nov. 21, 1960," *TOR,* p. 314; Harold R. Tyler Jr., to the Solicitor General, Nov. 30, 1960, reel 99, CRDP; Diary of Richard Arnold, Nov. 21, 1960, in Anthony Lewis, "In Memoriam: William J. Brennan, Jr.," *Harvard Law Review* 111 (Nov. 1997): 29–30 (quotation on p. 29).

39. Harold R. Tyler, Jr., to the Solicitor General, Nov. 30, 1960 (quotation), reel 99, CRDP; David A. Nichols, *A Matter of Justice: Eisenhower and the Beginning of the Civil Rights Revolution* (New York: Simon & Schuster, 2007), pp. 214–63.

40. Tyler to the SG, Nov. 30, 1960 (first quotation on p. 5; second quotation on p. 6).

41. BJT to J. Lee Rankin, Dec. 8, 1960, reel 99, CRDP; author interview with BJT, March 29, 2006, Washington, D.C.

42. BJT to Rankin, Dec. 8, 1960 (quotations on p. 2).

43. Ibid. (first quotation on p. 3; all other quotations on p. 4).

44. Ibid. (quotations on p. 5).

45. Ibid. (quotations on p. 6).

5. INTO THE POLITICAL THICKET

1. J. Lee Rankin, "RE: *Charles W. Baker* v. *Joe C. Carr* . . . Participation of the United States as *Amicus Curiae* Authorized," Dec. 1960, reel 99, CRDP; Ken Gormley, *Archibald Cox: Conscience of a Nation* (Cambridge, MA: Perseus Publishing, 1997), pp. 140–47.

2. AC Calendar, Feb. 3, 1961, box 13, "Cox Diaries (S.G.)," KGP; AC, *The Court and the Constitution* (Boston: Houghton Mifflin, 1987), pp. 287–94 (first quotation on p. 289; second quotation on p. 294); Gormley, *Archibald Cox,* pp. 146, 163–65; Graham, *One Man, One Vote,* pp. 206–17.

3. Author interview with BJT; BJT to the SG, Dec. 8, 1960; "Brief for the United States as *Amicus Curiae,*" *Baker* v. *Carr,* no. 103, OT 1960, SCUS, filed March 14, 1961, pp. 8–19, in *Landmark Briefs,* 56:286–97.

4. AC Calendar, April 19, 1961, box 13, "Cox Diaries (S.G.)," KGP; OA of Charles Rhyne, *Baker* v. *Carr,* no. 103, OT 1960, April 19, 1961, pp. 1–2 (quotations on p. 1), in *Landmark Briefs,* 56:550–51; Graham, *One Man, One Vote,* pp. 218–25.

5. OA of Charles Rhyne, April 19, 1961, pp. 3, 9–10 (quotation on p. 10), in *Landmark Briefs,* 56:552, 558–59; Graham, *One Man, One Vote,* pp. 225–33.

6. OA of AC, April 19, 1961, p. 17, in *Landmark Briefs,* 56:566.

7. Ibid., pp. 17–18 (first quotation on p. 17; second quotation on p. 18), in *Landmark Briefs,* 56:566–67.

8. Ibid., pp. 23–24 (second quotation), in *Landmark Briefs,* 56:572–73; Graham, *One Man, One Vote,* pp. 234–35 (first quotation on p. 235).

9. OA of AC, April 19, 1961, pp. 19–20 (first, second, and third quotations on p. 19; fourth quotation on p. 20), in *Landmark Briefs,* 56:568–69.

10. OA of AC, April 19, 1961, pp. 20–21 (first quotation on p. 20; second quotation on pp. 20–21), in *Landmark Briefs*, 56:569–70; OA of Charles Rhyne, April 20, 1961, p. 27, in *Landmark Briefs*, 56:612.

11. OA of James Glasgow and Jack Wilson, April 20, 1961, pp. 1–22 (quotation on p. 10), in *Landmark Briefs*, 56:586–607; *Kidd* v. *McCanless*, 352 U.S. 920 (1956).

12. Graham, *One Man, One Vote*, pp. 241–42.

13. Roger K. Newman, *Hugo Black: A Biography* (New York: Pantheon, 1994), pp. 621–22.

14. WJB, Conference Notes on No. 103, *Baker* v. *Carr* (quotation), box 43, folder 16, part I, WJBP; WOD, Conference Notes on No. 103, *Baker* v. *Carr*, April 21, 1961, box 1267, "*Baker* v. *Carr* Misc. Memos," WODP; Dickson, *Supreme Court in Conference*, p. 845; *South* v. *Peters*, 339 U.S. 276 (1950); Newman, *Hugo Black*; Steve Suitts, *Hugo Black of Alabama* (Montgomery, AL: NewSouth Books, 2005).

15. Michael E. Parrish, *Felix Frankfurter and His Times: The Reform Years* (New York: Free Press, 1982); WOD, Conference Notes on No. 103, *Baker* v. *Carr*, April 21, 1961, box 1267, "*Baker* v. *Carr* Misc. Memos," WODP; Dickson, *Supreme Court in Conference*, pp. 845–46 (quotations).

16. WOD, Conference Notes on No. 103, *Baker* v. *Carr*, April 21, 1961, box 1267, "*Baker* v. *Carr* Misc. Memos," WODP; Dickson, *Supreme Court in Conference*, p. 846; WOD, *Go East, Young Man: The Early Years* (New York: Random House, 1974), esp. pp. 159–75 (quotation on p. 167); WOD, *The Court Years, 1939–1975* (New York: Random House, 1980), esp. pp. 43–56.

17. WOD, Conference Notes on No. 103, *Baker* v. *Carr*, April 21, 1961, box 1267, "*Baker* v. *Carr* Misc. Memos," WODP; Dickson, *Supreme Court in Conference*, p. 846 (quotations); Alexander Wohl, *Father, Son, and Constitution: How Justice Tom Clark and Attorney General Ramsey Clark Shaped American Democracy* (Lawrence: University Press of Kansas, 2013).

18. WOD, Conference Notes on No. 103, *Baker* v. *Carr*, April 21, 1961, box 1267, "*Baker* v. *Carr* Misc. Memos," WODP; Dickson, *Supreme Court in Conference*, p. 846 (quotations); Tinsley E. Yarbrough, *John Marshall Harlan: Great Dissenter of the Warren Court* (New York: Oxford University Press, 1992), pp. 3–113, 274–77.

19. WOD, Conference Notes on No. 103, *Baker* v. *Carr*, April 21, 1961, box 1267, "*Baker* v. *Carr* Misc. Memos," WODP; Dickson, *Supreme Court in Conference*, p. 846 (quotations); Seth Stern and Stephen Wermiel, *Justice Brennan: Liberal Champion* (Boston: Houghton Mifflin Harcourt, 2010), pp. 3–95.

20. Craig Alan Smith, *Failing Justice: Charles Evans Whittaker on the Supreme Court* (Jefferson, NC: McFarland, 2005).

21. WOD, Conference Notes on No. 103, *Baker* v. *Carr*, April 21, 1961, box 1267, "*Baker* v. *Carr* Misc. Memos," WODP; Dickson, *Supreme Court in Conference*, pp. 846–47 (first quotation on p. 846; second quotation on p. 847); Roy A. Schotland and Frank I. Michelman, "Notes: Opinions of William J. Brennan, Jr., October Term 1961," pp. i–ii (third quotation on p. ii), box 6, folder 4, part II, WJBP; Newman, *Hugo Black*, p. 517 (fourth quotation); Lewis, "In Memoriam," pp. 30–31.

22. Schotland and Michelman, "Notes," pp. i–ii (first quotation); Lewis, "In Memoriam," pp. 30–31; Newman, *Hugo Black*, p. 517 (second quotation).

23. Joel Jacobsen, "Remembered Justice: The Background, Early Career, and Judicial Appointments of Justice Potter Stewart," *Akron Law Review* 35, no. 2 (2002): 227–50.

24. WOD, Conference Notes on No. 103, *Baker* v. *Carr*, April 21, 1961, box 1267, "*Baker* v. *Carr* Misc. Memos," WODP; Dickson, *Supreme Court in Conference*, p. 847 (all quotations except fourth); Lewis, "In Memoriam," p. 31 (fourth quotation); *Baker* v. *Carr*, 366 U.S. 907 (1961).

25. FF to PS, April 24, 1961, reel 3, frames 418–19, part III, FFP-H.

26. FF to PS, May 1, 1961 (first quotation), box 135, folder "No. 6 Memoranda, etc.," JMHP; FF to CEW, May 17, 1961 (second and third quotations), reel 4, frame 931, part III, FFP-H; FF to CEW, Oct. 6, 1961, reel 80, frames 514–15 (fourth and fifth quotations), part II, FFP-H.

27. *Journal of the Supreme Court of the United States*, Monday, Oct. 2, 1961, p. 1; Graham, *One Man, One Vote*, pp. 244–50; AC, Diary entries, Oct. 5–8, 1961, box 13, "Cox Diaries (S.G.)," KGP.

28. OA, *Baker* v. *Carr*, Oct. 9, 1961, pp. 63–69, in *Landmark Briefs*, 56:678–84; Ken Gormley interview with Harris Gilbert, box 5, KGP; Graham, *One Man, One Vote*, pp. 250–51; WJB, "Memorandum to the Conference," Oct. 12, 1961 (quotation), box 353, "*Baker* v. *Carr*," Hugo L. Black Papers, Manuscript Division, LOC.

29. "Brief for the United States as *Amicus Curiae* on Reargument," *Baker* v. *Carr*, No. 6, OT 1961, pp. 8–17 (first quotation on p. 9; second, third, and fourth quotations on p. 10; fifth and sixth quotations on p. 11), in *Landmark Briefs*, 56:367–76; OA of AC, Oct. 9, 1961, p. 29 (seventh quotation), in *Landmark Briefs*, 56:644.

30. OA of AC, Oct. 9, 1961, pp. 36–37 (quotations on p. 37), in *Landmark Briefs*, 56:651–52.

31. "Brief for the United States as *Amicus Curiae* on Reargument," pp. 59–69 (first and second quotations on p. 61), in *Landmark Briefs*, 56:418–28; OA of AC, Oct. 9, 1961, p. 39 (third quotation), in *Landmark Briefs*, 56:654; Ken Gormley interview with Harris Gilbert (fourth quotation), box 5, KGP; Graham, *One Man, One Vote*, p. 252 (fifth quotation).

32. OA of AC, Oct. 9, 1961, p. 39 (quotations), in *Landmark Briefs*, 56:654.

33. "Brief *Amici Curiae* of the National Institute of Municipal Law Officers," filed July 22, 1960, "Brief *Amici Curiae* of the National Institute of Municipal Law Officers," filed Feb. 23, 1961, in *Landmark Briefs*, 56:75–87, 533–48; "Brief as *Amici Curiae* for John F. English, Eugene H. Nickerson, et al.," filed March 3, 1961, in *Landmark Briefs*, 56:471–87; "Brief *Amicus Curiae*, Bernard F. Bowling, Mayor City of St. Matthews, Kentucky," filed Feb. 25, 1961.

34. "Brief for Marvin Fortner, W. D. Alberts, et al.," filed Feb. 18, 1961 (first quotation on p. 14); "Brief of J. Howard Edmondson, Governor of the State of Oklahoma," filed Sept. 3, 1961, in *Landmark Briefs*, 56:447–69; "Brief for J. P. Harris, Peter MacDonald, John McCormally, and Ernest W. Johnson, as *Amici Curiae*," filed Sept. 29,

1961 (second quotation on p. 23; third quotation on p. 35), in *Landmark Briefs*, 56:489–531.

35. FF, "Memorandum for the Conference," Oct. 10, 1961, box 479, "No. 6, *Baker* v. *Carr*, Frankfurter Dissenting Opinion, folder No. 1," EWP; Schotland and Michelman, "Notes," p. ii; JMH to CEW and PS, Oct. 11, 1961 (first, second, third, and fourth quotations on p. 2), FF to JMH, Oct. 11, 1961 (fifth and sixth quotations), box 135, "No. 6—Memoranda, etc.," JMHP.

36. WOD, Conference Notes, Oct. 13, 1961, box 1267, "*Baker* v. *Carr*, Miscellaneous Memos," WODP; Dickson, *Supreme Court in Conference*, pp. 847–48 (all quotations except fifth); *Colegrove* v. *Green*, 328 U.S. 549 (fifth quotation at p. 570).

37. Schotland and Michelman, "Notes," p. iii (first, fifth, and sixth quotations); WOD, Conference Notes, Oct. 13, 1961, box 1267, "*Baker* v. *Carr*, Miscellaneous Memos," WODP; Dickson, *Supreme Court in Conference*, pp. 848–89 (second, third, and fourth quotations on p. 849).

38. WOD, Conference Notes, Oct. 13, 1961, box 1267, "*Baker* v. *Carr*, Miscellaneous Memos," WODP; Dickson, *Supreme Court in Conference*, p. 850 (quotations).

39. WOD, Conference Notes, Oct. 13, 1961, box 1267, "*Baker* v. *Carr*, Miscellaneous Memos," WODP; Dickson, *Supreme Court in Conference*, pp. 850–51 (first quotation on p. 851); PS, Conference Notes, Oct. 13, 1961 (second quotation; emphasis in original), box 383, folder 4689, Docket Books, OT 1961, "No. 6, *Baker* v. *Carr*," Potter Stewart Papers, Yale University Library. Anthony Lewis, the *New York Times*'s Supreme Court correspondent, confidentially told the journalist Victor Navasky that the federal government's support of the Tennessee plaintiffs in *Baker* v. *Carr* had influenced the votes of Tom Clark and Potter Stewart. According to Lewis, Stewart considered it particularly important that Lee Rankin, Cox's Republican predecessor as solicitor general, had also planned to support the plaintiffs. Anthony Lewis to Victor Navasky, May 8, 1969, box 10, "Anthony Lewis," Victor Navasky Personal Papers, JFKL.

40. Schotland and Michelman, "Notes," pp. iii–iv; WJB to WOD and WOD to WJB, [Oct. 23, 1961], box 65, folder 1, part I, WJBP.

41. Schotland and Michelman, "Notes," pp. iv–vii; Lewis, "In Memoriam," pp. 33–34; "Justiciability" and "Political Questions," in Hall, *Oxford Companion to the Supreme Court*, pp. 478, 651–52; WJB to EW, HLB, and WOD, Jan. 27, 1962 (quotation), box 63, folder 2, part I, WJBP.

42. WJB to PS, Jan. 22, 1962, WJB to EW, HLB, and WOD, Jan. 27, 1962, WJB to HLB, Jan. 31, 1962, WJB to EW, HLB, WOD, and PS, Feb. 1, 1962, PS to WJB, Feb. 1, 1962, TCC to WJB, Feb. 2, 1962, box 63, folder 2, part I, WJBP; TCC to FF, Feb. 3 (quotation), 1962, reel 80, frame 250, part II, FFP-H; JMH to FF, Feb. 5, 1962, box 135, "No. 6—Memoranda, etc.," JMHP; Schotland and Michelman, "Notes," pp. iv–vii.

43. PS to WJB, Feb. 13, 1962, box 63, folder 2, part I, WJBP; Schotland and Michelman, "Notes," pp. iv–vii; Lewis, "In Memoriam," pp. 33–34.

44. TCC to FF, Feb. 3, 1962, CEW to FF, Feb. 14, 1962, reel 80, frames 250–51, part II, FFP-H; FF to JMH, Feb. 1962, JMH to PS, Feb. 8, 1962 (quotation), PS to JMH, Feb.

8, 1962, box 135, "No. 6—Memoranda, etc.," JMHP; CEW to JMH, Feb. 14, 1962, box 134, "JMH Memorandum—2nd. Circulation & Votes," JMHP.

45. Concurring opinion of TCC, *Baker* v. *Carr*, 369 U.S. 254 (1962); TCC to FF, March 7, 1962, reel 80, frame 704, part II, FFP-H; Schotland and Michelman, "Notes," pp. vii–viii.

46. Smith, *Failing Justice*, pp. 214–16; author interview with James Adler, March 17, 2010, Los Angeles; author interview with Jerome Libin, April 9, 2010, Washington, D.C. (quotations).

47. "Calendar of the Chief Justice," Feb. 24–March 5, 1962, box 32, "Personal Calendar, Jan.–June 1962," EWP; Smith, *Failing Justice*, pp. 217–21 (quotations on p. 221).

48. "Calendar of the Chief Justice," March 15, 1962, box 32, "Personal Calendar, Jan.–June 1962," EWP; "Medical Board Proceedings," March 16, 1962 (quotation), EW to JFK, March 16, 1962, EW, "Certificate of Disability," March 16, 1962, CEW to JFK, March 16, 1962, box 358, "Whittaker, Charles E., 1957–73," EWP; Smith, *Failing Justice*, p. 222.

49. "Bigger Voice for the Cities," *Newsweek* 59 (April 9, 1962): 29–30 (first quotation on p. 29); WJB, Bench Announcement (second quotation on p. 1), box 65, folder 1, part 1, WJBP; *Baker* v. *Carr*, 369 U.S. 186 (1962); EW to WJB (third and fourth quotations), box 64, folder 4, part I, WJBP; Smith, *Failing Justice*, p. 222.

50. "Bigger Voice for the Cities" (first and second quotations on p. 29); "Political Upheaval? Cities to Gain if High Court's Ruling Spurs Reapportionment," *WSJ*, March 27, 1962, pp. 1, 19 (third and fourth quotations on p. 1); "Supreme Court Gives U.S. Judges Voice in States' Reapportioning: Urban-Rural Struggle at Issue," *NYT*, March 27, 1962, p. 1; Anthony Lewis, "Decision on Reapportionment Points Up Urban-Rural Struggle," *NYT*, April 1, 1962, p. E3; James E. Clayton, "Court Performs Heart Surgery on Our System," *WP*, April 1, 1962, p. E1 (fifth quotation); "Remap Case Returned Here," *Nashville Tennessean*, March 27, 1962, pp. 1–2.

51. "The President's News Conference of March 29, 1962," Item 115, in *Public Papers of the Presidents of the United States: John F. Kennedy, Containing the Public Messages, Speeches, and Statements of the President, January 1 to December 31, 1962* (Washington, D.C.: GPO, 1963), pp. 271–77 (first quotation on p. 271; fourth and fifth quotations on p. 274); Statement of Charles Evans Whittaker, March 29, 1962 (second and third quotations), box 194, "FG 535/A Executive," White House Central Subject Files, JFKL.

52. Ed Cray, *Chief Justice: A Biography of Earl Warren* (New York: Simon & Schuster, 1997), pp. 382–83; Ed Cray, telephone interview with Murray Bring, Feb. 14, 1994, box 53, folder 10, Ed Cray Papers, Department of Special Collections, Charles E. Young Research Library, UCLA; Smith, *Failing Justice*, pp. 216–17; CEW to FF, Feb. 14, 1962, reel 80, frame 251, part II, FFP-H; CEW to JMH, Feb. 14, 1962, various draft opinions of FF, box 134, "*Baker* v. *Carr*," JMHP; Circulation Notes, *Baker* v. *Carr*, box A211, folder 1, TCCP. In a telephone interview with Warren biographer Ed Cray, former Warren clerk Murray Bring discussed Whittaker's vacillations, and Frankfurter's response, at the time of the first *Baker* conference in April

1961. Cray, however, mistakenly assumed that Bring was talking about events a year later, and thus makes the erroneous claim that Whittaker was prepared to switch his vote and join the majority.

53. FF to Alexander Bickel, April 4, 1962, reel 32, frame 962, part III, FFP-H.

54. Schotland and Michelman, "Notes," p. viii (quotation). For more on Rutledge, see John M. Ferren, *Salt of the Earth, Conscience of the Court: The Story of Justice Wiley Rutledge* (Chapel Hill: University of North Carolina Press, 2004).

55. NML, "Court Cases on Apportionment and/or Districting," Sept. 1963, JWMP; Graham, *One Man, One Vote*, pp. 256–58.

56. "Amending the United States Constitution to Strengthen the States in the Federal System: Action of the Sixteenth Biennial General Assembly of the States," Chicago, Dec. 6, 1962 (Chicago: Council of State Governments, 1963); Robert L. Riggs, "States' Votes Quietly Push Court Curbs," *Louisville Courier-Journal*, April 28, 1963, pp. 1, 24.

57. George R. Prentice, "Report to Florida Commission on Constitutional Government," Sept. 13, 1963, pp. 1–2, 8 (quotation on p. 2), box 23, folder 10, Thomas D. Graham Papers, Missouri State Archives, Jefferson City; Riggs, "States' Votes Quietly Push Court Curbs," p. 24.

58. George Lewis, "Virginia's Northern Strategy: Southern Segregationists and the Route to National Conservatism," *Journal of Southern History* 72 (Feb. 2006): 111–46 (quotation on p. 121).

59. Riggs, "States' Votes Quietly Push Court Curbs," pp. 1, 24; AJF, "Roll of the States on Resolutions of the Council of State Governments to Amend the United States Constitution," Dec. 31, 1963, box 659, "Constitutional Amendments 1963," EWP. The fifteen were Alabama, Arkansas, Florida, Idaho, Illinois, Kansas, Missouri, Montana, New Hampshire, Oklahoma, South Dakota, Texas, Utah, Washington, and Wyoming. Riggs's article in the *Courier-Journal* failed to include Alabama, but the Alabama legislature filed its petition with Congress on April 1. Utah's resolution—to overturn *Baker* v. *Carr*—appeared in slightly different form from the resolution passed by the other states. The early tally would have risen to sixteen as the unicameral Nebraska legislature passed a resolution to overturn *Baker* v. *Carr*, but the governor vetoed it.

60. "Rewriting the Constitution in Committee," *Louisville Courier-Journal*, April 30, 1963, p. 8 (first quotation); "Challenging the Constitution Wreckers," *Louisville Courier-Journal*, May 5, 1963, section 4, p. 3 (second quotation); EW to AJF, May 2, 1963 (third quotation), box 660, "Constitutional Amendments 1963," EWP; AJF to AC, Jan. 9, 1963, AJF to WOD, Jan. 9, 1963, WOD to AJF, Jan. 15, 1963, AJF to WOD, Jan. 18, 1963 (fourth quotation), box 330, "Arthur Freund," WODP; AJF to EW, Feb. 22, 1963, Charles L. Black to AJF, Jan. 7, 1963 (fifth and sixth quotations), AJF to EW, April 29, 1963, box 660, "Constitutional Amendments 1963," EWP.

61. Charles L. Black, Jr., "The Proposed Amendment of Article V: A Threatened Disaster," *Yale Law Journal* 72 (April 1963): 957–66 (first quotation on p. 957); Paul A. Freund, quoted in AJF, "A Clear and Present Danger," *Washington University*

Magazine 34 (Fall 1963): 42–45 (second quotation on p. 45), copy in box 659, "Constitutional Amendments 1963," EWP; EW, "Address at the Dedication of the New Law Building, Duke University, April 27, 1963," "Address, Annual Meeting of the American Law Institute, May 22, 1963," box 810, EWP; EW, "Dedication of the New Duke Law School Building," *Duke Law Journal* 1963 (Summer 1963): 386–94 (third and fourth quotations on p. 394); "Change the Constitution? Warren Urges Great Debate," *U.S. News & World Report* 54 (June 3, 1963): 19; "Warren Cautions on Amendments," *NYT*, May 23, 1963, p. 1.

62. AJF, "Memorandum: The First Seventeen Months of the States' Rights Amendments: December 6, 1962–May 6, 1964," box 659, "Constitutional Amendments 1963," EWP; Burton C. Bernard to EW, Jan. 16, 1964, and Bernard, "Bibliography for the Three States' Rights Amendments," Dec. 16, 1963, box 660, "Constitutional Amendments 1964," EWP; "Statement by the AFL-CIO Executive Council on the Attack on the American Form of Government," May 14, 1963, box 660, "Constitutional Amendments 1963," EWP; William Chappell and Randolph Hodges to the President, Aug. 20, 1962, T. J. Reardon to Chappell and Hodges, Sept. 11, 1962, Chappell to the President, Oct. 15, 1962, Reardon to Chappell, unsent draft, Norbert Schlei to Reardon, Nov. 20, 1962, box 929, "ST 2-16-62," White House Central Subject Files, JFKL; "Justice Aide Declares States' Rights Amendments Could Cost Negroes Votes," *NYT*, May 2, 1963, p. C17; Joseph Dolan, "Some New Year's Resolutions on Law Day," May 1, 1963, box 1139, folder 2, ACLU Papers, Seely G. Mudd Manuscript Library, Princeton University; BM to Lawrence Hudson, July 30, 1963, box 96, section 6, RG 60; AC, "Understanding the Supreme Court: Address Before the Cleveland Bar Association," May 4, 1963, box 109, folder 17, Archibald Cox Papers, Law School Library, Harvard University; RFK, "Government Under Law in a Dynamic Age," address at the University of Virginia Law School, May 4, 1963, box 6, "Constitutional Amendments—Three Proposed," RFK-1964 Campaign Papers, JFKL; "Record Number Returns for Law Day Program," *Virginia Law Weekly* 15 (May 9, 1963): 1; JFK, "The President's News Conference," May 8, 1963, Question 8, *Public Papers of the Presidents: John F. Kennedy*, pp. 374–75.

63. FF to PS, May 27, 1963, box 584, folder 118, Potter Stewart Papers, Yale University Library.

64. Norman Isaacs to EW, May 7, 1963 (quotation), box 660, "Constitutional Amendments 1963," EWP; AJF, "Roll of the States on Resolutions of the Council of State Governments to Amend the United States Constitution," Dec. 31, 1963, box 659, "Constitutional Amendments 1963," EWP. Nevada and South Carolina passed resolutions in June 1963. Wyoming was the only state outside the South to call for the establishment of a Court of the Union.

6. ONE PERSON, ONE VOTE

1. Baker, *Rural versus Urban Political Power*, p. 5 (first quotation); Gene Graham interview with Charles Rhyne, July 25, 1969, Washington, D.C., pp. 12–13 (second

quotation on p. 13), box 4, "Charles Rhyne," GGP; MBA, *The Day Is Short* (New York: Harcourt, 1982), p. 50 (third quotation).

2. "Reply Brief of Petitioner," *Hartsfield* v. *Sloan*, No. 683 Misc., OT 1957, SCUS, p. 4, box 35, MBAP; "Life, Death of Unit Plan Awaits Ruling by Court," *Atlanta Journal*, April 28, 1962, p. 1; Pat Watters, "Attorney Abram Did a Fine Job, Unit Decision Clears the Air," *Atlanta Journal*, April 30, 1962, p. 20.

3. Baker, *Rural versus Urban Political Power*, pp. 5–10; Nelson Mandela, "The Shifting Sands of Illusion," *Liberation* (June 1953), "The Freedom Charter," adopted June 25–26, 1955, "Mandela's Testimony, 1960," in Nelson Mandela, *The Struggle Is My Life* (New York: Pathfinder Press, 1986), pp. 43–45, 50–54, 87–90 (first quotation on p. 43; second quotation on p. 51); Nelson Mandela, interview by Brian Widlake, "The New Republic," *ITN Roving Report*, May 1961, clip 5 of 8 (X21066101 14862), www.itnsource.com (third quotation); Nelson Mandela, *Long Walk to Freedom* (Boston: Little, Brown, 1994), pp. 148–53; Martin Legassick, "South Africa in Crisis: What Route to Democracy?" *African Affairs* 84 (Oct. 1985): 587–603.

4. Twentieth Century Fund, *One Man–One Vote* (New York: Twentieth Century Fund, 1962), p. 5 (first quotation); John Lewis, *Walking with the Wind: A Memoir of the Movement* (New York: Simon & Schuster, 1998), pp. 216–34 (second quotation on p. 217).

5. Sachs, "*Scholle* v. *Hare*," pp. 1605–24 (first and second quotations on p. 1607); *Scholle* v. *Hare*, 360 Mich. 1 (1960) (third quotation at 360 Mich. 61).

6. Sachs, "*Scholle* v. *Hare*," pp. 1616–24 (first quotation on p. 1616; second quotation on p. 1623, n83).

7. Daniel B. Magraw to Mayne M. Miller, March 21, 1961, box 2, "Magraw, Daniel," GGP; Theodore Sachs to WC, June 9, 1960, WC to Sachs, July 27, 1960, box 1, "Walter Chandler Letters," GGP; Alfred Scanlan to Sachs, March 28, 1960, Sachs to Scanlan, May 3, 1962, MBA to Sachs, Dec. 3, 1962, Sachs to August Scholle, Sept. 12, 1963, box 14, "Scholle Suit—Correspondence Only," ASC; Sachs to Tom Downs, Oct. 28, 1959, folder "Reapportionment—#2," "This Is Detroit," transcript of interview with Theodore Sachs, broadcast on WDTM, July 22, 1962, esp. pp. 1–5, unlabeled folder, box 1, ASC.

8. WC to Sachs, July 27, 1960, box 1, "Walter Chandler Letters," GGP; John Silard to Joseph L. Rauh, Jr., May 8, 1961, Rauh to Sachs, May 8, 1961 (quotation), Sachs to Rauh, May 10, 1961, box 14, "Scholle Suit—Correspondence Only," ASC.

9. Sachs, "*Scholle* v. *Hare*," p. 1618 (first, second, and third quotations); "Brief of August Scholle, *Amicus Curiae*," filed Sept. 20, 1961, in *Baker* v. *Carr*, No. 6, OT 1961, SCUS, p. 13 (fourth quotation).

10. Jimmy Carter, *Turning Point: A Candidate, a State, and a Nation Come of Age* (New York: Times Books, 1992), pp. 25–42 (first quotation is the title of the book; second quotation on p. 26; third quotation on p. 28); *Sanders* v. *Gray*, 203 F. Supp. 158 (1962); *Toombs* v. *Fortson*, 205 F. Supp. 248 (1962); *Wesberry* v. *Vandiver and Fortson*, 206 F. Supp. 276 (1962); MBA, *The Day Is Short*, pp. 48–50, 101–109.

11. MBA, *The Day Is Short*, pp. 9–77.

12. "Complaint," filed March 27, 1962, in *TOR*, *Gray* v. *Sanders*, No. 112, OT 1962, SCUS, pp. 5–9, 25–34; Larry Sabato, *The Democratic Party Primary in Virginia: Tantamount to Election No Longer* (Charlottesville: University of Virginia Press, 1977), p. vii (quotation).

13. MBA, *The Day Is Short*, pp. 77–104; "Appellants' Brief on Petition for Rehearing," p. 13 (first quotation), filed in *South* v. *Peters*, No. 724, OT 1949, SCUS; *South* v. *Peters*, 339 U.S. 276 (1950) (all other quotations at pp. 278–80); *Cox* v. *Peters*, 342 U.S. 936 (1952); *Hartsfield* v. *Sloan*, 357 U.S. 916 (1958).

14. MBA, *The Day Is Short*, pp. 104–105; William B. Hartsfield, "What Georgia Thinks of the County Unit System," 1958, box 34, folder 10, William B. Hartsfield Papers, Manuscript, Archives, and Rare Book Library, Emory University, Atlanta; "Complaint," filed March 27, 1962, Civil Action No. 7872, *Sanders* v. *Gray*, in the District Court for the Northern District of Georgia, Atlanta Division, in *TOR*, *Gray* v. *Sanders*, pp. 1–38.

15. MBA, *The Day Is Short*, pp. 105–106; "House Okays Unit Plan, 147–37, as Court Hints Quick Ruling," *Atlanta Journal*, April 27, 1962, p. 1; "Life, Death of Unit Plan Awaits Ruling by Court," p. 1.

16. *Sanders* v. *Gray*, 203 F. Supp. 158 (1962) (quotation at p. 168); "U.S. Court Rejects New Georgia Law on Unit Elections," *NYT*, April 29, 1962, pp. 1, 55; "Unit Law 'in Present Form,' Ruled Invalid by U.S. Court," *Atlanta Journal and Atlanta Constitution*, April 29, 1962, pp. 1, 6.

17. Victor Navasky interview with AC, Oct. 1970, p. 2 (quotation), box 3, "Archibald Cox," Victor Navasky Personal Papers, JFKL; Larry J. Hackman, Jr., interview with BM, Jan. 19–20, 1970, Bedford, NY, p. 64, RFK Oral History Program, JFKL.

18. AC to RFK, Dec. 20, 1962, folder 4, *Gray* v. *Sanders*, "Notes for Oral Arguments" and handwritten notes of RFK, folder 10, box 489, Arthur M. Schlesinger, Jr., Papers, Manuscripts and Archives Division, New York Public Library; Victor Navasky interview with BJT, Dec. 12, 1968, box 19, "Bruce Terris," Victor Navasky Personal Papers, JFKL; author interview with BJT, March 29, 2006, Washington, D.C.; Arthur M. Schlesinger, Jr., *Robert Kennedy and His Times* (Boston: Houghton Mifflin, 1978), p. 398.

19. AC to RFK, Dec. 20, 1962, pp. 1–4 (all quotations on pp. 2–3), folder 4, box 489, Arthur M. Schlesinger, Jr., Papers, Manuscripts and Archives Division, New York Public Library.

20. "Brief on Behalf of Appellee," filed Dec. 6, 1962, in *Gray* v. *Sanders*, No. 112, OT 1962, SCUS, esp. pp. 14–15; MBA, *The Day Is Short*, pp. 107–108 (first quotation on p. 107; second and third quotations on p. 108).

21. Mary McGrory, "Bobby's Court Debut Socially Brilliant: Kennedys Outnumber Justices," *WES*, Jan. 18, 1963, pp. 1, 6 (first quotation on p. 1); "Robert F. Kennedy Argues First Case," *NYT*, Jan. 18, 1963, pp. 1, 4; "12 Kennedys Hear Attorney General's Courtroom Debut," *WP*, Jan. 18, 1963, p. A5; Doris Lockerman, "County Unit Suit Attracts Social Set," *Atlanta Constitution*, Jan. 23, 1963, p. 17; Victor Navasky interview with BJT, p. 2 (second quotation), Victor Navasky Personal Papers, JFKL.

22. OA of B. D. Murphy and E. Freeman Leverett, Jan. 17, 1963 (quotations), in *Gray* v. *Sanders*; "Broad Unit Ruling Urged by Abram," *Atlanta Constitution*, Jan. 18, 1963, pp. 1, 8; "Robert F. Kennedy Argues First Case," *NYT*, Jan. 18, 1963, p. 4.

23. OA of MBA, Jan. 17, 1963 (quotations), in *Gray* v. *Sanders*; "Broad Unit Ruling Urged by Abram," p. 1.

24. McGrory, "Bobby's Court Debut Is Socially Brilliant"; James E. Clayton, *The Making of Justice: The Supreme Court in Action* (New York: Dutton, 1964), pp. 141–55 (first and second quotations on p. 141); OA of RFK, Jan. 17, 1963 (all other quotations), in *Gray* v. *Sanders*; MBA, *The Day Is Short*, pp. 108–109; Navasky, *Kennedy Justice*, pp. 277–79.

25. McGrory, "Bobby's Court Debut Is Socially Brilliant" (first and second quotations on p. 6); OA of RFK, Jan. 17, 1963 (all other quotations), in *Gray* v. *Sanders*; "Robert F. Kennedy Argues First Case," pp. 1, 4.

26. Lucas A. Powe Jr., *The Warren Court and American Politics* (Cambridge, MA: Harvard University Press, 2000), pp. 241–42 (first quotation on p. 242); Cray, *Chief Justice*, p. 435; OA of E. Freeman Leverett, Jan. 17, 1963 (other quotations), in *Gray* v. *Sanders*.

27. Thomas G. Walker, "White, Byron Raymond," in Hall, *Oxford Companion to the Supreme Court*, pp. 926–27; Dennis J. Hutchinson, *The Man Who Once Was Whizzer White: A Portrait of Justice Byron R. White* (New York: Free Press, 1998).

28. Ibid.

29. Donald M. Roper, "Goldberg, Arthur Joseph," in Hall, *Oxford Companion to the Supreme Court*, pp. 340–41.

30. Ibid.; Laura Kalman, "Fortas, Abe" and "Fortas Resignation," in Hall, *Oxford Companion to the Supreme Court*, pp. 308–309; Bob Woodward and Scott Armstrong, *The Brethren: Inside the Supreme Court* (New York: Avon Books, 1979), pp. 11–18.

31. Roper, "Goldberg, Arthur Joseph."

32. WOD, Conference Notes, Jan. 18, 1963, "No. 112—*Gray* v. *Sanders*," box 1293, folder "No. 112, *Gray* v. *Sanders*, Misc. Memos, Cert. Memos," part II, WODP.

33. WOD, handwritten draft and first typed draft (first and second quotations), "No. 112 *Gray* v. *Sanders*, Penciled Draft," box 1293, part II, WODP; *Gray* v. *Sanders*, 372 U.S. 368 (1963) (first quotation at 372 U.S. 381).

34. WOD, handwritten draft and first typed draft (quotation), "No. 112 *Gray* v. *Sanders*, Penciled Draft," comments from clerk on typed draft, Jan. 30, 1963, "No. 112 *Gray* v. *Sanders*, Law Clerk," box 1293, part II, WODP; *Gray* v. *Sanders*, 372 U.S. 368 (1963) (quotation at 372 U.S. 381).

35. List of Circulations, *Gray* v. *Sanders*, folder 2, box A211, TCCP; *Gray* v. *Sanders*, 372 U.S. 368 (1963) (first and second quotations at 372 U.S. 390; third quotation at 372 U.S. 381–82; fourth quotation at 372 U.S. 382). For his concurrence, Stewart leaned on *United States* v. *Classic*, 313 U.S. 299 (1941).

36. "High Court Smashes Unit Plan," *Atlanta Journal*, March 18, 1963, p. 1, "Unit System Illegal, Says High Court," *Atlanta Constitution*, March 19, 1963, "Death of Unit Fails to Surprise State," *Atlanta Constitution*, March 19, 1963, "High Court

Dooms County-Unit Voting," *CSM*, March 19, 1963, "Supreme Court Declares Unconstitutional County-Unit Voting Procedure in Georgia," *WSJ*, March 19, 1963, and "One Person, One Vote," *NYT*, March 20, 1963, all in box 35, Scrapbook of Newspaper Clippings Re: *Gray* v. *Sanders*, MBAP; "Toward 'One Voter, One Vote,'" *New York Post*, March 20, 1963, p. 48 (quotation).

37. Robert G. Dixon, Jr., to AC, Nov. 15, 1968 (quotations on p. 2), box 44, folder 7, Archibald Cox Papers, Law School Library, Harvard University.

38. LWV-US, "League Favors 'One Man, One Vote,'" Jan. 12, 1966, box 258, "Government and Apportionment: Basic Documents, 1959–71," part IV, LWVP; Jean M. Whittet, Young Women's Christian Association of the USA, to Mrs. Robert J. Stuart, President, LWV-US, Feb. 25, 1966, box 259, "Government Apportionment Miscellany 1965–66," part IV, LWVP; SNCC, "Lowndes County Freedom Organization: One Man—One Vote," *The Voice* 6 (Dec. 20, 1965): 1, in Clayborne Carson, ed., *The Student Voice, 1960–1965* (Westport, CT: Greenwood Press, 1990), p. 231; OA of E. Freeman Leverett, Jan. 17, 1963 (quotations), in *Gray* v. *Sanders*.

7. THE MAKING OF *REYNOLDS* V. *SIMS*

1. Author interview with CJS, Nov. 8, 2005, Birmingham, AL.

2. CJS, "Little Counties Play Big Role in Senate," *BPH*, May 10, 1961, p. 1; CJS, "Some of Lawmakers Break Oath Each Time," *BPH*, May 11, 1961, p. 1. Figure of 1,000 bills in CJS, "'At-Large' Legislative Race Sought," *BPH*, March 30, 1962, pp. 1–2.

3. Amended Complaint, *M. O. Sims, et al.* v. *Bettye Frink, et al.*, Civil Action No. 1744-N, USDC for the Middle District of Alabama (Northern Division), filed Aug. 26, 1961, Exhibit B, pp. 1–3.

4. Author interview with CJS.

5. CJS recalls a fourteen-part series, but the author has located an eight-part series that ran in the *BPH* between May 10 and May 19, 1961. The *BPH* published many subsequent articles on the subject written by CJS, including another series in 1962.

6. CJS, "Little Counties Play Big Role in Senate," pp. 1, 4; CJS, "Some of Lawmakers Break Oath Each Term," pp. 1, 2; CJS, "Will Tax Inequities Be Solved This Year?" *BPH*, May 12, 1961, p. 1 (all quotations); CJS, "Courts May Take Hand in Reapportionment," *BPH*, May 16, 1961, p. 13; CJS, "Alabama Not Only State Needing Reapportionment," *BPH*, May 17, 1961, p. 2; CJS, "Reapportionment Might Be Forced by Supreme Court," *BPH*, May 18, 1961, p. 12; CJS, "Black Belt Reapportionment Is a 'Lame Duck' Shuffle," *BPH*, May 19, 1961, p. 6.

7. GPT, unpublished memoir, pp. 25–33, in possession of the author; interview with GPT, Nov. 9, 2005, Birmingham, AL (first three quotations); Anthony Paul Underwood, "A Progressive History of the Young Men's Business Club of Birmingham, Alabama, 1946–1970" (master's thesis, Samford University, 1980); Diane McWhorter, *Carry Me Home* (New York: Simon & Schuster, 2002), p. 189; "Resolution," file 960.1.8, YMBC Research Files (fourth quotation), Anthony Paul Underwood Papers, BPL; "YMBC Urges Sit-ins Here Be Halted," *BPH*, April 9, 1963,

copy in file 960.1.8, YMBC Research Files, Anthony Paul Underwood Papers, BPL.

8. Interview with CJS. Stallworth remembered that when he suggested a federal lawsuit, Morgan chimed in "we're working on that," a claim that conforms with records that show that the YMBC's State Affairs Committee first discussed reapportionment at a meeting on May 16, 1961. But even if Morgan and other members of the YMBC had discussed the possibility of a lawsuit prior to Stallworth's talk, the timing of the committee meeting suggests that the committee discussed reapportionment as a direct result of Stallworth's series. See David Vann to YMBC State Affairs Committee, May 16, 1961, box 26, file 11, David Vann Papers, BPL.

9. Author interview with GPT; CM, *A Time to Speak* (New York: Harper, 1964), chaps. 3–4; McWhorter, *Carry Me Home*, pp. 171–72, 188–89 (first and second quotations on p. 188; third quotation on p. 172).

10. Interview with GPT; CM, *A Time to Speak*, chaps. 3–5.

11. CM, *A Time to Speak*, chaps. 6–7; McWhorter, *Carry Me Home*, pp. 150–55, 168–73.

12. CM, *A Time to Speak*, chaps. 12–13. For more on Bob Zellner, see Lewis, *The Shadows of Youth*.

13. Author interview with GPT; "Memorials—George Peach Taylor," *Alabama Lawyer*, March 2009, pp. 94–95.

14. GPT, unpublished memoir, pp. 25–33 (first quotation on page 32); author interview with GPT (second quotation); WC to CM, Aug. 23, 1961, box 2 (1976 accession), CMP.

15. Leonard Chamblee, "Nettles Fears Small Counties Will Lose Roads if Reapportioned," *BPH*, July 3, 1961, pp. 1, 2.

16. "Cut-Up Defeat Possible," *BPH*, Aug. 10, 1961, p. 1.

17. CM, *A Time to Speak*, pp. 103–104 (first quotation); "Agreement," Aug. 7, 1961, box 2 (1976 accession), CMP; GPT, unpublished memoir, p. 27 (second quotation); author interview with GPT; Richard T. Tannehill to CM, Aug. 14, 1961, David R. Baker to CM, Aug. 21, 1962, Baker to GPT, Jan. 17, 1963, GPT to Baker, Jan. 23, 1963, Baker to GPT, Jan. 29, 1963, in box 1 (1976 accession), CMP.

18. CJS, "Jefferson Fate Up to Gov. Patterson," *BPH*, Aug. 14, 1961, pp. 1–2; CJS, "Suit in Federal Court Seeks to Force Reapportionment," *BPH*, Aug. 14, 1961, pp. 1–2.

19. Amended Complaint, filed Aug. 26, 1961, *M. O. Sims, et al. v. Bettye Frink, et al.*, Civil Action No. 1744-N, in the USDC for the Middle District of Alabama (Northern Division), box 75A, folder 1, Record Group 21, NARA-SE; GPT, unpublished memoir, pp. 28–29; Jack Bass, *Taming the Storm* (New York: Anchor Books, 1993), pp. 107–17.

20. Amended Complaint, filed Aug. 26, 1961, *Sims* v. *Frink* (first quotation on p. 13; second quotation on p. 17).

21. "An Editorial—Let's Face the Facts on State's Redistricting," *BPH*, Aug. 16, 1961, pp. 1, 10.

22. CJS, "Filibuster Halts Chop-Up," *BPH*, Aug. 30, 1961, pp. 1–2; CJS, "Modified '9-8' Bill Due for OK," *BPH*, Sept. 15, 1961, pp. 1–2; CJS, "Legislators Pass '9-8' Plan, State Money Bill, Go Home," *BPH*, Sept. 16, 1961, pp. 1–2; *Moore* v. *Moore*, 229 F. Supp. 435 (S.D. Ala. 1964).

23. Author interview with GPT (first quotation); GPT, unpublished memoir (second quotation on p. 29); CM, *A Time to Speak*, pp. 104–108; Ivan Swift, "Business Club Blasts YMBC in Federal Suit," *Birmingham News*, Sept. 13, 1961 (third quotation), clipping located in file 960.1.12, YMBC Research Files, Anthony Paul Underwood Papers, BPL.

24. WC to CM, Aug. 23, 1961, box 2 (1976 accession), CMP; author interview with GPT; GPT, unpublished memoir, p. 31.

25. Jerome Cooper, "'Segregating Together': Memories of a Birmingham Labor Lawyer," pp. 69–71, edited by C. Roger Nance, file 1633.1.2, Jerome A. Cooper Papers, BPL; "Motion to Intervene," Nov. 1, 1961, "Motion to Dismiss the Plea of Intervention," Nov. 15, 1961, Civil Action #1744-N, box 75A, folder 1, RG 21, NARA-SE.

26. "Motion for a Preliminary Injunction," March 29, 1962, and "Affidavit to Support Motion," March 29, 1962, in box 75A, folder 1, #1744-N, RG 21, NARA-SE; "At-Large Legislative Race Sought," *BPH*, March 30, 1962, pp. 1–2; "Hearing Set for April 14 on Reapportion Injunction," *BPH*, March 31, 1962, p. 1; "Order Setting Hearing of Application for Interlocutory Injunction," March 30, 1962, *TOR*, No. 23, *B. A. Reynolds* v. *M. O. Sims*, No. 27, *David J. Vann* and *Robert S. Vance* v. *Bettye Frink, et al.*, No. 41, *John W. McConnell, Jr.*, v. *Bettye Frink, et al.*, OT 1963, SCUS, pp. 57–59 (quotation).

27. Testimony from Hearing of April 14, 1962, Civil Action #1744-N, box 75A, folder 1, RG 21, NARA-SE (first quotation on p. 5; all other quotations on p. 7).

28. Ibid.

29. "Opinion on Hearing of Application for Interlocutory Injunction," April 14, 1962, #1744-N, box 75A, folder 1, RG 21, NARA-SE; "Political Leaders Urge Reapportionment," *BPH*, April 16, 1962, pp. 1–2; "Reapportionment Order Quite Clear," *BPH*, April 16, 1962, p. 8; CJS, "Judges Say 'You Reapportion or We Will,'" *BPH*, April 16, 1962, p. 8.

30. "Legislature Meets Today on Issue," *BPH*, June 12, 1962, pp. 1, 3; "Legislators Urged to Beat Deadline," *BPH*, June 13, 1962, pp. 1–2 (quotations).

31. CJS, "'67' Plan Passage Could Give Wallace Power to Pick Lawmakers," *BPH*, June 15, 1962, p. 2; "67-Senator Reshuffle Passed—Patterson Signs Standby Bill," *BPH*, July 13, 1962, p. 1; "Reapportionment Suit Dismissal Is Sought," *BPH*, July 14, 1962, pp. 1–2; CJS, "Legislature Changes Few in Crawford Bill," *BPH*, July 14, 1962, p. 12.

32. *Sims* v. *Frink*, Hearings Before Hon. Richard T. Rives, Hon. Daniel H. Thomas, and Hon. Frank M. Johnson, Jr., July 16, 1962, #1744-N, box 75, folder "Exhibits," RG 21, NARA-SE (first quotation on p. 25; second quotation on p. 32; third and fourth quotations on p. 31; fifth quotation on p. 34); "Reapportion Bills Go to U.S. Judges," *BPH*, July 16, 1962, pp. 1–2; CJS, "Prompt Reapportion Decision Is Promised," *BPH*, July 17, 1962, pp. 1–2.

33. "Motion for Leave to Intervene," April 9, 1962, box 75A, folder 1, #1744-N, RG 21, NARA-SE; "Jeffco Demo Committee Votes to Join Suit," *BPH*, April 4, 1962, p. 1; McWhorter, *Carry Me Home*, pp. 187–99, 282–320; Ray Jenkins, *Blind Vengeance: The Roy Moody Mail Bomb Murders* (Athens: University of Georgia Press, 1997), pp. 83–85.

34. McWhorter, *Carry Me Home*, pp. 282–83 (first quotation on p. 282); CM to the Rt. Rev. George H. Murray, Oct. 16, 1963, "Correspondence October 1963," box 16 (8/24/1981 accession), "Fight the So-Called Civil Rights Bill—Your Help Is Needed Now!" folder "Correspondence Q–T," box 11 (8/24/1981 accession), CMP; Jenkins, *Blind Vengeance*, chaps. 5, 8, 10, 12, 13; Al Fox, "Bob Vance Just a 'Bookwormish' Lawyer," *Birmingham News*, Nov. 6, 1977 (second quotation), "Robert Vance" clipping file, BPL.

35. David Vann to YMBC State Affairs Committee, May 16, 1961, folder 26.11, David Vann Papers, BPL; David Vann to CM, Oct. 11, 1961, box 2 (1976 accession), CMP; Jenkins, *Blind Vengeance*, pp. 83–85.

36. David Vann to JWM, April 26, 1962, David Vann to JWM, May 9, 1962, CM to David Vann and JWM, May 14, 1962, box 2 (1976 accession), CMP; "Amended Complaint," Aug. 26, 1961, "Motion for Leave to Amend Complaint in Intervention," June 28, 1962, "Joindure in Motion for Summary Judgment," July 3, 1962, #1744-N, box 75A, folder 1, RG 21, NARA-SE. The plan put forward by David Vann and Robert Vance is detailed in "Motion for Leave to Amend Complaint in Intervention."

37. "Order," April 20, 1962, "Motion for Leave to Intervene," June 27, 1962, #1744-N, box 75A, folder 1, RG 21, NARA-SE; author interview with JWM, May 9, 2006 (quotation), Memphis; JWM, "The Problem of the Reapportionment of the Alabama Legislature and a Recommended Solution," JWM biographical statement, Aug. 29, 2005, in possession of author.

38. *Sims* v. *Frink*, Hearings Before Hon. Richard T. Rives, Hon. Daniel H. Thomas, and Hon. Frank M. Johnson Jr., July 16, 1962, #1744-N, box 75, folder "Exhibits," RG 21, NARA-SE, pp. 45–52 (quotations on p. 49).

39. *Sims* v. *Frink*, Hearings Before Hon. Richard T. Rives, Hon. Daniel H. Thomas, and Hon. Frank M. Johnson Jr., July 16, 1962, #1744-N, box 75, folder "Exhibits," RG 21, NARA-SE, pp. 53–76 (all quotations on pp. 59–60); "Up to the Court," *BPH*, July 18, 1962, p. 8.

40. "Personality Conflicts Are Cited by Webb," *BPH*, July 17, 1962, p. 2; *Eighteenth Decennial Census of the United States, Census of Population: 1960*, Vol. 1, *Characteristics of the Population*, part 2: Alabama, table 28, pp. 2-92 to 2-96; "Brief on Behalf of Appellee," filed Dec. 6, 1962, in *Gray* v. *Sanders*, No. 112, OT 1962, SCUS, esp. pp. 11–14.

41. "Decree," July 25, 1962, *Sims* v. *Frink*, #1744-N, box 75A, folder 1, RG 21, NARA-SE (first quotation on p. 2); *Sims* v. *Frink*, 208 F. Supp. 431 (D.C.M.D. Ala. 1962) (other quotations at 208 F. Supp. 441–42).

42. "Special Primaries up to Patterson: Demo Nominee Changes Must Be Made in 46 Days," *BPH*, July 23, 1962, pp. 1, 4 (quotation on p. 1); "Great Victory, Great Challenge," *BPH*, July 23, 1962, p. 8.

43. "Decree," July 25, 1962, p. 15, *Sims* v. *Frink*, #1744-N, box 75A, folder 1, RG 21, NARA-SE; "Funds Voted for Reshuffle Court Fight," newspaper clipping from *BPH* or *Birmingham News*, week of August 14, 1961, YMBC *Weekly Bulletin*, Aug. 7, 1962, both in file 960.1.12, YMBC Research Files, Paul Anthony Underwood Papers, BPL; Underwood, "Progressive History of the Young Men's Business Club," pp. 111–12; CJS, "Among the Clatter," *Birmingham* 2, no. 3 (March 1963): 9, 24; JWM to T. G. Greaves Jr., Sept. 4, 1962, JWM to Joseph Langan, William Williams, and Garet Van Antwerp, Aug. 30, 1963, JWMP; CM to Jerome Cooper, Aug. 1, 1962, box 2 (1976 accession), CMP; author interview with GPT; author interview with CJS.

44. "Motion for Rehearing and Modification of Proposed Decree," July 25, 1962, "Order Denying Motion for Rehearing and Modification," July 25, 1962, *Sims* v. *Frink*, #1744-N, box 75A, folder 1, RG 21, NARA-SE; "Special Primaries up to Patterson," pp. 1, 4 (first quotation on p. 4); CM to Martha McPherson, July 31, 1962 (second quotation), folder "Through July 1962," box 10 (1976 accession), CMP.

45. "Demos to Arrange Special Primaries: Committee Will Decide on Details," *BPH*, July 24, 1962, p. 1; Richard C. Cortner, *The Apportionment Cases* (New York: Norton, 1972), pp. 189–90.

46. Robert Vance to JWM, Aug. 10, 1962, JWMP.

47. Ibid.

48. Vance to JWM, Aug. 10, 1962 (first and third quotations), JWMP; Vance to AC, Oct. 19, 1962 (second quotation), file 113.26.31, David J. Vann Papers, BPL.

49. Notes from meeting of Aug. 7, 1962, folder 4, "Federal Reapportionment Decision," SG 22375, Executive Papers of George Wallace, Alabama Department of Archives and History, Montgomery; letter from Robert Vance to Richard C. Cortner, July 1, 1965, in Cortner, *Apportionment Cases*, p. 189; "Notice of Appeal of B. A. Reynolds," filed Aug. 17, 1962, *TOR*, No. 23, *B. A. Reynolds* v. *M. O. Sims*, No. 27, *David J. Vann and Robert S. Vance* v. *Bettye Frink*, No. 41, *John W. McConnell, Jr.,* v. *Bettye Frink*, pp. 197–201.

50. "Notice of Appeal (Cross Appeal) of David Vann, et al.," Aug. 23, 1962, *TOR*, *Reynolds* v. *Sims*, pp. 201–203; Robert Vance to JWM, Sept. 10, 1962 (all quotations), JWMP; "Well-Intentioned Goof," *BPH*, Aug. 25, 1962, editorial page.

51. CM to JWM, Sept. 22, 1962 (first quotation), Jerome Cooper to JWM, Sept. 10, 1962, box 1 (1976 accession), CMP; author interview with GPT (second and third quotations).

52. Robert Vance to JWM, Sept. 10, 1962 (first quotation), JWMP; Jerome Cooper, "Segregating Together," pp. 70–71 (second quotation), Jerome Cooper Papers, BPL; author interview with GPT.

53. McWhorter, *Carry Me Home*, pp. 172, 282–83 (quotations on p. 282); CM, *A Time to Speak*, p. 74.

54. JWM to CM, Sept. 5, 1962, Jerome Cooper to JWM, Sept. 10, 1962, CM to JWM, Sept. 12, 1962, JWM to CM, Sept. 17, 1962, CM to JWM, Sept. 22, 1962, box 1 (1976 accession), CMP; author interview with JWM; "Notice of Appeal (Cross Appeal) of John McConnell, Jr.," *TOR*, *Reynolds* v. *Sims*, pp. 204–205.

55. See McWhorter, *Carry Me Home*; J. Mills Thornton, III, *Dividing Lines: Municipal Politics and the Struggle for Civil Rights in Montgomery, Birmingham, and Selma* (Tuscaloosa: University of Alabama Press, 2002); Glenn T. Eskew, *But for Birmingham: The Local and National Movements in the Civil Rights Struggle* (Chapel Hill: University of North Carolina Press, 1997).

56. John F. Davis to JWM, June 10, 1963, Davis to JWM, June 11, 1963, JWMP; "Order Noting Probable Jurisdiction," June 10, 1963, *TOR*, *Reynolds* v. *Sims*, p. 206. Wallace was elected governor in November 1962 and inaugurated in January 1963.

57. Statement of CM, Sept. 16, 1963, "Speeches and Lecture Material 1963," box 15 (8/24/1981 accession), CMP; CM, *A Time to Speak*, pp. 161–70. Morgan delivered his remarks to the YMBC using only notes, so it is impossible to know to what extent his original remarks differed from the version he made available for publication. Three days later, Senator Maurine Neuberger of Oregon quoted extensively from the speech on the floor of the U.S. Senate. See "The Universal Guilt of Birmingham," *CR* 88th Cong., 1st Sess., Senate, vol. 109, n. 148, Sept. 18, 1963. Two weeks after that, the *Christian Century* ran Morgan's speech in full. See "Who Is Guilty in Birmingham?" *Christian Century* 80 (Oct. 2, 1963): 1195–96 (quotation). Excerpts of the speech appeared in "Birmingham: An Alabaman's Great Speech Lays the Blame," *Life* 55 (Sept. 27, 1963): 44 B–C; "I Saw a City Die," *Look* 27 (Dec. 3, 1963): 23–25.

58. CM, *A Time to Speak*, pp. 161–77; T. C. Reeves to CM, Oct. 11, 1963, CM to Reeves, Oct. 23, 1963 (first quotation), CM to George M. Murray, Oct. 16, 1963 (second quotation), "Correspondence October 1963," box 16 (8/24/1961 accession), CMP; McWhorter, *Carry Me Home*, 582–83.

59. Jerome Cooper to CM, Oct. 10, 1963, "Correspondence October 1963," box 16 (8/24/1981 accession), CMP.

8. CONVERGING ON WASHINGTON, D.C.

1. EDC to CM, Leonard B. Sand, Alfred L. Scanlan, et al., June 18, 1963, box 2 (1976 accession), CMP; CM to EDC, July 2, 1963, box 15 (8/24/1981 accession), "Personal File, June–Dec. 1963," CMP; HEH to Scanlan, Sand, CM, et al., Sept. 25, 1963, box 7, "Correspondence 1963," HEHP.

2. NML, "Court Cases on Apportionment and/or Districting," Sept. 1963, copy in JWMP.

3. Powe, *Warren Court and American Politics*, p. 246.

4. OA of E. Freeman Leverett, Jan. 17, 1963, in *Gray* v. *Sanders*, No. 112, OT 1962, SCUS.

5. James H. Hershman, Jr., "Campbell, Edmund Douglas," in Sara B. Bearss et al., eds., *Dictionary of Virginia Biography* (Richmond: Library of Virginia, 2001),

2:563–64; Hershman, "Massive Resistance Meets Its Match: The Emergence of a Pro-School Majority," in Matthew D. Lassiter and Andrew B. Lewis, eds., *The Moderates' Dilemma: Massive Resistance to School Desegregation in Virginia* (Charlottesville: University of Virginia Press, 1998), pp. 104–33; Andrew Lewis, "Wandering in Two Worlds: Race, Education, and Citizenship in Virginia Since 1945" (Ph.D. diss., University of Virginia, 2000), esp. chaps. 3–4.

6. "Complaint," filed April 9, 1962, in *Mann* v. *Davis*, Civil Action No. 2604, USDC, Eastern District of Virginia, in *TOR, Davis* v. *Mann*, No. 69, OT 1963, SCUS, pp. 1–9. On Hampton Roads after World War II, see Thomas C. Parramore et al., *Norfolk: The First Four Centuries* (Charlottesville: University of Virginia Press, 1994).

7. Armistead L. Boothe, "A Handbook of Redistricting the Senate and House of Delegates of Virginia, 1952," box 10, "Redistricting," Armistead Lloyd Boothe Papers, Albert and Shirley Small Special Collections Library, University of Virginia; Douglas Smith, "When Reason Collides with Prejudice," *Virginia Magazine of History and Biography* 102, no. 1 (Jan. 1994): 14–15.

8. Boothe, "Handbook of Redistricting," pp. 10–13, 18–21; "Exhibits A and B," filed April 9, 1962, in *TOR, Davis* v. *Mann*, pp. 11–17.

9. "Complaint" and "Exhibits C and D," filed April 9, 1962, "Intervening Petition," filed May 25, 1962, in *TOR, Davis* v. *Mann*, pp. 1–9, 18–24, 33–43; Report of the Commission on Redistricting, "Reapportionment of the State for Representation," House Document No. 8 (Richmond: Commonwealth of Virginia, 1961); Albertis S. Harrison, Jr., "Statement re HB 250 and SB 145," April 7, 1962, copy in box 5, folder "Correspondence Prior to Verdict, 1962," HEHP; "Redistricting Verdict Brings Plan to Light," *Richmond Times-Dispatch*, Dec. 2, 1962, pp. 1, 5.

10. "Henry E. Howell, Jr., 76, Leader of Liberal Democrats in Virginia," *NYT*, July 9, 1997, p. B11; "Biography," Guide to the HEHP.

11. "Henry E. Howell, Jr., 76,"; Garrett Epps, *The Shad Treatment* (New York: Putnam, 1977).

12. HEH to EDC, June 5, 1962, HEH to EDC and E. A. Prichard, June 13, 1962, EDC to HEH, June 19, 1962, HEH to Ralph Eisenberg and Paul T. David, June 27, 1962, Eisenberg to HEH, July 11, 1962, HEH to Eisenberg, July 16, 1962, EDC to HEH, July 25, 1962, box 5, "Correspondence Prior to Verdict, 1962," HEHP; Ralph Eisenberg, "Legislative Apportionment: How Representative Is Virginia's Present System?" *University of Virginia News Letter* 37 (April 15, 1961): 29–32; David and Eisenberg, *Devaluation of the Urban & Suburban Vote*; "Plaintiffs' Trial Brief," filed July 20, 1962, pp. 16–20, "Plaintiffs' Reply and Supplemental Briefs," filed Oct. 10, 1962, "Brief on Behalf of Intervening Petitioners," pp. 24–25, "Reply Brief on Behalf of Intervening Petitioners," *Mann* v. *Davis*, Civil Action No. 2604, box 4, HEHP.

13. "Plaintiffs' Trial Brief," pp. 4–7 (quotation on p. 6), *Mann* v. *Davis*, Civil Action No. 2604, box 4, HEHP; "Exhibits C and D," filed April 9, 1962, in *TOR, Davis* v. *Mann*, pp. 18–24.

14. "Plaintiffs' Trial Brief" (second quotation on p. 9), "Brief on Behalf of Intervening Petitioners" (first quotation on p. 34), *Mann v. Davis*, Civil Action No. 2604, box 4, HEHP.

15. James R. Sweeney, ed., *Race, Reason, and Massive Resistance: The Diary of David J. Mays, 1954–1959* (Athens: University of Georgia Press, 2008); Joseph J. Thorndike, " 'The Sometimes Sordid Level of Race and Segregation': James J. Kilpatrick and the Virginia Campaign Against *Brown*," in Lassiter and Lewis, *The Moderates' Dilemma*, pp. 51–71. For the most complete set of pamphlets published by the Virginia Commission on Constitutional Government, see the holdings of the Library of Virginia in Richmond. On Mays and his critique of the Warren Court, see Diary of David J. Mays, Dec. 4, 1962, box 2, David J. Mays Papers, Virginia Historical Society, Richmond.

16. "Brief on Behalf of Defendants," *Mann v. Davis*, Civil Action No. 2604, box 4, HEHP.

17. James J. Kilpatrick to DJM, June 22, 1962 (quotations on p. 2), box 1, Virginia Commission on Constitutional Government Papers, Library of Virginia, Richmond.

18. Diary of DJM, Aug. 10, 15, 16, and 24, and Sept. 6 and 12, 1962, box 2, David J. Mays Papers, Virginia Historical Society, Richmond; "Brief on Behalf of Defendants," *Mann v. Davis*, Civil Action No. 2604, box 4, HEHP; "Defendants' Exhibits 4, 5, and 6," in *TOR, Davis v. Mann*, pp. 254–73.

19. *Mann v. Davis*, 213 F. Supp. 577 (1962) (first quotation on p. 584; all other quotations on p. 589); Hershman, "Massive Resistance Meets Its Match," pp. 117–18; "Defendants' Exhibits 4 and 5," in *TOR, Davis v. Mann*, pp. 254–67. Hoffman cited Alaska, Maine, Massachusetts, New Hampshire, Oregon, West Virginia, and Wisconsin as the seven states deemed more representative than Virginia.

20. Diary of DJM, Dec. 3, 1962 (quotations), box 2, David J. Mays Papers, Virginia Historical Society, Richmond; "Appeal the Decision," *Richmond News Leader*, Dec. 4, 1962, editorial page; "VA. to Appeal Decision," *Richmond News Leader*, Dec. 7, 1962, p. 1; "High Court Gets Appeal by State," *Richmond Times-Dispatch*, Dec. 11, 1962, pp. 1, 3.

21. *Mann v. Davis*, 213 F. Supp. 589 (1962); "Defendants' Exhibit 5," in *TOR, Davis v. Mann*, pp. 262–67; Calvin B. T. Lee, *One Man, One Vote: WMCA and the Struggle for Equal Representation* (New York: Scribner, 1967), pp. 3–11.

22. Lee, *One Man, One Vote*, pp. 4–5; FXB, "Bench Memorandum," Nov. 5, 1963, pp. 2–9 (quotation on p. 3), *WMCA v. Lomenzo*, No. 20, OT 1963, SCUS, in box 246, "Conference Memos OT 1963, Appellate #20-22," EWP; "Defendants' Exhibit 4" in *TOR, Davis v. Mann*, pp. 255–61.

23. Lee, *One Man, One Vote*, pp. 4–5 (quotation on p. 5); FXB, "Bench Memorandum," Nov. 5, 1963, pp. 2–9, *WMCA v. Lomenzo*, in box 246, "Conference Memos OT 1963, Appellate #20-22," EWP; "Defendants' Exhibit 4" in *TOR, Davis v. Mann*, pp. 255–61.

24. Lee, *One Man, One Vote*, pp. 15–25.

25. Ibid., pp. 26–28, 42–47 (quotation on p. 46).

26. Ibid., pp. 49–59 (first quotation on p. 51; second quotation on p. 55).

27. Royce Hanson, *Fair Representation Comes to Maryland*, Cases in Practical Politics, Eagleton Institute (New Brunswick, NJ: Rutgers University, 1964), pp. 2–3; Strout, "The Next Election Is Already Rigged."

28. Hanson, *Fair Representation*, pp. 3–4.

29. Maryland Committee for Fair Representation, "The Case for Fair Representation in Maryland" (quotation), box 1137, folder 17, ACLU Papers, Seely G. Mudd Manuscript Library, Princeton University; *Maryland Committee for Fair Representation v. J. Millard Tawes*, "Bill of Complaint," filed Aug. 20, 1960, in *TOR, Maryland v. Tawes*, No. 29, OT 1963, SCUS, pp. 4–6, 31–33.

30. Hanson, *Fair Representation*, pp. 6–9; "Bill of Complaint," in *TOR, Maryland v. Tawes*, pp. 18–20 (quotation on p. 19).

31. "Opinion," April 25, 1962, *Maryland v. Tawes*, no. 52, September Term 1961, Court of Appeals of Maryland, in *TOR, Maryland v. Tawes*, pp. 54–78 (first and second quotations on p. 71); Hanson, *Fair Representation*, p. 21 (third quotation).

32. "Opinion," May 24, 1962, No. 13,920 Equity, Circuit Court for Anne Arundel County, in *TOR, Maryland v. Tawes*, pp. 100–11.

33 "Supplemental Opinion," June 28, 1962, in *TOR, Maryland v. Tawes*, pp. 113–22.

34. "Appeal" and "Motion for Reargument," filed Aug. 2, 1962, in *TOR, Maryland v. Tawes*, pp. 123–62; "Opinion," filed Sept. 25, 1962, and "Dissenting Opinion," filed Sept. 25, 1962, in the Court of Appeals of Maryland, No. 140-Adv., September Term 1962, in *TOR, Maryland v. Tawes*, pp. 163–91 (first quotation on p. 176; second quotation on p. 179; third quotation on p. 183).

35. "Notice of Appeal," filed Sept. 28, 1962, and "Order Noting Probable Jurisdiction," June 10, 1963, in *TOR, Maryland v. Tawes*, pp. 193–97; EDC to Alfred L. Scanlan, CM, Leonard B. Sand, et al., June 18, 1963, box 2 (1976 accession), CMP; HEH to Leonard Bert Sachs, July 18, 1963, box 8, "Correspondence 1963," HEHP.

36. *Sanders v. Gray*, 203 F. Supp. 158 (1962), which on appeal to the Supreme Court became *Gray v. Sanders*, 372 U.S. 368 (1963); *Toombs v. Fortson*, 205 F. Supp. 248 (1962); *Wesberry v. Vandiver*, 206 F. Supp. 276 (1962), which on appeal to the Supreme Court became *Wesberry v. Sanders*, 376 U.S. 1 (1964).

37. "Complaint," filed April 17, 1962, "Defendants' Exhibit 1: Congressional Districts Ranked According to Populations," *Wesberry v. Vandiver*, Civil Suit No. 7889, USDC for the Northern District of Georgia, in *TOR, Wesberry v. Sanders*, No. 22, OT 1963, SCUS, pp. 7–8, 79.

38. "Preliminary Brief of the Plaintiffs," pp. 8–13 (first quotation on p. 13), Civil Suit No. 7889, box 283, RG 21, NARA-SE; "Complaint," in *TOR, Wesberry v. Sanders*, pp. 1–4 (quotation on p. 4).

39. "Preliminary Brief of the Defendants," filed May 23, 1962, pp. 1–14, "Supplemental Brief of the Defendants," filed June 6, 1962 (quotation on p. 3), Civil Suit No. 7889, box 283, RG 21, NARA-SE.

40. "Opinion," June 20, 1962, in *TOR, Wesberry v. Sanders*, pp. 36–51 (quotation on p. 41).

41. "Opinion of Elbert Tuttle," June 20, 1962, in *TOR*, *Wesberry* v. *Sanders*, pp. 51–55 (quotation on p. 53).

42. Harold H. Greene to BM, July 22, 1963, box 6, "General Correspondence July 1963," Burke Marshall Papers, JFKL.

9. AMICUS CURIAE

1. BM to J. Edgar Hoover, April 30, 1962, Harold H. Greene to BM, May 3, 1962, section 3, box 95, BM to U.S. Attorneys, May 2, 1962, section 2, box 95, BM to Hoover, Feb. 4, 1962, section 8, box 96, BM to Edmund Campbell, May 10, 1962, section 4, box 95, BM to Campbell, Aug. 13, 1962, Campbell to Greene, Aug. 17, 1962, Theodore Sachs to BM, Aug. 16, 1962, Sachs to BM, Aug. 24, 1962, Alfred L. Scanlan to BM, Nov. 1, 1962, BM to Scanlan, Nov. 28, 1962, section 5, box 96, RG 60; "Memorandum for the Attorney General," May 14, 1962, p. 3, box 16, "Civil Rights Division, Monday and Wednesday Reports, April–June 1962," Burke Marshall Papers, JFKL.

2. BM to Nicholas Katzenbach, April 23, 1962, box 1, "Chronological File April 1962," Burke Marshall Papers, JFKL; RFK, "Address at the Law Day Ceremonies of the Virginia State Bar," May 1, 1962, box 1, Speeches, RFK Attorney General Papers, JFKL; BM, "Address to Alumni, University of Connecticut Law School," May 1, 1962, box 13, Burke Marshall Papers; Nicholas Katzenbach, "Address at Vanderbilt University," April 27, 1962 (quotation on p. 11), box 31, Nicholas deB. Katzenbach Papers, JFKL; BM to Nicholas Katzenbach, April 23, 1962, box 1, "Chronological File April 1962," Burke Marshall Papers.

3. AC, "Law and the People," May 1, 1962, box 35, "Material Collected CL–CO," Burke Marshall Papers, JFKL; AC, "Current Constitutional Issues," June 8, 1962 (quotations on p. 3; emphasis in original), box 1, "Archibald Cox," GGP.

4. Author interview with BJT, March 29, 2006, Washington, D.C.

5. BJT to AC, "The Substantive Standards Under the Fourteenth Amendment for Apportioning State Legislatures," July 3, 1963, reel 99, CRDP.

6. Ibid., p. 1.

7. Ibid., pp. 1–2.

8. Ibid., p. 4.

9. Ibid., p. 5.

10. Ibid., pp. 6–7.

11. Ibid., pp. 8–10 (quotations); AC, "Current Constitutional Issues," June 8, 1962, box 1, "Archibald Cox," GGP; AC, "The Constitutional Aspects of Legislative Apportionment," July 1, 1963, box 109, folder 18, Archibald Cox Papers, Law School Library, Harvard University.

12. Author interview with BJT (first quotation); BJT to AC, "Substantive Standards," pp. 10–11 (other quotations).

13. BJT to J. Lee Rankin, Dec. 8, 1960, p. 5, reel 99, CRDP.

14. David Rubin and Howard A. Glickstein to Harold H. Greene, July 15, 1963, reel 99, CRDP.

15. Harold H. Greene to Burke Marshall, July 19, 1963, reel 99, CRDP.

16. AC to RFK, Aug. 19, 1963 (first quotation on p. 1), AC to RFK, Aug. 21, 1963, reel 99, CRDP; Navasky, *Kennedy Justice*, p. 311 (second quotation).

17. AC to RFK, Aug. 19, 1963, pp. 13–14 (quotations); Helen J. Knowles, "May It Please the Court? The Solicitor General's Not-So-'Special' Relationship: Archibald Cox and the 1963–1964 Reapportionment Cases," *Journal of Supreme Court History* 31 (Nov. 2006): 279–97.

18. AC to RFK, Aug. 19, 1963, pp. 14–17.

19. Ibid., pp. 17–18.

20. Ibid., pp. 18–19.

21. Ibid., pp. 21–28.

22. Ibid., pp. 29–31.

23. Ibid., p. 2; AC to RFK, Aug. 21, 1963, p. 2; BJT to AC, "Substantive Standards," p. 2n2.

24. AC to RFK, Aug. 21, 1963, p. 3 (all quotations except third and fourth); AC to RFK, Aug. 19, 1963, p. 32 (third and fourth quotations).

25. Anthony Lewis, "Seventh Oral History Interview with Robert F. Kennedy and Burke Marshall," Dec. 22, 1964, p. 575 (first and second quotations), RFK Oral History Program, JFKL; Larry O'Brien to RFK, Aug. 27, 1963 (all other quotations), folder 4, box 489, Arthur M. Schlesinger, Jr., Papers, Manuscripts and Archives Division, New York Public Library; Navasky, *Kennedy Justice*, p. 314.

26. Lewis, Oral History Interview with RFK and BM, p. 577.

27. AC, *The Court and the Constitution*, pp. 297–98 (quotation on p. 297); Navasky, *Kennedy Justice*, pp. 314–15; AC Diaries, Sept. 1963, box 13, "Cox Diaries (S.G.)," KGP.

28. Author interview with BJT (first quotation); Navasky, *Kennedy Justice*, pp. 314–15 (second quotation on p. 314; seventh quotation on p. 315); AC interview with Victor Navasky, Oct. 1970, p. 2 (third, fourth, and fifth quotations), box 3, "Archibald Cox," Victor Navasky Personal Papers, JFKL; AC, *The Court and the Constitution*, pp. 297–99 (sixth quotation on p. 298).

29. Navasky, *Kennedy Justice*, p. 315 (first quotation; emphasis in original); AC interview with Victor Navasky, Oct. 1970, p. 2 (second quotation); author interview with BJT.

30. "Brief for the United States as *Amicus Curiae*," filed Sept. 25, 1963, *Maryland* v. *Tawes*, No. 29, OT 1963, SCUS; "Appendix B to the Brief for the United States as *Amicus Curiae*," filed Sept. 30, 1963, *Maryland* v. *Tawes*, No. 29, OT 1963, SCUS; "Brief for the United States as *Amicus Curiae*," filed Sept. 30, 1963, *WMCA* v. *Simon*, No. 20, OT 1963, SCUS (second quotation on p. 13); "Brief for the United States as *Amicus Curiae*," filed Oct. 18, 1963, *Reynolds* v. *Sims*, No. 23, OT 1963, SCUS; "Brief for the United States as *Amicus Curiae*," filed Oct. 17, 1963, *Davis* v. *Mann*, No. 69, OT 1963, SCUS (first quotation on p. 2).

31. Author interview with BJT.

32. Ibid.; author telephone interview with Nicholas Katzenbach, Feb. 14, 2008.

33. "Brief for the United States as *Amicus Curiae*," *WMCA* v. *Simon*, p. 13.
34. "Brief for the United States as *Amicus Curiae*," *Maryland* v. *Tawes*, pp. 24–25.

10. NOVEMBER 1963

1. "Argument Before the Court: Legislative Apportionment," *United States Law Week* 32 (Nov. 26, 1963): 3189–93 (quotation on p. 3189).
2. OA of Leonard Sand, *WMCA* v. *Lomenzo*, No. 20, OT 1963, SCUS, Nov. 12, 1963.
3. "Brief for Appellants on Appeal from the Court of Appeals for Maryland," filed Aug. 22, 1963, *Maryland* v. *Tawes*, No. 29, OT 1963, SCUS, pp. 70–71; OA of Alfred Scanlan, *Maryland* v. *Tawes*, Nov. 13, 1963.
4. OA of CM, *Reynolds* v. *Sims*, No. 23, OT 1963, SCUS, Nov. 13, 1963, transcript in *Landmark Briefs*, 58:997–1003 (first quotation on p. 997; all other quotations on pp. 1000–1001).
5. OA of AC, *WMCA* v. *Lomenzo*, Nov. 12, 1963 (first quotation); OA of AC, *Reynolds* v. *Sims*, Nov. 13, 1963, in *Landmark Briefs*, 58:1024–34; OA of AC, *Maryland* v. *Tawes*, Nov. 14, 1963 (second quotation); OA of AC, *Davis* v. *Mann*, No. 69, OT 1963, SCUS, Nov. 18, 1963.
6. OA of JWM, *Reynolds* v. *Sims*, Nov. 13, 1963, in *Landmark Briefs*, 58:1012–13 (quotations on p. 1013).
7. David Collins to JWM, Nov. 14, 1963, H. J. McDevitt to JWM, Dec. 2, 1963 (first quotation), JWMP; OA of JWM, pp. 1013–19 (second quotation on p. 1014; third quotation on p. 1017).
8. OA of JWM, *Reynolds* v. *Sims*, Nov. 13, 1963, pp. 1013–19 (first quotation on p. 1013; second and third quotations on p. 1019).
9. OA of JWM, *Reynolds* v. *Sims*, Nov. 13, 1963, pp. 1013–21 (first quotation on p. 1015; second quotation on p. 1021; third quotation on p. 1013); *Gray* v. *Sanders*, 372 U.S. 368 (1963); OA of AC, *WMCA* v. *Lomenzo*, Nov. 12, 1963.
10. OA of Irving Galt, *WMCA* v. *Lomenzo*, Nov. 12, 1963.
11. OA of W. McLean Pitts, *Reynolds* v. *Sims*, Nov. 13, 1963, in *Landmark Briefs*, 58:979–90 (first quotation on p. 987; second quotation on p. 979; third quotation on p. 982).
12. OA of Robert S. Bourbon, *Maryland* v. *Tawes*, Nov. 14, 1963.
13. OA of Theodore I. Botter, *Maryland* v. *Tawes*, Nov. 14, 1963 (first quotation); rebuttal oral argument of Alfred L. Scanlan, *Maryland* v. *Tawes*, Nov. 14, 1963 (second quotation).
14. OA of DJM and Robert D. McIlwaine, III, *Davis* v. *Mann*, Nov. 14, 1963.
15. DJM Diary, Nov. 12, 1963, box 2 of 4, "July 14–December 31, 1963," David J. Mays Papers, Virginia Historical Society, Richmond.
16. Ibid., Nov. 13, 1963.
17. Ibid., Nov. 14, 1963.
18. Ibid.

19. Ibid.

20. "Conference Lists," Nov. 15, 1963, box 28, folder 8, part I, Byron R. White Papers, Manuscript Division, LOC; Bernard Schwartz, *Super Chief* (New York: New York University Press, 1983), p. 503.

21. WOD, Conference Notes, "No. 20—*WMCA, Inc.* v. *Simon,*" Nov. 15, 1963 (all quotations except final one), box 1301, "OT 1963 Argued Cases No. 19–22," part II, WODP; JMH, Conference Notes, "No. 20," Nov. 15, 1963 (final quotation), box 190, "No. 20 *WMCA* v. *Simon,*" JMHP. William O. Douglas kept the most detailed notes of the Court's discussions about the reapportionment cases; notes from John Marshall Harlan and Tom Clark also survive. Unless otherwise noted, all references and quotations are from WOD.

22. JMH Conference Notes (first quotation); WOD Conference Notes (all other quotations).

23. WOD Conference Notes (all quotations except final one); JMH Conference Notes (final quotation).

24. WOD Conference Notes (all quotations); JMH Conference Notes.

25. WOD Conference Notes (first and second quotations); JMH to FF, Nov. 15, 1963, reel 1, frames 672–73 (third quotation on frame 673), part III, FFP-H.

26. WOD Conference Notes.

27. Ibid. (all quotations); JMH Conference Notes.

28. WOD Conference Notes; JMH Conference Notes; TCC Conference Notes, "State Reapportionment Cases," box A152, folder 5, TCCP.

29. WOD Conference Notes (all quotations except second); TCC Conference Notes (second quotation).

30. OA of Robert D. McIlwaine, *Davis* v. *Mann,* Nov. 18, 1963.

31. OA of EDC, *Davis* v. *Mann,* Nov. 18, 1963.

32. OA of HEH, *Davis* v. *Mann,* Nov. 18, 1963.

33. OA of AC, *Davis* v. *Mann,* Nov. 18, 1963.

34. DJM Diary, Nov. 18, 1963 (first and second quotations); AC, "The Constitutional Aspects of Legislative Apportionment," July 1, 1963, p. 11 (other quotations), box 109, folder 18, Archibald Cox Papers, Law School Library, Harvard University.

35. DJM Diary, Nov. 18, 1963.

36. Author interview with EJB, Jan. 5, 2007, Atlanta; EJB to Clement F. Haynsworth Jr., Sept. 16, 1963, Haynsworth to EJB, Sept. 17, 1963, EJBP.

37. Author interview with EJB; "Brief *Amicus Curiae* of Emmet J. Bondurant," filed May 23, 1962, *Sanders* v. *Gray,* Civil Action No. 7872, USDC for the Northern District of Georgia, p. 21 (quotation), NARA-SE; EJB, "A Stream Polluted at Its Source: The Georgia County Unit System," *Journal of Public Law* 12, no. 1 (1963): 86–121; EJB to Robert G. Edge, Dec. 4, 1963, EJBP.

38. OA of EJB, *Wesberry* v. *Sanders,* Nov. 18, 1963, in *Landmark Briefs,* 58:238–53 (all quotations except final one on p. 241; final quotation on p. 250); "Argument Before the Court: Legislative Apportionment," *United States Law Week* 32 (Nov. 26, 1963): 3192–93.

39. OA of EJB, *Wesberry* v. *Sanders*, Nov. 18, 1963, in *Landmark Briefs*, 58:238–53 (first and second quotations on p. 246; third quotation on p. 247); "Argument Before the Court: Legislative Apportionment"; Charles L. Weltner to EJB, Nov. 22, 1963, EJBP; "Chosen by the People," *WP*, Nov. 22, 1963, p. A22.

40. OA of BJT, *Wesberry* v. *Sanders*, Nov. 18, 1963, in *Landmark Briefs*, 58:253–69 (quotation on p. 255).

41. EJB to Gordon Gooch, Sept. 30, 1963 (first quotation), EJBP; OA of BJT, *Wesberry* v. *Sanders*, Nov. 18, 1963, in *Landmark Briefs*, 58:253–69 (second quotation on p. 265); "High Court Urged to Realign House," *NYT*, Nov. 19, 1963, p. 25; "Argument Before the Court: Legislative Apportionment," p. 3193 (third quotation); author interview with BJT.

42. OA of Paul Rodgers, *Wesberry* v. *Sanders*, Nov. 18, 1963, in *Landmark Briefs*, 58:269–82 (first quotation on p. 280; second quotation on p. 277).

43. OA of Paul Rodgers, *Wesberry* v. *Sanders*, Nov. 19, 1963, in *Landmark Briefs*, 58:284–96 (first quotation on p. 294); OA of Frank Cash, *Wesberry* v. *Sanders*, Nov. 19, 1963, in *Landmark Briefs*, 58:296–301 (second quotation on p. 301).

44. "Conference Lists," Nov. 22, 1963, box 28, folder 8, part I, Byron R. White Papers, Manuscripts Division, LOC; WOD, Conference Notes, "No. 22—*Wesberry* v. *Sanders*," Nov. 22, 1963, box 1301, "OT 1963 Argued Cases No. 19–22," part II, WODP. Douglas's notes are transcribed and printed in Dickson, *Supreme Court in Conference*, pp. 852–53.

45. WOD, Conference Notes, "No. 22—*Wesberry* v. *Sanders*," Nov. 22, 1963, box 1301, "OT 1963 Argued Cases No. 19–22," part II, WODP.

46. Ibid.

47. Author interview with FXB, June 4, 2010, Columbus, Ohio; Newton, *Justice for All*, pp. 409–10; Cray, *Chief Justice*, p. 412.

48. Newton, *Justice for All*, pp. 410–11; Cray, *Chief Justice*, pp. 412–13 (quotation on p. 413).

49. Newton, *Justice for All*, pp. 412–13 (first quotation on p. 412; other quotations on p. 413); Cray, *Chief Justice*, pp. 413–14.

11. LEGISLATORS REPRESENT PEOPLE, NOT TREES OR ACRES

1. Woodward and Armstrong, *The Brethren*, pp. 3–4.

2. Author interview with FXB, June 4, 2010.

3. Ibid.; Robert B. McKay, "Political Thickets and Crazy Quilts: Reapportionment and Equal Protection," *Michigan Law Review* 61 (Feb. 1963): 645–710; Jo Desha Lucas, "Legislative Apportionment and Representative Government: The Meaning of *Baker* v. *Carr*," *Michigan Law Review* 61 (Feb. 1963): 711–804.

4. Author interview with FXB; Newton, *Justice for All*, pp. 410–11.

5. Author interview with FXB.

6. Author interview with FXB; FXB, "General Discussion of State Legislative Apportionment Cases Argued During November 1963," Nov. 27, 1963, box 246,

"Conference Memos OT 1963, Appellate #20-22," FXB, "Bench Memorandum, No. 20, *WMCA* v. *Lomenzo*," Nov. 5, 1963, box 246, FXB, "Bench Memorandum, No. 23, *Reynolds* v. *Sims*," Oct. 8, 1963, box 246, FXB, "Bench Memorandum, No. 29, *Maryland* v. *Tawes*," Nov. 7, 1963, box 246, FXB, "Bench Memorandum, No. 69, *Davis* v. *Mann*," Nov. 9, 1963, box 247, EWP.

7. Author interview with FXB; FXB, "Bench Memorandum, No. 20, *WMCA* v. *Lomenzo*" (first quotation on p. 32), FXB, "General Discussion of State Legislative Apportionment Cases Argued During November 1963," Nov. 27, 1963 (remaining quotations on pp. 6–8), box 246, "Conference Memos OT 1963, Appellate #20-22," EWP.

8. Stephen R. Barnett, "Standards for State Legislative Apportionment Under the Fourteenth Amendment" (first quotation on p. 348; second and third quotations on p. 142a), box 96, folder 6, part I, WJBP.

9. Author interview with FXB (quotation); Newton, *Justice for All*, pp. 414–16.

10. Author interview with FXB; Newton, *Justice for All*, pp. 416–23.

11. Author interview with FXB; Newton, *Justice for All*, pp. 423–24; Cray, *Chief Justice*, pp. 432–34.

12. FXB, "Bench Memorandum, No. 307, *Roman* v. *Sincock*," Dec. 4, 1963, p. 19 (first quotation), box 250, EWP; "Brief for the United States as *Amicus Curiae*," filed Dec. 4, 1963, *Roman* v. *Sincock*, No. 307, OT 1963, SCUS (second quotation on p. 13); WOD, Conference Notes, "No. 307—*Roman* v. *Sincock*," Dec. 13, 1963 (third quotation), box 1305, part II, WODP; "Statehouse Shuffle: Will Business Be the Loser?" *Nation's Business* 53 (June 1965): 75.

13. *Lucas* v. *Forty-Fourth General Assembly of Colorado*, 375 U.S. 938 (1963); WOD, Conference Notes, "No. 20—*WMCA, Inc.* v. *Simon*," Nov. 15, 1963, box 1301, "OT 1963 Argued Cases No. 19–22," part II, WODP; author interview with FXB (quotation); Schwartz, *Super Chief*, pp. 504–505.

14. FXB, "Nos. 23, 27, 41, et al., Reapportionment Cases," Jan. 15, 1964, box 608, "*Reynolds* v. *Sims*, Folder No. 1," EWP; HLB, "Memorandum for the Conference," Jan. 31, 1964, box 381, "*Wesberry* v. *Sanders* I," Hugo L. Black Papers, Manuscript Division, LOC.

15. HLB, "Memorandum for the Conference," Jan. 31, 1964 (quotation); Circulation History, "*Wesberry* v. *Sanders*," box A211, folder 3, TCCP.

16. *Wesberry* v. *Sanders*, 376 U.S. 1 (1964) (quotations at pp. 7–8).

17. Ibid. (first quotation at p. 20; all other quotations at pp. 18–19).

18. EJB to Clement F. Haynsworth, March 6, 1964, EJBP.

19. LWV-US, *Inventory of Work on Reapportionment*, pp. 2–3 (quotations on p. 2); Advisory Commission on Intergovernmental Relations, *Apportionment of State Legislatures* (Washington, D.C., Dec. 1962), Appendix B, p. A-7.

20. LWV-US, *Inventory of Work on Reapportionment*, pp. 2–3 (quotations on p. 3); LWV-Colorado, "Report of *Voter* Campaign for Reapportionment—Colorado, 1962," Dec. 14, 1962, box 258, "Government Apportionment Miscellany 1960–1965," part IV, LWVP.

21. LWV-Colorado, "Report of *Voter* Campaign for Reapportionment," pp. 2–3.

22. *Lisco* v. *McNichols*, 208 F. Supp. 471 (1962); "Jurisdictional Statement and Appendices," filed Sept. 30, 1963, pp. 30–45, 46–50 (quotations on pp. 49–50), *Lucas* v. *Colorado*, No. 508, OT 1963, SCUS; LWV-Colorado, "Report of *Voter* Campaign for Reapportionment," pp. 2–6.

23. LWV-Colorado, "Report of *Voter* Campaign for Reapportionment," pp. 2–6.

24. Ibid., pp. 5–6; Conrad L. McBride, "The 1964 Election in Colorado," *Western Political Quarterly* 18 (June 1965): 475–80.

25. *Lisco* v. *Love*, No. 7501, and *Myrick* v. *Forty-Third General Assembly of the State of Colorado*, No. 7637, 219 F. Supp. 922 (1963); "Jurisdictional Statement and Appendices," filed Sept. 30, 1963, pp. 46–102, "Motion to Dismiss or Affirm," filed Oct. 24, 1963, *Lucas* v. *Colorado*, No. 508, OT 1963, SCUS.

26. Stephen H. Hart to AC, Dec. 13, 1963, AC to Hart, Dec. 16, 1963, box 96, section 7, RG 60; Joseph W. Halpern, "Six of the Greatest," *The Colorado Lawyer* 32 (July 2003): 19.

27. Richard S. Kitchen, Sr., to AC, Jan. 10, 1964, Stephen H. Hart to AC, Jan. 13, 1964, box 96, section 7, RG 60; author interview with William Murane, May 15, 2012, Denver; Denver Research Institute, "An Economic Analysis of State Senatorial Districts in Colorado" (Denver, April 15, 1963); testimony of Dean C. Coddington, May 6, 1963, *Lisco* v. *McNichols*, No. 7501 and *Myrick* v. *Forty-Third General Assembly of Colorado*, No. 7637, in "Appendix to Briefs of Appellees and Added Appellees," filed March 16, 1964, in *Lucas* v. *Colorado*, pp. 116–26.

28. AC Diary, Jan. 21, 1964, box 13, "Cox Diaries (S.G.), KGP; Richard S. Kitchen, Sr., to AC, Jan. 24, 1964, box 96, section 7, RG 60; BM to AC [no date, but just prior to Feb. 4, 1964], box 96, section 8, RG 60.

29. BM to AC, pp. 7–12, box 96, section 8, RG 60.

30. BJT to AC, Feb. 3, 1964, pp. 2–7, box 96, section 8, RG 60.

31. AC to RFK, Feb. 4, 1964, pp. 1–3, box 96, section 8, RG 60.

32. Ibid., pp. 5–6.

33. Ibid., pp. 7–8 (all quotations; emphasis added), BJT to AC, Feb. 3, 1964, David Rubin to Harold H. Greene, Feb. 3, 1964, box 96, section 8, RG 60.

34. Knowles, "May It Please the Court?" pp. 279–97; Schlesinger, *Robert Kennedy and His Times*, p. 399 (first quotation); AC, *The Court and the Constitution*, p. 302 (second and third quotations); AC to RFK, Feb. 4, 1963, p. 6 (final quotation).

35. Theodore C. Sorensen to RFK, Feb. 10, 1964, box 12, "Colorado Apportionment Case," General Correspondence, RFK Attorney General Papers, JFKL.

36. Nicholas Katzenbach to RFK, Feb. 11, 1964, box 12, "Colorado Apportionment Case," General Correspondence, RFK Attorney General Papers, JFKL; author interview with BJT.

37. John W. Douglas to RFK, Feb. 11, 1964, box 12, "Colorado Apportionment Case," General Correspondence, RFK Attorney General Papers, JFKL.

38. Anthony Lewis, Oral History Interview with RFK and BM, pp. 576–81; Lewis to Victor Navasky, May 8, 1969, box 10, "Anthony Lewis," Victor Navasky Personal Papers, JFKL.

39. AC Diary, Feb. 11, 1964, box 13, "Cox Diaries (S.G.)," KGP; RFK Diary, Feb. 11, 1964, box 1, RFK Attorney General Papers, JFKL; LBJ Daily Diary, Feb. 11, 1964, box 1, LBJL; Lewis, Oral History Interview with RFK and BM, pp. 576–81; AC, *The Court and the Constitution*, p. 300 (quotations).

40. Lewis, Oral History Interview with RFK and BM, pp. 576–81 (quotations on p. 579).

41. Author interview with FXB (quotations); author telephone interview with FXB, June 20, 2013; *Reynolds* v. *Sims*, draft opinions, Jan. 31 and Feb. 26, 1964, box 608, "*Reynolds* v. *Sims*, Folder No. 1," EWP.

42. Typewritten draft, *Reynolds* v. *Sims*, Jan. 31, 1964 (first quotation on p. 13; second quotation on p. 14; third quotation on p. 35; fourth quotation on p. 21), box 608, "Nos. 23, 27, 41, *Reynolds* v. *Sims*, Folder No. 1," EWP.

43. Author telephone interview with FXB (quotation); typewritten draft, *Reynolds* v. *Sims*, Feb. 26, 1964, pp. 44–54, box 608, "Nos. 23, 27, 41, *Reynolds* v. *Sims*, Folder No. 1," EWP.

44. Author interview with FXB; Calendar of EW, box 33, "1964 Jan.–June," EWP; Cray, *Chief Justice*, p. 436 (third quotation); Schwartz, *Super Chief*, pp. 503–504 (all other quotations).

45. "Memorandum from the Chief Justice," March 1964, box 609, "*Reynolds* v. *Sims*, Folder No. 2," WOD to EW, March 12, 1964, Arthur J. Goldberg to EW, March 13, 1964, HLB to EW, March 17, 1964, box 509, "Reapportionment Cases: Opinions and Returns from Associate Justices," EWP.

46. Draft Opinion, *Reynolds* v. *Sims*, circulated March 16, 1964, box 33, folder 7, part I, Byron R. White Papers, Manuscript Division, LOC.

47. Author interview with FXB.

48. Author interview with William E. Murane (quotation); Doris Kal, *Fragile Advocate: Remembrance of a Legendary Trial Lawyer* (Aurora, CO: Verbal Imagery, 1975).

49. OA of George Louis Creamer, *Lucas* v. *Colorado*, No. 508, OT 1963, SCUS, March 31, 1964.

50. OA of AC, *Lucas* v. *Colorado*, March 31 and April 1, 1964.

51. OA of Anthony F. Zarlengo, *Lucas* v. *Colorado*, April 1, 1964 (emphasis added).

52. OA of Stephen H. Hart, *Lucas* v. *Colorado*, April 1, 1964.

53. TCC to EW, March 18, 1964 (first quotation), box 509, "Reapportionment Cases: Opinions and Returns from Associate Justices," EWP; WOD, Conference Notes, April 3, 1964 (all other quotations), No. 508—*Lucas* v. *Colorado*, box 1305, "OT 1963 Argued Cases No. 498–508," WODP.

54. WOD, Conference Notes, April 3, 1964 (all quotations except first), No. 508—*Lucas* v. *Colorado*, box 1305, "OT 1963 Argued Cases No. 498–508," WODP; PS, Conference Notes (first quotation), No. 508, *Lucas* v. *Colorado*, Docket Book, OT 1963, box 388, folder 4768, Potter Stewart Papers, Yale University Library.

55. Byron R. White to EW, June 10, 1964, box 509, "Reapportionment Cases: Opinions and Returns from Associate Justices," EWP; Hutchinson, *The Man Who Was Once Whizzer White*, pp. 2–3.

56. "Announcement of the Court's Legislative Apportionment Decisions by the Chief Justice on June, 15, 1964," p. 1, box 609, "*Reynolds* v. *Sims*, Folder No. 3," EWP.

57. "Supreme Court Holds States Must Apportion Legislatures on Basis of Equal Population: Historic Decision," *NYT*, June 16, 1964, pp. 1, 28; *Reynolds* v. *Sims*, 377 U.S. 533 (quotation at 377 U.S. 567); OA of AC, *Baker* v. *Carr*, April 19, 1961, p. 20, and Oct. 9, 1961, p. 29, in *Landmark Briefs*, 56:569, 644.

58. Author interview with FXB (first quotation); *Reynolds* v. *Sims*, 377 U.S. 562 (second quotation); typewritten draft, *Reynolds* v. *Sims*, Jan. 31, 1964, p. 13 (second quotation), box 608, "*Reynolds* v. *Sims*, Folder No. 1," EWP.

59. "Announcement of the Court's Legislative Apportionment Decisions by the Chief Justice on June 15, 1964," p. 1, box 609, "*Reynolds* v. *Sims*, Folder No. 3," EWP; *Reynolds* v. *Sims*, 377 U.S. 533 (first quotation at p. 558; second quotation at p. 559; third quotation at p. 568).

60. "Announcement of the Court's Legislative Apportionment Decisions by the Chief Justice on June 15, 1964," p. 1, box 609, "*Reynolds* v. *Sims*, Folder No. 3," EWP; *Lucas* v. *Forty-Fourth General Assembly of Colorado*, 377 U.S. 713 (1964) (quotations at pp. 736–37); author interview with FXB; Powe, *Warren Court and American Politics*, pp. 249–50.

61. *Reynolds* v. *Sims*, 377 U.S. 533 (1964); *WMCA* v. *Lomenzo*, 377 U.S. 633 (1964); *Maryland* v. *Tawes*, 377 U.S. 656 (1964); *Davis* v. *Mann*, 377 U.S. 678 (1964); *Roman* v. *Sincock*, 377 U.S. 695 (1964); *Lucas* v. *Forty-Fourth General Assembly of Colorado*, 377 U.S. 713 (first quotation at p. 750); "Supreme Court Holds States Must Apportion Legislatures on Basis of Equal Population"; "Present Divisions in Six States Are Voided; Ruling Hits Others," *WP*, June 16, 1964, pp. A1, A6 (second quotation on p. A6).

62. "Districts Voided in 9 More States," *NYT*, June 23, 1964, p. 16.

63. Stephen R. Barnett and Stephen J. Friedman, "Notes," *Opinions of William J. Brennan, Jr., October Term, 1963*, p. xxvii, box 6, "Case Histories, 1958–74," folder 6, part II, WJBP.

64. Roy A. Schotland and Frank I. Michelman, "Notes," pp. vii–viii; Schwartz, *Super Chief*, pp. 417–19. *New York Times* reporter Anthony Lewis, who covered the Court at the time of the reapportionment rulings, has argued persuasively that the Court would have lacked the votes for so sweeping a standard as "one-person, one-vote" if not for the appointment of two new justices between the decisions in *Baker* and *Reynolds*. See Anthony Lewis, Oral History Interview with Nicholas Katzenbach, Washington, D.C., Nov. 16, 1964, pp. 78–80, JFKL.

65. BJT to J. Lee Rankin, Dec. 8, 1960, p. 5, reel 99, CRDP; Victor Navasky interview with AC, Oct. 1970 (quotation on p. 6), box 3, "Archibald Cox," Victor Navasky Personal Papers, JFKL.

12. THE LITTLE FILIBUSTER

1. "Constitutional Revolution," *NYT*, June 16, 1964, p. 38 (first and second quotations); "The Court and the States," *NYT*, June 21, 1964, p. E8; "Urban Voters Win a

Smashing Victory," *Washington Daily News*, June 16, 1964, p. 16 (third quotation); "Sweeping Decision," *Newsweek* 63 (June 29, 1964): 22 (fourth quotation); Walter Lippmann, "The Frankfurter-Harlan Dissents," *NYHT*, June 18, 1964, p. 18; Roscoe Drummond, "After Reapportionment, Urban Power Will Grow," *NYHT*, June 19, 1964, p. 19; Drummond, "Behind Dirksen's Ploy," *NYHT*, Aug. 23, 1964, p. 22.

2. "Muzzling Minorities," *WSJ*, June 18, 1964, p. 14 (first quotation), "The Case Against the Court," *WSJ*, June 22, 1964 (second quotation), "A Fateful Decision," *Chicago Tribune*, June 21, 1964, "Court and Its Critics," *Dallas Morning News*, July 13, 1964 (third quotation), William F. Buckley, Jr., "Warren's Destructive Court," June 28, 1964 (fourth quotation), clippings in oversize box 852, EWP; Lawrence, "Apportionment Ruling Deplored"; White, "Historic Balance Being Destroyed by Highest Court," p. 6.

3. "Redistricting: A Warren View in '48," *U.S. News & World Report* 57 (July 6, 1964): 34; "Warren—Then and Now," *Richmond Times-Dispatch*, July 8, 1964, p. 18, "Warren Once Approved California Senate Plan," *Reading (CA) Record Searchlight*, July 9, 1964, editorial page, *Jackson (MS) Clarion-Ledger*, July 14, 1964, p. 4, clippings in oversize box 852, EWP; Schwartz, *Super Chief*, pp. 503–504; author interview with FXB.

4. Edwin C. Johnson, "Shall We the People Rule?" *Western Farm Life*, Jan. 1965, pp. 7, 9 (quotations on p. 7).

5. Robert B. McKay to JWM, June 16, 1964, JWM to McKay, July 17, 1964, James E. Larson to JWM, June 19, 1964, JWM to Larson, July 17, 1964, JWM to Roscoe C. Martin, July 17, 1964, JWMP; Anthony Lewis, "Supreme Court Moves Again to Exert Its Powerful Influence," *NYT*, June 21, 1964, p. E3.

6. James E. Clayton, "Court Ruling May Shatter Old Political Machines," *WP*, June 16, 1964, p. A6.

7. Lee, *One Man, One Vote*, p. 103; Clayton, "Court Ruling"; "Democratic Gain in State Is Seen," *NYT*, June 16, 1964, p. 1; Claude Sitton, "South Faces Era of Vast Changes," *NYT*, June 16, 1964, p. 32; Roscoe Drummond, "After Reapportionment, Urban Power Will Grow," *NYHT*, June 19, 1964, p. 19; "Where States May See Changes in Taxes, Welfare, Highways," *U.S. News & World Report* 57 (July 6, 1964): 34–36; "Sweeping Decision," *Newsweek* 63 (June 29, 1964): 23. *Newsweek* predicted gains for Democrats in California, Connecticut, Illinois, Iowa, Kansas, Maine, Maryland, Massachusetts, Michigan, Missouri, Nevada, New Hampshire, New York, Ohio, Pennsylvania, Rhode Island, Utah, Vermont, Washington, and Wyoming. Republicans' fortunes, according to the weekly, looked promising in six southern states—Alabama, Florida, Georgia, Louisiana, South Carolina, and Tennessee—plus five others—Arizona, Montana, New Mexico, Oklahoma, and Wisconsin.

8. Definition of "metropolitan" at http://quickfacts.census.gov/qfd/meta/long_metro .htm (first quotation); Richard M. Scammon, "Vanishing Farmer Losing His Lever," *WP*, June 28, 1964, p. E1 (second quotation); Congressional Quarterly, *Representation and Apportionment*, pp. 38–44; David and Eisenberg, *Devaluation of the*

Urban and Suburban Vote, pp. 11–16; *Reynolds* v. *Sims*, 377 U.S. 533 (third quotation at p. 568n43); "Where States May See Changes in Taxes, Welfare, Highways," p. 36; William J. D. Boyd, "Suburbia Takes Over," *National Civic Review* 54 (June 1965): 294–98 (fourth quotation on p. 294).

9. Elizabeth Yadlowsky, "Action with Respect to Apportionment of State Legislatures and Congressional Redistricting: 88th Congress" (Washington, D.C.: Legislative Reference Service, July 16, 1964, revised, Dec. 14, 1964), p. 16 (quotation).

10. Nick Kotz, *Judgment Days: Lyndon Baines Johnson, Martin Luther King Jr., and the Laws That Changed America* (Boston: Houghton Mifflin, 2005), pp. 112–55; Nicholas deB. Katzenbach, *Some of It Was Fun: Working with RFK and LBJ* (New York: Norton, 2008), pp. 136–44; Neil MacNeil, *Dirksen: Portrait of a Public Man* (Cleveland: World Publishing Company, 1970), pp. 208–38 (quotation on p. 238); *Time* 83 (June 19, 1964): cover; *Time* 84 (July 10, 1964): cover.

11. MacNeil, *Dirksen*, pp. 215, 236; Kotz, *Judgment Days*, p. 150; author interview with Nicholas Katzenbach, Oct. 12, 2009, Exeter, NH (first quotation); Katzenbach, *Some of It Was Fun*, pp. 140–41 (second quotation on p. 141).

12. MacNeil, *Dirksen*, pp. 238–44; Byron C. Hulsey, *Everett Dirksen and His Presidents* (Lawrence: University Press of Kansas, 2000), pp. 199–203.

13. MacNeil, *Dirksen*, pp. 238–44; Halsey, *Everett Dirksen*, pp. 202–203; "Dirksen Orders Study of Plan for Apportioning Amendment," *NYT*, June 22, 1964, p. 37 (first quotation); Minutes, U.S. Senate Republican Policy Committee, Meeting #18, June 23, 1964 (second quotation on p. 2), box 70, "Republican Policy Committee, Minutes 1964," Senate Republican Memo, 2n26 (July 2, 1964), pp. 1–2 (third quotation on p. 2), box 71, "Republican Policy Committee, Publications, Senate Republican Memoranda, 1964," Political File, National Politics, Bourke B. Hickenlooper Papers, Herbert Hoover Library, West Branch, IA. Byron Halsey makes the explicit connection between Dirksen's attack on the Supreme Court and the need to unify the Republican Party in the wake of the civil rights debate. See *Everett Dirksen*, p. 203.

14. Ben H. Bagdikian, "The Oil Can Is Mightier than the Sword," *NYT Magazine*, March 14, 1965, pp. 30–31, 82–88 (first and second quotations on p. 31); Kotz, *Judgment Days*, p. 116 (third quotation).

15. David E. Kyvig, "Everett Dirksen's Constitutional Crusades," *Journal of the Illinois State Historical Society* 95 (Spring 2002): 68–86; Frank H. Mackaman, introduction to Everett Dirksen, *The Education of a Senator* (Champaign: University of Illinois Press, 1998).

16. "Redistricting Upset? Drive in Congress Tries to Guard Rural Power in State Legislatures," *WSJ*, July 9, 1964, pp. 1, 20 (quotation on p. 1).

17. "The 1964 Platform of Republican National Convention," *CR*, 88th Cong., 2nd Sess., vol. 110, no. 140, July 22, 1964, copy in "Remarks/Releases, July 1964 (2)," Dirksen Congressional Center, Pekin, IL; "Rights Law Incites Hatred, Barry Says: GOP Nominee Blames New Act for Violence," *WP*, Sept. 11, 1964, pp. A1, A12; "Goldwater Criticizes High Court," *NYT*, Sept. 12, 1964, p. A1; "Partial Text of Goldwater Speech," *WP*, Sept. 12, 1964, p. A6.

18. TDG to the President, July 15, 1964, Lee C. White to TDG, July 24, 1964, "Comment on Republican Platform," July 15, 1964, Phillip S. Hughes to White, July 27, 1964, TDG to White, July 28, 1964, White to Bill Moyers, Aug. 5, 1964, White to TDG, Aug. 10, 1964, LE/FG box 46, folder "LE/FG 410, 11/23/63–9/5/64 (General)," WHCF, LBJL.

19. Yadlowsky, "Action with Respect to Apportionment," pp. 28–29; "Move on Districts Is Begun in House," *NYT*, July 23, 1964, p. 16; MacNeil, *Dirksen*, pp. 245–49; "Dirksen Would Block Districting by Court Until States Can Act," *NYT*, Aug. 4, 1964, p. 17; "Dirksen Bill Would Stay Reapportionment Cases," *WP*, Aug. 4, 1964, p. A5; Walter Lippmann, "The Dirksen Breather," *WP*, Aug. 18, 1964, p. A13.

20. Mossback McKinley to All Republican Party Workers, "Confidential Bulletin No. 1" and "Confidential Bulletin No. 2"; "After Redistricting Decision—Where States May See Changes in Taxes, Welfare, Highways," *U.S. News & World Report*, July 6, 1964, pp. 34–36; "Reapportionment Slashes Ranks of 1965 Legislature in Michigan," *WP*, Sept. 6, 1964, p. A4; "Court Orders Oklahoma to Realign Legislature," *NYHT*, Aug. 1, 1964, p. 2; "Congressional Districts Ranked According to Population," Defendants' Exhibit 1, pp. 79–92, and Defendants' Exhibit 8, pp. 122–37, *TOR, Wesberry v. Sanders*, No. 22, OT 1963, SCUS.

21. Chalmers Roberts, "Dirksen Move Seen as Shortsighted," *WP*, Aug. 12, 1964, p. A10.

22. David Halberstam, *The Powers That Be* (New York: Knopf, 1979), p. 387 (first quotation); MacNeil, *Dirksen*, p. 242 (second quotation).

23. "Reapportionment of State Legislatures," *CR-Senate*, 88th Cong., 2nd Sess., vol. 110, Aug. 3, 1964, pp. 17189–91, attached to Myer Feldman to the President, Aug. 4, 1964, LE/ST box 155, folder "LE/ST (Executive)," WHCF, LBJL; MacNeil, *Dirksen*, p. 246 (first quotation); "Districting Curb Gains in Senate," *NYT*, Aug. 5, 1964, p. 14 (second quotation); "Districting Stay Voted by Senators," *WP*, Aug. 5, 1964, pp. A1, A8; "Crisis for the Court," *WP*, Aug. 9, 1964, p. E8; "Dirksen's Aid-Bill Rider Faces Stiff Opposition," *WP*, Aug. 9, 1964, p. A4.

24. "Law Experts Wary on Dirksen's Move," *NYT*, Aug. 7, 1964, pp. 1, 56; "Law Deans, Professors Oppose Curbing Reapportioning Powers," *WP*, Aug. 10, 1964, p. A1; "63 in House Threaten Bolt on Aid Bill," *WP*, Aug. 7, 1964, p. A2; "Dirksen's Aid-Bill Rider Faces Stiff Opposition," p. A4 (quotation).

25. "Senate Ready to Modify Reapportionment Rider," *WP*, Aug. 11, 1964, p. A1 (first and last quotations); "Accord to Delay Districting Near," *NYT*, Aug. 11, 1964, p. 8; "Apportion—Senate 'Go Slow,'" *NYHT*, Aug. 11, 1964, p. 1; Mike Manatos to Larry O'Brien, Aug. 10, 1964 (second and third quotations), GEN FG 405 box 332, folder 1, WHCF, LBJL.

26. "Senate in Upheaval Over Dirksen Rider," *WP*, Aug. 12, 1964, pp. A1, A9; "Mansfield Still Hopeful of Aug. 22 Close," *WP*, Aug. 10, 1964, p. A6; Question 5, Presidential News Conference, Aug. 15, 1964, *Public Papers of the Presidents: Lyndon B. Johnson, 1963–64* (Washington, D.C.: GPO, 1965), 2:516.

27. "Senate in Upheaval Over Dirksen Rider"; "Districting Delay Mapped in Senate," *NYT*, Aug. 13, 1964, pp. 1, 19 (first five quotations on p. 19); "Deal in Senate on Aid—Redistricting Delay," *NYHT*, Aug. 13, 1964, pp. 1, 12 (sixth quotation on p. 12).

28. "Redistricting Fight Flares in Congress," *NYHT*, Aug. 14, 1964, pp. 1, 13 (first quotation on p. 1; second quotation on p. 13); "Redistricting Faces New Threat," *WP*, Aug. 14, 1964, pp. A1, A13; "Court-Ripper Bill," *WP*, Aug. 15, 1964, p. A10 (third quotation); "Districting Fight Forced to Floor by House Panel," *NYT*, Aug. 14, 1964, pp. 1, 12 (fourth quotation on p. 1); "House Votes Ban on Court Power to Reapportion," *NYT*, Aug. 20, 1964, pp. 1, 18.

29. "Redistricting Faces New Threat," pp. A1, A13 (quotations on p. A13); "Districting Fight Forced to Floor by House Panel."

30. "Liberals Keep Up Districting Fight," *NYT*, Aug. 18, 1964, p. 20.

31. Mackaman, introduction to Dirksen, *The Education of a Senator*; Drew Pearson, "Illinois Senators Vie Over Cloture," *WP*, Sept. 10, 1964, p. F15; Paul H. Douglas, *In the Fullness of Time: The Memoirs of Paul H. Douglas* (New York: Harcourt, 1972), pp. 101–29 (quotation on p. 126); Roger Biles, *Crusading Liberal: Paul H. Douglas of Illinois* (DeKalb: Northern Illinois University Press, 2002), chaps. 1–2; "M'Keough Lead in Senate Race Nears 285,000," *Chicago Daily Tribune*, April 15, 1942, p. 1; "Democratic Vote by Counties in U.S. Senator Race," *Chicago Daily Tribune*, April 15, 1942, p. 2.

32. Douglas, *In the Fullness of Time*, pp. 546–58; Biles, *Crusading Liberal*, chap. 2.

33. Douglas, *In the Fullness of Time*, pp. 554–55 (first quotation); "Apportion Fight Dims Adjournment Hopes," *WP*, Aug. 15, 1964, pp. A1, A4; "Mansfield Drops Plan to Adjourn," *NYT*, Aug. 16, 1964, p. 53 (second quotation); "Liberals Keep Up Districting Fight," *NYT*, Aug. 18, 1964, p. 20 (third quotation).

34. "Congress—The Angry Impasse," *NYHT*, Aug. 15, 1964, pp. 1, 12 (first quotation on p. 1); "Districting Fight Threatens Drive for Adjournment," *NYT*, Aug. 15, 1964, p. 1; "Congress Turns to Johnson on Districting," *NYHT*, Aug. 16, 1964, p. 2; "Liberals Keep Up Districting Fight," p. 20 (second quotation); Question 5, Presidential News Conference, Aug. 15, 1964, *Public Papers of the Presidents: Lyndon B. Johnson, 1963–64*, 2:516; "Congress Faces Stay of Weeks," *WP*, Aug. 19, 1964, p. A2; Ted Lewis, "Capitol Stuff," *NYHT*, Aug. 19, 1964, p. 4; HEH to the President, Aug. 11, 1964, LE/FG box 46, "LE/FG 410, 11/22/63—9/5/64 (General)," WHCF, LBJL; George Louis Creamer to the President, Aug. 5, 1964, FG 410 box 333, folder 1, WHCF, LBJL.

35. "Districting—Irate House Slaps Court," *NYHT*, Aug. 20, 1964, pp. 1, 14; "House Votes Ban on U.S. Courts in Reapportioning," *WP*, Aug. 20, 1964, pp. A1, A20; "Court Supported on Redistricting," *NYHT*, Aug. 19, 1964, p. 2; Roscoe Drummond, "Dirksen Acts in Unseemly Haste," *WP*, Aug. 23, 1964, p. E7; "Districting Delay Fought by Mayors," *NYT*, Aug. 19, 1964, p. 16; letters from various mayors in box 96, section 13, RG 60, and in LE/FG box 47, "LE/FG 410, 9/6/64—9/25/64 (General)," WHCF, LBJL.

36. Kotz, *Judgment Days*, chap. 8. For more on Freedom Summer, which spawned the Mississippi Freedom Democratic Party, see Doug McAdam, *Freedom Summer* (New York: Oxford University Press, 1988), and Elizabeth Sutherland Martínez, ed., *Letters from Mississippi* (Brookline, MA: Zephyr Press, 2007).

37. "Democrats Urged to Support Court on Redistricting," *NYT*, Aug. 22, 1964, pp. 1, 7; "Repudiate Rights Act, Wallace Urges Party," *WP*, Aug. 22, 1964, p. A5.

38. "Democrats Weigh Policy on Seating and Districting," *NYT*, Aug. 20, 1964, pp. 1, 18 (quotation on p. 18).

39. Ibid. (quotation on p. 1).

40. "Democrats Urged to Support Court on Redistricting"; "Johnson Opposes a District Plank," *NYT*, Aug. 23, 1964, p. 82; "Democrats United on Platform," *WP*, Aug. 25, 1964, pp. A1, A6; "Party Platforms Differ Sharply on Rights, Taxes, Urban Woes," *WP*, Aug. 30, 1964, p. A4; Royce Hanson, *The Political Thicket: Reapportionment and Constitutional Democracy* (Englewood Cliffs, NJ: Prentice-Hall, 1966), p. 87.

41. "Mansfield Drops Plan to Adjourn," *NYT*, Aug. 16, 1964, p. 53 (first quotation); "Redistricting—The Pat Hand and the Joker," *NYHT*, Aug. 23, 1964, p. 11.

42. "Redistricting—The Pat Hand and the Joker," p. 11.

43. "Dirksen Asks Cloture on Apportionment Rider," *WP*, Sept. 9, 1964, pp. A1, A2; Question 16, Presidential News Conference, Sept. 9, 1964 (quotation), *Public Papers of the Presidents: Lyndon B. Johnson, 1963–64*, 2:1057; Chalmers Roberts, "Reapportionment Bind: No Help from Johnson," *WP*, Sept. 10, 1964, p. A21.

44. "Apportionment Roll Calls," *NYT*, Sept. 11, 1964, p. 42; "Cloture Move Fails in Senate," *WP*, Sept. 11, 1964, p. A1; "Senate Refuses to Vote Closure on Redistricting," *NYT*, Sept. 11, 1964, p. 1.

45. "Johnson Presses Liberals in Senate on Districting," *NYT*, Sept. 14, 1964, pp. 1, 22; "Apportioning Strategy Talk Slated Today," *WP*, Sept. 14, 1964, p. A6; "Dirksen Rider Reworded; Showdown Due Today," *WP*, Sept. 15, 1964, p. A1; "Districting Accord Is Near Among Liberals in Senate," *NYT*, Sept. 15, 1964, pp. 1, 26; "Humphrey Plans Two More Moves to End Stalemate," *WP*, Sept. 16, 1964, pp. A1, A6 (quotation on p. A1); Mike Manatos to Larry O'Brien, Sept. 11, 1964, O'Brien to the President, Sept. 11, 1964, LE/ST box 155, folder "LE/ST (Executive)," WHCF, LBJL; Manatos to O'Brien, Sept. 15, 1964, Manatos to O'Brien, Sept. 16, 1964, box 9 (2 of 2), "Reapportionment Act," White House Staff Files, Mike Manatos, LBJL; "Roll Call on Redistricting," *NYT*, Sept. 16, 1964, p. 20; "Senate Keeps Dirksen Rider, 42–40," *WP*, Sept. 16, 1964, p. A1.

46. Larry O'Brien, Memorandum for the President, Sept. 24, 1964 (first quotation), box 1 (1 of 2), "Legislation 1964—General Info—Mr. O'Brien," White House Staff Files, Mike Manatos, LBJL; "Mansfield Offers New Plan to End Senate Impasse," *WP*, Sept. 24, 1964, pp. A1, A9 (second quotation on p. A9).

47. "Senate Approves Compromise on Reapportioning," *WP*, Sept. 25, 1964, pp. A1, A8 (first quotation on p. 8); "Roll Call in Senate on District Substitute," *NYT*, Sept. 25, 1964, p. 31; "Senate Ends Reapportionment Filibuster, Passes Mansfield 'Sense

of Congress' Plan," *WSJ*, Sept. 25, 1964, p. 4; Mike Manatos, Memorandum to the President, Oct. 1, 1964 (second quotation), box 1 (1 of 2), "Legislation 1964—General Info—Mr. O'Brien," White House Staff Files, Mike Manatos, LBJL; "Congress Votes $3.25 Billion Aid," *NYT*, Oct. 3, 1964, p. 12.

48. Dan Cordtz, "Anatomy of a Filibuster," *WSJ*, Sept. 25, 1964, p. 16.
49. Dan Cordtz to the author, May 6, 2009.
50. Cordtz, "Anatomy of a Filibuster," p. 16; Cordtz to the author, May 6, 2009.
51. Cordtz, "Anatomy of a Filibuster," p. 16.

13. SCARED STIFF

1. "Town Hall Gives Plan for House," *Arizona Republic*, Oct. 14, 1964, p. 17, clipping in box 2, "DJM Speeches," Virginia Commission on Constitutional Government Papers, Library of Virginia, Richmond.
2. Ernest A. Tupper to W. F. Bramstedt, March 12, 1965, box 96, "Congressional Statements Section 3," W&BP.
3. "Resolution Adopted by the Seventeenth Biennial General Assembly of the States," Chicago, Dec. 3, 1964, box 1320, folder "Pro Groups," PHDP; Peter Irons, "The Race to Control the States," *Progressive* 29, no. 5 (May 1, 1965): 11–14; "Districting Foes Press New Drive," *NYT*, Dec. 13, 1964, p. 54 (first and second quotations); "The Seventeenth Biennial General Assembly of the States: Closing Business—Adoption of Resolutions," *State Government* 38 (Winter 1965): 61–64 (third quotation on p. 61).
4. Prentice, "Report to Florida Commission on Constitutional Government"; AJF, "Memorandum: The First Seventeen Months of the States' Rights Amendments: Dec. 6, 1962–May 6, 1964," p. 6, box 659, "Constitutional Amendments 1963," EWP; "New States Rights Unit Will Push Amendments," *Lincoln (NE) Star*, Feb. 7, 1964, p. 1; "Clarification Called Commission's Aim," *Lincoln (NE) Star*, March 1, 1964, p. B5. Initially incorporated as the Commission on Constitutional Government, Inc., the group soon referred to itself in all correspondence as the National Commission on Constitutional Government (NCCG).
5. Irons, "Race to Control the States," pp. 11–12; *Wesberry* v. *Sanders*, 376 U.S. 1 (1964); AJF to EW, Jan. 31, 1964, AJF to Paul H. Douglas, Feb. 13, 1964, Information Service, American Bar Association, "Proposals for Amending the Constitution . . . A Summary of State Legislative Action (May 1964)," box 660, "Constitutional Amendments 1964," EWP; George Prentice, "Report from Washington on Reapportionment," Sept. 11, 1964, SG 22375, folder 4, George Wallace Papers, Alabama Department of Archives and History, Montgomery; TDG to Officers and Members of the Board of Directors of the NCCG, Oct. 2, 1964, box 22, folder 11, Thomas D. Graham Papers, Missouri State Archives, Jefferson City. See also chapter 12 on effort by TDG and NCCG to insert a plank into the Democratic platform.
6. Ernest Tupper to TDG, Dec. 9, 1964 (first quotation), box 22, folder 11, Thomas D. Graham Papers; Tupper to W. F. Bramstedt, March 12, 1965 (second quotation), box 96, "Congressional Statements Section 3," W&BP.

7. "Districting Foes Press New Drive," *NYT*, Dec. 13, 1964, p. 54 (both quotations).
8. NCCG, "Questions and Answers on Reapportionment," Jan. 14, 1965, box 9, "Reapportionment," Virginia Commission on Constitutional Government Papers, Library of Virginia, Richmond; Ernest A. Tupper to "Participants in U.S. Chamber of Commerce's Fourth Annual Public Affairs Conference," Feb. 1965, TDG, "Dear Sir," Feb. 1965 fund-raising letter (first quotation), box 96, "Congressional Statements Section 3," W&BP; Council of State Governments, "State Legislative Action on Proposals to Amend the Constitution of the United States to Permit the Apportionment of One House of a Bicameral Legislature on Factors Other Than Population," July 15, 1965, folder 2351, DWP; Elizabeth Yadlowsky, "State Petitions and Memorials to Congress on the Subject of Apportionment of State Legislatures" (Washington, D.C.: Legislative Reference Service, June 11, 1965, revised and updated by Johnny H. Killian, Feb. 1, 1968); Irons, "Race to Control the States," pp. 11–14 (second quotation on p. 13). The twenty-five states that passed the resolution between December 1964 and October 1965 in the form suggested by the General Assembly of the States were Alabama, Arizona, Arkansas, Florida, Georgia, Idaho, Kansas, Kentucky, Louisiana, Maryland, Minnesota, Mississippi, Missouri, Montana, Nebraska, New Hampshire, New Mexico, North Carolina, Oklahoma, South Carolina, South Dakota, Tennessee, Texas, Utah, and Virginia. Wyoming and Washington both passed resolutions in 1963 that asked Congress to call a constitutional convention for the purpose of allowing states to reapportion without federal interference, but they did not adopt the more narrow, and differently worded, petition in 1965 that sought to reapportion only one house on factors other than population. Nevada passed the same reapportionment resolution in 1963, and did adopt a new resolution in 1965, but asked Congress to initiate proceedings rather than call directly for a convention. The NCCG and its allies included all three states in their numbers on the grounds that each state had called at one point since 1963 for a convention to deal with reapportionment. See TDG, Press Release, April 20, 1965, box 96, "Background Materials, Miscellaneous," W&BP; NCCG, "Constitutional Amendment Action by State Legislatures," box 292, folder "1," ECP.
9. Peter Irons, "Race to Control the States," pp. 11–14 (first and third quotations on p. 12; second quotation on p. 11).
10. Jeffrey D. Howison emphasizes this point in "'This Is Not a Cotton Picker's Dream': Reapportionment, Conservative Ideology, and the Urban-Rural Divide," *Journal of Urban History* 37 (Sept. 2011): 680–93.
11. "How Reapportionment Threatens Business," *Nation's Business* 52 (Dec. 1964): 94–97 (quotation on p. 94).
12. Ibid. (first and third quotations on p. 94; second, fourth, and fifth quotations on p. 95).
13. Irons, "Race to Control the States"; "How Reapportionment Threatens Business"; EMD, "Reapportionment: America's Greatest Constitutional Crisis," *NAM Reports* 11 (March 14, 1966): 5–6.

14. "GOP Will Unite on Redistricting," *NYT*, Jan. 6, 1965, p. 1; "Dirksen Introduces Amendment to Void '1-Man 1-Vote' Rule," *WP*, Jan. 7, 1965, p. A4; "Senate Panel Opens District Hearings," *NYT*, March 4, 1965, p. 32.

15. Transcript of Panel Discussion, Fourth Annual Association Public Affairs Conference of the Chamber of Commerce of the United States, "Effect of Supreme Court Decision on Legislative Reapportionment," Feb. 4, 1965 (Findlay quotations on p. 7; Proxmire quotation on p. 5), box 292, "Reapportionment 2," ECP.

16. Bayh Report (quotation on p. 384); EMD, "Reapportionment: America's Greatest Constitutional Crisis," p. 6.

17. Martin S. Griglak to Senator Joseph S. Clark, March 9, 1965 (first and second quotations), "Legislative Apportionment," *The Citizen*, March 5, 1965, box 97, section 15, RG 60; "Let the People Decide," *Standard Oiler* (March/April 1965), copy in box 96, folder "Background Materials: Clippings from Newspapers, Magazines, etc.," W&BP.

18. Edwin J. Regan to "Dear Editor," Aug. 21, 1964 (quotation) and "Reapportionment of California Legislature," Aug. 21, 1964, LP 229:334, Senator Randolph Collier Papers, CSA; Regan to Members of the California Senate, Aug. 18, 1964, League of California Cities, "Apportionment of Both Houses of a Bicameral Legislature on a Population Basis," Jesse Unruh, "Reapportionment: One Man, One View," Sept. 30, 1964, LP 87:29, James A. Cobey Papers, CSA.

19. EMD, "The Supreme Court Is Defying the People," *Saturday Evening Post* 237 (Sept. 12, 1964): 10–11 (first three quotations on p. 10); draft of letter from Edwin J. Regan to the Editor, *Saturday Evening Post*, Sept. 22, 1964 (fourth and fifth quotations), box 98, folder "Statement Edwin J. Regan," W&BP. Regan's letter to the editor of the *Saturday Evening Post* was never published.

20. James Dorais to Sigvald Nielson, Nov. 16, 1960, box 58, folder 1, Herbert M. Baus to Nielson, Nov. 10, 1960, box 58, folder 4, CW to Nielson, Jan. 26, 1965, box 102, "Hold File: Reapportionment Current," William F. Bramstedt to Ralph B. Johnson, Nov. 4, 1965, box 99, "Contributions," W&BP. For a complete record of Whitaker & Baxter's management of Proposition 15 in 1960 and Proposition 23 in 1962, see boxes 58–59 and 81–82, W&BP.

21. CW to Sigvald Nielson, Jan. 26, 1965, box 102, "Hold File: Reapportionment Current," W&BP.

22. CW to Sigvald Nielson, Feb. 9, 1965, Nielson to various recipients, Feb. 12, 1965, box 101, "Reapportionment 1965: Sig Nielson," W&BP; James Mussatti to Elmer Bromley, March 4, 1965, Mussatti to various recipients, March 5, 1965, box 96, "Mussatti Letters," W&BP; Press Release, March 8, 1965, LP 87:30, James A. Cobey Papers, CSA.

23. James Mussatti to James A. Cobey, April 8, 1965, April 19, 1965, May 6, 1965, June 28, 1965, LP 87:30, Cobey Papers, CSA; Robert L. Pierce to Alan C. Furth, March 5, 1965, box 97, "Southern Pacific," untitled background memorandum, box 97, "Background," "Results of mailing to California organization executives," box 97, "Letter Writing Campaign," "Memorandum," April 23, 1965, box 98, "Progress

Report," W&BP; Don A. Allen, "A Los Angeles Assemblyman Recalls the Reapportionment Struggle," interview by James R. Rowland, 1979, pp. 39–40, Regional Oral History Office, Bancroft Library, University of California, Berkeley; CW to EMD, June 28, 1965, file 2264, DWP; "Reapportionment Drive Pushed," *WP*, July 1, 1965, p. A4.

24. Whitaker & Baxter, "Report on No. 23," pp. 11–20, Senator Randolph Collier Papers, LP 229: 334, CSA; James Mussatti to Congressman, June 26, 1965, box 292, folder 1, ECP; William F. Bramstedt to Ralph B. Johnson, Nov. 4, 1965, box 99, folder "Contributions," W&BP; Lists of Donations, box 99, "Contributions (Solicitation Lists)," W&BP; CW to Robert W. Jackson, May 1, 1967, box 99, "Correspondence (General) 1965–1966," W&BP. Clem Whitaker spent one-third of his budget on office expenses, one-third on travel (which included the cost of sending California legislators all over the country), and one-third on personnel (half of which covered Whitaker & Baxter's fee). See CW to R. W. Rood, March 1, 1965, box 97, "Correspondence," CW to T. S. Petersen, June 11, 1965, CW to Si Fluor, June 29, 1965, box 96, "Whitaker & Baxter Out-of-State Names," W&BP.

25. Ernest A. Tupper to William F. Bramstedt, March 12, 1965, Bramstedt to Tupper, March 17, 1965, box 96, "Congressional Statements Section 3," W&BP.

26. Hanson, *Political Thicket*, pp. 91–92.

27. ADA, *Legislative Newsletter*, 89th Cong., 1st Sess., no. 14 (Aug. 11, 1965): 2–3, box 292, "Reapportionment Folder 1," ECP; "The Vote Shrinkers Are on the Move Again," box 117, "Constitutional Amendment—Reapportionment," ACLU of Southern California Papers, Department of Special Collections, Charles E. Young Research Library, UCLA; NCFR to "Dear Friends," Feb. 22, 1965, box 1139, folder 10, ACLU Papers, Seely G. Mudd Manuscript Library, Princeton University; ADA, "List of Organizations to Contact," Feb. 26, 1965, box 1320, "NCFR," PHDP; Hanson, *Political Thicket*, pp. 92–93.

28. Hanson, *Political Thicket*, pp. 92–93.

29. Testimony of EMD, March 3, 1965, Bayh Report, pp. 7–12 (quotations on p. 8).

30. Testimony of Paul Douglas, Joseph Tydings, and William Proxmire, March 4, 1965, Bayh Report, pp. 35–80; Hanson, *Political Thicket*, pp. 93–95; NCFR, Minutes of Organizational Meeting, March 16, 1965, p. 2, box 1320, "NCFR," PHDP.

31. NCFR, Minutes of Organizational Meetings, March 8 and 16, 1965, box 1320, "NCFR," PHDP; Marvin H. Caplan, *Farther Along: A Civil Rights Memoir* (Baton Rouge: Louisiana State University Press, 1999), pp. 181–235.

32. NCFR, Minutes of Organizational Meetings; Bayh Report, pp. 236–38, 316–18, 485–87.

33. NCFR, Minutes of Organizational Meetings, March 8 and 16, 1965, and Minutes of Regular Meetings, April 8 and 26, 1965, box 1320, "NCFR," PHDP. The NCFR listed its address as 2027 Massachusetts Avenue, NW, a building purchased in 1962 by the Religious Action Center.

34. "Brief on Behalf of Appellee," *Gray v. Sanders*, No. 112, OT 1962, SCUS, pp. 12–13; testimony of Douglas S. Webb, *Sims v. Frink*, No. 1744-N, USDC for the Middle

District of Alabama, July 16, 1962, p. 59, box 75, "Exhibits," RG 21, NARA-SE; "Personality Conflicts Are Cited by Webb," *BPH*, July 17, 1962, p. 2.

35. NCFR, Minutes of Organizational Meetings, March 8 and 16, 1965, and Minutes of Regular Meetings, April 8 and 26; ADA, *Legislative Newsletter*, no. 14 (Aug. 11, 1965): 3 (quotation), box 292, "Reapportionment Folder 1," ECP.

36. See David J. Garrow, *Protest at Selma: Martin Luther King, Jr., and the Voting Rights Act of 1965* (New Haven: Yale University Press, 1980); Thornton, *Dividing Lines*; Kotz, *Judgment Days*.

37. Alan Reitman to Larry Speiser, April 30, 1965, Speiser to Executive Committee, NCFR, May 4, 1965, box 1320, "NCFR," PHDP; ADA, *Legislative Newsletter*, no. 14, pp. 3–4.

38. Testimony of RFK, May 6, 1965, Bayh Report, pp. 775–84 (first quotation on p. 778; second quotation on p. 777).

39. Testimony of BM, May 14, 1965, Bayh Report, pp. 852–65 (first four quotations on pp. 853–54); ADA, *Legislative Newsletter*, no. 14, p. 5 (fifth quotation).

40. Testimony of J. Lee Rankin, May 14, 1965, Bayh Report, pp. 865–74 (first quotation on p. 865; second and third quotations on p. 867).

41. Testimony of Theodore Sachs, May 20, 1965, Bayh Report, pp. 903–13 (first quotation on p. 905; second quotation on p. 904).

42. Joseph D. Tydings, "Reapportionment—The Rotten Borough Amendments," *CR-Senate*, 89th Cong., 1st Sess., vol. 111 (June 2, 1965): 12284–95 (first quotation on p. 12291); CW to James Mussatti, June 7, 1965 (second and third quotations), box 96, "Whitaker & Baxter Out-of-State Names," W&BP; National Council of Churches, "Equal Representation Is a Right of Citizenship," June 3, 1965, box 562, "Policy Statement on Equal Representation," PHDP; NCFR, *News Bulletin* 2 (June 21, 1965): 2, box 79, "Reapportionment: Dirksen Amendment," MBAP.

43. NCFR, *News Bulletin* 3 (June 30, 1965): 1–3, box 79, "Reapportionment: Dirksen Amendment," MBAP; "Districting Plan Gains in Senate," *NYT*, June 24, 1965, p. 21; "Dirksen Sees No Block to Apportioning Action," *WES*, July 7, 1965, p. A21; "Reapportionment: Dirksen's Battle for His 'Brainchild,'" *NYHT*, July 15, 1965; "Districting Showdown Is Blocked by Dirksen," *WES*, July 20, 1965, p. A3; "Dirksen Blocks Districting Vote," *NYT*, July 21, 1965, p. 17.

44. "Districting Showdown Is Blocked by Dirksen," *WES*, July 20, 1965, p. A3 (first quotation); Roman Hruska, "Let the People Decide Fair Apportionment," *CR-Senate*, 89th Cong., 1st Sess., vol. 111, no. 131 (July 20, 1965): 16811–42; "Dirksen Going to Bat on One Man, One Vote Bill," *NYHT*, July 23, 1965, pp. 1, 10 (second quotation on p. 1); NCFR, *News Bulletin* 4 (July 26, 1965): 1, box 79, "Reapportionment: Dirksen Amendment," MBAP.

45. Phillip S. Hughes to Lee White, March 16, 1965, LE/FG box 45, "LE/FG 410 (Executive)," WHCF, LBJL; Rowland Evans and Robert Novak, "L.B.J. Help Needed to Kill Redistricting Ban," *LAT*, May 25, 1965, p. A5; Bill Moyers to Jerome T. Orans, June 5, 1965, GEN FG 410 box 333, folder 3, WHCF, LBJL; LBJ, Press Conference, June 1, 1965, question 11 (quotation), in *Public Papers of the Presidents:*

Lyndon B. Johnson, 1965 (Washington, D.C.: GPO, 1966), 2:614; "Senate Showdown: Dirksen's Bid to Void Reapportionment Edict to Ignite Major Fight," *WSJ*, June 29, 1965, pp. 1, 10; Harold S. Stern to LBJ, June 29, 1965, Lee C. White to Stern, July 7, 1965, White to Moyers, July 7, 1965, LE/ST box 155, "LE/ST (General)," WHCF, LBJL.

46. William Proxmire to Philip A. Hart, July 7, 1965, box 116, "Reapportionment: Dirksen Amendment," ASC; Pennsylvania Democratic State Committee to Hubert H. Humphrey and others, July 23, 1965, Joseph S. Clark to LBJ, July 29, 1965, Lawrence O'Brien to Clark, July 31, 1965, GEN FG 405 box 332, folder 1, WHCF, LBJL; Joseph D. Tydings to RFK, July 8, 1965, box 96, "Reapportionment of State Legislatures, 7/1/65–7/15/65," Legislative Subject Files, RFK-Senatorial Papers, JFKL; Herman W. Goldner to LBJ, June 30, 1965, Frank F. McDonald to LBJ, July 1, 1965, Terry D. Schrunk to LBJ, July 20, 1965, box 97, section 16, George D. Johnson to LBJ, July 6, 1965, Henry W. Maier to LBJ, July 6, 1965, James H. J. Tate to LBJ, July 14, 1965, Theodore R. McKeldin to LBJ, July 15, 1965, John J. Barton to LBJ, Aug. 4, 1965, box 97, section 17, RG 60; "Mayors Condemn Dirksen Proposal," *NYT*, July 29, 1965, p. 15.

47. Nick Kotz, "Humphrey Opposes Dirksen Remap Plan," *Minneapolis Tribune*, July 3, 1965, pp. 1, 7 (first quotation on p. 1); "Johnson, Dirksen Paths May Part," *WES*, July 21, 1965, p. A23; "Johnson to Keep Hands Off Senate Apportioning Fight," *WES*, July 23, 1965, p. A2; Mary McGrory, "The Poet on Battle's Eve," *WES*, Aug. 4, 1965, p. A2 (second quotation); EMD, Statement, Aug. 1965, file 2378, DWP; "Dirksen Asks End to Humphrey Lobby," *Philadelphia Inquirer*, Aug. 4, 1965 (third quotation), copy in file 2247, DWP; Malcolm MacLean to LBJ, July 1, 1965, Aug. 4, 1965 (fourth quotation), GEN FG 410 box 333, folder 4, WHCF, LBJL.

48. "It's D-Day in the Senate: Douglas vs. Dirksen in the Big Debate," *WP*, Aug. 4, 1965, p. 1; "Dirksen Proposal on Redistricting Beaten in Senate," *NYT*, Aug. 5, 1965, p. 1.

49. *CR-Senate*, 89th Cong., 1st Sess., vol. 111, no. 142 (Aug. 4, 1965): 18633–39 (Dirksen quotations on p. 18633; Douglas quotations on p. 18638).

50. "Dirksen Proposal on Redistricting Beaten in Senate," p. 1 (quotation); "Senate Roll-Call Vote on Dirksen Proposal," *NYT*, Aug. 5, 1965, p. 11; NCFR, *News Bulletin* 5 (Aug. 30, 1965): 1, copy in box 79, "Reapportionment: Dirksen Amendment," MBAP. Of the four senators, all Democrats, who did not vote, two were announced as paired in favor of the amendment and one in opposition. The fourth senator, Carl Hayden of Arizona, did not vote and was not paired, but he did vote in favor of the Dirksen amendment the following year. Therefore, the final vote would have been 60–40 if all one hundred senators had voted. Among the thirty-two Republicans, twenty-nine supported their leader. Clifford Case of New Jersey, Jacob Javits of New York, and Caleb Boggs of Delaware voted against the measure. Boggs had initially sponsored the Dirksen amendment but switched his vote during the course of deliberations.

14. LET THE PEOPLE DECIDE

1. "Congress Produces," *NYT*, Aug. 8, 1965, p. E1; Kotz, *Judgment Days*, pp. 278–337.

2. Ibid.

3. "Dirksen Submits New Amendment," *NYT*, Aug. 12, 1965, p. 17; NCFR, *News Bulletin* 5 (Aug. 30, 1965): 1-4, copy in box 79, "Reapportionment: Dirksen Amendment," MBAP.

4. Joseph D. Tydings, "Legislative Apportionment," *CR-Senate*, 89th Cong., 1st Sess., vol. 111, Aug. 18, 1965, pp. 20126–29 (quotation on p. 20126), in Johnny H. Killian, "State Legislative Apportionment: An Analysis of Proposed Constitutional Amendments" (Washington, D.C.: Legislative Reference Service, Dec. 7, 1965), pp. 64–68; NCFR, *News Bulletin* 5 (Aug. 30, 1965): 1–4; ADA, *Legislative Newsletter*, 89th Cong., 2nd Sess., no. 7 (April 13, 1966): 1–5, copy in box 292, "Reapportionment Folder 1," ECP.

5. "Dodd Helps Dirksen on Reapportioning," *NYT*, Aug. 27, 1965, p. 58; "Alien Bill Freed by Dirksen Deal," *NYT*, Sept. 9, 1965, pp. 1, 19 (quotation on p. 19).

6. CW to Clyde Flynn, Aug. 11, 1965, file 2264, DWP; "The Plan of Campaign for the Committee for Government of the People," Sept. 17, 1965 (quotation on p. 4), box 98, W&BP, also in file 2265, DWP; EMD to J. Ed. Warren and nine others, Oct. 1, 1965, file 2266, DWP.

7. EMD, invitation to Sept. 17 dinner, Sept. 1, 1965, file 2265, DWP; materials related to Sept. 17 dinner, box 189, yellow binder, W&BP; EMD to J. Ed. Warren and nine others, Oct. 1, 1965, file 2266, DWP; CW to Warren and eight others, Oct. 16, 1965, file 2267, DWP; EMD to William J. Young, Dec. 15, 1965, file 2273, DWP.

8. John M. Lupton to Robert Smalley, Jan. 5, 1966, file 2274, DWP; "Draft of a statement George Champion or anyone else soliciting funds could use in talking with another businessman," box 99, "Solicitations (suggested letter to donors)," W&BP; "Reapportionment of State Legislatures and Its Relationship to Business" [Fall 1965] (first quotation on p. 1), J. Ed. Warren, excerpts of talk before Independent Petroleum Association of America, Dallas, Oct. 25, 1965 (second quotation), file 2273, DWP.

9. "Reapportionment of State Legislatures and Its Relationship to Business," file 2273, DWP; "14(b)—Victory for Labor," *NYT*, Aug. 1, 1965, p. E3; "14(b) Issue Saw Sharp Turnabout by Dirksen," *LAT*, Nov. 15, 1965, p. 7.

10. "Senate Vote Backs Filibuster," *LAT*, Oct. 12, 1965, p. 1; "14(b) Issue Saw Sharp Turnabout by Dirksen"; "Closure Fails, 14(b) Survives," *NYT*, Feb. 13, 1966, p. 166.

11. Archie Robinson, *George Meany and His Times: A Biography* (New York: Simon & Schuster, 1981), pp. 244–47 (first and second quotations on p. 246; third quotation on p. 247); "Political Memo from COPE," Nov. 29, 1965, box 192, "AFL-CIO," W&BP.

12. W. C. Schade to EMD, Sept. 27, 1965 (first quotation), file 2266, DWP; William F. Bramstedt to Ralph B. Johnson, Nov. 4, 1965 (second quotation), box 99, "Contributions," W&BP.

13. John M. Lupton to Robert Smalley, Jan. 5, 1966, file 2274, DWP; EMD to J. Ed. Warren and nine others, Oct. 1, 1965, file 2266, DWP; William F. Bramstedt to Ralph B. Johnson, Nov. 4, 1965 (quotation), box 99, "Contributions," W&BP.

14. L. du P. Copeland to CW, Oct. 27, 1965, James Dorais to Walter Baird, Oct. 28, 1965, box 99, "Contributions," W&BP; "National Corporations ($30,000 quota)," box 99, "Contributions (Solicitation Lists)," W&BP; various lists of solicitations and donations, box 189, three-ring binder, W&BP.

15. "National Corporations (Oil Industry)," box 99, "Contributions (Solicitation Lists)," W&BP; Carstens Slack to Clyde Flynn, Dec. 20, 1965, file 2273, DWP.

16. "Foes Losing Fight on 1 Man, 1 Vote," NYT, Oct. 26, 1965, p. 27; "A Fateful Year for 'One Vote,'" WP, Nov. 7, 1965, pp. E1, E3 (first quotation on p. E3); "Statehouse Shift: Widespread Redrawing of Legislative Districts Benefits Urban Areas," WSJ, Dec. 2, 1965, pp. 1, 10 (second quotation on p. 1).

17. "Lobbying Campaign Is Mapped for Dirksen's Districting Plan," NYT, Jan. 19, 1966, p. 28; "Dirksen Outlines New Apportionment Battle," WES, Jan. 19, 1966, copy in file 2252, DWP.

18. List of Advisory Committee, Jan. 14, 1966, file 2275, DWP; Paul Hope, "Dirksen Drive Picks Up Helpers," WES, Feb. 18, 1966, copy in file 2253, DWP; George H. Buschmann to James Dorais, Jan. 24, 1966, CW to Buschmann, Jan. 26, 1966, box 99, "Correspondence (George H. Buschmann)," W&BP. In addition to EMD, the members of the advisory committee were Senators Frank Church (D-Idaho), Roman L. Hruska (R-Nebraska), Frank J. Lausche (D-Ohio), Hugh Scott (R-Pennsylvania), and Spessard L. Holland (D-Florida), and Representatives B. F. Fisk (D-California), Richard Ichord (D-Missouri), William M. McCullough (R-Ohio), William M. Tuck (D-Virginia), and Carleton J. King (R-New York).

19. "Publicity Check List," box 185, "Publicity Outline," W&BP; "Report to the Advisory Committee, Committee for the Government of the People, on the Campaign of Public Information in Behalf of the Reapportionment Constitutional Amendment (S.J. Res. 103)," May 6, 1966, files 2284–88, esp. "Distribution of Materials" and "Publicity," file 2286, DWP; "Let the People Decide," box 99, W&BP; William Elkins to Committee for the Government of the People, April 6, 1966, Mrs. Mabel Abbott to CGOP, March 15, 1966, Miss Loyola T. Haenel to CGOP, March 13, 1966, Mrs. John F. Hector to CGOP, March 7, 1966, Mrs. Carolyn MacCormack to CGOP, Mrs. Ruth Hutchins to CGOP, Miss Amelia Coy to CGOP, box 192, "Small Contributions," W&BP.

20. "Campaign Organization," in "Report to the Advisory Committee," May 6, 1966, file 2285, DWP; "Card Signers by States," box 193, W&BP; card signed by George [H. W.] Bush, box 187, "Texas," W&BP.

21. "3 Senators Fight Dirksen Proposal," NYT, Jan. 22, 1966, p. 12; ADA, Legislative Newsletter no. 7 (April 13, 1966): 3–5 (quotation on p. 4), box 292, "Reapportionment Folder 1," ECP; "Dirksen Hires Publicity Firm to Promote His Amendment," St. Louis Post-Dispatch, Feb. 6, 1966, copy in box 192, "Clippings—columns," W&BP.

22. "Roll Call in Senate on Dirksen Amendment," *NYT*, April 21, 1966, p. 26; "Senate Again Balks Dirksen by 7 Votes in Districting Fight," *NYT*, April 21, 1966, pp. 1, 26 (quotation on p. 26); "Congress: Three-Time Loser," *Newsweek* 67 (May 2, 1966): 19–20. Willis Robertson of Virginia, a staunch supporter of Dirksen's position, was the only senator not to vote or be announced one way or the other.

23. "Legislative Reapportionment Completed in 46 States," *WP*, June 23, 1966, p. E7; Congressional Quarterly, *Representation and Apportionment*, esp. p. 65; Douglas Smith, "Apportionment Politics, 1920–1970," in William Deverell and David Igler, eds., *Companion to California History* (Malden, MA: Wiley-Blackwell, 2008), pp. 384–85; "Dirksen Plowed Under," *WP*, April 10, 1966, p. E6 (quotation).

24. CW to EMD, Dec. 21, 1966, box 100, "State Check 1967," W&BP.

25. CW to EMD, Dec. 21, 1966, Memorandum to EMD and Roman Hruska, May 31, 1967, box 100, "State Check 1967," W&BP; "Iowa," "Indiana," "Oregon," "Vermont" (quotation), box 100, "Contacts (1967)," W&BP; "Colorado," Feb. 15, 1967, box 193, "Colorado," W&BP; Clyde Flynn to EMD, June 15, 1967, file 2310, DWP; "Statehouse Shuffle: Will Business Be the Loser?" pp. 69–70, 75.

26. CW to EMD, Dec. 21, 1966, box 100, "State Check 1967," W&BP; memorandum, dated Feb. 21, 1967, file 2291b, DWP; telegram, Ted Stevens to CGOP and EMD, Feb. 28, 1967, box 192, "Alaska," W&BP; "Efforts to Amend the Constitution on Districts Gain," *NYT*, March 18, 1967, p. 1. Whitaker had identified Indiana, Illinois, and Colorado, along with Iowa and Alaska, as the five states most likely to petition for a convention. Curiously, North Dakota did not appear on his initial list of states inclined to act favorably.

27. "Efforts to Amend the Constitution on Districts Gain"; LWV-US, "News Release," March 21, 1967, Mrs. Robert J. Stuart to Joseph D. Tydings, March 21, 1967, LWV-US, "Status of Legislative Resolutions Asking Congress to Call a Constitutional Convention," March 21, 1967, box 258, "Government and Apportionment: Basic Documents, 1959–1971," part IV, LWVP. The six petitions considered legitimate by Stuart were those passed by the legislatures of Colorado, Illinois, Indiana, Kentucky, Oklahoma, and North Dakota. Furthermore, a degree of confusion clouded the status of Nevada. In 1963, Nevada had adopted two petitions, one that memorialized Congress to call a convention to strip the federal courts of jurisdiction in all reapportionment matters and a second one that asked Congress to propose an amendment along the same lines. In 1965, Nevada joined California, Alaska, and Rhode Island in asking Congress to pass the Dirksen amendment but did not petition Congress to convene a convention. Whitaker & Baxter, however, later claimed that in 1965 Nevada had adopted convention and amendment petitions that conformed to the language of the Dirksen amendment, but that the state never officially sent the convention petition to the federal government. No other evidence supports this claim. Nevertheless, the League of Women Voters included Nevada in its list of thirty states that had petitioned for a convention, when in fact its petition for a convention was identical to those passed by Wyoming and Washington in 1963. See Ed Fike to EMD, Jan. 24, 1967, file 2298, DWP; "States Which

Have Passed Resolutions Calling for Constitutional Convention," Feb. 24, 1967, box 100, "States Action," W&BP; Yadlowsky, "State Petitions and Memorials to Congress," pp. 19–21, 76–77.

28. "Efforts to Amend the Constitution on Districts Gain"; "Constitutional Convention Faces Many Hurdles," *WP*, March 19, 1967, p. A6; "Senators Belittle Attempts to Alter 1-Man, 1-Vote," *Baltimore Sun*, March 19, 1967, copy in file 2255, DWP; "Assault on the Constitution," *WP*, March 21, 1967, p. A10; "26 District Petitions Invalid, Proxmire Says," *WES*, March 22, 1967, copy in box 192, W&BP; "Congress May Kill Constitutional Call," *WP*, April 16, 1967, p. A2 (quotation).

29. "The Mysterious Convention," *NYT*, March 23, 1967, p. 34 (quotation); "Assault on the Constitution"; "Tearing at the Fabric," *WP*, April 24, 1967, p. A18; "Battle Royal Looms If Two States Act," *Torrance (CA) South Bay Daily Breeze*, April 29, 1967, copy in box 192, W&BP; "Constitutional Convention: Unlikely Road to Amendment," *CSM*, April 3, 1967, second section, p. 1; "A Pandora's Box?" *CSM*, April 4, 1967, copy in file 2257, DWP.

30. David Lawrence, "Anti-Convention Points Rebutted," *WES*, March 24, 1967, copy in file 2256, DWP; Lawrence, "Constitution Specific on Convention," April 1967, copy in file 2257, DWP; James J. Kilpatrick, "Congress 'Shall' Call a Convention," *WES*, May 16, 1967, copy in file 2258, DWP; United Press International, "Apportionment," May 10, 1967, copy in file 2306, DWP; "Interview with Senator Everett Dirksen: Rewrite the U.S. Constitution?" *U.S. News & World Report* 62 (June 5, 1967): 63–66.

31. "A Constitutional Convention—The Facts," *U.S. News & World Report* 62 (June 5, 1967): 62; "Dirksen Presses for Constitutional Parley," *WES*, May 10, 1967, copy in file 2258, DWP; "Dirksen and Hruska Again Urge End to One-Man, One-Vote Rule," *NYT*, May 11, 1967, p. 43 (quotations); "A Convention to Amend the Constitution?" *Washington Sunday Star*, April 2, 1967, editorial page, copy in Legislative File 1178, Dirksen Congressional Center, Pekin, IL.

32. "Let the People Decide," *Standard Oiler*; CW and James Dorais to Sigvald Nielson, Jan. 26, 1965, box 102, "Hold File: Reapportionment Current," W&BP; CW to Robert Jackson, May 1, 1967, box 99, "Correspondence (General) 1965–1966," W&BP; EMD to Joseph B. Campbell, Augusta, Maine, April 3, 1967, EMD to Maurice A. Hartnett III, Dover, Delaware, April 4, 1967, EMD to R. P. Knowles, Madison, Wisconsin, April 6, 1967, EMD to Brad Phillips, Juneau, Alaska, April 7, 1967, file 2305, DWP; David E. Kyvig, "Everett Dirksen's Constitutional Crusade," *Journal of the Illinois State Historical Society* 95 (Spring 2002): 79.

33. Theodore C. Sorensen, "The Quiet Campaign to Rewrite the Constitution," *Saturday Review* 50 (July 15, 1967): 17–20 (all quotations on pp. 17–18).

34. Hugh J. Wade to the President, March 12, 1965, box 97, section 15, RG 60; Herman E. Slotnick, "The 1966 Election in Alaska," *Western Political Quarterly* 20 (June 1967): 524–28; "Legislatures Meeting in 1967 Which Have Not Completed Action on Reapportionment Resolution," box 100, "State Check 1967," W&BP; EMD to Walter Hickel, Jan. 30, 1967, CW to Carl D. McMurray, Feb. 16, 1967, CW,

"Alaska," Feb. 16, 1967 (quotation), telegram, Ted Stevens to CGOP, Feb. 28, 1967, box 192, "Alaska," W&BP; CW to Theodore Stevens, Feb. 16, 1967, box 101, "Alaska," W&BP.

35. "Alaska Rejects Reapportion Move," *WP*, April 9, 1967, p. A2; "Congress May Kill Constitutional Call," *WP*, April 16, 1967, p. A2; CW, "Alaska," Feb. 16, 1967, "Phillips' Grandstanding Needn't Halt Progress," *Fairbanks Daily News-Miner*, April 6, 1967, box 192, "Alaska," W&BP; Clyde Flynn to EMD, March 20, 1967, file 2304, DWP; telegram, EMD to Brad Phillips, April 7, 1967, file 2305, DWP.

36. Ted Stevens to CW, April 14, 1967 (quotations), box 101, "Alaska," W&BP; CW to Roman Hruska, March 28, 1968, box 102, "Hold File: Reapportionment Current," W&BP.

37. Verne Scoggins to CW, June 15, 1965, box 96, "Scoggins Letters," W&BP; "Legislatures Meeting in 1967 Which Have Not Completed Action on Reapportionment Resolution"; two memoranda titled "Iowa," undated, box 100, "Contacts (1967)," W&BP; untitled memorandum, Feb. 21, 1967, file 2291b, DWP.

38. Gerald Bogan to Robert M. Smalley, May 1, 1967, Gerald Bogan, "Special Memorandum on Dirksen Amendment," undated, box 192, "Correspondence—Smalley," W&BP; memorandum to EMD and Roman Hruska, May 17, 1967, file 2307, DWP; memorandum to EMD and Hruska, May 31, 1967, box 100, "State Check 1967," W&BP.

39. "To Save the Constitution," *WP*, May 25, 1967, p. A22; CGOP checkbook confirms that activity in the D.C. office ceased as of August 1, 1967, box 196, W&BP.

40. Ted Stevens to EMD, Dec. 26, 1967, file 2311, DWP.

41. EMD to Ted Stevens, April 4, 1968, file 2311, DWP; CW to Roman Hruska, March 28, 1968, CW to EMD, June 11, 1968, box 102, "Hold File: Reapportionment Current," W&BP.

42. "Dirksen Revives Fight Against Apportionment," *LAT*, Dec. 6, 1968, pp. 10–11 (first quotation on p. 10; second quotation on p. 11).

43. Robert B. McKay, *Reapportionment Reappraised* (New York: Twentieth Century Fund, 1968), pp. 18–19; "Senate's Young Pup Lames Old Growler," *Washington Daily News*, June 9, 1967, p. 12 (quotation); "Kennedys Swing Passage of 1 Man, 1 Vote Now," *WP*, June 9, 1967, pp. A1, A7; "Districting Compromise," *WP*, June 10, 1967, p. A10; "The Lion Cub of the Senate," *NYT*, Aug. 27, 2009, p. A27.

44. EMD to Floyd Edgington, Des Moines, Iowa, March 14, 1969, file 2312, DWP; "Constitutional Convention Bill," *WP*, April 12, 1969, p. A10; "33rd State Backs Dirksen Proposal," *NYT*, May 1, 1969, p. 60.

45. Sam Ervin to EMD, May 7, 1969, file 2314, DWP; "Senators Take Up Charter Parley," *NYT*, June 14, 1969, p. 27; "Mr. Dirksen's Time Bomb," *NYT*, June 16, 1969, p. 46 (first quotation); Anona Teska, LWV-US, to William Boyd, NML, June 27, 1969 (second quotation), box 259, "Government Apportionment Miscellany, 1967–1973," part IV, LWVP; "Symposium on the Article V Convention Process," *Michigan Law Review* 66 (March 1968): 837–1016; "Dirksen Push: 1 More State," *WP*, July 10, 1969, pp. H1, H7 (third quotation on p. H7); U.S. Senate, Committee on

the Judiciary, Subcommittee on Separation of Powers, 90th Cong., 1st Sess., "Hearings on S. 2307," Oct. 30–31, 1967 (Washington, D.C.: GPO, 1968); Sam J. Ervin, Jr., "Proposed Legislation to Implement the Convention Method of Amending the Constitution," *Michigan Law Review* 66 (March 1968): 875–902.

46. EMD to Warren P. Knowles, May 6, 1969, file 2314, DWP; "Delaware Senate Backs U.S. Parley," *NYT,* June 27, 1969, p. 22; Anona Teska, LWV-US, to William Boyd, NML, June 27, 1969, box 259, "Government Apportionment Miscellany, 1967–1973," part IV, LWVP; "Constitutional Convention Drive Gets Mixed Response in Nation," *NYT,* June 28, 1969, p. 17; "2d Wisconsin Drive Seeks Convention on U.S. Constitution," *NYT,* July 10, 1969, p. 16; "Wisconsin Panel Against Convention on U.S. Constitution," *NYT,* July 11, 1969, p. 42; "Support Is Found for Redistricting," *NYT,* July 17, 1969, p. 55.

47. "Efforts to Rescind," May 31, 1967, box 100, "State Check 1967," W&BP; Richard Norvell to EMD, Jan. 29, 1968, file 2311, DWP; "Texas Senate Approves Bill to Halt Petition to Congress," *NYT,* June 1, 1969, p. 64; "Constitutional Convention Drive Gets Mixed Response in Nation"; "Oklahoma May Quit Convention Drive," *NYT,* Aug. 8, 1969, p. 19; "Constitutional Ploy Bogging Down," *LAT,* Sept. 2, 1969, p. A6; David L. Russell to Finis W. Smith, Aug. 1, 1969 (quotation), Smith to EMD, Aug. 18, 1969, file 2922, DWP.

48. David L. Russell to Finis W. Smith, Aug. 1, 1969 (first quotation), Smith to EMD, Aug. 18, 1969 (second quotation), file 2922, DWP; "Dirksen's Last Days," *Pekin* (IL) *Daily Times,* Sept. 7, 2004, www.dirksencenter.org/print_emd_lastdays.htm; E. W. Kenworthy, "A Political Phenomenon," *NYT,* Sept. 8, 1969, p. 1; "Nixon Leads Mourning for Sen. Dirksen," *LAT,* Sept. 8, 1969, p. 9; "Legacy of Everett Dirksen," *LAT,* Sept. 9, 1969, p. A6.

49. "Dirksen Amendment Gains in Wisconsin," *NYT,* Oct. 22, 1969, p. 31; "Wisconsin Refuses to Become the 34th State to Adopt Dirksen Plan," *NYT,* Nov. 5, 1969 (first quotation); AJF to A. Wally Sandack, May 8, 1970, AJF to EW, June 8, 1970 (second quotation), box 660, "Constitutional Amendments 1964 to Date," EWP; Anona Teska, LWV-US, to Harold A. Katz, April 23, 1971, box 259, "Government Apportionment Miscellany 1967–1973," Series IV, LWVP.

EPILOGUE

1. An unnamed associate of Dirksen's told the *Los Angeles Times* that if the senator's opponents in 1967 had remained in the dark about his progress for "one more week, we would have won. We were so close to winning you could taste it." "Dirksen Revives Fight Against Apportionment," *LAT,* Dec. 6, 1968, pp. 10–11 (quotation on p. 11).

2. George B. Merry, "Putting the Houses in Order," *CSM,* Oct. 29, 1968, second section, p. 1; Cortner, *Apportionment Cases,* p. 253; Johnny H. Killian, "Legislative Apportionment: The Background and Current Status of Developments in Each of the Fifty States" (Washington, D.C.: Legislative Reference Service, Jan. 1966),

pp. 227–29; NML, *Apportionment in the Nineteen Sixties*, especially sections on Alaska, Hawaii, Massachusetts, Oregon, and South Carolina; Robert G. Dixon Jr., *Democratic Representation: Reapportionment in Law and Politics* (New York: Oxford University Press, 1968), p. 3 (quotation). Oregon, the only state in which no legislative reapportionment took place between the *Baker* ruling and the end of October 1968, had been reapportioned in 1961. That reapportionment did not meet a precise one person, one vote standard, but it came sufficiently close so that it remained unchallenged until the next regularly scheduled reapportionment after the 1970 census.

3. Armbrister, "The Octopus in the State House," pp. 25–29, 70–80; William J. D. Boyd, "Suburbia Takes Over," *National Civic Review* 54 (June 1965): 294–98; "One Person, One Vote—Who Wins, Who Loses," *U.S. News & World Report* 59 (Aug. 23, 1965): 42–44; Congressional Quarterly, *Representation and Apportionment*, pp. 38–41; William Schneider, "The Suburban Century Begins," *Atlantic* 270 (July 1992): 33–44. In New York, for example, the suburbs exploded by 75 percent between 1950 and 1960, in Los Angeles by 83 percent, in Chicago by 71 percent, and in Detroit by nearly 80 percent.

4. Boyd, "Suburbia Takes Over," p. 298.

5. "Legislators Across the Country Respond to Additional Burdens," *NYT*, Sept. 1, 1969, p. 9 (quotation); Bill Kovach, "Some Lessons of Reapportionment," *Reporter* 37 (Sept. 21, 1967): 26, 31–32; James U. Blacksher and Larry T. Menefee, "From *Reynolds* v. *Sims* to *City of Mobile* v. *Bolden*: Have the White Suburbs Commandeered the Fifteenth Amendment?" *Hastings Law Journal* 34 (Sept. 1982): 1–64; Matthew D. Lassiter, *The Silent Majority: Suburban Politics in the Sunbelt South* (Princeton: Princeton University Press, 2006); Kevin M. Kruse, *White Flight: Atlanta and the Making of Modern Conservatism* (Princeton: Princeton University Press, 2005); Stephen Ansolabehere and James M. Snyder Jr., *The End of Inequality: One Person, One Vote and the Transformation of American Politics* (New York: Norton, 2008), esp. chaps. 10–11 (quotation on p. 233).

6. Bruce F. Norton, "Recent Supreme Court Decisions on Apportionment" (Washington, D.C.: Legislative Reference Service, Aug. 12, 1964), p. 28 (first quotation); "The Governor's Vetoes," *NYT*, May 29, 1965, p. 26 (second quotation); "Reshaping Congress: Drawing New Districts Bogs Down as States Bicker, Gerrymander," *WSJ*, July 21, 1971, pp. 1, 18; Robert Draper, "The League of Dangerous Mapmakers," *Atlantic* 310 (Oct. 2012): 50–59 (third quotation on p. 50).

7. Ward Elliott, "Prometheus, Proteus, Pandora, and Procrustes Unbound: The Political Consequences of Reapportionment," *University of Chicago Law Review* 37 (Spring 1970): 474–92 (first and second quotations on pp. 474–75; third quotation on p. 490); Alexander M. Bickel, "The Supreme Court and Reapportionment," in Nelson W. Polsby, ed., *Reapportionment in the 1970s* (Berkeley: University of California Press, 1971), pp. 57–74 (fourth quotation on p. 69).

8. *Vieth* v. *Jubelirer*, 541 U.S. 267 (2004); *Cox* v. *Larios*, 542 U.S. 947 (2004); *League of United Latin American Citizens* v. *Perry*, 126 S. Ct. 2594 (2006); Sam Wang, "The

Great Gerrymander of 2012," *NYT*, Feb. 3, 2013, pp. 1, 5; Adam Liptak, "Smaller States Find Outsize Clout Growing in Senate," *NYT*, March 11, 2013, pp. A1, A12–13.

9. David E. Kyvig, *Explicit and Authentic Acts: Amending the U.S. Constitution, 1776–1995* (Lawrence: University Press of Kansas, 1996), pp. 426–47; Kevin Klose, "Michigan Lawmaker Stalls Budget-Amendment Drive," *WP*, Sept. 14, 1984, p. A7; *Citizens United* v. *Federal Election Commission*, 558 U.S. 310 (2010); Bennet, "The New Price of American Politics."

10. "'One Person, One Vote'—Who Wins, Who Loses," *U.S. News & World Report* 59 (Aug. 23, 1965): 42–43; Ansolabehere and Snyder, *The End of Inequality*, esp. chaps. 10–11 (first quotation on p. 241; second quotation on p. 240); Mathew D. McCubbins and Thomas Schwartz, "Congress, the Courts, and Public Policy: Consequences of the One Man, One Vote Rule," *American Journal of Political Science* 32 (May 1988): 388–415; Cox and Katz, *Elbridge Gerry's Salamander*, esp. pp. 3–28.

11. Author interview with CJS, Nov. 8, 2005, Birmingham, Alabama; author telephone interview with CJS, Oct. 14, 2005 (first quotation); "A Conversation with Earl Warren," *Brandeis Television Recollections*, p. 17 (second quotation); testimony of Theodore Sachs in Bayh Report, p. 910 (third quotation).

ACKNOWLEDGMENTS

The process of researching and writing this book has been at times a solitary enterprise, but in fact has depended on the camaraderie, goodwill, and professionalism of scores of people. Nearly a decade has passed since Matt Lassiter and Andy Lewis encouraged me to think about a book on reapportionment. Little did I imagine then where that journey would lead. A project initially conceived within the context of my previous work on the history of the American South became a broad study of national politics in the post–World War II period. At critical points along the way, numerous individuals and organizations supported the research and writing of this book. For quite some time I have looked forward to thanking them, and I do so now.

One of the great joys of this project was the opportunity to meet and spend time with a number of individuals central to the stories told in these pages. I am particularly indebted to Frank Beytagh, Emmet Bondurant, John McConnell, George Peach Taylor, Clarke Stallworth, and Bruce Terris, for sharing their thoughts and recollections with me. In addition, I am immensely grateful to Camille Morgan, the widow of Chuck Morgan, who graciously invited me to her home and made arrangements for me to gain access to her husband's papers even though they remained closed to researchers at the time. My one regret is that I was not able to write fast enough to share the final product with George Taylor and Clarke Stallworth.

I owe an immeasurable debt to the American Council of Learned Societies, the National Endowment for the Humanities (Ref: FB-52686-06), and the John Randolph and Dora Haynes Foundation. Fellowships from each of these organizations allowed me the time to complete most of the research for this project. The John F. Kennedy Library, the Lyndon Baines Johnson Library, the Everett M. Dirksen Congressional Center, the Huntington Library, and the American Historical Association provided additional research assistance. Roy Ritchie, the Director of Research Emeritus at the Huntington Library, and Steve Hindle, the current Director of Research, graciously provided office space in which I drafted the entire manuscript. My thanks also to dozens of librarians and archivists across the country, but especially the Interlibrary Loan staff at Occidental College, who fielded numerous requests for often obscure documents and reports.

Matt Lassiter and Ed Ayers each read every word of the manuscript. As they have done repeatedly over the two decades that I have had the good fortune to count them as friends and colleagues, Matt and Ed offered deeply insightful observations that shaped the final draft in important ways. Deanne Maynard, an appellate lawyer, former Supreme Court law clerk, and close family friend, fielded numerous questions and no doubt saved me from embarrassment on a number of occasions as I tried to navigate the nuances of Supreme Court jurisprudence. My editors at Hill and Wang, Alex Star and Dan Gerstle, have been phenomenal partners. Alex encouraged me to rethink and clarify key portions of the story told in these pages, while Dan's superb editing skills greatly improved the final product. Closer to home, Bill Deverell and David Igler are the best of friends, providing constant support and encouragement, both personally and professionally. My oldest friends, Peter Hatcher and Rudi Colloredo-Mansfeld, remain as important as ever.

The research and writing of this book took place as my wife, Julie, and I discovered what it means to be parents. When I started this project, we had one dog and no children. Now we have no dog and two amazing children—Zoe and Jack—who both ask incessantly when they can have a dog. In my office, I have a small chalkboard on which Zoe once wrote, "Please finish your book! P.S. How soon will you finish?" The answer, it turned out, was a lot longer than she imagined. But at last I am finished, and I owe a great deal of thanks to Zoe and Jack for their limitless reservoirs of unconditional love, their almost constant good humor, their excellent company, their occasional interest in what their father does all day, and their general acceptance when that meant a few more hours at the office.

Without a doubt, my greatest thanks are reserved for Julie, to whom this book is dedicated. For more than twenty years, Julie has been my greatest friend and champion. Whatever I have not learned from my children about the meaning of unconditional love, I have learned from her. I marvel at Julie every day and cannot begin to adequately express my feelings of love, admiration, and gratitude for who she is and for what she means to me.

INDEX

Abram, Morris: background of, 103; and coining of term "one man, one vote," 99; connection between racial discrimination and minority rule made by, 131; Georgia's county-unit system challenged by, 99, 101, 102, 104, 105, 106, 107–109, 113, 114, 115, 186, 231

ACLU Foundation of Northern California, 31

Adams, Charles Francis, vii, 15

AFL-CIO, 38, 96, 101, 112, 151, 200, 254, 255, 258, 266

African Americans, 15, 19, 160, 231, 276; civil rights of, *see* civil rights movement; Dirksen amendment and, 257; voting rights denied to, 14, 161

African National Congress, 99

Agricultural Council, California, 251

Alabama, 16, 116–38, 141, 151, 154, 161, 166, 167, 170, 255, 285, 310, 333, 339; constitution of, 118, 126; House seat lost by, 122; Supreme Court reapportionment case in, 173, 174–77, 178, 180, 182–83, 184, 193, 196, 201, 203, 212, 213, 214–15; *see also Reynolds* v. *Sims*

Alabama, University of, 120, 137

Alabama Council on Human Relations, 120, 136

Alameda, Calif., 25, 26

Alaska, 274–75, 276–77, 281, 346

Albert, Carl, 226, 235

All-Parties Reapportionment Commission, 25

Almond, Lindsay, 142

Amendment No. 7 (Colorado plan), 200–201, 202, 203, 211, 214–15, 264

American Bar Association, 63

American Civil Liberties Union, 53, 76, 96, 97, 252, 254, 255

American Farm Bureau Federation, 247

American Jewish Congress, 254

American Law Institute, 96

American Medical Association, 34, 63

American Metal Climax, Inc., 265

American Municipal Association, 60, 63

American Political Science Association, 18, 155

Americans for Democratic Action (ADA), 252–53, 254, 258

Anderson, Clinton, 237

Ansolabehere, Stephen, 285

apportionment, 14, 17; area vs. population as basis for, 14–15; and city vs. countryside power struggle, 11–12, 15–17, 18, 24, 26–27, 29, 47–48, 50, 54–55, 220; in Massachusetts, 14–15, 16; state legislative, 287–90; *see also* malapportionment; reapportionment

Arizona, 16, 18, 333, 339

Arkansas, 310

Armstrong, Scott, 192

Arnold, Richard S., 67

Aspinall, Wayne, 19

Associated Industries, 245

Atkins, Hobart, 57–58, 62, 63
Atkinson, Brooks, 227
Atlanta, Ga., 19
Atlantic, 283

Bailey, John, 220
Baker, Charles W., 58
Baker, Gordon, 99, 101
Baker, Howard, 277–78
Baker v. Carr, 46, 59, 61–70, 77–78, 81,
    105, 125, 142, 158, 159, 167, 180, 188,
    209, 215, 216, 258; amicus briefs
    in, 63–64, 71, 72, 84–85, 101–102;
    decision making in, 75–76, 80–81,
    85–88, 149; Fourteenth Amendment
    and, 60, 65, 67, 69–70, 73, 74, 75, 78,
    82, 83, 179; importance and legacy of,
    3–4, 80–81, 93–94, 103, 106, 107, 114,
    118, 122, 125, 132, 135, 139, 140, 152,
    154, 156, 157, 162, 172, 176, 177, 183,
    192–93, 242, 281–82, 284, 310; JFK's
    endorsement of decision in, 92, 97;
    opinion and dissent in, 6, 88–89,
    91–92, 100, 101, 126, 144, 145–46, 165,
    181, 186, 211; oral arguments in, 51,
    72–75, 81–84, 118, 213; rearguing of,
    81–84, 147–48; Tennessee state
    historian's report in, 59–60;
    Whittaker's depression exacerbated
    by, 79, 89–90, 92
Ball Brothers, 267
Baltimore, Md., 50, 51, 282–83
Bankers Association, California, 251
Barnett, Stephen, 194
Bartlett, E. L., 275
Baxter, Leone, 31–34
Bayh, Birch, 246, 250, 253, 257, 259,
    260, 269
Beasley, I. D., 54
Beebe, James L., 48–49
Bell, Griffin, 155
Bell Telephone Company, 248

Beytagh, Frank, 192–96, 207–209, 212,
    213–14
Bickel, Alexander, 92, 284
Biemiller, Andy, 255, 266
Big Mules, 116, 122, 124–25, 174
Billig, Sebby, 52, 54
Birmingham, Ala., 19, 97, 116, 118–19,
    121, 135–36; church bombing in,
    137–38; civil rights protest in, 136–37
Birmingham Post-Herald, 116, 117, 124,
    127, 131, 132, 135
Birmingham Southern College, 120
Black, Charles, 96
Black, Hugo, 126, 128; *Baker v. Carr* and,
    74, 76, 77, 85–86, 87, 88, 180, 78, 79;
    Colegrove v. Green dissent of, 45, 86,
    93, 104, 197; Georgia congressional
    reapportionment case assigned to,
    193, 196–97; *Gomillion v. Lightfoot*
    opinion of, 66, 67; *Gray v. Sanders*
    and, 107, 113; *Hartsfield v. Sloan* and,
    105; individual rights and, 112;
    population equality embraced by, 217;
    South v. Peters dissent of, 104–105,
    106; in state reapportionment case,
    175, 176, 180–81, 211–12, 216
Black Belt, 116–17, 118, 122, 124, 134
Blue Ballot Reapportionment
    Amendment, Illinois, 40–41
Boggs, Caleb, 343
Bondurant, Emmet, 186–87, 189, 198
Bonelli, Frank, 48–49
Boston, Mass., 50, 233, 234
Botter, Theodore I., 176–77
Bourbon, Robert S., 176
Boyarsky, Bill, 29
Boyd, William, 221, 282
Bramstedt, William F., 249, 251, 252, 267
Brant, Irving, 93
Brennan, William, 93, 96, 97; *Baker v.
    Carr* and, 67, 76, 78, 79, 82, 85, 86, 87,
    88, 89, 90, 91, 179; in Georgia
    congressional reapportionment case,